McGRAW-HILL ON-SITE GUIDE TO BUILDING CODES 2000: COMMERCIAL AND RESIDENTIAL INTERIORS

McGRAW-HILL ON-SITE GUIDE TO BUILDING CODES 2000: COMMERCIAL AND RESIDENTIAL INTERIORS

William David Smith III
Laura Holland Smith

McGRAW-HILL
New York San Francisco Washington D.C. Auckland Bogotá
Caracas Lisbon London Madrid Mexico City Milan
Montreal New Delhi San Juan Singapore
Sydney Tokyo Toronto

Cataloging-in-Publication Data is on file with the Library of Congress

McGraw-Hill

A Division of The McGraw-Hill Companies

1 2 3 4 5 6 7 8 9 0 DOC/DOC 0 7 6 5 4 3 2 1

ISBN 0-07-136127-8

*The sponsoring editor for this book was Wendy Lochner and the production
supervisor was Sherri Souffrance. It was set in Times Roman by Lone Wolf
Enterprises, Ltd.*

Printed and bound by R.R. Donnelley & Sons Company.

This book is printed on recycled, acid-free paper containing
a minimum of 50% recycled, de-inked fiber.

McGraw-Hill books are available at special quantity discounts to use as premiums
and sales promotions, or for use in corporate training programs. For more
information, please write to the Director of Special Sales, McGraw-Hill,
Professional Publishing, Two Penn Plaza, New York, NY 10121-2298. Or contact
your local bookstore.

This book is dedicated to our parents, Mr. and Mrs. William David Smith II (Jane and Bill David) and Mr. and Mrs. Lyman Faith Holland Jr. (Leannah and Lyman), who have given us so many advantages and so much support, and to our children, Will, Foster, and Ella.

CONTENTS

Chapter 8 Accessibility   8.1

Chapter 9 Interior Finishes   9.1

Chapter 10 Other Issues   10.1

FOREWORD

This book, the *McGraw-Hill On-Site Guide to Building Codes 2000: Commercial and Residential Interiors*, is not a building code. This book is a guide to the codes described herein, primarily *The 2000 International Building Code* (IBC), *The 2000 Life Safety Code* (LSC), and *ICC/ANSI A 117.1 Accessible and Usable Buildings and Facilities*. Other codes are included by reference or in appendices. This book is intended to supplement, not replace, the building codes. Reading this book should familiarize the reader with important code concepts and reference applicable parts of the codes.

Anyone who has used the building codes knows they are highly technical and complex documents, subject to interpretation and revision. The codes also conflict one with one another on certain specific subjects. Important concepts, however, are common to all building codes, such as allowable building height and area, protection of building elements, occupancy, means of egress provisions, accessibility, and interior finish ratings. We have tried to emphasize the importance of these concepts and have organized this book around them. Extensive references make it clear what code and section is relied upon for the concepts discussed.

Our writing focuses on portions of the building codes applicable to the design and construction of interiors. The building codes are not divided conveniently into "Interior" and "Exterior" content, so we have made judgments about which codes and concepts are most applicable to this title. A second book, the *McGraw-Hill On-Site Guide to Building Codes 2000: Exteriors*, addresses a wider range of code issues.

We believe this book about Interiors will be of use to interior designers, architects, contractors, building owners, developers, students, and others who need or want to study the building codes.

ABOUT THE AUTHORS

WILLIAM DAVID SMITH III

Mr. Smith is a Registered Architect in the states of Alabama and Tennessee with more than 20 years of professional experience. His experience includes all aspects of architectural practice—planning, design, specifications, construction documents, contract negotiation, and construction administration. In addition to working in a range of residential, commercial, and institutional building types, Mr. Smith has specialized experience in medical architecture, education and recreational facilities, space planning, industrial architecture, and building rehabilitation. Mr. Smith has served as expert witness in litigation involving personal injury, construction disputes and design matters. He is a graduate of Birmingham-Southern College and Mississippi State University.

LAURA HOLLAND SMITH

Ms. Smith is a registered interior designer with more than 15 years of professional experience. Her experience includes interior space planning, selection of interior finish materials, furniture design, selection and procurement, and preparation of construction documents. Ms. Smith has designed interiors for a variety of building types including medical, retail, office, and educational facilities. She has worked most of her career with architecture firms, understands the relationship of interiors to architecture, and is familiar with building and life safety codes. She is a graduate of Auburn University.

Laura and David are owners of Holland Smith Architects in Huntsville, Alabama. They spend lots of time with their sons, ages 6 and 9, at sports, reading, and computer games. David is an avid golfer, and Laura enjoys gardening.

ACKNOWLEDGEMENTS

Thanks to the International Code Council and to the National Fire Protection Association for granting permission to use many of their illustrations, primarily from the code commentaries.

Special thanks to Lyman Holland, for legal work in connection with the author's agreement for this book.

Special thanks also to James Munger, CFPS, of Munger and Associates Code Consultants, and James Lee Caudle, AIA, of NewSouth Architects, for use of their technical library resources.

Note:
† Reprinted with permission from NFPA101-2000 Life Safety Code®, Copyright© *2000, NFPA*. This reprinted material is not the complete and official position of the NFPA on the referenced subject which is represented only by the standard in its entirety.

†† Reprinted from the Life Safety Code® Handbook—1997, Copyright© 1997 NFPA. All rights reserved.

CHAPTER 1

INTRODUCTION TO BUILDING CODES

BUILDING CODES—A DEFINITION

Dozens of regulations govern the built environment—municipal, county, state, federal, and (recently) international. This book covers the two major codes affecting design and construction of interiors in the United States—the *ICC, International Building Code 2000,* published by the International Code Congress, and the *Life Safety Code* (NFPA 101), published by the National Fire Protection Association. Chapter 8, *Accessibility,* is based on the 1998 ICC/ANSI A117.1 "*Accessible and Usable Buildings and Facilities*." Other codes related to design and construction of interiors are included by reference or in the appendices.

In order to understand the building codes, we must recognize who writes, interprets, and promotes them, how they are adopted into law, and who enforces them. This chapter provides an overview of the major building codes and the organizations that promote them. We will survey the typical methods of code adoption and enforcement and try to understand what to expect when dealing with officials.

HISTORY OF BUILDING CODE ORGANIZATIONS

Building code and safety organizations have existed in the United States since the 19th century [1]. These organizations promote public health and safety and, therefore, develop standards for building design and construction. Their membership primarily is composed of building inspection officials or fire prevention officials but also includes other professionals from the design and construction industry. Building officials traditionally enforce one of the regional model building codes, and fire officials enforce the life safety codes. This concept is illustrated in Figure 1.1.

REGIONAL MODEL BUILDING CODES

Regional model building codes cover a variety of structural, environmental, weatherproofing, and building systems topics, as well as life safety concerns, such as means of egress, fire resistance, fire protection, and control. The three model building code organizations in the United States are the Building Officials and Code Administrators (BOCA), the International Conference of Building Officials (ICBO), and the Southern Building Code Congress International (SBCCI). All three organizations maintain, revise, and publish the codes, provide plan reviews, code interpretations, education and the certification of building officials. The IBC and SBC operate testing and evaluation services for building products and systems [2, 3, 4].

Figure 1.2 shows the approximate regional areas in which each of the model building codes has been adopted. Some states, such as Wisconsin and New York, and even some counties, such as Dade County (Miami) in Florida, have written and adopted their own building codes [5]. This book, however, does not address these local codes.

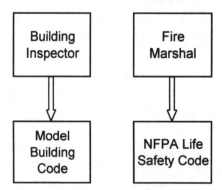

FIGURE 1.1 Building inspector, fire marshal, relevant codes.

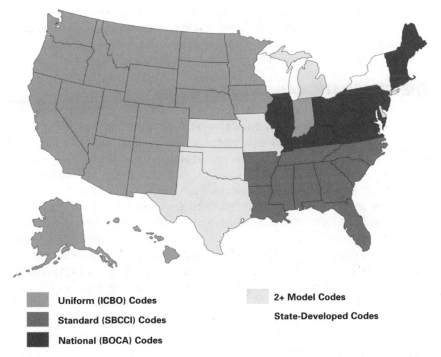

FIGURE 1.2   Regional model building codes currently observed in each state. *(Source: NCSBCS, Introduction to Building Codes 2000)*

Building Officials and Code Administrators International

Building Officials and Code Administrators International (BOCA) was founded in 1915. Its codes are used in the Midwest and from New England to Oklahoma. BOCA publishes building, mechanical, plumbing, fire prevention, and property maintenance codes called The National Code Series [2].

International Conference of Building Officials

The International Conference of Building Officials (ICBO) founded in 1922, publishes the *Uniform Building Code* (UBC). The UBC is used in the western states, Texas, Missouri, and Indiana. It is also the model code for the U.S. departments of defense and energy and is used in Japan, Brazil, and other countries. The ICBO also publishes a mechanical code and fire code [3].

Southern Building Code Congress International

Founded in 1940, the Southern Building Code Congress International (SBCCI) publishes the *Standard Building Codes*, which is used mainly in the southern states and Puerto Rico. SBCCI publishes plumbing, fire prevention, mechanical, and gas codes, and codes concerning housing, swimming pools, amusement devices, existing buildings, and unsafe building abatement [4].

THE INTERNATIONAL BUILDING CODE

The model code groups formed the Congress of American Building Officials (CABO) in 1972. CABO has enabled the code groups to address editorial and technical differences in the model codes, adopt a common format for the various codes, and create the International Code Council (ICC). The ICC's five technical committees, consisting of members from each code group, have worked since 1996 to create the *ICC, International Building Code 2000*, "a building code that is consistent with and inclusive of the scope and content of the existing model building codes" [5]. The IBC eventually will replace the regional model codes currently used by building officials throughout the United States. Fire officials will continue to enforce the NFPA *Life Safety Code* [5]. The IBC already has been adopted by the state of South Carolina and the city of Richardson, Texas [8].

NFPA GOES ITS OWN WAY

Attempts to integrate the NFPA into the ICC have failed for several reasons, including an inability to determine which fire and fuel gas codes the IBC would govern and which group would have authority. The NFPA allows any active member to vote on code changes, while the ICC and model code organizations allow only active building officials to vote. These differences, along with the old conflict of authority between fire and building officials, are too great a divide to be bridged at present [5].

The ICC has published the *International Fire Code,* along with *the International Plumbing Code, International Mechanical Code,* and *International Private Sewage Disposal Code.* The NFPA has announced an agreement with the International Association of Plumbing and Mechanical Officials (IAPMO) to publish a new building code. Although the IBC still references NFPA codes extensively, the ICC likely will revise its code to eliminate any reference to NFPA when that organization publishes its own building code. Designers, contractors, and owners, therefore, must continue to deal with two separate sets of building codes for the foreseeable future.

Figure 1.3 illustrates the parallel development of the model codes and the IBC with the *Life Safety Code* and other NFPA codes. You will notice that much attention is given in critical areas of this book to comparing and contrasting these two major codes.

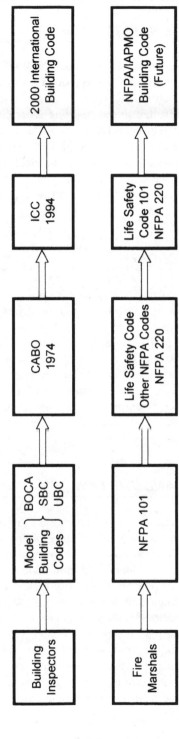

FIGURE 1.3 Parallel development of ICC and NFPA codes.

NFPA AND THE LIFE SAFETY CODE

The National Fire Protection Association (NFPA), with headquarters in Quincy, Mass., was "founded in 1896 to protect people, their property and the environment from destructive fire" [2]. A series of documents relating to fire drills and fire escapes resulted in the *Building Exits Code* published in 1927. The NFPA publishes and maintains hundreds of standards about fire prevention and safety, including the *Life Safety Code* (NFPA 101). Other publications include a fire prevention code, a fuel gas code, an electrical code, and a standard for building construction types. NFPA also publishes codes governing fire extinguishers, fire sprinklers, fire doors, grandstands, racetracks, and roof coverings [1].

NOT A BUILDING CODE?

Although the *Life Safety Code* (LSC) says it "does not address building construction features," it does include provisions typically associated with a building code and "identifies the minimum criteria for the design of egress facilities" [7]. LSC Chapters 7, 8, 9, and 10 contain prescriptive (code) requirements for the location, number, and size of exits, and also the design and construction of doors, stairs, ramps, finishes, walls, lighting, and ventilation equipment. Chapters 12 and 13 contain detailed construction requirements for all health-care structures. Some of those requirements conflict with the model building codes. Since the *Life Safety Code* affects design and construction, we will consider it to be a building code.

BUILDING CODES AND THE LAW

Local and/or state governments adopt codes into law, along with exceptions and additions recommended by local building or fire officials. Updated versions of the codes usually are adopted a few years after the code group revises them. This approach allows problems with new code revisions to be worked out by conferences and officials, who thoroughly review and amend them before their enactment. Most states have adopted the *Life Safety Code* and some version of one of the regional model building codes. Some state and federal agencies that build or provide plan reviews also adopt various codes. Some states adopt codes statewide and some allow local governments to adopt the codes. The map in Figure 1.4 shows which states adopt codes statewide [6]. Since some cities and counties also adopt codes as ordinances, buildings on opposite sides of a street might be in different municipalities and fall under different jurisdictions.

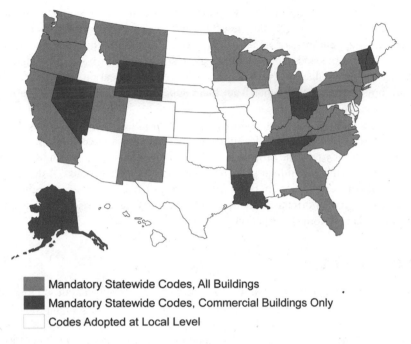

Mandatory Statewide Codes, All Buildings

Mandatory Statewide Codes, Commercial Buildings Only

Codes Adopted at Local Level

FIGURE 1.4 Code adoption and application across the U.S. *(Source: NCSBCS, Introduction to Building Codes, 2000)*

Code Enforcement and Plan Review

Local building and fire officials usually enforce the codes, but they also may be enforced by state agencies. In Alabama, the State Building Commission reviews plans for schools, dormitories, hotels, theaters, and other public facilities. The Department of Public Health reviews plans for health-care and food-preparation facilities. The Department of Human Resources reviews plans for day-care facilities. Other states have similar governmental entities that review and enforce the codes.

Cities and other areas that require a building permit also enforce the codes when the permit application is submitted. The permitting authority might review plans, inspect the work, and require changes if the plans or work do not meet code. Local building inspectors usually are the most common code enforcement agents.

Overlapping Jurisdictions

Codes do not always coincide and can conflict in situations of overlapping jurisdiction. The designer, with assistance from code enforcement officials, must sort out which code(s) will govern on a given project.

When there is a difference of opinion about code interpretation, the model code or NFPA staff usually decide which will govern. The codes also have commentaries, appendices, or annexes that expand on the text. We have included many illustrations and quotations from these sources in this book. Although individual code staff may interpret the code differently, appeal procedures are available in all jurisdictions, either from local appeal boards or through litigation in civil court.

One cannot be too circumspect about which codes are applicable and who will enforce them; states and localities have no specific sources for that information. An attorney near the project should be able to advise you which code(s) and code versions the governments that have jurisdiction have adopted. A design professional with experience in a specific building or occupancy type might be the best source for information about which agencies have jurisdiction and must approve plans before construction.

A Cautionary Tale

We know about one instance in which an architect designed an addition to a medical outpatient clinic. This steel and wood frame building had a high pitched roof with space for a partial second floor. Other tenants in the building (physician's offices and the architect's own office) had second-floor areas, so the addition to the outpatient clinic was designed for the second floor. The city building official permitted the project since the design complied with the model building code (SBC). After the addition was built, the state health agency inspector ruled (correctly) that the facility violated the *Life Safety Code* provision that does not allow health-care facilities in wood-frame buildings to be higher than one story (contradicting the SBC). The outpatient clinic paid for an office and then paid to have it torn down. Our firm inherited that work after the owner's relationship with the original architect was terminated.

Code Enforcement After Occupancy

In areas where no plan review or permit is required, the codes are enforced during a fire official's inspection, typically after occupancy. It is difficult to modify an occupied building, so complete enforcement is usually not possible without plan review and permitting. The building or fire official typically inspects for violations but also has limited authority to require building modifications.

Another Tale

We once worked on a project in a county that had no building permit authority. The state fire marshal inspected a pool hall after it opened and ruled that the building was a place of assembly because of its size and the amount of open floor space. The owner had to hire an architect to draw plans (now as-builts). In the process, we found a long list of code violations, and that the modifications required would be quite costly. In fact, the retrofit was so costly that the pool hall was forced out in favor of a better paying tenant—an exotic dance club.

Let's assume that, whether you are an owner, designer, or builder, you want to know what the codes are and how to comply with them. This book will examine the codes in more detail and show you how to design facilities that comply with the *International Building Code,* the *Life Safety Code,* and the ICC/ANSI *Accessible and Usable Buildings and Facilities.*

REFERENCES

1. NFPA Web site: http://www.nfpa.org/About_NFPA/about_nfpa.html
2. BOCA Web site: http://www.bocai.org/about_boca.htm
3. ICBO Web site: http://www.icbo.org/General_Information/History,_Mission,_Purpose/
4. SBC Web site: http://www.sbcci.org/SBCCIInfo/sbcci.htm
5. ICC Web site: http://www.intlcode.org/abouticc.htm
6. NCSBCS. 2000 Edition. *Introduction to Building Codes*, National Conference of States on Building Codes and Standards, Inc. Herndon, VA
7. NFPA. 2000 Edition. *NFPA 101 Life Safety Code,* National Fire Protection Association. Quincy, MA
8. SBC Web site: sbcci.org/ICC.icc.htm

CHAPTER 2
THE PROFESSIONAL INTERIOR DESIGNER

DEFINITION

The National Council for Interior Design Qualification (NCIDQ) offers the following definition of the professional interior designer:

The Professional Interior Designer is qualified by education, experience, and examination to enhance the function and quality of interior spaces.

For the purpose of improving the quality of life, increasing productivity, and protecting the health, safety, and welfare of the public, the Professional Interior Designer:

- *analyzes the client's needs, goals, and life and safety requirements;*
- *integrates findings with knowledge of interior design;*
- *formulates preliminary design concepts that are appropriate, functional, and aesthetic;*
- *develops and presents final design recommendations through appropriate presentation media;*
- *prepares working drawings and specifications for non-load bearing interior construction, materials, finishes, space planning, furnishings, fixtures and equipment;*
- *collaborates with licensed practitioners who offer professional services in the technical areas of mechanical, electrical, and load-bearing design as required for regulatory approval;*
- *prepares and administers bids and contract documents as the client's agent; reviews and evaluates design solutions during implementation and upon completion* [1].

DECORATOR VS. DESIGNER

Although many people make no distinction between *interior designer* and *interior decorator*, the job description offered by NCIDQ doesn't fit the term *decorator* at all. The interior designer we discuss in this book designs interior spaces (among other activities) and is unavoidably involved in using the building codes. The issues of building construction and life safety addressed in this book will help designers understand the codes and their impact on the designer's work.

NATIONAL COUNCIL FOR INTERIOR DESIGN QUALIFICATION

NCIDQ was created in 1972 by the two national interior design membership organizations that subsequently formed the American Society of Interior Designers (ASID). By charter, the NCIDQ has a membership consisting of state (or provincial) licensing agencies and professional interior design organizations. The professional organizations that are members of NCIDQ are:

- ASID—American Society of Interior Designers
- IDC—Interior Designers of Canada
- IIDA—International Interior Design Association
- IDEC—Interior Design Educators Council

LEGAL RECOGNITION

Twenty jurisdictions in the United States, including the District of Columbia, as well as Puerto Rico and eight Canadian provinces, currently have a registration, certification, or licensing requirement for interior designers. Several states license interior designers through the same board that licenses engineers, architects, surveyors, and landscape architects. Figure 2.1 shows the states that offer interior design licensing. More than 23 countries outside the United States also recognize the professional practice of interior design or interior architecture.

TITLE VS. PRACTICE LAWS

Most states have enacted *title laws* for interior designers, laws that govern who can use the title *interior designer*. Other design professionals, such as architects,

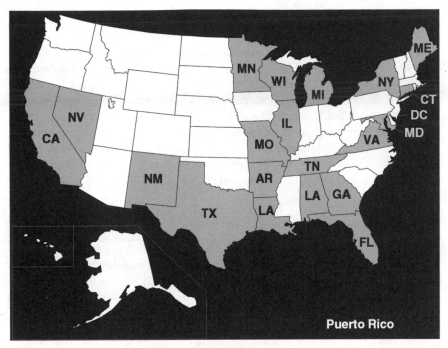

FIGURE 2.1   States that offer interior design licensing. *(Source: NCIDQ, www.ncidq.org)*

surveyors, and engineers, have *practice laws*, which restrict who may perform or supervise the design of certain types of facilities. Interior designers and organizations around the United States are working to enact and/or revise interior design laws to allow more freedom and responsibility for interior designers. Political controversy surrounds this issue.

OPPOSITION

The American Institute of Architects (AIA) is keenly interested in the state certification activities of the NCIDQ and of interior designers because it sees an infringement of its practice area [3]. The NCIDQ definition of interior designer overlaps most of what traditionally has been considered architecture. In fact, many architects use the term *interior architecture* to describe part of their business. Architects argue that the education and experience required for NCIDQ certification do not qualify interior designers to design large facilities.

EDUCATION

The Foundation for Interior Design Education (FIDER), created in 1970, establishes standards for interior design education. Participating institutions are reviewed periodically for student achievement in several areas, including theory, design, technical, communication, professional concerns, history, and information gathering. FIDER proposes standards with increased emphasis on understanding and applying codes in the area of life safety, exits, fire suppression, indoor air quality, sanitation, acoustics, lighting, ergonomics, and barrier-free design. Most of these topics will be discussed in later chapters. A list of FIDER qualified college programs is included in an appendix [2].

QUALIFICATION

NCIDQ maintains and administers the examination recognized by the member state boards for licensing interior designers. To qualify to take the exam, a candidate must meet minimum education and experience requirements, generally a combination of at least two years of education and three years of experience.

EXAMINATION AND CERTIFICATION

The NCIDQ examination, given in six parts over 12 hours, includes (in descending order of importance) building systems, building codes, pre-design activities, contract documents, theory, business, project coordination, furniture and equipment, finishes, history, and communication methods. Passing the NCIDQ exam qualifies you for registration as a Professional Interior Designer in the state or states where you practice [4].

PROFESSIONAL PRACTICE

Professional interior design organizations in the United States have approximately 30,000 members. The largest 100 firms in commercial practice employ about 8,000 designers. During 1998, they designed more than 431 million square feet, specified more than $22 billion in construction, equipment, and furniture, and generated more than $1.13 billion in fees. The other 22,000 interior designers work in a wide range of businesses, including small and medium-sized interior design practices, architect's offices, furniture dealers, and facilities management offices. Interior designers can work alone or in tandem with other professionals to design all types of residential, commercial, governmental, and institutional facilities [5].

ASSOCIATING WITH AN ARCHITECT OR ENGINEER

Many times, especially on large and complex projects, the interior designer functions as part of a larger team of design professionals. An interior designer might associate with an architect or engineer when the size or complexity of a project cause state registration laws to require an architect or engineer. Architects usually are qualified to design building structures and enclosures and are typically *generalists*. Engineers usually are qualified to design only one part of the building and are *specialists*. You might need several engineers in various disciplines, such as structural, mechanical, electrical, and acoustical. This relationship is illustrated in Figure 2.2.

CONTRACT DOCUMENTS

Whether or not working in a team, the interior designer produces plans, specifications, instructions, renderings, sample boards, and other documents that convey the design intent to potential bidders or contractors. This package is referred to as the *contract documents* and is the basis for the contract between the owner and the contractor. Many interior design projects are multiple contract types, in which several packages are bid out, with each *bid package* configured around the work of a specific trade or group of trades.

CONSTRUCTION

Several types of contractual relationships can be employed to develop a project. The most commonly used are Owner In-House Forces, Single Prime Contract, Multiple Prime Contract, Construction Manager, and Design Build, as illustrated in Figure 2.3. A more detailed illustration of the owner-designer-contractor relationship in the traditional method of design/bid/build project delivery is shown in Figure 2.4. Many interior designers provide some portion of the work under direct contract with the owner, especially floor and wall covering, window treatment, and furnishings. This type of project delivery option is illustrated in Figure 2.5. Furniture, fixtures, and equipment typically are delivered and installed by separate contractors; these items must be coordinated with the activities of the construction contractor.

Interior designers often certify payments to contractors and suppliers and can find themselves involved in disputes about payment or performance. The Construction Specifications Institute and other professional societies are sources for guides and checklists about the administration of construction projects. It is safest to use a time-tested contract form of agreement between owner and design pro-

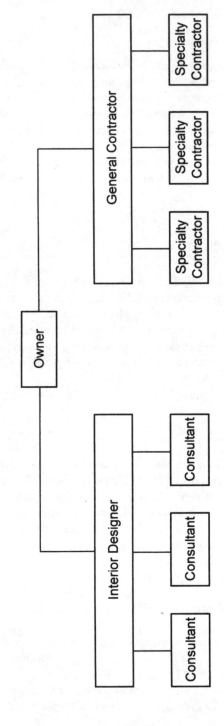

FIGURE 2.2 Traditional relationships between owner, designer, and contractors.

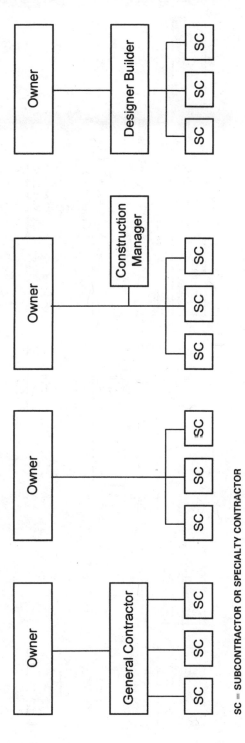

SC = SUBCONTRACTOR OR SPECIALTY CONTRACTOR

FIGURE 2.3 Optional construction delivery relationships.

2.7

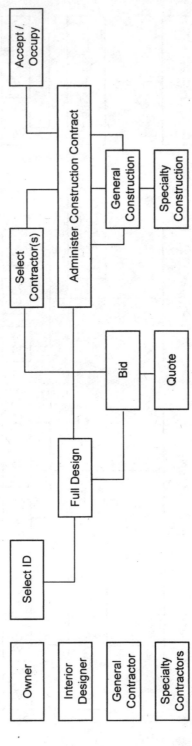

FIGURE 2.4 Traditional project delivery flow diagram.

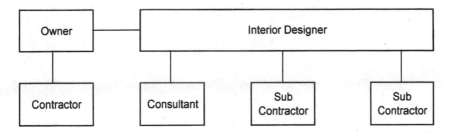

FIGURE 2.5 Optional project delivery flow diagram.

fessional and between owner and contractor. The AIA sells a complete series of documents, as does the Engineers Joint Construction Documents Committee. An attorney should review contracts for changes. Keep accurate records; document conversations and activities. One essential thing to remember—*communicate*. Ineffective communication, poor contract documents, and failure to interpret the documents correctly create most of the problems during construction. The design professional is part of a team whose common goal is to deliver a quality project to the owner.

REFERENCES

1. NCIDQ Web site. http.//www.ncidq.org/fr_who.htm
2. FIDER Web site: http://www.fider.org/direc.htm
3. NCIDQ Web site. http://www.ncidq.org/fr_certification.htm
4. NCIDQ Web site: http://www.ncidq.org/fr_exinfo.htm
5. Koffel, W.E., 1999, *"What is a Registered Interior Designer."* Southern Building Magazine July/August 1999, Birmingham, AL.

CHAPTER 3
USE AND OCCUPANCY

CLASSIFYING OCCUPANCIES

The building codes define occupancy of a building or space according to how it is used. The International Building Code (IBC) and the Life Safety Code (LSC) classify occupancies according to a different set of categories. Sometimes the codes define one project under two different classifications. It is the designer's task not only to determine which codes are applicable but also to resolve sometimes contradictory requirements between the codes [1].

LSC Chapters 1-4 and 5-11 describe the basic components for means of egress and fire resistance applicable to all buildings. Chapters 12-42 contain requirements for specific occupancy classifications. The LSC has a recommended procedure for using the code, which starts at Chapter 6, *Occupancy*. This procedure is shown in a chart as Figure 3.1a.

The IBC also is organized around occupancy classifications. No recommended procedure is included in the IBC, so we have included the chart from the 1997 Standard Building code as Figure 3.1b.

OCCUPANT LOAD

The codes provide methods of calculating occupant load, primarily based on an allowance of a given number of square feet per occupant. The LSC specifies a floor area allowance in the code section for each occupancy. The occupant load is used to determine minimum exit width, unless there is a limiting factor such as fixed seating. We discuss exits in Chapter 7, *Means of Egress*.

(1) Determine the occupancy classification by referring to the occupancy definitions in Chapter 6 and the occupancy Chapters 12 through 42 *(see 6.1.14 for buildings with more than one use).*

(2) Determine if the building or structure is new or existing *(see the definitions in Chapter 3).*

(3) Determine the occupant load *(see 7.3.1).*

(4) Determine the hazard of contents *(see Section 6.2).*

(5) Refer to the applicable occupancy chapter of the *Code* (Chapters 12 through 42) *(see Chapters 1 through 4 and 6 through 11, as needed, for general information (such as definitions) or as directed by the occupancy chapter).*

(6) Determine the occupancy subclassification or special use condition, if any, by referring to Chapters 18 and 19, health care occupancies; Chapters 22 and 23, detention and correctional occupancies; Chapters 28 and 29, hotels and dormitories; Chapters 32 and 33, residential board and care occupancies; and Chapters 36 and 37, mercantile occupancies, which contain subclassifications or special use definitions.

(7) Proceed through the applicable occupancy chapter to verify compliance with each referenced section, subsection, paragraph, subparagraph, and referenced codes, standards, and other documents.

(8) Where two or more requirements apply, the occupancy chapter generally takes precedence over the base Chapters 1 through 4 and 6 through 11.

(9) Where two or more occupancy chapters apply, such as in a mixed occupancy *(see 6.1.14),* the most restrictive requirements apply.

FIGURE 3.1a Procedure for determining Life Safety Code Requirements. *(Source: NFPA, 101 Life Safety Code, 2000)†*

OCCUPANCY CLASSIFICATIONS

Assembly: Large gatherings of more than 50 people in one room, as classified by both the IBC and LSC. Some regional model codes previously defined *assembly* as more than 100. The IBC divides *assembly* into five groups (Groups A-1 through A-5) based on the number of occupants and specific use. The codes are very restrictive for this classification because of the number of occupants.

Business: Offices for professional service providers, banks, outpatient clinics, laboratories, higher education, government offices, and post offices. Do not confuse with *mercantile* occupancy. Business includes medical outpatient clinics that do not involve certain types of anesthesia.

1. Determine Occupancy Classification of the structure. Select occupancy classification which most accurately fits the use of the building. (Chapter 3)

2. Determine actual physical properties of building.
   (a) Determine building area each floor. (Area definition Chapter 2)
   (b) Determine grade elevation for building. (Grade definition Chapter 2)
   (c) Determine building height in feet above grade. (Height definition Chapter 2)
   (d) Determine building height in stories. (Story definition Chapter 2)
   (e) Determine separation distance from exterior walls to assumed and common property lines. (Property line definition Chapter 2)
   (f) Determine percent of exterior openings per floor.

3. Determine minimum Type of Construction necessary to accommodate proposed structure. (Chapter 6)
   (a) Determine maximum allowable heights and floor areas for Types of Construction and Occupancy classification. (Table 500)
   (b) Check allowable height and area increases permitted. (Chapter 5)

4. Check detailed Occupancy requirements. (Chapter 4)

5. Check detailed Construction requirements.
   (a) Fire Protection of Structural Members (Chapter 6 and Table 600)
   (b) Fire Protection Requirements (Chapter 7 and Table 705.1.2)
   (c) Means of Egress Requirements (Chapter 10)
   (d) Special restrictions if in Fire District. (Appendix F. The provisions of Appendix F are applicable only where specifically adopted by ordinance.)

6. Review design as related to standards. (Chapters 16-26)

7. Check other requirements as necessary.
   (a) Construction projecting into public property (Chapter 32)
   (b) Elevators and conveying systems (Chapter 30)
   (c) Sprinklers, standpipes and alarm systems (Chapter 9)
   (d) Use of combustible materials on the interior (Chapter 8)
   (e) Roofs and roof structures (Chapter 15)
   (f) Light, ventilation and sanitation (Chapter 12)
   (g) Other

These steps are naturally varied in sequence by individual preferences; however, the first three are standard steps which should be followed in proper order to assist in design or review of buildings.

FIGURE 3.1b   Procedure for determining Standard Building Code requirements. *(Source: SBCCI, Standard Building Code Commentary, 1997)*

Detention: Jails, prisons, and detention facilities of all types, as classified by the LSC. The IBC includes detention facilities under *institutional*.

Educational: Any educational use for six or more people through high school. This includes kindergarten, nursery schools, and day care. The IBC defines *educational* as any use for *education, supervision, or personal care of persons over 2½ years old*[1]. The codes are especially restrictive for early childhood facilities because young children cannot exit without assistance in an emergency.

Factory and industrial: Manufacturing and processing of all types of goods and materials, power plants, refineries, and laundries. The IBC divides *factory* into two groups based on hazard. The LSC uses the term *industrial* instead of *factory*. If the process involves certain types and amounts of hazardous materials, it falls into a *high hazard* classification.

High hazard: *"Manufacturing, processing, generation or storage of materials that constitute a physical or health hazard,"* according to the IBC [1]. This occupancy is divided into five groups (Groups H-1 through H-5), based on quantity and type of material involved. The LSC has no separate *hazard* classification, but classifies all buildings as *low, ordinary,* or *high hazard* and provides special means of egress requirements for *high hazard* occupancies.

Health care: Hospitals, nursing homes, and outpatient treatment clinics, as classified by the LSC. The code is very restrictive for this occupancy because of the inability of occupants to be aware of an emergency or to escape without assistance. The IBC classifies outpatient treatment clinics not involving certain types of anesthesia as *business* occupancy.

Ambulatory Health Care: This definition from LSC section 3.3.134.1 includes outpatient treatment facilities that provide medical procedures requiring anesthesia or which otherwise *"render the patient incapable of taking action for self-preservation."* This may include outpatient surgery, dialysis, sleep therapy and other types of outpatient care.

Institutional: The IBC uses this classification to include all of the uses the LSC defines as health care, as well as prisons and other types of detention facilities. *Institutional* is divided into four groups: Group I-1 (mental health facilities); Group I-2 (hospitals and other 24-hour care facilities, including overnight childcare centers); Group I-3 (detention facilities, which are divided into Conditions 1 through 4 based on the amount of restraint and supervision the occupants need); and Group I-4 (childcare facilities). The IBC classifies 24-hour childcare facilities as I-2.

Mercantile: Department stores, supermarkets, drug stores, shopping centers, and markets of all kinds involved in the *"display and sale of merchandise,"* as classified by both the IBC and LSC. Since *mercantile* establishments often sell materials that can be dangerous in large quantities, limits are placed on how much of these materials can be stored in the store. The codes have special rules for covered shopping malls, which are outlined in Chapter 4, *Special Use and Occupancies*.

Residential: All places where people sleep, including one- and two-family dwellings, apartments, condominiums, hotels, boarding houses, and convents. This classification applies to board and care or assisted living facilities that house no more than 16 residents. The IBC divides *residential* into four groups (R-1 through R-4) and the LSC divides it into five groups (*a* through *e*). Both codes have specific requirements for each group based on the number of residents in one place.

Storage: Facilities for bulk storage of goods or materials. The IBC divides this use into two groups based on the hazard of contents. The LSC includes storage of animals in this classification. Large amounts of dangerous materials can cause a storage facility to be classified as *high hazard*. Minor storage incidental to another use generally is not considered separately.

Utility: Agricultural facilities, barns, and stables, as classified by the IBC.

Miscellaneous: Tanks, greenhouses and other structures.

Special uses: Covered malls, high rise buildings, atriums, parking structures, movie projection rooms, amusement buildings, and aircraft-related buildings, as classified by the IBC [1, 2].

MIXED USE—TO SEPARATE OR NOT

The codes have methods of dealing with mixed use, but generally recognize that any occupancy has a certain amount of mixed use. The issue of separation of occupancies is an important difference between the two major codes.

The LSC simply requires that the construction and means of egress for any mixed occupancy must meet the requirements of the most restrictive occupancy. Specific fire separations are not prescribed. This method also is accepted under the IBC [2].

The model codes always have recognized a need to separate uses with fire-rated walls. The IBC, however, has incorporated two methods of dealing with mixed uses: *separated* or *non-separated*. The IBC and LSC treat non-separated uses the same, applying the construction requirements of the most restrictive occupancy to both occupancy areas. Separated uses require use of the matrix shown in Figure 3.2 to calculate required fire separation.

REFERENCES

1. ICC, 2000 Edition. International Code Congress. Falls Church, VA.
2. NFPA, 2000 Edition, NFPA 101 Life Safety Code, National Fire Protection Association

TABLE 302.3.3
REQUIRED SEPARATION OF OCCUPANCIES (HOURS)[a]

USE	A-1	A-2	A-3	A-4	A-5	B[b]	E[e]	F-1	F-2	H-1	H-2	H-3	H-4	H-5	I-1	I-2	I-3	I-4	M[b]	R-1	R-2	R-3,R4	S-1	S-2[c]	U
A-1	2	2	2	2	2	2	2	3	2	NP	4	3	2	4	2	2	2	2	2	2	2	2	3	2	1
A-2[h]	—	2	2	2	2	2	2	3	2	NP	4	3	2	4	2	2	2	2	2	2	2	2	3	2	1
A-3[d,f]	—	—	2	2	2	2	2	3	2	NP	4	3	2	4	2	2	2	2	2	2	2	2	3	2	1
A-4	—	—	—	2	2	2	2	3	2	NP	4	3	2	4	2	2	2	2	2	2	2	2	3	2	1
A-5	—	—	—	—	2	2	2	3	2	NP	4	3	2	4	2	2	2	2	2	2	2	2	3	2	1
B[b]	—	—	—	—	—	2	2	3	2	NP	2	1	1	1	2	2	2	2	2	2	2	2	3	2	1
E	—	—	—	—	—	—	2	3	2	NP	4	3	2	3	2	2	2	2	2	2	2	2	3	2	1
F-1	—	—	—	—	—	—	—	3	3	NP	2	1	1	1	3	3	3	3	3	3	3	3	3	3	3
F-2	—	—	—	—	—	—	—	—	2	NP	2	1	1	1	2	2	2	2	2	2	2	2	3	2	1
H-1	—	—	—	—	—	—	—	—	—	4	NP	NP	NP	NP	NP	NP	NP	NP	NP	NP	NP	NP	NP	NP	NP
H-2	—	—	—	—	—	—	—	—	—	—	4	1	2	2	4	4	4	4	2	4	4	4	2	2	1
H-3	—	—	—	—	—	—	—	—	—	—	—	3	1	1	4	3	3	3	1	3	3	3	1	1	1
H-4	—	—	—	—	—	—	—	—	—	—	—	—	2	2	4	4	4	3	1	4	4	4	1	1	1
H-5	—	—	—	—	—	—	—	—	—	—	—	—	—	—	4	4	4	2	2	2	2	2	1	1	3
I-1	—	—	—	—	—	—	—	—	—	—	—	—	—	—	2	2	2	2	2	2	2	2	4	3	2

FIGURE 3.2a Required separation of occupancies (*Source: ICC, International Building Code, 2000*)

USE	A-1	A-2	A-3	A-4	A-5	B^b	E^e	F-1	F-2	H-1	H-2	H-3	H-4	H-5	I-1	I-2	I-3	I-4	M^b	R-1	R-2	R-3,R-4	S-1	S-2^c	U
I-1	—	—	—	—	—	—	—	—	—	—	—	—	—	1	2	2	2	2	2	2	2	2	4	3	2
I-2	—	—	—	—	—	—	—	—	—	—	—	—	—	—	—	2	2	2	2	2	2	2	3	2	1
I-3	—	—	—	—	—	—	—	—	—	—	—	—	—	—	—	—	2	2	2	2	2	2	3	2	1
I-4	—	—	—	—	—	—	—	—	—	—	—	—	—	—	—	—	—	2	2	2	2	2	3	2	1
M^b	—	—	—	—	—	—	—	—	—	—	—	—	—	—	—	—	—	—	2	2	2	2	3	2	1
R-1	—	—	—	—	—	—	—	—	—	—	—	—	—	—	—	—	—	—	—	2	2	2	3	2	1
R-2	—	—	—	—	—	—	—	—	—	—	—	—	—	—	—	—	—	—	—	—	2	2	3	2	1
R-3, R-4	—	—	—	—	—	—	—	—	—	—	—	—	—	—	—	—	—	—	—	—	—	2	3	2^g	1^g
S-1	—	—	—	—	—	—	—	—	—	—	—	—	—	—	—	—	—	—	—	—	—	—	3	3	3
S-2^c	—	—	—	—	—	—	—	—	—	—	—	—	—	—	—	—	—	—	—	—	—	—	—	3	1
U	—	—	—	—	—	—	—	—	—	—	—	—	—	—	—	—	—	—	—	—	—	—	—	—	1

For SI: 1 square foot = 0.0929 m². NP = Not permitted.

a. See Exception 1 to Section 302.3.3 for reductions permitted.

b. Occupancy separation need not be provided for incidental storage areas within Groups B and M if the:
   1. Area is less than 10 percent of the floor area, or
   2. Area is provided with an automatic fire-extinguishing system and is less than 3,000 square feet, or
   3. Area is less than 1,000 square feet.

c. Areas used only for private or pleasure vehicles may reduce separation by 1 hour.

d. Accessory assembly areas are not considered separate occupancies if the floor area is 750 square feet or less.

e. Assembly uses accessory to Group E are not considered separate occupancies

f. Accessory religious educational rooms and religious auditoriums with occupant loads of less than 100 are not considered separate occupancies.

g. See exception to Section 302.3.3.

h. Commercial kitchens need not be separated from the restaurant seating areas that they serve.

FIGURE 3.2a (continued) Required separation of occupancies (Source: ICC, International Building Code, 2000)

CHAPTER 4
SPECIAL USE AND OCCUPANCIES

INTENT AND SCOPE OF SPECIAL OCCUPANCIES

The IBC devotes an entire chapter about special occupancies considered as unique building types that require special rules and exceptions beyond those contained in other parts of the code. The types of special occupancies that involve design and construction of interiors are covered mall buildings, high-rise buildings and atriums. The rules for these types apply beyond the code requirements based on occupancy, height and area, and fire resistance. It might be possible, for example, to have a mall, an atrium, and a high-rise in the same building. The requirements for these special occupancies supersede, or are in addition to, the requirements specified in other sections of the code.

COVERED MALL BUILDINGS

A covered mall building, defined in IBC 402.2 and in LSC 3.3.25.3, is not more than three stories high and contains two or more tenants with main entrances opening into a pedestrian way. The tenants, according to the IBC, may include retail stores, restaurants, entertainment or amusement facilities, and transportation facilities.

A *lease plan* showing the location of each tenant and its exits must be provided to both building and fire authorities. Modifications to the lease plan may not be made without approval by code authorities.

MALLS

IBC Occupant Load

The IBC calculates mall occupant loads with a special formula, shown in Figure 4.1, to determine the means of egress requirements for malls.

Figure 4.1 shows a sample mall plan and how to calculate the *gross leasable area* (GLA). The GLA is used in the formula shown in Figure 4.1 to determine the *occupant load factor* (OLF), which is expressed in square feet per occupant. OLF is used to determine the requirements for means of egress, discussed in Chapter 7. The occupant load is not required to be less than 30 and shall not exceed 50. Mall buildings all have an OLF between 30 and 50 square feet per occupant, regardless of the calculated occupant load [1].

LSC Occupant Load

The LSC provides the chart shown in Figure 4.1a for calculating the occupant load. This chart starts at an occupant load of 30, which matches the IBC, but the maximum extends past 50. This means that a mall building larger than 30,000 square feet can have an occupant load of more than 50 square feet per occupant. When both codes apply, use the IBC maximum of 50 square feet per occupant.

The occupant load of food courts is added to the occupant load of malls, since means of egress from food courts is the same as from the mall. The occupant load of anchor tenant buildings is not included occupant load calculation for mall buildings because they have means of egress separate from the mall [2].

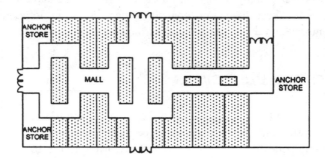

$$OLF = (0.00007) (GLA) + 25$$

where:

OLF = The occupant load factor (square feet per person).
GLA = The gross leasable area (square feet).

FIGURE 4.1   Mall gross leasable area and occupant load formula. *(Source: ICC, International Building Code, 2000 and SBCCI, Standard Building Code Commentary, 1997)*

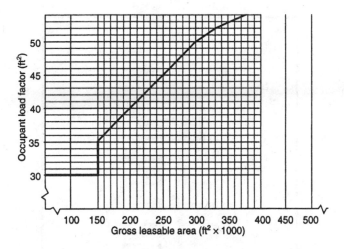

FIGURE 4.1a   Mall occupant load table. *(Source: NFPA, 101 Life Safety Code, 2000)*†

Anchor Tenants

Anchor tenants are usually large stores that open into the mall pedestrian way, but they also must have means of egress independent of the mall building. Figure 4.1b shows a sample mall plan with two large tenants, one that qualifies as an anchor tenant with independent means of egress and one that does not.

Means of Egress

The minimum mall width is 20 feet but the width also must be sufficient to serve the required occupant load. The maximum travel distance from any point within a mall to an exit is 200 feet. The length of dead-end malls may not exceed twice the width of the mall. The minimum width of an exit corridor from a mall is 66 inches. Ten feet clear exit width is required at any location between tenants, kiosks, displays, or other obstructions within the mall. Dead-end mall corridors are allowed only when the distance is less than twice the mall width, as illustrated in Figure 4.2.

Two Exits Required

Tenants with public area travel distance to the mall greater than 75 feet or with an occupant load of more than 50 people must have two means of egress. Figure 4.2 shows plans and sample calculations to show where a second means of egress is required.

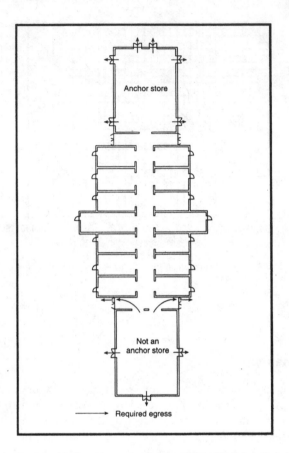

FIGURE 4.1b   Anchor tenant exit requirements. *(Source: NFPA, Life Safety Code Handbook, 1997)*††

Assembly Tenants

Assembly occupancy tenants (more than 50 people) must be located adjacent to a mall building's principal entrance. This would apply to a restaurant or a similar establishment. Half the exits from an assembly occupant tenant must lead directly to the exterior.

Construction Type and Fire Separation

Mall buildings of Construction Types I, II, III, and IV may be unlimited in area when they are surrounded on all sides by a dedicated open space of 60 feet or more. Fire-resistance-rated separation is not required between the mall and tenant spaces or between a food court and adjacent tenant spaces. Each tenant space must be separated from other tenants by a fire partition. Fire Partitions are discussed in Chapter 7, *Fire Resistance Rated Construction*.

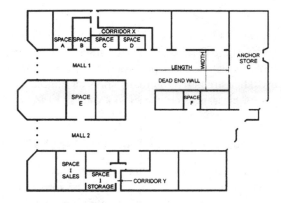

1. Space A exceeds the size and travel distance and must have two egress doors. (See 413.4.5.1.) Door to corridor X must be 1-hour with closers. (See 413.4.5.2 and Item 4 below.)
2. Space B is less than 2,250 sq ft, but exceeds 75 ft travel distance, therefore, 2 egress doors are required. (See 413.4.5.1.)
3. Spaces C and D do not exceed 2,250 sq ft or 75 ft travel, therefore, they may have a single egress door opening to the mall. (See 413.4.5.1.)
4. Corridor X, built as one of the listed exit elements, may serve as a termination of travel distance measurement from the mall. (See 413.4.3.) Storage is prohibited. (See 413.4.5.2.) Minimum width is 66 inches. (See 413.4.6.2.)
5. Space E has exposure on two malls and, due to size and travel distance, must have two doors. Each door may open into different malls as shown. (See 413.4.5.4.)
6. Space F has exposure on two malls, but is only required to have one egress door because of size and travel distance. (See 413.4.5.4.)
7. Mall 1 has a dead end that terminates at an anchor store. This is allowed as long as the length does not exceed twice the width. (See 413.4.8 and 1005.2 commentary.)
8. Store G qualifies as an anchor store because all of its exit requirements are satisfied by doors directly to the exterior.
9. Corridor Y must be 66 inches wide (See 413.4.6.2.) and meet the requirements for exit passageways with 1-hour opening protectives and closers. (See 413.4.5.2.)
10. Space I is required to have two exits. One of the means of egress is through an intervening storage room, as specifically allowed by 413.4.5.3.

FIGURE 4.2   Mall tenant exit requirements. *(Source: SBCCI, Standard Building Code Commentary, 1997)*

Kiosks

Temporary or permanent kiosks may not exceed 300 square feet, must be constructed of non-combustible material or fire-retardant treated wood, be provided with approved smoke detection and suppression equipment, and allow 10 feet of clearance from any other structure. Figure 4.3 shows a sample mall plan with the critical dimensions for clearances around kiosks shown.

Sprinkler, Emergency Communications, and Smoke Control

The mall building and all connected buildings are required to have an automatic sprinkler system and standpipe system throughout. The sprinkler system must be active even in vacant or unoccupied parts of the mall building. The sprinkler control system for tenant spaces must be independent from the sprinkler control system for the mall building. Mall buildings larger than 50,000 square feet are required to have an emergency communication system with standby power accessible to the fire department. The LSC requires smoke control systems in malls and in all tenant spaces when smoke barriers are not provided between tenants.

Plastic Signs

Plastic signs shall not exceed 20 percent of the tenant mall frontage area. The maximum height for horizontal signs and maximum width for vertical signs is 36

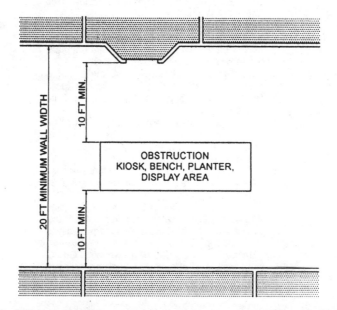

FIGURE 4.3   Mall kiosk critical clearances. *(Source: SBCCI, Standard Building Code Commentary, 1997)*

inches. The signs must be located at least 18 inches from adjacent tenants and have minimum flame and smoke ratings. For other requirements, see IBC Section 402.14. Figure 4.4 illustrates the requirements for allowable location, size, and construction of plastic signs in malls.

HIGH-RISE BUILDINGS

The IBC and the LSC define a high rise as any building having occupied floors more than 75 feet above the lowest level of fire department access, as illustrated in Figure 4.5. Exceptions include airport control towers, parking garages, stadiums, and similar outdoor assembly facilities (for which there are separate requirements), industrial process facilities, and certain hazardous occupancies.

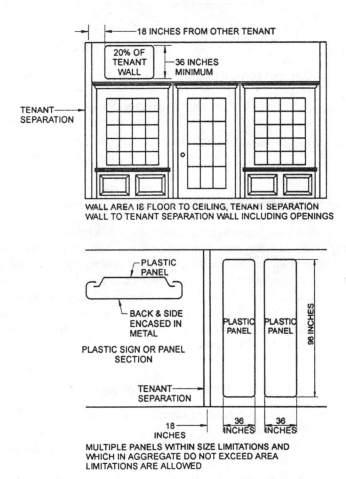

FIGURE 4.4 Mall sign location, dimensions, and construction. *(SBCCI, Standard Building Code Commentary, 1997)*

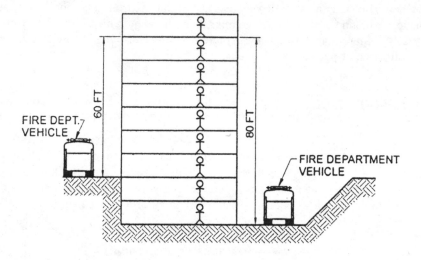

LEVEL OF FIRE DEPARTMENT VEHICLE ACCESS

HIGH RISE BUILDINGS

FIGURE 4.5   Definition of high-rise building. *(Source: SBCCI, Standard Building Code Commentary, 1997)*

Fire Sprinkler and Detection, Emergency Operations

All high-rise buildings, under the IBC, must have automatic sprinkler and fire detection systems, an emergency communication system, a fire department communication system, and a command center. They also must have stairway doors that meet fire and temperature rise requirements and have stairway communication systems. The LSC covers this topic in Chapter 32, *Special Structures and High Rise Buildings*. The LSC requires standby power sufficient to operate emergency lighting, the fire alarm, fire pump, central control station, elevator for firefighter access, and the smoke control system [2].

Reduction in Fire Resistance and Shaft Ratings

In high-rise buildings, which have supervisory sprinkler controls on each floor, the IBC allows special reductions in fire resistance ratings. Fire resistance ratings of building elements also may be reduced from that required under height and area limitations in the IBC. Height and area are discussed in Chapter 5. Vertical shafts, such as ducts or elevators, must have a one-hour fire resistance rating when automatic sprinklers are installed [1].

ATRIUMS

IBC Definition and Requirements

The IBC defines an *atrium* as an opening through two or more floor levels that is not a stairway, hoistway, or equipment chase. Materials and decorations in atriums must comply with the International Fire Code [3]. With certain exceptions, the entire building with an atrium must have sprinklers. No sprinklers are required in portions of the building that are protected from the atrium by a two-hour rated fire barrier. No sprinklers are required in an atrium when the ceiling is more than 55 feet above the atrium floor. These concepts are illustrated in Figure 4.6 [1].

The atrium must be separated from adjacent spaces by a one-hour rated fire barrier, with certain exceptions. The one-hour separation is not required when adjacent spaces are separated from the atrium by a 45-minute rated glass block wall. No rating is required when the adjacent spaces are separated from the atrium with glass walls protected by a sprinkler *water curtain*, with sprinkler heads spaced one foot off the glass and at six feet on center on both sides of the glass. The glass also must be held in place by substantial framing members, which will retain the glass in the framing during a fire. A qualified professional should, and in some jurisdiction must, design the water curtain and all fire protection sprinkler systems [1, 2].

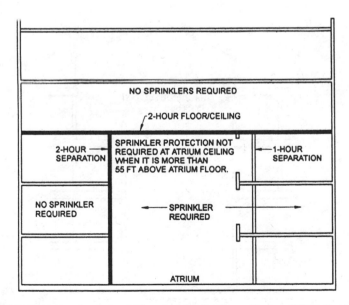

FIGURE 4.6 Fire separation and sprinkler protection in atriums. *(Source: SBCCI, Standard Building Code Commentary, 1997)*

An atrium may be used for any low-hazard occupancy, but when sprinklers are installed any use is permitted. The interior finish of walls and ceilings in atriums must be Class B, with no reduction allowed for installing sprinklers. Travel distances from levels above the atrium floor through an atrium may not exceed 150 feet.

Fire Detection and Smoke Control

An automatic fire detection and alarm system is required in atriums; the specific requirements are found in IBC Chapter 9, *Fire Protection Systems*. Figure 4.7 shows recommended locations for smoke detectors in an atrium. A smoke control (smoke venting) system with standby power for emergency operation also is required in atriums. A qualified professional should design the smoke control system.

Life Safety Code Definitions and Requirements

The LSC covers *Atriums* in Chapter 8, *Features of Fire Protection*, in the section about Vertical Openings. The definition and requirements for atriums differ slightly from those in the IBC. The LSC requires the atrium to be separated from the remainder of the building by a one-hour fire-rated barrier, with exceptions allowed, similar to the IBC, for glass walls with sprinklers. The entire building must be protected by an automatic sprinkler system, and there must be a smoke control system. The atrium floor may be used for any low hazard occupancy.

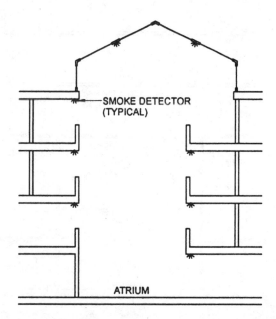

FIGURE 4.7   Smoke detector locations in an atrium. *(Source: SBCCI, Standard Building Code Commentary, 1997)*

MINI-ATRIUMS—ALTERNATIVE TO ATRIUMS

The LSC provides for "unenclosed floor openings forming a communicating space between floor levels" of three floors or less, called a *mini-atrium* in the LSC Commentary [2]. The requirements for a mini-atrium are less restrictive than the LSC requirements for a true atrium of more than three floors. The bottom floor of a mini-atrium must be located at, or one floor below, street or grade level, as shown in Figure 4.8. The mini-atrium must be separated from the remainder of the building with a one-hour rated fire barrier, as shown in Figure 4.9. Open stairs are allowed within the atrium with exits arranged from adjacent spaces as shown in Figure 4.10.

The IBC has similar means to achieve a mini-atrium but refers to this type of space as *a shaft enclosure*. The requirements for shaft enclosures are covered in Chapter 6, *Fire-Resistance-Rated Construction*.

REFERENCES

1. ICC, 2000 Edition. 2000 International Building Code, International Code Council, Falls Church, VA
2. NFPA, 2000 Edition, 2000 Life Safety Code, National Fire Protection Association, Quincy, MA

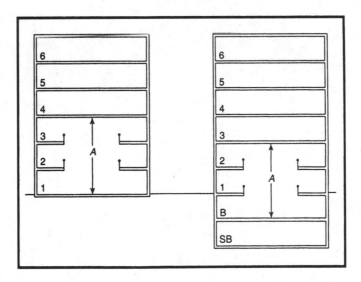

FIGURE 4.8　LSC required location of mini-atrium. *(Source: NFPA, Life Safety Code Handbook, 1997)*††

CHAPTER 5

HEIGHT, AREA, AND CONSTRUCTION TYPES

DEFINITIONS AND SCOPE

We will assume that most projects involving determinations of height, area, and construction type would require an architect or engineer. Certain projects involving interior construction for existing buildings, however, might require use and knowledge of the International Building Code Chapter 5, *General Building Heights and Areas*, and Chapter 6, *Types of Construction*, and the Life Safety Code Chapter 12, *New Health Care Occupancies*. This chapter examines the interior design and construction issues covered in these chapters.

HEIGHT AND AREA—IBC

When interior design and construction projects involve the addition of floor area, it is necessary to determine the total allowable area. IBC Table 503, shown in Figure 5.1, is used to determine the maximum allowable height and area of a building. This table has been developed using three main factors to set allowable area: occupancy, type of construction, and sprinklers. The building code allows larger buildings with a higher level of building protection, and restricts the area of buildings with a lower level of building protection. For instance, Construction Type IA buildings (the most restrictive building protection) may be of unlimited area for all occupancies except hazardous. Type VI buildings (the least restrictive building protection) may be no larger than 13,500 square feet and two stories.

ALLOWABLE HEIGHT AND BUILDING AREAS
Height limitations shown as stories and feet above grade plane.
Area limitations as determined by the definition of "Area, building", per floor.

		TYPE OF CONSTRUCTION								
		TYPE I		TYPE II		TYPE III		TYPE IV	TYPE V	
		A	B	A	B	A	B	HT	A	B
GROUP	HGT(ft) Hgt(S)	UL	160	65	55	65	55	65	50	40
A-1	S	UL	5	3	2	3	2	3	2	1
	A	UL	UL	15,500	8,500	14,000	8,500	15,000	11,500	5,500
A-2	S	UL	11	3	2	3	2	3	2	1
	A	UL	UL	15,500	9,500	14,000	9,500	15,000	11,500	6,000
A-3	S	UL	11	3	2	3	2	3	2	1
	A	UL	UL	15,500	9,500	14,000	9,500	15,000	11,500	6,000
A-4	S	UL	11	3	2	3	2	3	2	1
	A	UL	UL	15,500	9,500	14,000	9,500	15,000	11,500	6,000
A-5	S	UL	UL	UL	UL	UL	UL	UL	UL	UL
	A	UL	UL	UL	UL	UL	UL	UL	UL	UL
B	S	UL	11	5	4	5	4	5	3	2
	A	UL	UL	37,500	23,000	28,500	19,000	36,000	18,000	9,000
E	S	UL	5	3	2	3	2	3	1	1
	A	UL	UL	26,500	14,500	23,500	14,500	25,500	18,500	9,500
F-1	S	UL	11	4	2	3	2	4	2	1
	A	UL	UL	25,000	15,500	19,000	12,000	33,500	14,000	8,500
F-2	S	UL	11	5	3	4	3	5	3	2
	A	UL	UL	37,500	23,000	28,500	18,000	50,500	21,000	13,000
H-1	S	1	1	1	1	1	1	1	1	NP
	A	21,000	16,500	11,000	7,000	9,500	7,000	10,500	7,500	NP
H-2	S	UL	3	2	1	2	1	2	1	1
	A	21,000	16,500	11,000	7,000	9,500	7,000	10,500	7,500	3,000
H-3	S	UL	6	4	2	4	2	4	2	1
	A	UL	60,000	26,500	14,000	17,500	13,000	25,500	10,000	5,000
H-4	S	UL	7	5	3	5	3	5	3	2
	A	IL	UL	37,500	17,500	28,500	17,500	36,000	18,000	6,500
H-5	S	3	3	3	3	3	3	3	3	2
	A	UL	UL	37,500	23,000	28,500	19,000	36,000	18,000	9,000
I-1	S	UL	9	4	3	4	3	4	3	2
	A	UL	55,000	19,000	10,000	16,500	10,000	18,000	10,500	4,500
I-2	S	UL	4	2	1	1	NP	1	1	NP
	A	UL	UL	15,000	11,000	12,000	NP	12,000	9,500	NP
I-3	S	UL	4	2	1	2	1	2	2	1
	A	UL	UL	15,000	10,000	10,500	7,500	12,000	7,500	5,000
I-4	S	UL	5	3	2	3	2	3	1	1
	A	UL	60,500	26,500	13,000	23,500	13,000	25,500	18,500	9,000

FIGURE 5.1 Table 503 Allowable height and area. *(Source: ICC, International Building Code, 2000)*

Figure 5.2 illustrates the definition of building area. The building area calculation must include the area of mezzanines but may exclude the basement(s), when they are smaller in area than the first floor. Figure 5.2a demonstrates the IBC definition for a basement. The maximum height is expressed in number of stories or height above grade. Basements are not counted as a story unless the use

		TYPE OF CONSTRUCTION								
		TYPE I		TYPE II		TYPE III		TYPE IV	TYPE V	
		A	B	A	B	A	B	HT	A	B
GROUP	HGT(ft) / Hgt(S)	UL	160	65	55	65	55	65	50	40
M	S	UL	11	4	4	4	4	4	3	1
	A	UL	UL	21,500	12,500	18,500	12,500	20,500	14,000	9,000
R-1	S	UL	11	4	4	4	4	4	3	2
	A	UL	UL	24,000	16,000	24,000	16,000	20,500	12,000	7,000
R-2ª	S	UL	11	4	4	4	4	4	3	2
	A	UL	UL	24,000	16,000	24,000	16,000	20,500	12,000	7,000
R-3ª	S	UL	11	4	4	4	4	4	3	3
	A	UL	UL	UL	UL	UL	UL	UL	UL	UL
R-4	S	UL	11	4	4	4	4	4	3	2
	A	UL	UL	24,000	16,000	24,000	16,000	20,500	12,000	7,000
S-1	S	UL	11	4	3	3	3	4	3	1
	A	UL	48,000	26,000	17,500	26,000	17,500	25,500	14,000	9,000
S-2	S	UL	11	5	4	4	4	5	4	2
	A	UL	79,000	39,000	26,000	39,000	26,000	38,500	21,000	13,500
U	S	UL	5	4	2	3	2	4	2	1
	A	UL	35,500	19,000	8,500	14,000	8,500	18,000	9,000	5,500

FIGURE 5.1 *(continued)*   Table 503 Allowable height and area. *(Source: ICC, International Building Code, 2000)*

is assembly or educational. Mezzanines never are counted as a story. A detailed discussion of mezzanines is included in this chapter.

HEIGHT AND AREA—LSC

The LSC regulates the allowable height and area of buildings with requirements specified in the occupancy chapters (12-42). "Minimum Construction Requirements" at LSC Section XX.1.6. shows "no special requirements" at all occupancies except assembly, health care, ambulatory health care and detention spaces. LSC construction requirements for assembly occupancies are included as Figure 5.3, and do not allow assembly facilities of Type V construction (wood or other combustible materials) of more than one story. This is in direct conflict with IBC Table 503, which allows a Type V sprinkled assembly facility to be 11,500 square feet, before the area increases. LSC construction requirements for new health-care facilities are included as Figure 5.3a, and do not allow new health-care facilities of Type V(000) construction (unprotected wood), even when sprinkled. This is in direct conflict with IBC Table 503, which allows a Type V (unprotected wood) health-care facility to be 7500 square feet, before area increases, when sprinkled. These examples prove that allowable height and area must be cross-checked carefully when both codes apply.

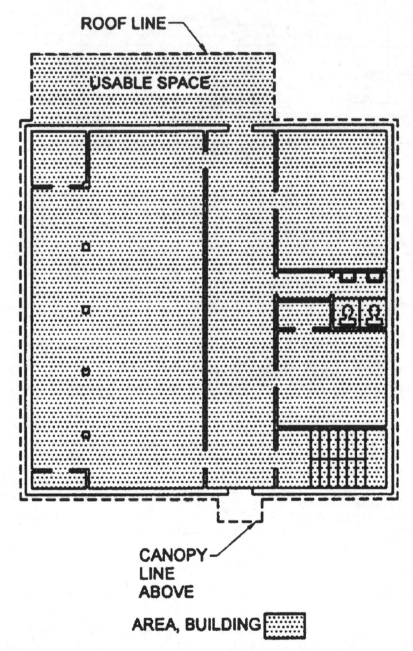

FIGURE 5.2 Calculation of building area. *(Source: SBCCI, Standard Building Code Commentary, 1997)*

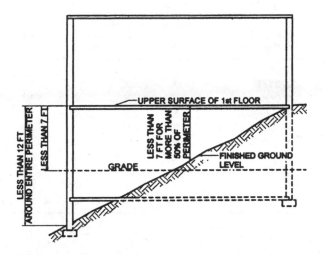

FIGURE 5.2a Qualification for basement. *(Source: SBCCI, Standard Building Code Commentary, 1997)*

Type of Construction	Below LED	LED	Number of Levels above LED				
			1	2	3	4
I(443)[†‡§] I(332)[†‡§] II(222)[†‡§]	Any assembly[◊]	Any assembly	Any assembly	Any assembly	Any assembly	Any assembly; If OL > 300[◊]
II(111)[†‡§]	Any assembly[◊] Limited to 1 level below LED	Any assembly	Any assembly	Any assembly; If OL > 1000[◊]	Assembly with OL ≤ 1000[◊]	NP
III(211)[‡] IV(2HH) V(111)	Any assembly[◊] Limited to 1 level below LED	Any assembly	Any assembly	Any assembly; If OL > 300[◊]	Assembly with OL ≤ 1000[◊]	NP
II(000)	Assembly with OL ≤ 1000[◊] Limited to 1 level below LED	Any assembly; If OL > 1000[◊]	Assembly with OL ≤ 300[◊]	NP	NP	NP
III(200) V(000)	Assembly with OL ≤ 1000[◊] Limited to 1 level below LED	Assembly with OL ≤ 1000	Assembly with OL ≤ 300[◊]	NP	NP	NP

NP: Not permitted.
LED: Level of exit discharge.
OL: Occupant load.
Note: For the purpose of this table, a mezzanine is not counted as a level.
[†]Where every part of the structural framework of roofs in Type I or Type II construction is 20 ft (6.1 m) or more above the floor immediately below, omission of all fire protection of the structural members shall be permitted, including protection of trusses, roof framing, decking, and portions of columns above 20 ft (6.1 m).
[‡]Where seating treads and risers serve as floors, such seating treads and risers shall be permitted to be of 1-hour fire resistance–rated construction. Structural members supporting seating treads and risers shall conform to the requirements of Table 12.1.6. Joints between seating tread and riser units shall be permitted to be unrated, provided that such joints do not involve separation from areas containing high hazard contents and the facility is constructed and operated in accordance with 12.4.2.
[§]In open-air fixed seating facilities, including stadia, omission of fire protection of structural members exposed to the outside atmosphere shall be permitted where substantiated by an approved engineering analysis.
[◊]Permitted if all the following are protected throughout by an approved, supervised automatic sprinkler system in accordance with Section 9.7:
(1) The level of the assembly occupancy
(2) Any level below the level of the assembly occupancy
(3) In the case of an assembly occupancy located below the level of exit discharge, any level intervening between that level and the level of exit discharge, including the level of exit discharge

. **FIGURE 5.3** Table 12-1.6 Construction Type Limitations—Assembly. *(Source: NFPA, 101 Life Safety Code 2000)*[†]

Construction Type	Stories			
	1	2	3	4 or More
I(443)	X	X	X	X
I(332)	X	X	X	X
II(222)	X	X	X	X
II(111)	X	X	X	NP
II(000)	X	NP	NP	NP
III(211)	X	NP	NP	NP
III(200)	NP	NP	NP	NP
IV(2HH)	X	NP	NP	NP
V(111)	X	NP	NP	NP
V(000)	NP	NP	NP	NP

X: Permitted type of construction.
NP: Not permitted.

FIGURE 5.3a Table 18.1.6.2 Construction Type Limitations—Health Care. *(Source: NFPA, 101 Life Safety Code 2000)*†

AREA MODIFICATIONS

The IBC allows a building area increase based on sprinklers or frontage on open spaces, like streets. For sprinklers alone, the area increase (over Table 503 allowable area) is 200 percent for multi-story and 300 percent for single-story buildings. The area increase allowed for open frontage alone is included as Figure 5.4.

The increase allowed for sprinklers and open frontage in combination is derived from the values determined for sprinklers and open frontage alone and combined according to the formula shown in Figure 5.5 [1].

UNLIMITED HEIGHT AND AREA BUILDINGS

The IBC allows certain buildings to be of unlimited height and area. One-story buildings surrounded on all sides by an open space may be unlimited in area for low-hazard factory and storage uses. One- or two-story buildings with sprinklers surrounded on all sides by an open space may be unlimited when used for business, factory, mercantile, or storage uses. Educational buildings may be unlimited in area when sprinkled and surrounded by an open space, and each classroom has an exit, if the building is construction Type II, IIIA, or IV. The height of multi-story buildings may be unlimited for business, mercantile, or residential uses when extra fire protection is provided for building elements. Exceptions are made for residential uses based on open space frontage and increased fire resistance ratings.

506.2 Frontage increase. Every building shall adjoin or have access to a public way to receive an area increase for frontage. Where a building has more than 25 percent of its perimeter on a public way or open space having a minimum width of 20 feet (6096 mm), the frontage increase shall be determined in accordance with the following:

$$I_f = 100 \left[\frac{F}{P} - 0.25 \right] \frac{W}{30}$$ (Equation 5-2)

where:
I_f = Area increase due to frontage (percent).
F = Building perimeter which fronts on a public way or open space having 20 feet (6096 mm) open minimum width.
P = Perimeter of entire building.
W = Minimum width of public way or open space.

FIGURE 5.4 Area modifications for open (street) frontage. *(Source: ICC, International Building Code 2000)*

506.1 General. The areas limited by Table 503 shall be permitted to be increased due to frontage (I_f) and automatic sprinkler system protection (I_s) in accordance with the following:

$$A_a = A_t + \left[\frac{A_t I_f}{100} \right] + \left[\frac{A_t I_s}{100} \right]$$ (Equation 5-1)

where:
A_a = Allowable area per floor (square feet).
A_t = Tabular area per floor in accordance with Table 503 (square feet).
I_f = Area increase due to frontage (percent) as calculated in accordance with Section 506.2.
I_s = Area increase due to sprinkler protection (percent) as calculated in accordance with Section 506.3.

FIGURE 5.5 Area modifications for combination of sprinklers and open (street) frontage. *(Source: ICC, International Building Code 2000)*

MEZZANINES

A mezzanine is defined by the LSC and the IBC as an intermediate level between the floor and ceiling of any story. Mezzanines do not count as a story, but the area is included in Table 503 area and occupant load for means of egress. Mezzanines are granted this special status because they must be open to the room they are in, and it is assumed the occupants are immediately aware of an emergency situation requiring egress. Mezzanines are often a useful way to increase the usable area of a building without violating IBC Table 503. Mezzanine requirements are in IBC Section 505 and LSC Section 8.2.6.

The total area of all mezzanines may be no larger than one-third the area of the room or space in which they are located. Figure 5.6 shows how to calculate the allowable mezzanine area for three sample mezzanines. The area under the mezzanine illustrates how that area also must remain open to be included in the calculation for allowable mezzanine size, as shown in Figure 5.6a. Mezzanine partitions may not exceed 42 in. high, and enclosed spaces on the mezzanine may not exceed 10 percent of the mezzanine area, with an occupant load of not more than 10. Mezzanines may be totally enclosed when two means of egress are provided and the building is sprinkled. These concepts are illustrated by the

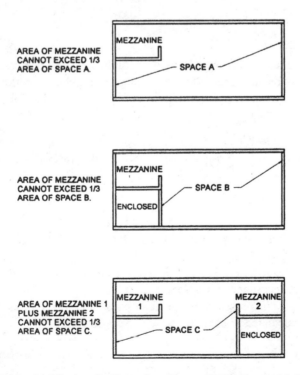

FIGURE 5.6   Qualifications for Mezzanine. (*Source: SBCCI, Standard Building Code Commentary, 1997*)

sample mezzanine plans shown in Figure 5.6b. Mezzanines may have one means of egress (stairway) when the allowable common path of travel is not exceeded. Please refer to Chapter 7, *Means of Egress*, later in this book.

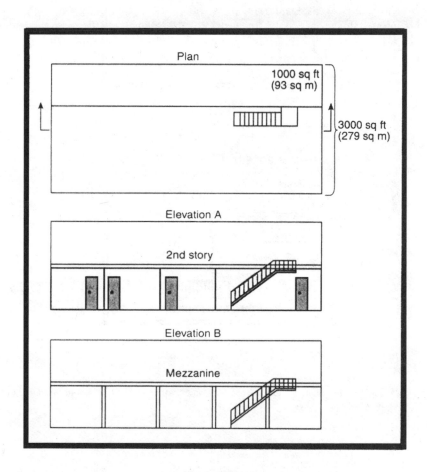

Determining whether a partial upper level meets the one-third area rule to qualify as a mezzanine. In elevation A, the enclosed space on the main floor reduces the area against which the area of the upper level is compared so that the maximum one-third area rule is exceeded. This makes the upper level in elevation A a story, not a mezzanine. In elevation B, the open space beneath the upper level is considered as part of the open area on the main floor. The maximum one-third area rule is met. This makes the upper level—in elevation B—a mezzanine.

FIGURE 5.6a Qualifications for Mezzanine. *(Source: NFPA, Life Safety Code Handbook 1997)*††

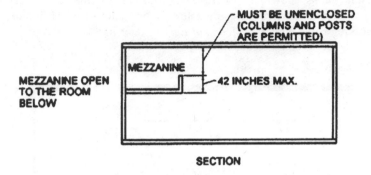

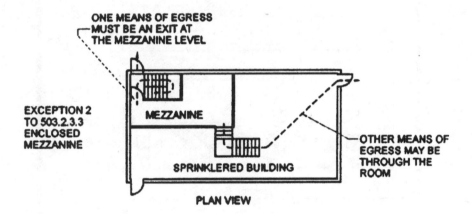

FIGURE 5.6b   Qualifications for Enclosed Mezzanine. *(Source: SBCCI, Standard Building Code Commentary, 1997)*

IBC CONSTRUCTION TYPES I, II, III, IV AND V

Any buildings that are "…erected, altered, or extended in height or area…" shall be classified in one of the five construction types defined in IBC Chapter 6. Construction Types I through V most closely resemble the Uniform Building Code classifications, with some changes. Those individuals familiar with the Standard Building Code or National (BOCA) Building Code need to read Chapter 6 of the 2000 IBC carefully. Building-construction types are defined based on fire-resistance rating, in hours, and for building elements shown in IBC Table 601, included here as Figure 5.7 [1].

FIRE-RESISTANCE RATING REQUIREMENTS FOR BUILDING ELEMENTS (hours)

BUILDING ELEMENT	TYPE I		TYPE II		TYPE III		TYPE IV	TYPE V	
	A	B	A^d	B	A^d	B	HT	A^d	B
Structural frame^a Including columns, girders, trusses	3^b	2^b	1	0	1	0	HT	1	0
Bearing walls Exterior^f	3^b	2	1	0	2	2	2	1	0
Interior	3^b	2^b	1	0	1	0	1/HT	1	0
Nonbearing walls and partitions Exterior^e	See Table 602								
Interior^e	See Section 603								
Floor construction Including supporting beams and joists	2	2	1	0	1	0	HT	1	0
Roof construction Including supporting beams and joists	1½^c	1^c	1^c	0^c	1^c	0	HT	1^c	0

For SI: 1 foot = 304.8 mm.

a. The structural frame shall be considered to be the columns and the girders, beams, trusses and spandrels having direct connections to the columns and bracing members designed to carry gravity loads. The members of floor or roof panels which have no connection to the columns shall be considered secondary members and not a part of the structural frame.

b. Roof supports: Fire-resistance ratings of structural frame and bearing walls are permitted to be reduced by 1 hour where supporting a roof only.

c. 1. Except in Factory-Industrial (F-1), Hazardous (H), Mercantile (M) and Moderate Hazard Storage (S-1) occupancies, fire protection of structural members shall not be required, including protection of roof framing and decking where every part of the roof construction is 20 feet or more above any floor immediately below. Fire-retardant-treated wood members shall be allowed to be used for such unprotected members.
   2. In all occupancies, heavy timber shall be allowed where a 1-hour or less fire-resistance rating is required.
   3. In Type I and Type II construction, fire-retardant-treated wood shall be allowed in buildings not over two stories including girders and trusses as part of the roof construction.

d. An approved automatic sprinkler system in accordance with Section 903.3.1.1 shall be allowed to be substituted for 1-hour fire-resistance-rated construction, provided such system is not otherwise required by other provisions of the code or used for an allowable area increase in accordance with Section 506.3 or an allowable height increase in accordance with Section 504.2. The 1-hour substitution for the fire resistance of exterior walls shall not be permitted.

e. For interior nonbearing partitions in Type IV construction, also see Section 602.4.6.

f. Not less than the fire-resistance rating based on fire separation distance (see Table 602.)

FIGURE 5.7 Table 601, Fire Resistance Rating Requirements for Building Elements. (*Source: ICC, International Building Code, 2000*)

CONSTRUCTION TYPES I AND II

Construction Types I and II allow the greatest building height and area and create a greater safety risk. Accordingly these construction types require the most protection of building elements. Types I and II typically require either a reinforced concrete structural frame or a heavily protected steel frame. Combustible materials in building Types II and I are restricted to a limited number and type of items. Partitions inside single-tenant offices or stores that do not establish a corridor for an occupant load of no more than 30 may be constructed of fire-retardant treated wood. Interior partitions not exceeding 6 ft in height may be constructed of wood or "similar light construction," including movable office partitions.

The code also allows other combustible materials, such as wood blocking and furring, interior wood floors and wall paneling, cabinets and millwork, wood doors and frames, stages and platforms. Draft stopping is required behind wood-finish floors or paneling. Other combustible materials allowed include Class A-rated interior finish materials; low flame spread insulation; joint sealers; certain types of plastic materials (complying with other code sections) including foam plastics, light transmitting plastics, and plastic veneers; combustible piping and ductwork (complying with other codes); and certain other materials. More information about this topic is included in Chapter 9, *Finishes Interiors.*

CONSTRUCTION TYPE III

Construction Type III requires exterior walls of noncombustible or fire-retardant treated wood. Interior walls supporting not more than two floors and a roof may be constructed of wood or other light construction. Allowable building height and area for Type III is considerably less than for Types I and II, since the required protection of building elements is reduced. See Figure 5.1, IBC Table 503.

CONSTRUCTION TYPE IV

Type IV is heavy timber construction, with structural frame members of wood or a glue-laminated wood composite of not less than the thickness required by the code (typically 3½ in). The construction of floors, walls, ceilings, and roofs is prescribed closely in the code. Interior partitions may be of a specified thickness of solid wood or one-hour fire-resistant construction. Allowable height and area are slightly higher than Type III.

CONSTRUCTION TYPE V

Type V allows construction of basically any material permitted by code. This includes light frame wood or other combustible materials. Allowable height and area for Type V are the smallest in Table 503, reflecting the minimal protection of building elements required.

FIRE RESISTANCE RATING OF BUILDING ELEMENTS—IBC

Various levels of protection of building elements are required by the code. IBC Table 601 (Figure 5.7), along with notes and exceptions, specifies the required fire-resistance rating of building structural frames, exterior load-bearing walls, floor construction, and roof construction. The level of protection is highest for Types I and II, and lowest for Type V, because of the relative size and risk posed. The code allows for a reduction of fire-resistance ratings if a fire protection sprinkler is installed as shown in Column A.

FIRE RESISTANCE RATING OF BUILDING ELEMENTS—LSC AND NFPA 220

LSC Chapters 20 and 21, *Ambulatory Health Care*, cover any outpatient medical facility within which patients undergo anesthesia (e.g., outpatient surgery) or treatments that render them incapable of self-preservation (e.g., dialysis or sleep-disturbance therapy) in an emergency. These chapters specifically allow one-story construction to be of any type allowed by NFPA 220, shown here as Figure 5.8. It is likely that other LSC occupancy chapters will refer to NFPA 220 in the future. A tabular comparison of fire resistance of construction required by NFPA 220 and IBC Table 601 is included in Figure 5.9 [2].

Table A.8.2.1 Fire Resistance Ratings (in hours) for Type I through Type V Construction

	Type I 443	Type I 332	Type II 222	Type II 111	Type II 000	Type III 211	Type III 200	Type IV 2HH	Type V 111	Type V 000
Exterior Bearing Walls –										
Supporting more than one floor, columns, or other bearing walls......	4	3	2	1	0*	2	2	2	1	0*
Supporting one floor only...................	4	3	2	1	0*	2	2	2	1	0*
Supporting a roof only.........................	4	3	1	1	0*	2	2	2	1	0*
Interior Bearing Walls –										
Supporting more than one floor, columns, or other bearing walls......	4	3	2	1	0	1	0	2	1	0
Supporting one floor only...................	3	2	2	1	0	1	0	1	1	0
Supporting a roof only.........................	3	2	1	1	0	1	0	1	1	0
Columns –										
Supporting more than one floor, columns, or other bearing walls......	4	3	2	1	0	1	0	H	1	0
Supporting one floor only...................	3	2	2	1	0	1	0	H	1	0
Supporting a roof only.........................	3	2	1	1	0	1	0	H	1	0
Beams, Girders, Trusses, and Arches –										
Supporting more than one floor, columns, or other bearing walls......	4	3	2	1	0	1	0	H	1	0
Supporting one floor only...................	3	2	2	1	0	1	0	H	1	0
Supporting a roof only.........................	3	2	1	1	0	1	0	H	1	0
Floor Construction	3	2	2	1	0	1	0	H	1	0
Roof Construction	2	1½	1	1	0	1	0	H	1	0
Exterior Nonbearing Walls	0*	0*	0*	0*	0*	0*	0*	0*	0*	0*

☐ Represents those members that are permittd to be of approved combustible material.
H: Heavy timber members (see NFPA 220, *Standard on Types of Building Construction*, for requirements).
*Requirements for fire resistance of exterior walls, the provision of spandrel wall sections, and the limitation or protection of wall openings are not related to construction type. Such requirements need to be specified in other standards and codes, where appropriate, and might be required in addition to the requirements of NFPA 220, *Standard on Types of Building Construction*, for the construction type.

FIGURE 5.8   Fire Resistance Rating Requirements LSC Table A.8.2.1. *(Source: NFPA, 101 Life Safety Code 2000)*†

NFPA 220	I(443)	I(332)	II(222)	II(111)	II(000)	III(211)	III(200)	IV(2HH)	V(111)	V(000)
UBC	----	I FR	II FR	II 1-HR	II N	III 1-HR	III N	IV HT	V 1-HR	V N
B0CA/NBC	1A	1B	2A	2B	2C	3A	3B	4	5A	5B
SBC	I	II	----	IV 1-HR	IV unp	V 1-HR	V unp	III	VI 1-HR	VI unp
IBC	----	I A	I B	II A	II B	III A	III B	IV	V A	V B

FIGURE 5.9   Allowable building construction types comparison

REFERENCES

1. ICC, 2000 Edition. 2000 International Building Codes, International Code Council, Falls Church, VA
2. NFPA 2000 Edition. 2000 Life Safety Code, National Fire Protection Association, Quincy, MA

CHAPTER 6

FIRE-RESISTANCE-RATED CONSTRUCTION

INTERNATIONAL BUILDING CODE VERSUS THE LIFE SAFETY CODE

As discussed in previous chapters, conflicts exist between the IBC and the LSC. LSC Chapter 8, *Features of Fire Protection*, covers the issues discussed in this chapter, including construction and compartmentation, fire barriers, and smoke barriers. Many LSC provisions, however, conflict with the IBC, and a section at the end of this chapter addresses these conflicts. The general concepts and standards for fire ratings are described in this chapter. Specific requirements and exceptions are covered in the LSC chapters.

FIRE-RESISTANCE RATINGS AND FIRE TESTS

ASTM E 119

The IBC requires that the fire-resistance rating of all building elements be tested according to the American Society of Testing and Materials (ASTM) E 119. This test determines the fire resistance of a material or assembly of materials under actual fire conditions. Many assemblies used in interior construction have not been tested according to ATSM E 119 because it is very expensive and most interior construction assemblies are composed of products from several suppliers. The IBC allows alternative methods for determining fire resistance as shown in Figure 6.1.

703.3 Alternative methods for determining fire resistance.
The application of any of the alternative methods listed in this section shall be based on the fire exposure and acceptance criteria specified in ASTM E 119. The required fire resistance of a building element shall be permitted to be established by any of the following methods or procedures:

1. Fire-resistance designs documented in approved sources.
2. Prescriptive designs of fire-resistance-rated building elements as prescribed in Section 719.
3. Calculations in accordance with Section 720.
4. Engineering analysis based on a comparison of building element designs having fire-resistance ratings as determined by the test procedures set forth in ASTM E 119.
5. Alternative protection methods as allowed by Section 104.11.

FIGURE 6.1   Alternative methods for determining fire resistance. *(Source: ICC, International Building Code, 2000)*

Alternate Sources

Alternate sources for fire-resistance ratings include Livermore Laboratories, Warnock-Hersey, and Underwriters Laboratory. Factory Mutual, the Insurance Services Organization, the Gypsum Association, the National Concrete Masonry Association, and the American Concrete Institute also conduct fire tests. A list of these organizations mentioned in the IBC is included in Appendix A. Most building officials and other regulatory agencies recognize the credibility of testing agencies and industry organizations and accept their test data as proof of code compliance. Figure 6.1a shows a number of designs for fire-rated gypsum drywall and the various sources used to establish fire ratings.

FIRE-RESISTANCE

Prescriptive

IBC Section 719, Prescriptive Fire Resistance, contains extensive tables about fire resistance for building structural elements. Fire resistance for walls and partitions is in Table 719.1, a portion of which is included as Figures 6.2a, 6.2b, and 6.2c. These wall assemblies are prescriptive, meaning that they must be built *exactly* as prescribed in the highly detailed system descriptions.

Partitions/Steel Framing

SINGLE LAYER—1 5/8" (41.3 mm) STUDS

FIRE – SOUND

No.	Fire Rating	Ref.	Design No.	Description		STC	Test No.
1	1 hr.	FM OSU	W1B–1 hr. T-3296	5/8" (15.9 mm) Fire-Shield Gypsum Wallboard or 5/8" Fire-Shield MR Board screw attached vertically to both sides 1 5/8" (41.3 mm) screw studs, 24" o.c. (610 mm). Wallboard joints staggered.		38	NGC 2384
		GA	WP 1340	2 1/2" (63.5 mm) glass fiber in cavity.		43	NGC 2383
2	1 hr.	UL	U420	Chase wall, 5/8" (15.9 mm) Fire-Shield Gypsum Wallboard screw attached vertically to both sides. Air space 9 1/2" (241.3 mm) between inside wallboard faces. Sound rating with 3 1/2" (88.9 mm) mineral wool or glass fiber. 1 5/8" (41.3 mm) screw studs, 24" o.c., (610 mm) cross braced at third points with 5/8" (15.9 mm) wallboard gussets 9 1/2" x 12" (241.3 mm x 305 mm) or 9 1/2" (241.3 mm) long stud track.		52	TL 76-155
		GA	WP 5015				

FIGURE 6.1a Fire-rated gypsum drywall. (*Source: National Gypsum Company, Gold Bond gypsum quick collector*)

6.3

Partitions/Steel Framing

No.	Fire Rating		Ref.	Design No.	Description	STC	Test No.

SINGLE LAYER—2 1/2" (63.5 mm) STUDS

No.	Fire Rating	Drawing	Ref.	Design No.	Description	STC	Test No.
3	1 hr.		FM	Based on W1B–1 hr.	5/8" (15.9 mm) Fire-Shield Gypsum Wallboard or 5/8" (15.9 mm) Fire-Shield MR Board screw attached vertically to both sides 2 1/2" (63.5 mm) screw studs, 24" o.c. (610 mm). Wallboard joints staggered.	40	NGC 2438
			OSU	Based On T-3296	With 2 1/2" (63.5 mm) of mineral wool or glass fiber in cavity.	45	NGC 2391
			GA	WP 1340			
4	1 hr.		UL FM	V401 W2A–1 hr. (WP-51)	1/2" (12.7 mm) Fire-Shield G Gypsum Wallboard screw attached vertically to both sides 2 1/2" (63.5 mm) screw studs, 24" o.c. (610 mm). 2" (51 mm) mineral wool [2 1/2 pcf (40 kg/m³)] in stud cavity. Wallboard joints staggered.	45	NGC 2179
			GA	WP 1070			
	1 hr.		UL FM	V401 W2B–1 hr. (WP-731)	1/2" (12.7 mm) Fire-Shield G Gypsum Wallboard screw attached horizontally to both sides, 2 1/2" (63.5 mm) screw studs, 24" o.c. (610 mm). 2" (51 mm) mineral wool [3 pcf (48 kg/m³)] in stud cavity. Horizontal joints not staggered with those on the opposite side of partition.		
			GA	WP 1071			
5			UL FM	U468 2B–1 hr.	1/2" (12.7 mm) Fire-Shield G Gypsum Wallboard applied vertically, screw attached 8" o.c. (203 mm) around perimeter, 12" o.c. (305 mm) in field, on 2 1/2" (63.5 mm) screw studs; 24" o.c. (610 mm). All Wallboard joints staggered. Wall cavity filled with Owens-Corning Fire-Core 60, Type FB, Insulation		

FIGURE 6.1a (*continued*) Fire-rated gypsum drywall. (*Source: National Gypsum Company, Gold Bond gypsum quick collector*)

Partitions/Steel Framing

No.	Fire Rating	Ref.	Design No.	Description	STC	Test No.
SINGLE LAYER—3 5/8" (92.1 mm) STUDS						
6	1 hr.	FM	W1A–1 hr. (WP 45)	5/8" (15.9 mm) Fire-Shield Gypsum Wallboard or 5/8" (15.9 mm) Fire-Shield MR Board screw attached horizontally to both sides 3 5/8" (92.1 mm) screw studs, 24" o.c. (610 mm). All wallboard joints staggered.	42	NGC 2385
		GA	WP-1200			
		OSU	T-1770	5/8" (15.9 mm) Fire-Shield Gypsum Wallboard screw attached vertically to both sides 3 5/8" (92.1 mm) screw studs, 24" o.c. (610 mm). Wallboard joints staggered.	47	NGC 2386
				2 1/2" (63.5 mm) mineral wool or glass fiber in cavity.		
7	45 min.	FM	Based on W2A–1 hr. (WP-51)	1/2" (12.7 mm) Fire-Shield G Gypsum Wallboard screw attached vertically to both sides 3 5/8" (92.1 mm) screw studs, 24" o.c. (610 mm). 2" (51 mm) glass fiber in stud cavity. Wallboard joints staggered.	45	NGC 2146
8	1 hr.	UL	Based on V401	1/2" (12.7 mm) Fire-Shield G Gypsum Wallboard screw attached vertically to both sides 3 5/8" (92.1 mm) screw studs, 24" o.c. (610 mm). 2" (51 mm) mineral wool [2 1/2 pcf (40 kg/m³)] in stud cavity. Wallboard joints staggered.	45	NGC 2149
		FM	Based on W2A–1 hr. (WP-51)			
		GA	WP1070			

FIGURE 6.1a (*continued*)   Fire-rated gypsum drywall. (*Source: National Gypsum Company, Gold Bond gypsum quick collector*)

TABLE 719.1(2)

RATED FIRE-RESISTANCE PERIODS FOR VARIOUS WALLS AND PARTITIONS [a,o,p]

MATERIAL	ITEM NUMBER	CONSTRUCTION	MINIMUM FINISHED THICKNESS FACE-TO-FACE [b] (inches)			
			4 hour	3 hour	2 hour	1 hour
1. Brick of clay or shale	1-1.1	Solid brick of clay or shale [c]	6	4.9	3.8	2.7
	1-1.2	Hollow brick, not filled.	5.0	4.3	3.4	2.3
	1-1.3	Hollow brick unit wall, grout or filled with perlite vermiculite or expanded shale aggregate.	6.6	5.5	4.4	3.0
	1-2.1	4" nominal thick units at least 75 percent solid backed with a hat-shaped metal furring channel 3/4" thick formed from 0.021" sheet metal attached to the brick wall on 24" centers with approved fasteners, and 1/2" Type X gypsum wallboard [e] attached to the metal furring strips with 1"-long Type S screws spaced 8" on center.	—	—	5 [d]	—
2. Combination of clay brick and load-bearing hollow clay tile	2-1.1	4" solid brick and 4" tile (at least 40 percent solid).	—	8	—	—
	2-1.2	4" solid brick and 8" tile (at least 40 percent solid).	12	—	—	—
3. Concrete masonry units	3-1.1 [f,g]	Expanded slag or pumice.	4.7	4.0	3.2	2.1
	3-1.2 [f,g]	Expanded clay, shale or slate.	5.1	4.4	3.6	2.6
	3-1.3 [f]	Limestone, cinders or air-cooled slag.	5.9	5.0	4.0	2.7
	3-1.4 [f,g]	Calcareous or siliceous gravel.	6.2	5.3	4.2	2.8
4. Solid concrete [h,i]	4-1.1	Siliceous aggregate concrete.	7.0	6.2	5.0	3.5
		Carbonate aggregate concrete.	6.6	5.7	4.6	3.2
		Sand-lightweight concrete.	5.4	4.6	3.8	2.7
		Lightweight concrete.	5.1	4.4	3.6	2.5

FIGURE 6.2a Prescribed fire resistance ratings—Various walls. (*Source: ICC, International Building Code, 2000*)

TABLE 719.1(2)—continued

RATED FIRE-RESISTANCE PERIODS FOR VARIOUS WALLS AND PARTITIONS [a,o,p]

MATERIAL	ITEM NUMBER	CONSTRUCTION	MINIMUM FINISHED THICKNESS FACE-TO-FACE [b] (inches)			
			4 hour	3 hour	2 hour	1 hour
13. Noncombustible studs—interior partition with gypsum wallboard each side	13-1.1	0.018 inch (No. 25 carbon sheet steel gage) channel-shaped studs 24" on center with one full-length layer of $5/8$" Type X gypsum wallboard [e] applied vertically attached with 1" long No. 6 drywall screws to each stud. Screws are 8" on center around the perimeter and 12" on center on the intermediate stud. The wallboard may be applied horizontally when attached to $3\frac{5}{8}$" studs and the horizontal joints are staggered with those on the opposite side. Screws for the horizontal application shall be 8" on center at vertical edges and 12" on center at intermediate studs.	—	—	—	$2\frac{7}{8}$d
	13-1.2	0.018 inch (No. 25 carbon sheet steel gage) channel-shaped studs 25" on center with two full-length layers of $1/2$" Type X gypsum wallboard [e] applied vertically each side. First layer attached with 1"-long, No. 6 drywall screws, 8" on center around the perimeter and 12" on center on the intermediate stud. Second layer applied with vertical joints offset one stud space from first layer using $1\frac{5}{8}$" long, No. 6 drywall screws spaced 9" on center along vertical joints, 12" on center at intermediate studs and 24" on center along top and bottom runners.	—	—	$3\frac{5}{8}$d	—
	13-1.3	0.055-inch (No. 16 carbon sheet steel gage) approved nailable metal studs [e] 24" on center with full-length $5/8$" Type X gypsum wallboard [e] applied vertically and nailed 7" on center with 6d cement-coated common nails. Approved metal fastener grips used with nails at vertical butt joints along studs.	—	—	—	$4\frac{7}{8}$
	14-1.1 [h,m]	2" x 4" wood studs 16" on center with two layers of $3/8$" regular gypsum wallboard [e] each side, 4d cooler [e] or wallboard [e] nails at 8" on center first layer, 5d cooler [e] or wallboard [e] nails at 8" on center second layer with laminating compound between layers, joints staggered. First layer applied full length vertically, second layer applied horizontally or vertically	—	—	—	5

FIGURE 6.2b Prescribed fire resistance ratings—Various walls. (*Source: ICC, International Building Code, 2000*)

TABLE 719.1(2)—continued
RATED FIRE-RESISTANCE PERIODS FOR VARIOUS WALLS AND PARTITIONS [a,b,c]

14. Wood studs—interior partition with gypsum wallboard each side	14-1.1[h,m]	2" x 4" wood studs 16" on center with two layers of 3/8" regular gypsum wallboard each side, 4d cooler[e] or wallboard[n] nails at 8" on center first layer, 5d cooler[e] or wallboard[b] nails at 8" on center second layer, with laminating compound between layers, joints staggered. First layer applied full length vertically, second layer applied horizontally or vertically	—	—	—	5
	14-1.2[i,m]	2" x 4" wood studs 16" on center with two layers 1/2" regular gypsum wallboard[e] applied vertically or horizontally each side[k], joints staggered. Nail base layer with 5d cooler[e] or wallboard[b] nails at 8" on center face layer with 8d cooler[e] or wallboard[n] nails at 8" on center.	—	—	—	5½
	14-1.3[l,m]	2" x 4" wood studs 24" on center with 5/8" Type X gypsum wallboard[e] applied vertically or horizontally nailed with 6d cooler[e] or wallboard[b] nails at 7" on center with end joints on nailing members. Stagger joints each side.	—	—	—	4¾
	14-1.4[l]	2" x 4" fire-retardant-treated wood studs spaced 24" on center with one layer of 5/8" Type X gypsum wallboard[e] applied with face paper grain (long dimension) parallel to studs. Wallboard attached with 6d cooler[e] or wallboard[b] nails at 7" on center.	—	—	—	4 3/4[d]
	14-1.5[l,m]	2" x 4" wood studs 16" on center with two layers 5/8" Type X gypsum wallboard[e] each side. Base layers applied vertically and nailed with 6d cooler[e] or wallboard[b] nails at 9" on center. Face layer applied vertically or horizontally and nailed with 8d cooler[e] or wallboard[b] nails at 7" on center. For nail-adhesive application, base layers are nailed 6" on center. Face layers applied with coating of approved wallboard adhesive and nailed 12" on center.	—	—	6	—

FIGURE 6.2c Prescribed fire resistance ratings—Various walls. *(Source: ICC, International Building Code, 2000)*

Calculated

IBC Section 720, Calculated Fire Resistance, is more flexible than the prescriptive type. Fire-resistance values are listed for each type, composition, and thickness of the building material used. The designer may select materials based on the values listed to "build" the needed fire resistance into a wall. Table 720.2.1, included here as Figure 6.3, gives the *time-assigned* fire-resistance values for various finish materials.

TABLE 720.2.1.4(2)
TIME ASSIGNED TO FINISH MATERIALS ON
FIRE-EXPOSED SIDE OF WALL

FINISH DESCRIPTION	TIME (minute)
Gypsum wallboard	
³/₈ inch	10
¹/₂ inch	15
⁵/₈ inch	20
2 layers of ³/₈ inch	25
1 layer ³/₈ inch, 1 layer ¹/₂ inch	35
2 layers ¹/₂ inch	40
Type X gypsum wallboard	
¹/₂ inch	25
⁵/₈ inch	40
Portland cement-sand plaster applied directly to concrete masonry	See Note a
Portland cement-sand plaster on metal lath	
³/₄ inch	20
⁷/₈ inch	25
1 inch	30
Gypsum sand plaster on ³/₈-inch gypsum lath	
¹/₂ inch	35
⁵/₈ inch	40
³/₄ inch	50
Gypsum sand plaster on metal lath	
³/₄ inch	50
⁷/₈ inch	60
1 inch	80

For SI: 1 inch = 25.4 mm.

a. The actual thickness of Portland cement-sand plaster, provided it is ⁵/₈ inch or less in thickness, shall be permitted to be included in determining the equivalent thickness of the masonry for use in Table 720.3.2.

FIGURE 6.3 Calculated fire resistance ratings—Various finishes. *(Source: ICC, International Building Code, 2000)*

Table 720.6.2(1), shown as Figure 6.4, gives the time assigned for various types of wallboard and wood framing. These tables can help you to design the wall or ceiling to the required fire resistance standard. Table 720.3.2, shown as Figure 6.5, gives the time assigned fire resistance for concrete (block) masonry. This table gives the time values in inches for various block materials. Therefore, it is necessary to measure the thickness and test for composition (if existing block) or determine from the block supplier the composition and actual face shell thickness. Lightweight aggregate is common in today's market because it is easy to lay, but it has a lower fire-resistance rating than other types.

Other Methods for Determining Fire Resistance

The code recognizes other methods of establishing fire-resistance ratings for walls, ceilings, floors, and other building elements, such as an engineering analysis based on a comparison between similar building elements that have been tested according to ASTM E 136. IBC Section 703.3, the part of the code that discusses methods of determining fire resistance, is included in its entirety as Figure 6.1. Since the code allows the use of *any* of the methods described, one method may be used for one building element and another method for a different element.

IBC Section 104.11 allows alternative methods when approved by the building official (Figure 6.6). This section not only applies to fire-resistance ratings, but to all code provisions. This section could be helpful when code-designated sources are not available.

LSC Performance-Based Option

The LSC 2000 has a new concept for code compliance described in Chapter 5, Performance Based Option. This concept, similar to the IBC provision for alternative methods, allows the designer to use methods not prescribed by the code and *prove* to the code authority that the new system or design will work. Most of the prescriptive requirements specified in LSC Chapter 7, *Means of Egress*, are retained, but other requirements contained in the occupancy chapters (12-42) can be substituted with the *performance-based* design. We have reservations about this approach and believe most code enforcement officials also will have reservations about it. Although this approach might seem like a panacea for designers (who love to create), it ultimately might be to their disadvantage when they cannot quote a code to defend their designs.

FIRE WALLS, BARRIERS, AND PARTITIONS, AND SMOKE BARRIERS

The 2000 IBC introduces a new group of terms to describe building elements that must resist the passage of smoke or fire. *Fire walls* separate areas of a building

TIME ASSIGNED TO WALLBOARD MEMBRANES[a,b,c,d]

DESCRIPTION OF FINISH	TIME[e] (minutes)
3/8-inch wood structural panel bonded with exterior glue	5
15/32-inch wood structural panel bonded with exterior glue	10
19/32-inch wood structural panel bonded with exterior glue	15
3/8-inch gypsum wallboard	10
1/2-inch gypsum wallboard	15
5/8-inch gypsum wallboard	30
1/2-inch Type X gypsum wallboard	25
5/8-inch Type X gypsum wallboard	40
Double 3/8-inch gypsum wallboard	25
1/2 + 3/8-inch gypsum wallboard	35
Double 1/2-inch gypsum wallboard	40

For SI: 1 inch = 25.4 mm.

a. These values apply only when membranes are installed on framing members which are spaced 16 inches o.c.

b. Gypsum wallboard installed over framing or furring shall be installed so that all edges are supported, except 5/8-inch Type X gypsum wallboard shall be permitted to be installed horizontally with the horizontal joints staggered 24 inches each side and unsupported but finished.

c. On wood-framed floor/ceiling or roof/ceiling assemblies, gypsum board shall be installed with the long dimension perpendicular to framing members and shall have all joints finished.

d. The membrane on the unexposed side shall not be included in determining the fire resistance of the assembly. When dissimilar membranes are used on a wall assembly, the calculation shall be made from the least fire resistant (weaker) side.

e. The time assigned is not a finish rating.

TABLE 720.6.2(2)

TIME ASSIGNED FOR CONTRIBUTION OF WOOD FRAME[a,b,c]

DESCRIPTION	TIME ASSIGNED TO FRAME (minutes)
Wood studs 16 inches o.c.	20
Wood floor and roof joists 16 inches o.c.	10

For SI: 1 inch = 25.4 mm.

a. This table does not apply to studs or joists spaced more than 16 inches o.c.

b. All studs shall be nominal 2 x 4 and all joists shall have a nominal thickness of at least 2 inches.

c. Allowable spans for joists shall be determined in accordance with Sections 2308.8, 2308.10.2 and 2308.10.3.

FIGURE 6.4 Calculated fire resistance ratings—Wallboard. (*Source: ICC, International Building Code, 2000*)

TABLE 720.3.2
MINIMUM EQUIVALENT THICKNESS (inches) OF BEARING OR NONBEARING CONCRETE MASONRY WALLS[a,b,c,d]

TYPE OF AGGREGATE	FIRE-RESISTANCE RATING (hours)														
	½	¾	1	1¼	1½	1¾	2	2¼	2½	2¾	3	3¼	3½	3¾	4
Pumice of expanded slag	1.5	1.9	2.1	2.5	2.7	3.0	3.2	3.4	3.6	3.8	4.0	4.2	4.4	4.5	4.7
Expanded shale, clay or slate	1.8	2.2	2.6	2.9	3.3	3.4	3.6	3.8	4.0	4.2	4.4	4.6	4.8	4.9	5.1
Limestone, cinders, or unexpanded slag	1.9	2.3	2.7	3.1	3.4	3.7	4.0	4.3	4.5	4.8	5.0	5.2	5.5	5.7	5.9
Calcareous of siliceous gravel	2.0	2.4	2.8	3.2	3.6	3.9	4.2	4.5	4.8	5.0	5.3	5.5	5.8	6.0	6.2

For SI: 1 inch = 25.4 mm.

a. Values between those shown in the table can be determined by direct interpolation.
b. Where combustible members are framed into the wall, the thickness of solid material between the end of each member and the opposite face of the wall, or between members set in from opposite sides, shall not be less than 93 percent of the thickness shown in the table.
c. Requirements of ASTM C 55, C 73 or C 90 shall apply.
d. Minimum required equivalent thickness corresponding to the hourly fire-resistance rating for units with a combination of aggregate shall be determined by linear interpolation based on the percent by volume of each aggregate used in manufacture.

FIGURE 6.5 Calculated fire resistance ratings—Concrete block. (*Source: ICC, International Building Code, 2000*)

> **104.11 Alternative materials, design and methods of construction and equipment.** The provisions of this code are not intended to prevent the installation of any material or to prohibit any design or method of construction not specifically prescribed by this code, provided that any such alternative has been approved. An alternative material, design or method of construction shall be approved where the building official finds that the proposed design is satisfactory and complies with the intent of the provisions of this code, and that the material, method or work offered is, for the purpose intended, at least the equivalent of that prescribed in this code in quality, strength, effectiveness, fire resistance, durability and safety.

FIGURE 6.6 Alternative methods for determining fire resistance. *(Source: ICC, International Building Code, 2000)*

into what is recognized by the IBC as "separate buildings," and normally would not be included in the design and construction of interiors. *Fire barriers* separate occupancies, divide a single occupancy into separate fire areas, enclose exit passageways and separate incidental-use areas. *Fire partitions* separate residential dwelling units, hotel guestrooms, tenant separation walls in covered malls, and, most important, corridor walls. *Smoke barriers* divide a building into separate smoke compartments and also are fire rated. The definition of each term is shown below, and each is discussed in detail later in this chapter.

FIRE BARRIERS

Types and Examples

Several types of building elements are included under fire barriers. The requirements for various types of fire barriers are addressed in IBC Chapter 10 and LSC Chapter 5, both titled *Means of Egress*, with modifications in the LSC individual occupancy chapters (12-42). This book covers the subject in detail in Chapter 7, *Means of Egress*. This chapter summarizes the fire-resistance rating requirements for each type of rated enclosure.

Vertical Exit Enclosures

Vertical exit enclosures (interior stairways) must comply with IBC Section 1005, fire rated for one hour when serving less than four floors or two hours when serving more than four floors. Section 1005 allows exceptions for many situations not serving large occupant loads, including stairs inside dwellings or guestrooms and open stairs not required for egress.

Exit Passageways

Exit passageways typically are used to connect exit stairs that do not stack vertically. Exit passageways must comply with IBC Section 1005.3.3 and must be fire rated for at least one hour, but the fire rating must not be less than the rating for any connected exit enclosures. For example, an exit passageway that connects exit stairs in a building more than four stories high will be fire rated for two hours.

Horizontal Exits

Horizontal exits are fire-rated hallways that provide an egress to an *area of refuge* beyond a fire wall rather than to the outside. Typically used to reduce travel distance in large buildings, horizontal exits may provide up to half the required exits and are fire rated two hours. Openings in the horizontal exit must be protected, and the size and character of the refuge area are specified in the codes.

Accessory and Incidental Use Areas

IBC Section 302.2 defines *accessory use areas* as parts of a building or tenant space with uses other than those allowed by the occupancy classification, and uses that do not comprise more than 10 percent of the total area. No fire separation is required for accessory uses when they do not qualify as *incidental use areas*. Incidental use areas, illustrated in Figure 6.7, must be separated with barriers of the fire-resistance rating shown and/or protected by fire protection sprinklers. When accessory use areas are permitted to be protected by sprinklers only, a smoke barrier also must separate the room or space. IBC requirements for openings are shown in Figure 6.12.

The LSC provides for fire-resistance-rated separation of accessory or incidental uses under *protection from hazards*. Hazardous areas must be separated from other spaces by a fire barrier of the rating specified in the individual occupancy chapters (12-42), typically one hour with ¾ hour (45 minute) opening protectives and sprinklers. Hazards include general storage, boiler or furnace rooms and maintenance shops, which include janitor closets and any gas-fired heating, ventilating and air conditioning equipment. The fire separation and protection of both codes should be considered separately and incorporated into any design when required.

Separation of Occupancies

Separation of occupancies requires the use of fire barriers according to the mixed occupancies chart in IBC Table 302.3.3 (Figure 3.2a in Chapter 3 of this book).

TABLE 302.1.1
INCIDENTAL USE AREAS

ROOM OR AREA	SEPARATION[a]
Furnace room where largest piece of equipment is over 400,000 Btu per hour input	1 hour or provide automatic fire-extinguishing system
Boilers over 15 psi and 10 horsepower	1 hour or provide automatic fire-extinguishing system
Refrigerant machinery rooms	1 hour or provide automatic fire-extinguishing system
Automotive parking garage in other than Group R-3	2 hours
Incinerator rooms	2 hours and automatic sprinkler system
Paint shops, not classified as a Group H, located in occupancies other than Group F	2 hours; or 1 hour and provide automatic fire-extinguishing systems
Laboratories and vocational shops, not classified as Group H, located in Group E and I-2 occupancies	1 hour or provide automatic fire-extinguishing system
Laundry rooms over 100 square feet	1 hour
Storage rooms over 100 square feet	1 hour
Group I-3 padded cells	1 hour
Waste and linen collection room over 100 square feet	1 hour
Stationary lead-acid battery systems having a liquid capacity of more than 100 gallons used for facility standby power, emergency power or uninterrupted power supplies	1-hour fire barriers and floor-ceiling assemblies in Group B, F, H, M, S and U occupancies. 2-hour fire barriers and floor-ceiling assemblies in Group A, E, I and R occupancies

For SI: 1 square foot = 0.0929 m², 1 pound per square inch = 6.9 kPa,
1 British thermal unit = 0.293 watts, 1 horsepower = 746 watts,
1 gallon = 3.785 L.

a. Where an automatic fire-extinguishing system is provided, it need only be provided in the incidental use room or area.

FIGURE 6.7 Incidental use areas—Required separation. (*Source: ICC, International Building Code, 2000*

Refer to the table for the fire resistance rating required. This table also is used to determine the required fire separation for dividing a single occupancy into fire areas for establishing horizontal exits. As discussed in Chapter 3, the codes allow mixed occupancies to be designed as single occupancy when the fire protection and egress requirements of the more restrictive occupancy are incorporated into the facility. This approach usually works better than separation when the areas of different occupancies are so intermingled that separation is impractical.

FIRE PARTITIONS

IBC Section 708 requires fire partitions to have a minimum fire resistance rating of one hour. No rating is required for corridor walls in educational facilities where exits are provided from each room directly to the exterior, businesses for which only one exit is required, residences and guestrooms, and open parking garages. The fire rating between guestrooms is reduced to ½ hour when sprinklers are installed.

SMOKE BARRIERS

Smoke barriers are one-hour smoke and fire resistive rated membranes extending from outside wall to outside wall and from the floor deck to the roof or floor deck above. Other parts of the codes require smoke barriers to divide buildings into *smoke compartments.*

CONTINUITY

Fire barriers, fire partitions, and smoke partitions must extend from, and be attached securely to, the floor (floor/ceiling assembly) below to the roof or floor deck (roof/ceiling or floor/ceiling assembly) above. Fire barriers must extend through concealed spaces such as suspended acoustical ceilings. Where the ceiling is part of a fire-rated roof/ceiling or floor/ceiling assembly, the fire barrier may stop at the ceiling, as shown in Figure 6.8. The construction supporting fire barriers also must be one-hour fire rated, with exceptions for certain incidental use separations. Where fire barrier walls extend through more than one floor, fire blocking must be provided at each floor. One important exception allows fire partitions with an equivalent fire-rated ceiling to form a corridor tunnel, as illustrated in Figure 6.9, and not extend to the roof or floor deck above. Fire partitions dividing tenants in a code-compliant mall building may terminate at a non-fire-rated ceiling.

Partitions used for tenant separation, occupancy
separation, exit access corridors, horizontal exits,
or any other rated partition must extend from the
top of the floor below to the ceiling above, provided that the ceiling is part of a rated assembly having a fire resistance rating at least equal to that
required for the partition. When the ceiling is not
part of a fire resistant assembly, the partition
should extend to either the floor deck above or the
roof deck above.

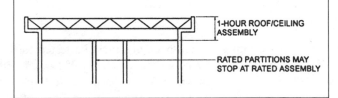

1-HOUR ROOF/CEILING ASSEMBLY

RATED PARTITIONS MAY STOP AT RATED ASSEMBLY

FIGURE 6.8 Fire partitions extending to rated roof-ceiling. *(Source: SBCCI, Standard Building Code Commentary, 1997)*

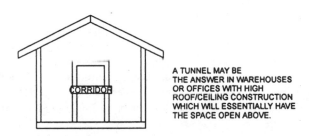

CORRIDOR

A TUNNEL MAY BE
THE ANSWER IN WAREHOUSES
OR OFFICES WITH HIGH
ROOF/CEILING CONSTRUCTION
WHICH WILL ESSENTIALLY HAVE
THE SPACE OPEN ABOVE.

FIGURE 6.9 Corridor "tunnel" with open space above. *(Source: SBCCI, Standard Building Code Commentary, 1997)*

Special Opening Restrictions

The area of any single opening in a fire barrier may not exceed 120 square feet
and the total of all openings may not exceed 25 percent of the wall in which they
are located. Openings are not limited to 120 square feet where automatic sprinklers are provided or where the opening protective has been tested according to
ASTM E 119.

OPENING PROTECTIVES

Fire Rating

Opening protectives include any device used to close an opening in a fire wall, fire barrier, fire partition, or smoke barrier and must be protected according to IBC Section 714. Opening protectives may include doors, windows, glass walls, shutters, or access doors. Fire-rating tests are specified in the code for each type of protective. Figure 6.10 contains the fire resistive rating requirements for opening protectives in various types of fire resistive building elements.

Other Requirements

In addition to the fire rating, certain openings must be tested for hose stream integrity, air transmission, and temperature rise. NFPA 252 or UL 10B requires corridor or smoke barrier doors to withstand a hose stream test that demonstrates that the protective material will remain in place during firefighting. UL 1784 requires smoke doors to resist air leakage. Doors in exit enclosures also must be tested for temperature rise, except in buildings with automatic sprinklers.

Glazing, Labeling, and Hardware

Fire-rated door glazing must be wired glass or fire-rated glass. Wired glass is restricted in area according to the table shown in Figure 6.11. Fire-rated glass is restricted in size and anchorage by the qualifying test. All glazing is subject to the temperature rise test mentioned above, except in buildings with automatic sprinklers. Small view ports with minimum construction as specified are exempt. Exceptions also are allowed for certain types of institutional occupancies and multi-theater complexes.

An approved testing agency must test, rate, and label all fire doors and other fire-rated opening protectives. The labels must be affixed permanently (to remain in place after construction) and be visible for inspection.

All fire-rated doors must be self-closing or automatic-closing and have a latch bolt that engages automatically upon closing. Automatic-closing fire doors must be tested according to NFPA 80. Smoke-activated doors in most locations must be connected to a fire detection and alarm system.

SHAFT AND VERTICAL EXIT ENCLOSURES

This part of the IBC closely matches the LSC provisions for a *mini-atrium*, discussed in Chapter 4 of this book. IBC Section 707 defines shaft and vertical exit enclosures with a number of exceptions, which describe what is *not* a shaft enclosure. Shaft enclosures are required for any series of communicating openings in

TABLE 714.2
OPENING PROTECTIVE FIRE-PROTECTION RATINGS

TYPE OF ASSEMBLY	REQUIRED ASSEMBLY RATING (hours)	MINIMUM OPENING PROTECTION ASSEMBLY (hours)
Fire walls and fire barriers having a required fire-resistance rating greater than 1 hour	4 3 2 1½	3 3[b] 1½ 1½

Fire barriers of 1-hour fire-resistance-rated construction:
  Shaft and exit enclosure walls
  Other fire barriers
	
	1
	
	1
		
		1
		
		¾

Fire partitions: Exit access corridor enclosure wall	1	0.33[a]
Other fire partitions	1	¾
Exterior walls	3 2 1	1½ 1½ ¾

a. For testing requirements, see Section 714.2.3.
b. Two doors, each with a fire-protection rating of 1.5 hours, installed on opposite sides of the same opening in a fire wall, shall be deemed equivalent in fire-protection rating to one 3-hour fire door.

FIGURE 6.10 Opening protective fire ratings. *(Source: ICC, International Building Code, 2000)*

more than two floors when not covered by the following exceptions: within an individual residence; code-compliant masonry chimneys; escalators in buildings with sprinklers; penetrations for pipes, tubes, cables, and vents addressed by other parts of the code; malls or atriums, mezzanines and certain other situations.

Where shaft enclosures are required, they must be of fire resistive construction which is rated not less than the floors they penetrate, but the rating is not required to be more than two hours. Shaft enclosures, like fire-rated walls, must be continuous with protection of openings, penetrations, and joints as provided in other parts of the code. Fire-rated shaft enclosures, such as laundry or trash chutes, that terminate in a room at the bottom must enclose that room, as illustrated in Figure 6.12.

TABLE 714.3.2
LIMITING SIZES OF WIRED GLASS PANELS

OPENING FIRE-PROTECTION RATING	MAXIMUM AREA (square inches)	MAXIMUM HEIGHT (inches)	MAXIMUM WIDTH (inches)
3 hour	0	0	0
1½-hour doors in exterior walls	0	0	0
1 and 1½ hours	100	33	10
¾ hour	1,296	54	54
0.33 hour	Not Limited	Not Limited	Not Limited
Fire window assemblies	1,296	54	54

For SI: 1 inch = 25.4 mm, 1 square inch = 645.2 mm².

FIGURE 6.11   Limiting size of wire glass panels. *(Source: ICC, International Building Code, 2000)*

HORIZONTAL ASSEMBLIES

Horizontal assemblies are floors and roofs (floor/ceiling and roof/ceiling assemblies) that are required to have a fire-resistance rating, as determined by other parts of the code, primarily IBC Table 601. When the floor separates occupancies, the horizontal assembly must have the same rating required for occupancy separation. Horizontal assemblies, like fire-rated walls, must be continuous with protected openings, penetrations, and joints.

PENETRATIONS

Penetrations through all types of fire-resistance-rated building elements are required to maintain the rating of the penetrated element. The penetration always includes an opening, called the *annular space*, in the rated wall that is larger than the pipe or conduit, as shown in Figure 6.13. Penetration seals must fill this annu-

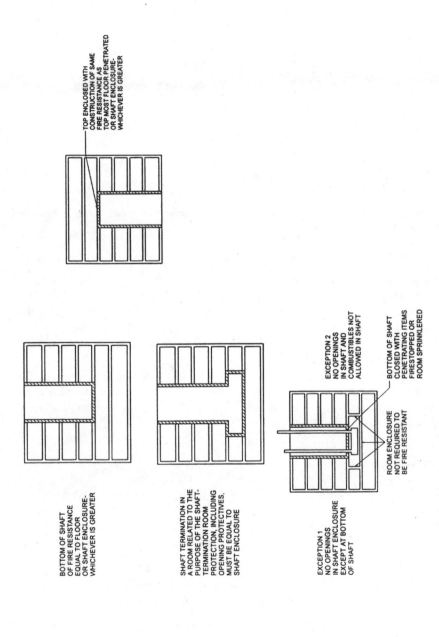

TOP ENCLOSED WITH CONSTRUCTION OF SAME FIRE RESISTANCE AS TOP MOST FLOOR PENETRATED OR SHAFT ENCLOSURE- WHICHEVER IS GREATER

BOTTOM OF SHAFT OF FIRE RESISTANCE EQUAL TO FLOOR OR SHAFT ENCLOSURE- WHICHEVER IS GREATER

SHAFT TERMINATION IN A ROOM RELATED TO THE PURPOSE OF THE SHAFT- TERMINATION ROOM PROTECTION, INCLUDING OPENING PROTECTIVES, MUST BE EQUAL TO SHAFT ENCLOSURE

EXCEPTION 1 NO OPENINGS IN SHAFT ENCLOSURE EXCEPT AT BOTTOM OF SHAFT

EXCEPTION 2 NO OPENINGS IN SHAFT AND COMBUSTIBLES NOT ALLOWED IN SHAFT

BOTTOM OF SHAFT CLOSED WITH PENETRATING ITEMS FIRESTOPPED OR ROOM SPRINKLERED

ROOM ENCLOSURE NOT REQUIRED TO BE FIRE RESISTANT

FIGURE 6.12 Requirements for shaft enclosures. *(Source: SBCCI, Standard Building Code Commentary, 1997)*

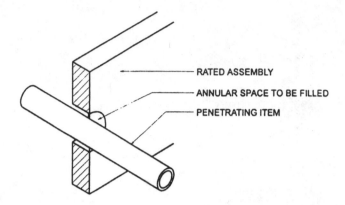

FIGURE 6.13   Annular space protection noncombustible penetration. *(Source: SBCCI, Standard Building Code Commentary, 1997)*

lar space and be installed as tested in the assembly rating or be tested individually as a *through penetration firestop system*. The test for firestops, ASTM E 114, includes a water pressure differential to simulate conditions experienced by the penetration during firefighting. Firestop products that have been tested in a variety of penetration conditions are the only option for most penetrations with combustible materials (e.g. plastic pipe).

An exception for metal pipe penetrations allows the annular space to be sealed with mortar at masonry walls. Another exception allows metal pipe to be sleeved and sealed with noncombustible filler, which will prevent the passage of fire-borne gases (Figure 6.14).

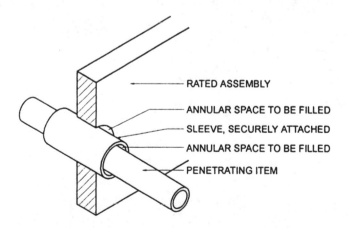

FIGURE 6.14   Annular space protection combustible penetration. *(Source: SBCCI, Standard Building Code Commentary, 1997)*

Penetrations through fire-rated membranes (walls) must not reduce the fire-rated integrity of the wall. Wall-mounted electrical boxes (typically not fire rated) are limited in size, number, and placement as illustrated in Figure 6.15 and in the exceptions listed in IBC 711.3.2.

FIRE RESISTANT JOINT SYSTEMS (SEALS)

Most construction systems are built with panels and parts with joints in the materials. Dissimilar materials, such as at the floor intersection with a wall, also form joints. The code requires continuity of any fire-rated elements. Joint systems must be tested according to UL 2079, which ensures stability and fire resistance of the joint under fire conditions.

CONCEALED SPACES

Concealed spaces are required to be fireblocked to prevent the undetected spread of fire and combustion gases between adjacent areas. Fireblocking must be installed in concealed wall spaces, between stair stringers, connections between horizontal and vertical elements, and other specified locations. Ceilings, walls, floors, and architectural trim installed over sleepers or blocking with concealed spaces must be fire blocked. Figures 6.16 and 6.17 show examples of where fireblocking is and is not required in stud wall and lay-in ceiling construction.

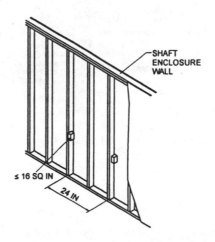

AGGREGATE AREA OF OUTLET BOXES MUST NOT EXCEED 100 SQ IN PER 100 SQ FT OF WALL AREA OR SHAFT ENCLOSURE WALL AREA.

FIGURE 6.15 Outlet boxes in fire-rated walls. *(Source: SBCCI, Standard Building Code Commentary, 1997)*

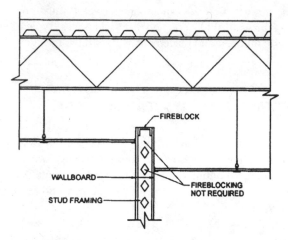

FIGURE 6.16   Fireblocking in noncombustible partition. *(Source: SBCCI, Standard Building Code Commentary, 1997)*

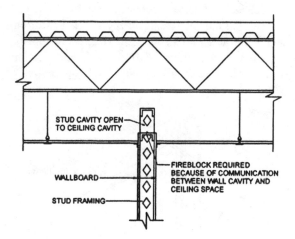

FIGURE 6.17   Fireblocking in noncombustible partition. *(Source: SBCCI, Standard Building Code Commentary, 1997)*

   Figure 6.18 shows the location of required fireblocking at the intersection of a floor and the exterior wall. Figure 6.19 shows the location of fireblocking at the stairs in wood-framed construction.

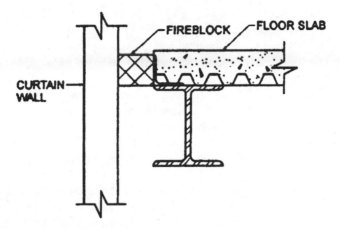

FIGURE 6.18 Fireblocking at floor-exterior wall intersection. *(Source: SBCCI, Standard Building Code Commentary, 1997)*

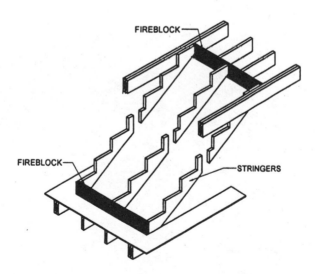

FIGURE 6.19 Fireblocking in wood-framed stairs. *(Source: SBCCI, Standard Building Code Commentary, 1997)*

LIFE SAFETY CODE—PROTECTION

The LSC in Chapter 6, *Classification of Occupancies and Classification of Hazards*, provides definitions for occupancies and classifies each according to low, medium, or high hazard. The individual occupancy chapters (12-42) provide requirements for fire-resistance-rated construction based on occupancy and hazard classification.

Protection from hazards covers uses or activities within a building considered hazardous and must be protected, typically with a one-hour fire rating. LSC Chapter 6 also provides for fire barriers, smoke barriers, openings, and penetrations. The fire ratings required for openings are similar to the IBC. Exceptions to the fire rating requirements in LSC Chapter 6 are included in each occupancy chapter, under the section titled Protection.

Protection of vertical openings covers required fire ratings of stairs, elevators, and other shafts. The requirements are similar to the IBC, with a fire rating of two hours for shafts of more than four floors, one hour for other shafts.

CHAPTER 7

MEANS OF EGRESS

EGRESS COMPONENTS—EXIT ACCESS, EXIT AND EXIT DISCHARGE

The International Building Code and the Life Safety Code use the same terminology to describe the components of an exit, and the requirements are very similar. This chapter discusses the concept of exits and exit components. Readers will note that they are surveyed generally in the order in which they are presented in IBC Chapter 10, *Means of Egress*. Figure 7.1 is a diagram that summarizes the components of means of egress. Figure 7.1a shows sample plans of ground and second floors with exit access, exit, and exit discharge paths marked.

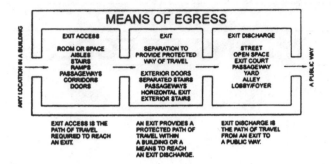

FIGURE 7.1   Means of egress. A continuous and unobstructed way of exit travel from any point in a building or structure to a public way, consisting of three separate and distinct parts: (1) the way of exit access; (2) the exit; and (3) the way of exit discharge. A means of egress comprises the vertical and horizontal ways of travel and shall include the intervening room space, doors, corridors, passageways, balconies, stairs, ramps, enclosures, lobbies, horizontal exits, courts, and yards. (*Source: SBCCI, Standard Building Code Commentary, 1997*)

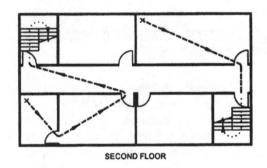

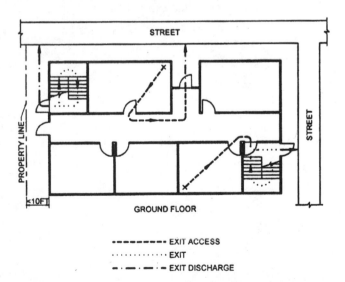

FIGURE 7.1a   Means of egress. (*Source: SBCCI, Standard Building Code Commentary, 1997*)

EXIT ACCESS

Exit access refers to the area within a building or space that must be traversed to reach an exit from the part of the building or space that normally is occupied. Obviously, exit access is the vast majority of the area to be designed or constructed. The arrangement and required number of exits, maximum travel distance, and common path of travel are described under exit access. The requirements for exit access are intended to allow persons to reach an exit during an emergency, typically a fire. Figure 7.2 illustrates various forms of exit access.

EXIT

An exit is typically a stairway enclosed by a fire barrier, with all of the other protection afforded under IBC Chapter 7, *Fire Resistance Rated Construction*, and LSC Chapter 6, *Features of Fire Protection*, plus other measures described in IBC Chapter 10, *Means of Egress*, and LSC Chapter 5, *Means of Egress*. An exit also can be a horizontal exit, exit passageway, exterior exit stair, or (of course) a door to the exterior. The most important concept here is that the exit provides protection for occupants during an emergency, and allows them to reach the exit discharge safely. Figure 7.3 illustrates various types of exits.

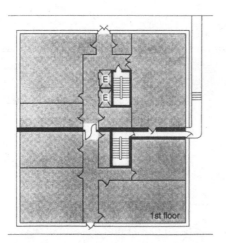
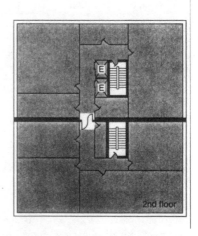

FIGURE 7.2   Spaces constituting exit access. All spaces occupied and traversed in reaching an exit are considered the exit access portion of the means of egress. From the shading shown in the figures, it is apparent that exit access comprises more floor area than either of the other components of means of egress—the exit and the exit discharge. *(Source: NFPA, Life Safety Code Handbook, 1997)*††

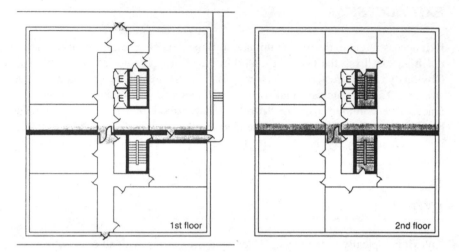

FIGURE 7.3   Various forms of exits. On the second floor, exits include (a) two exit stairs enclosed by fire-rated barriers including a rated self-closing door; and (b) a horizontal exit consisting of a fire-rated barrier, including rated self-closing doors, completely dividing the floor into two fire compartments. On the first floor, (a) two doors form the corridor directly to the outside at grade level; (b) a horizontal exit is a vertical extension of and therefore similar to the horizontal exit on the second floor; and (c) an exit passageway connects one of the second-floor exit stairs directly with the outside, separated from the remainder of the floor by fire-rated barriers, including rated self-closing doors. *(Source: NFPA, Life Safety Code Handbook, 1997)*††

EXIT DISCHARGE

Exit discharge is the part of a building or outside passageway that remains to be traversed before reaching a public way. The codes also allow exit discharge into an outside area that complies with the requirements for an *exit court*. The concept is that exit discharge allows the building occupants to escape the building during an emergency, or to reach an area of safety where they can be rescued. Figure 7.4 illustrates various types of exit discharge.

MEANS OF EGRESS—GENERAL REQUIREMENTS

General means of egress requirements apply to all exit components: exit access, exit, and exit discharge. General requirements include occupant load, minimum width and height, continuity, floors, changes in level, signage, lighting, doors, stairs, railings, and barriers. These topics are addressed in this chapter.

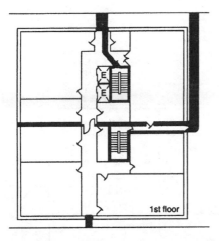

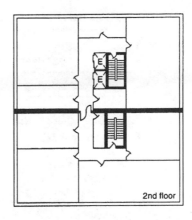

FIGURE 7.4   Exit discharge. Because occupants leave the building at the first floor only, no exit discharge occurs on the second floor. The first-floor exit discharge includes (a) the exterior space beginning at the exit doors from the corridor and continuing to the public way (street); (b) the exterior walkway along the side of the building beginning at the door from the exit passageway and continuing to the public way; and (c) the interior path of travel from the second-floor exit stair discharging through a portion of the first floor corridor. For an occupant of the second floor who must travel across a portion of the first floor, this area is considered exit discharge, yet an occupant of the first floor may travel across the same space and be considered to be within exit access. *(Source: NFPA, Life Safety Code Handbook, 1997)*††

CALCULATED OCCUPANT LOAD

Means of egress requirements are established by the *occupant load*, which is the calculated number of occupants within the facility. IBC Table 1003.2.2.2 Maximum Floor Area Allowances Per Occupant is included here as Figure 7.5. LSC Table 7.3.1.2 Occupant Load Factor is included here as Figure 7.6.

Although the allowances do not coincide entirely, the methods of calculating occupant load are identical. Floor areas are calculated using the gross building area or net room areas. A sample calculation for a business occupancy, which uses the gross building (or tenant) area, is included as Figure 7.7. A sample calculation for an educational occupancy, which uses net classroom area, is included as Figure 7.8 [1, 2].

Multiple- or mixed-occupancy loads are determined with the factors assigned to each individual use, and require a more complicated set of calculations. Figure 7.9 illustrates the occupant-load calculations for a mixed business and assembly use. Figure 7.10 offers occupant-load calculations for a mixed education and assembly use.

TABLE 1003.2.2.2
MAXIMUM FLOOR AREA ALLOWANCES PER OCCUPANT

OCCUPANCY	FLOOR AREA IN SQ. FT. PER OCCUPANT
Agricultural building	300 gross
Aircraft hangars	500 gross

Airport terminal
  Concourse
  Waiting areas
  Baggage claim
  Baggage handling
	
	100 gross
	15 gross
	20 gross
	300 gross

Assembly Gaming floors (keno, slots, etc.)	 11 gross
Assembly with fixed seats	See 1003.2.2.9

Assembly without fixed seats
  Concentrated (chairs only—not fixed)
  Standing space
  Unconcentrated (tables and chairs)
	
	7 net
	5 net
	15 net

Bowling centers, allow 5 persons for each lane including 15 feet of runway, and for additional areas	7 net
Business areas	100 gross
Courtrooms—other than fixed seating areas	40 net
Dormitories	50 gross

FIGURE 7.5   Table 1003.2.2.2. *(Source: ICC, International Building Code, 2000)*

MAXIMUM FLOOR AREA ALLOWANCES PER OCCUPANT

OCCUPANCY	FLOOR AREA IN SQ. FT. PER OCCUPANT

Educational
    Classroom area
    Shops and other vocational room areas
	
	20 net
	50 net

Exercise rooms	50 gross
H-5 Fabrication and manufacturing areas	200 gross
Industrial areas	100 gross

Institutional areas
    Inpatient treatment areas
    Outpatient areas
    Sleeping areas
	
	240 gross
	100 gross
	120 gross

Kitchens, commercial	200 gross

Library
    Reading rooms
    Stack area
	
	50 net
	100 gross

Locker rooms	50 gross

Mercantile
    Basement and grade floor areas
    Areas on other floors
    Storage, stock, shipping areas
	
	30 gross
	60 gross
	300 gross

Parking garages	200 gross
Residential	200 gross

Skating rinks, swimming pools
    Rink and pool
    Decks
	
	50 gross
	15 gross

Stages and platforms	15 net
Accessory storage areas, mechanical equipment room	300 gross
Warehouses	500 gross

FIGURE 7.5 *(continued)*   Table 1003.2.2.2. *(Source: ICC, International Building Code, 2000)*

Occupant Load Factor

Use	ft²† (per person)	m²† (per person)
Assembly Use		
Concentrated use, without fixed seating	7 net	0.65 net
Less concentrated use, without fixed seating	15 net	1.4 net
Bench-type seating	1 person/18 linear in.	1 person/45.7 linear cm
Fixed seating	Number of fixed seats	Number of fixed seats
Waiting spaces	*See 12.1.7.2 and 13.1.7.2.*	*See 12.1.7.2 and 13.1.7.2.*
Kitchens	100	9.3
Library stack areas	100	9.3
Library reading rooms	50 net	4.6 net
Swimming pools	50 — of water surface	4.6 — of water surface
Swimming pool decks	30	2.8
Exercise rooms with equipment	50	4.6
Exercise rooms without equipment	15	1.4
Stages	15 net	1.4 net
Lighting and access catwalks, galleries, gridirons	100 net	9.3 net
Casinos and similar gaming areas	11	1
Skating rinks	50	4.6
Educational Use		
Classrooms	20 net	1.9 net
Shops, laboratories, vocational rooms	50 net	4.6 net
Day-Care Use	35 net	3.3 net
Health Care Use		
Inpatient treatment departments	240	22.3
Sleeping departments	120	11.1

FIGURE 7.6 Table 7.3.1.2. *(Source: NFPA, 101, Life Safety Code, 2000)*†

Table 7.3.1.2 Occupant Load Factor

Use	ft^{2†} (per person)	m^{2†} (per person)
Detention and Correctional Use	120	11.1
Residential Use		
Hotels and dormitories	200	18.6
Apartment buildings	200	18.6
Board and care, large	200	18.6
Industrial Use		
General and high hazard industrial	100	9.3
Special purpose industrial	NA‡	NA‡
Business Use	100	9.3
Storage Use (other than mercantile storerooms)	NA‡	NA‡
Mercantile Use		
Sales area on street floor $^{\S\,\lozenge}$	30	2.8
Sales area on two or more street floors $^{\lozenge}$	40	3.7
Sales area on floor below street floor $^{\lozenge}$	30	2.8
Sales area on floors above street floor $^{\lozenge}$	60	5.6
Floors or portions of floors used only for offices	*See business use.*	*See business use.*
Floors or portions of floors used only for storage, receiving, and shipping, and not open to general public	300	27.9
Covered mall buildings	Per factors applicable to use of space $^{\#}$	Per factors applicable to use of space $^{\#}$

†All factors expressed in gross area unless marked "net".
‡Not applicable. The occupant load shall be not less than the maximum probable number of occupants present at any time.
§For the purpose of determining occupant load in mercantile occupancies where, due to differences in grade of streets on different sides, two or more floors directly accessible from streets (not including alleys or similar back streets) exist, each such floor shall be considered a street floor. The occupant load factor shall be one person for each 40 ft^2 (3.7 m^2) of gross floor area of sales space.
$^{\lozenge}$In mercantile occupancies with no street floor, as defined in 3.3.196, but with access directly from the street by stairs or escalators, the principal floor at the point of entrance to the mercantile occupancy shall be considered the street floor.
$^{\#}$The portions of the covered mall, where considered a pedestrian way and not used as gross leasable area, shall not be assessed an occupant load based on Table 7.3.1.2. However, means of egress from a covered mall pedestrian way shall be provided for an occupant load determined by dividing the gross leasable area of the covered mall building (not including anchor stores) by the appropriate lowest whole number occupant load factor from Figure 7.3.1.2.
   Each individual tenant space shall have means of egress to the outside or to the covered mall based on occupant loads figured by using the appropriate occupant load factor from Table 7.3.1.2.
   Each individual anchor store shall have means of egress independent of the covered mall.

FIGURE 7.6 *(continued)*   Table 7.3.1.2. *(Source: NFPA, 101, Life Safety Code, 2000)* $\dagger$

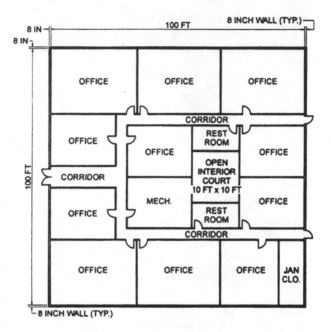

GROSS FLOOR AREA BASED OCCUPANT LOAD

SOLUTION: First, calculate gross floor area.

Gross Floor Area = (100 ft x 100 ft) – (10 ft x 10 ft courtyard)
= 9,900 sq ft

Notice that the only area excluded from the gross floor area is the open court. The corridor, mechanical rooms, rest rooms, and janitor's closet, as well as interior building components, are included in the gross floor area. Next, calculate the minimum occupant load. The occupant load for the building is based on 100 gross sq ft per occupant. The occupant load is calculated by dividing the gross area by 100.

$$\text{Occupant Load} = \frac{9{,}900 \text{ sq ft}}{100 \text{ sq ft/occupant}} = 99 \text{ occupants}$$

FIGURE 7.7 Gross floor area-based occupant load. *(Source: SBCCI, Standard Building Code Commentary, 1997)*

In occupant load densities based on gross floor area, the assumption is that, at any given time, the occupants will be uniformly distributed around the building. For this reason, the specified density is attributed to accessory common use areas, such as corridors and restrooms, as well as the office area itself.

Net floor area based occupant densities involve a different assumption. Net area is defined as the area actually occupied, not including accessory unoccupied areas, such as corridors, stairs, thickness of walls, columns, toilet rooms, and mechanical rooms. (See definition and commentary for AREA, NET FLOOR in 202.)

EXAMPLE: Calculate the occupant load for the following education building, a single-story Group E building.

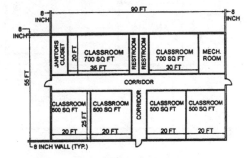

NET FLOOR AREA BASED OCCUPANT LOAD

SOLUTION: First, calculate area. The gross floor area of this building is:

   Gross Floor Area = 90 ft x 55 ft = 4,950 sq ft

However, the density for educational classroom areas in Table 1003.1 is based on 20 sq ft per person net area. Consequently, the actual classroom area is:

   Net Floor Area = 4 x 500 + 600 + 700 = 3,300 sq ft

The occupant load for the building, as determined from Table 1003.1, is based on 20 net sq ft per occupant. The occupant load is calculated by dividing the net area by 20.

$$\text{Occupant Load} = \frac{3,300 \text{ sq ft}}{20 \text{ sq ft/occupant}} = 165 \text{ occupants}$$

Using net floor area assumes that all building occupants will be in the principal-use area (classrooms) at any given time and not simultaneously in the accessory areas, such as corridors and rest rooms.

FIGURE 7.8   Net floor area-based occupant load. (*Source: SBCCI, Standard Building Code Commentary, 1997*)

EXAMPLE: Calculate the occupant load for the mixed use building shown.

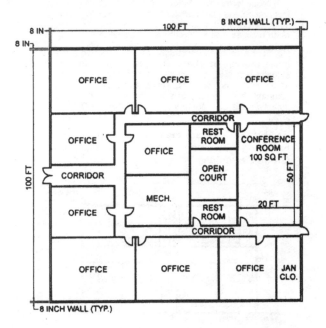

SOLUTION: The small assembly conference room constitutes a different use than the business area and must be considered separately. The previously calculated gross floor area was 9,900 sq ft. The net floor area of the conference room is 1,000 sq ft.

Therefore, the building contains 8,800 sq ft of gross floor area as Business use and 1,000 sq ft of net floor area as unconcentrated Assembly. The occupant load for the building would be:

$$\text{Business Use} = \frac{8{,}800 \text{ sq ft}}{100 \text{ sq ft/occupant}} = 88 \text{ occupants}$$

$$\text{Assembly Use} = \frac{1{,}000 \text{ sq ft}}{15 \text{ sq ft/occupant}} = 67 \text{ occupants}$$

Total Occupant Load   = 155

FIGURE 7.9   Mixed-occupancy business building occupant load. *(Source: SBCCI, Standard Building Code Commentary, 1997)*

EXAMPLE: Calculate the occupant load for the mixed use building shown.

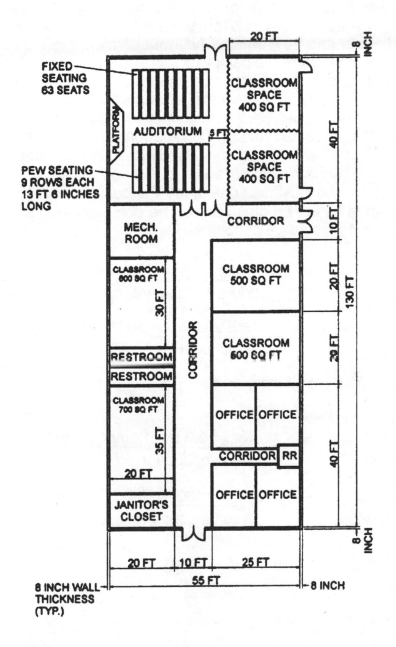

FIGURE 7.10 Mixed-occupancy education building occupant load. *(Source: SBCCI, Standard Building Code Commentary, 1997)*

SOLUTION: Two classrooms are now subdivided as administrative offices with an accessory corridor and a restroom, and an auditorium has been added on one end. The auditorium has an unusual combination of fixed seats and pew seating (without dividing arms). It also has an area at the back which is separated by folding partitions. Even though this space is designated as classroom space, it is likely that at some time the partitions will be pulled back and this area utilized as an extension of the auditorium. Consequently, it is conservative to consider it as concentrated Assembly. The corridor and restroom accessory to the office area is included in the Business use since the business density factor is based on gross area. The occupant load for the building would be as follows:

$$\text{Classroom Area} = \frac{500 + 500 + 700 + 600 \text{ sq ft}}{20 \text{ sq ft/occupant}} = 115$$

$$\text{Office Area} = \frac{25 \text{ ft} \times 40 \text{ ft}}{100 \text{ sq ft/occupant}} = 10 \text{ occupants}$$

Auditorium (Fixed Seats) = 63

$$\text{Auditorium (Pew Seats)} = \frac{9 \text{ rows} \times 13.5 \text{ ft} \times 12 \text{ in/ft}}{18 \text{ in/occupant}} = 115$$

$$\text{Auditorium (Concentrated)} = \frac{400 + 400 \text{ sq ft}}{7 \text{ sq ft/occupant}} = 115$$

Total Occupant Load = 384

FIGURE 7.10 *(continued)* Mixed-occupancy education building occupant load. *(Source: SBCCI, Standard Building Code Commentary, 1997)*

IBC AND LSC ALLOWABLE FLOOR AREA VARIATIONS

Notice that most of the floor area factors or allowance are the same in both the IBC and the LSC. However, some factors vary. The following list describes some of the floor areas in occupancies relating to interior design and construction that have different values in the IBC and LSC.

Occupancy	IBC allowance	LSC load factor
Kitchens	200	100
Swimming pool decks	15	30
Exercise rooms	50	15 (no equipment)
Day care	20 (educational)	35
Mercantile	60 (not grade floor or basement)	40 (w/ street access)

One must determine what code(s) will govern for a given project location and jurisdiction, and use the appropriate factor to determine occupant load. If both codes are applicable, the lower (more restrictive) factor should be applied.

INCREASED OCCUPANT LOAD

Under the International Building Code, if the *actual* number of building occupants known or designed for exceeds the *calculated* occupant load, the larger number of occupants is used to determine the required egress width. No occupant load may be less than 5 sq ft per occupant. Both codes require posting of occupant load in assembly occupancies [1].

MINIMUM EGRESS WIDTH—CALCULATED

Calculated minimum exit width is determined by using IBC Table 1003.2.3, Egress Width Per Occupant Served (Figure 7.11), and/or LSC 5-3.3.1, Egress Capacity (Figure 7.12). The value of exit units in inches per occupant is multiplied by the number of occupants to determine the minimum exit width. A building or space must have exits totaling not less than the required exit width.

The required egress width for most buildings and occupancies is the same in both codes: 0.3 in. per occupant for stairs, and 0.2 in. per occupant for other exit components (level hallways, doors, and compliant ramps). The minimum egress width specified in the Life Safety Code occupancy chapters (12-42) and special exit widths in other parts of the IBC supersede the exit width determined using

EGRESS WIDTH PER OCCUPANT SERVED

OCCUPANCY	WITHOUT SPRINKLER SYSTEM		WITH SPRINKLER SYSTEM[a]	
	Stairways (inches per occupant)	Other egress components (inches per occupant)	Stairways (inches per occupant)	Other egress components (inches per occupant)
Occupancies other than those listed below	0.3	0.2	0.2	0.15
Hazardous: H-1, H-2 H-3, and H-4	0.7	0.4	0.3	0.2
Institutional: I-2	0.4	0.2	0.3	0.2

FIGURE 7.11 Egress width per occupant served. (*Source: ICC, International Building Code, 2000*)

Area	Stairways (width per person)		Level Components and Ramps (width per person)	
	in.	cm	in.	cm
Board and care	0.4	1.0	0.2	0.5
Health care, sprinklered	0.3	0.8	0.2	0.5
Health care, nonsprinklered	0.6	1.5	0.5	1.3
High hazard contents	0.7	1.8	0.4	1.0
All others	0.3	0.8	0.2	0.5

FIGURE 7.12 Capacity factors. *(Source: NFPA, 101, Life Safety Code, 2000)*†

the egress width calculations. Special requirements for assembly occupancies are covered later in this chapter. Decreases in required exit width per occupant are allowed under both codes for sprinkled buildings [1, 2].

REQUIRED EXIT WIDTH—EXAMPLES

Figures 7.13 and 7.14 show examples of mercantile plans and the calculations for verifying required width of doors and stairs, respectively. Figure 7.15 shows a sample residential plan and the calculation to determine if the corridor width is adequate.

EXIT STAGING AND CONVERGENCE

In the design of both codes, it is assumed that occupants on the ground floor will exit before those on the second floor, and those on the second floor before those on the third floor, and so on, so that the building occupants never double up on the stairs. The exit components affected (stairs and exit discharge) then must be designed for the occupant load on the floor with the maximum occupant load, and not the total of all floors. This concept of exit staging is illustrated by Figure 7.16, where the required width of exits at the ground floor must accommodate 450 persons (the greatest *single* floor occupant load).

EXAMPLE: The figure below shows a 110 ft x 140 ft single-story mercantile building with three 34-inch clear width exit doors. Determine if the exit capacity is sufficient.

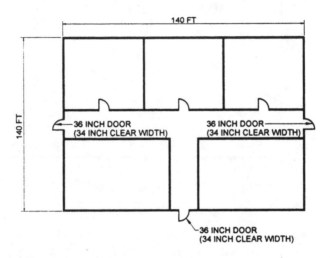

MERCANTILE DOORS — CAPACITY OF MEANS OF EGRESS

SOLUTION: The occupant load for this floor (calculated from Table 1003.1) is:

Occupant Load =

$$\frac{\text{Area}}{\text{Area per occupant}} = \frac{140 \text{ ft x } 100 \text{ ft}}{30 \text{ sq ft/occupant}} = 467$$
(Table 1003.1)

The capacity of the three 34-inch clear width exit doors (level travel from Table 1004) is:

$$\text{Capacity} = \frac{3 \text{ x } 34 \text{ inches}}{0.2 \text{ inches/person}} = 510 \text{ persons}$$

The exit capacity exceeds the occupant load.

FIGURE 7.13   Mercantile doors—capacity of means of egress. *(Source: SBCCI, Standard Building Code Commentary, 1997)*

EXAMPLE: Suppose that the mercantile story shown below was located at a basement level with three 44-inch wide stairs that led to the level of exit discharge. Determine if the exit capacity of the doors and stairs is sufficient.

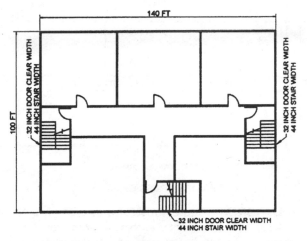

MERCANTILE STAIR — CAPACITY OF MEANS OF EGRESS

SOLUTION: The stair's exit doors have a clear width of 32 inches. The occupant load of 467 persons is the same as previously calculated. The exit capacity of the stair and of the doors must be checked.

For the doors (level travel):
$$\text{Capacity} = \frac{3 \times 32 \text{ inches}}{0.2 \text{ inches/person}} = 480 \text{ persons}$$

For the stairs:
$$\text{Capacity} = \frac{3 \times 44 \text{ inches}}{0.3 \text{ inches/persons}} = 440 \text{ persons}$$

The capacity of the doors exceeds the occupant load; however, the stair capacity is less than the occupant load. Since the capacity of the exit system is limited by the most restrictive component in the system, this exit example does not satisfy 1003.3.1. The total width of stairs that would be required to provide adequate exit capacity can be easily calculated.

Total Stair Width =
467 persons x 0.3 inches/person =140 inches

Three 47-inch stairs (141 inches total width) is sufficient.

FIGURE 7.14 Mercantile stair—capacity of means of egress. *(Source: SBCCI, Standard Building Code Commentary, 1997)*

EXAMPLE: Determine if the corridor shown below has sufficient egress capacity for the Residential occupancy.

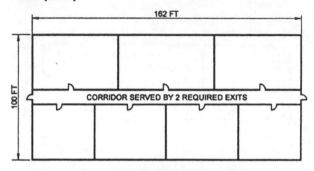

RESIDENTIAL OCCUPANCY

CORRIDOR EGRESS CAPACITY

SOLUTION: The figure above shows a 162 ft x 100 ft Residential occupancy with two grade-level exit doors connected by an exit access corridor. This section of the code establishes the following procedure to determine the required corridor width. First determine minimum occupant load.

$$\text{Occupant Load} = \frac{\text{Area}}{\text{Area per occupant}}$$
(Table 1003.1)

$$= \frac{162 \text{ ft} \times 200 \text{ ft}}{200 \text{ sq ft/occupant}} = 81 \text{ persons}$$

$$\text{Exit access corridor capacity} = \frac{81 \text{ persons}}{2 \text{ exits}} = 41 \text{ persons/exit}$$

Corridor width = 41 persons x 0.2 inches/person
= 8.2 inches

Obviously, a corridor 8.2 inches wide is unrealistic; consequently, the minimum corridor width in Table 1004 governs. Table 1004 requires a minimum 44-inch corridor with Notes 5 and 10. Note 5 does not apply since the corridor is outside the dwelling units. However, since the corridor occupant load is less than 50 (in this case 41), Note 10 to Table 1004 allows a 36-inch corridor to be used.

FIGURE 7.15   Corridor egress capacity. *(Source: SBCCI, Standard Building Code Commentary, 1997)*

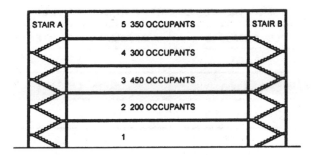

FIGURE 7.16 Exit staging. *(Source: SBCCI, Standard Building Code Commentary, 1997)*

When a building has floors above *and* below the level of exit discharge, the means of egress converge at the intermediate level. The occupants double up in the exit, so the width of egress components must equal the sum of the two floors. This concept of exit convergence is illustrated by Figure 7.17, where the required width of exits at the ground level is 500 occupants (the total of the *two* greatest floor occupant loads).

REQUIRED NUMBER OF EXITS— MINIMUM OF TWO

Every floor in the building must have a minimum of two exits as required by IBC Table 1005.2.1, included here as Figure 7.18. The Life Safety Code provisions are the same. Both codes require a minimum of two, but no more than four, exits per floor. The IBC and the LSC both allow one exit under certain circumstances. The IBC has summarized the types and sizes of facilities allowed to have one exit in Table 1004.2.1, included here as Figure 7.19. Multiplying the allowable number of occupants by the occupant load allowance gives the maximum size of these single-exit facilities. The Life Safety Code exceptions that allow one exit are contained in the occupancy chapters (12-42) [1, 2].

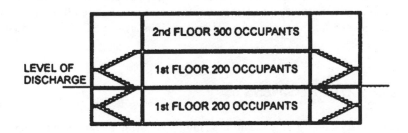

FIGURE 7.17 Converging exits. *(Source: SBCCI, Standard Building Code Commentary, 1997)*

MINIMUM NUMBER OF EXITS FOR OCCUPANT LOAD

OCCUPANT LOAD	MINIMUM NUMBER OF EXITS
1-500	2
501-1,000	3
More than 1,000	4

FIGURE 7.18   Table 1005.2.1. *(Source: ICC, International Building Code, 2000)*

SPACES WITH ONE MEANS OF EGRESS

Three or more exits: Access to three or more exits shall be provided from a floor area where required by Section 1005.2.1.

OCCUPANCY	MAXIMUM OCCUPANT LOAD
A, B, E, F, M, U	50
H-1, H-2, H-3	3
H-4, H-5, I-1, I-3, I-4, R	10
S	30

FIGURE 7.19   Table 1004.2.1. *(Source: ICC, International Building Code, 2000)*

SINGLE EXIT—MERCANTILE

Class C mercantile occupancies (less than 3000 sq ft) are allowed to have one exit under certain circumstances. Larger mercantile occupancies are allowed to have one exit under certain circumstances. The exceptions are at LSC 36.2.4, shown in Figure 7.19a.

SINGLE EXIT—BUSINESS

The Life Safety Code at 38.2.4.2 allows single exits from certain business spaces as listed in Figure 7.19b.

> *Exception No. 1: Exit access travel shall be permitted to be common for the distances permitted as common paths of travel by 36.2.5.3.*
>
> *Exception No. 2: A single means of egress shall be permitted in a Class C mercantile occupancy, provided that one of the following conditions is met:*
>
> *(a) The travel distance to the exit or to a covered mall (if it is considered a pedestrian way) does not exceed 75 ft (23 m).*
>
> *(b) The travel distance to the exit or to a covered mall (if it is considered a pedestrian way) does not exceed 100 ft (30 m), and the story on which the occupancy is located and all communicating levels that are traversed to reach the exit or covered mall are protected throughout by an approved, supervised automatic sprinkler system in accordance with Section 9.7.*
>
> *Exception No. 3: A single means of egress to an exit or to a covered mall (if it is considered a pedestrian way) shall be permitted from a mezzanine within any Class A, Class B, or Class C mercantile occupancy, provided that the common path of travel does not exceed 75 ft (23 m), or does not exceed 100 ft (30 m) if protected throughout by an approved, supervised automatic sprinkler system in accordance with Section 9.7.*

FIGURE 7.19a   36.2.4 Exceptions. *(Source: NFPA, 101, Life Safety Code, 2000)*†

WINDOWS AS SECONDARY MEANS OF EGRESS

Residential occupancies require two means of egress from any sleeping rooms. One means must be through normal exit components (e.g., corridors, doors, stairs, and ramps). A secondary means of egress also is required. Figure 7.20 illustrates two acceptable single-family floor plans, with acceptable secondary means of egress. Educational occupancies also require windows as a secondary means of egress for classrooms that do not have a door leading directly to the exterior [1, 2].

Egress windows must have 5.7 sq ft of open area, along with minimum horizontal and vertical dimensions, illustrated in Figure 7.21. These requirements are the same in both the IBC and the LSC. The window shown in Figure 7.22 does not qualify as a code-compliant means of egress, because it does not have the required minimum clear opening with the window in the open position. Below-grade sleeping rooms are allowed to have window openings into a window well, as shown in Figure 7.23 [1, 2].

Exception No. 1: Exit access travel shall be permitted to be common for the distances permitted as common paths of travel by 38.2.5.3.

Exception No. 2: A single exit shall be permitted for a room or area with a total occupant load of fewer than 100 persons, provided that the following criteria are met:

(a) The exit shall discharge directly to the outside at the level of exit discharge for the building.

(b) The total distance of travel from any point, including travel within the exit, shall not exceed 100 ft (30 m).

(c) Such travel shall be on the same floor level or, if traversing of stairs is necessary, such stairs shall not exceed 15 ft (4.5 m) in height, and the stairs shall be provided with complete enclosures to separate them from any other part of the building, with no door openings therein.

(d) A single outside stair in accordance with 7.2.2 shall be permitted to serve all floors permitted within the 15-ft (4.5-m) vertical travel limitation.

Exception No. 3: Any business occupancy not exceeding three stories, and not exceeding an occupant load of 30 people per floor, shall be permitted a single separate exit to each floor. This exception shall be permitted only where the total travel distance to the outside of the building does not exceed 100 ft (30 m) and where the exit is enclosed in accordance with 7.1.3.2, serves no other levels, and discharges directly to the outside. A single outside stair in accordance with 7.2.2 shall be permitted to serve all floors.

Exception No. 4: A single means of egress shall be permitted from a mezzanine within a business occupancy, provided that the common path of travel does not exceed 75 ft (23 m), or 100 ft (30 m) if protected throughout by an approved, supervised automatic sprinkler system in accordance with Section 9.7.

Exception No. 5: A single exit shall be permitted for a maximum two-story, single-tenant space/building protected throughout by an approved, supervised automatic sprinkler system in accordance with Section 9.7 where the total travel to the outside does not exceed 100 ft (30 m).

FIGURE 7.19b   38.2.4.2 Exceptions. *(Source: NFPA, 101, Life Safety Code, 2000)†*

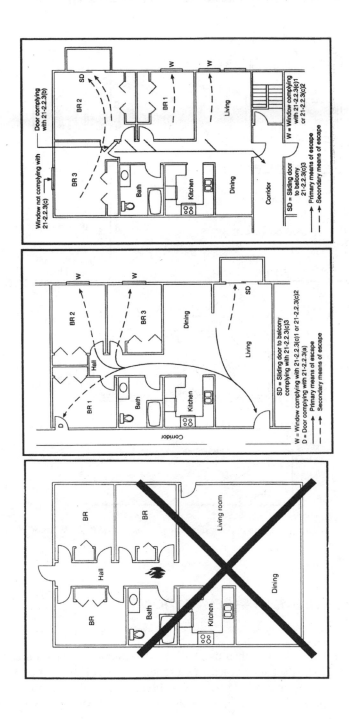

FIGURE 7.20 Acceptable and unacceptable means of egress. (*Source: NFPA, Life Safety Code Handbook, 1997*)††

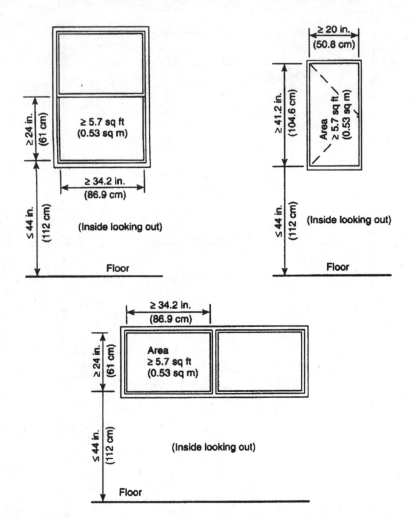

FIGURE 7.21 Emergency egress opening dimensions. *(Source: NFPA, Life Safety Code Handbook, 1997)*††

EXIT ARRANGEMENT—SEPARATION OF EXITS

A dimension that is not less than one-half the maximum diagonal dimension of the area served must separate at least two required exits. This is to prevent one fire or other event from blocking both exits. Figures 7.24 and 7.25 illustrate this concept with spaces of several different shapes. This is a concept on which both codes agree [1, 2].

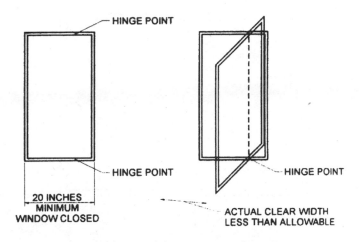

FIGURE 7.22   Insufficient opening size window. *(Source: SBCCI, Standard Building Code Commentary, 1997)*

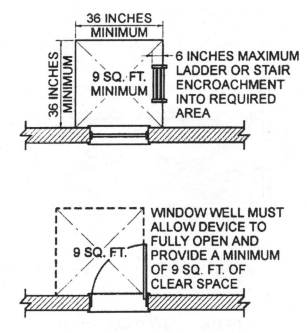

WINDOW WELLS

FIGURE 7.23   Window wells. *(Source: SBCCI, Standard Building Code Commentary, 1997)*

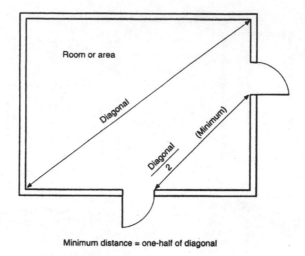

Minimum distance = one-half of diagonal

FIGURE 7.24   Exit arrangement. *(Source: NFPA, Life Safety Code Handbook, 1997)*††

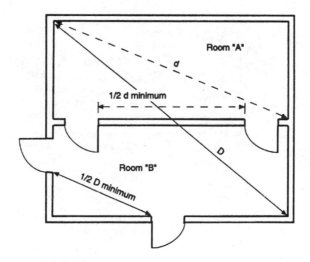

FIGURE 7.25   Exit arrangement. *(Source: NFPA, Life Safety Code Handbook, 1997)*††

SEPARATION OF EXITS—RATED CORRIDOR

When travel between required exits is along a one-hour fire rated corridor, the dimension between the two stairs may be measured *along* the length of corridor between the exits rather than on a straight line between the two exits. This is illustrated in Figures 7.26 and 7.27.

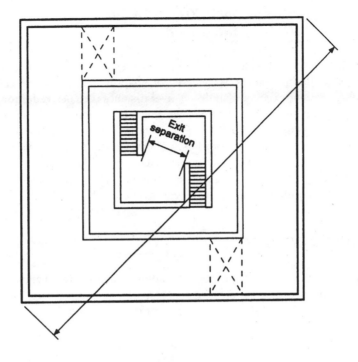

FIGURE 7.26   Separation of exits. *(Source: NFPA, Life Safety Code Handbook, 1997)*††

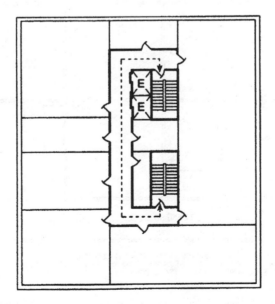

FIGURE 7.27   Separation of exits. *(Source: NFPA, Life Safety Code Handbook, 1997)*††

DEAD ENDS, COMMON PATH OF TRAVEL, AND TOTAL TRAVEL DISTANCE

Travel distance is limited to that which is considered safe according to the occupancy and building features, sprinklered or unsprinklered facilities, and (in the LSC only) new or existing facilities. Travel distances are derived through years of experience with building emergencies and the reactions of various types and conditions of occupants. The IBC and LSC both limit travel distance according to three measures: dead-end corridors, common path of travel, and total travel distance. Common path and total travel distance are illustrated in Figure 7.28. The Life Safety Code Annex has a table listing maximum travel distance for each occupancy and building feature, included as Figure 7.29.

DEAD-END CORRIDORS

A dead-end corridor is any corridor not leading to an exit. Dead ends are limited to 20 ft in unsprinklered buildings and 50 ft in sprinklered buildings, with certain exceptions. Figure 7.30 shows an example of dead-end corridors.

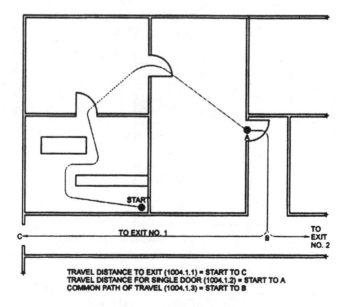

TRAVEL DISTANCE TO EXIT (1004.1.1) = START TO C
TRAVEL DISTANCE FOR SINGLE DOOR (1004.1.2) = START TO A
COMMON PATH OF TRAVEL (1004.1.3) = START TO B

FIGURE 7.28   Travel distance. *(Source: SBCCI, Standard Building Code Commentary, 1997)*

Type of Occupancy	Common Path Limit		Dead-End Limit		Travel Distance Limit	
	Unsprinklered ft (m)	Sprinklered ft (m)	Unsprinklered ft (m)	Sprinklered ft (m)	Unsprinklered ft (m)	Sprinklered ft (m)
Assembly						
New	20/75 (6.1/23)[a,b]	20/75 (6.1/23)[a,b]	0/20 (0/6.1)[b]	0/20 (0/6.1)[b]	150 (45)[c]	200 (60)[c]
Existing	20/75 (6.1/23)[a,b]	20/75 (6.1/23)[a,b]	0/20 (0/6.1)[b]	0/20 (0/6.1)[b]	150 (45)[c]	200 (60)[c]
Educational						
New	75 (23)	100 (30)	20 (6.1)	50 (15)	150 (45)	200 (60)
Existing	75 (23)	100 (30)	20 (6.1)	50 (15)	150 (45)	200 (60)
Day-Care						
New day-care center	75 (23)	100 (30)	20 (6.1)	50 (15)	150 (45)[d]	200 (60)[d]
Existing day-care center	75 (23)	100 (30)	20 (6.1)	50 (15)	150 (45)[d]	200 (60)[d]
Health Care						
New	NR	NR	30 (9.1)	30 (9.1)	NA	200 (60)[d]
Existing	NR	NR	NR	NR	150 (45)[d]	200 (60)[d]
Ambulatory Health Care						
New	75 (23)[e]	100 (30)[e]	20 (6.1)	50 (15)	150 (45)[d]	200 (60)[d]
Existing	75 (23)[e]	100 (30)[e]	50 (15)	50 (15)	150 (45)[d]	200 (60)[d]

FIGURE 7.29 Table A.7.6.1. (*Source: NFPA, 101, Life Safety Code, 2000*)†

Type of Occupancy	Common Path Limit		Dead-End Limit		Travel Distance Limit	
	Unsprinklered ft (m)	Sprinklered ft (m)	Unsprinklered ft (m)	Sprinklered ft (m)	Unsprinklered ft (m)	Sprinklered ft (m)
Detention and Correctional						
New — Use conditions II, III, IV	50 (15)	100 (30)	50 (15)	50 (15)	150 (45)[d]	200 (60)[d]
New — Use condition V	50 (15)	100 (30)	20 (6.1)	20 (6.1)	150 (45)[d]	200 (60)[d]
Existing — Use conditions II, III, IV, V	50 (15)[f]	100 (30)[f]	NR	NR	150 (45)[d]	200 (60)[d]
Residential						
One- and two-family dwellings	NR	NR	NR	NR	NR	NR
Lodging or rooming houses	NR	NR	NR	NR	NR	NR
Hotels and Dormitories						
New	35 (10.7)[g,i]	50 (15)[g,i]	35 (10.7)	50 (15)	175 (53)[d,h]	325 (99)[d,h]
Existing	35 (10.7)[g]	50 (15)[g]	50 (15)	50 (15)	175 (53)[d,h]	325 (99)[d,h]

FIGURE 7.29 (continued)   Table A.7.6.1. (Source: NFPA, 101, Life Safety Code, 2000) †

Type of Occupancy	Common Path Limit		Dead-End Limit		Travel Distance Limit	
	Unsprinklered ft (m)	Sprinklered ft (m)	Unsprinklered ft (m)	Sprinklered ft (m)	Unsprinklered ft (m)	Sprinklered ft (m)
Apartments						
New	35 (10.7)[g]	50 (15)[g]	35 (10.7)	50 (15)	175 (53)[d,h]	325 (99)[d,h]
Existing	35 (10.7)[g]	50 (15)[g]	50 (15)	50 (15)	175 (53)[d,h]	325 (99)[d,h]
Board and Care						
Small, new and existing	NR	NR	NR	NR	NR	NR
Large, new	NA	125 (38)[i]	NA	50 (15)	NA	325 (99)[d,h]
Large, existing	110 (33)	160 (49)	50 (15)	50 (15)	175 (53)[d,h]	325 (99)[d,h]
Mercantile						
Class A, B, C						
New	75 (23)	100 (30)	20 (6.1)	50 (15)	100 (30)	200 (60)
Existing	75 (23)	100 (30)	50 (15)	50 (15)	150 (45)	200 (60)
Open air	NR	NR	0 (0)	0 (0)	NR	NR

FIGURE 7.29 *(continued)* Table A.7.6.1. *(Source: NFPA, 101, Life Safety Code, 2000)* †

Type of Occupancy	Common Path Limit		Dead-End Limit		Travel Distance Limit	
	Unsprinklered ft (m)	Sprinklered ft (m)	Unsprinklered ft (m)	Sprinklered ft (m)	Unsprinklered ft (m)	Sprinklered ft (m)
Mercantile (Continued)						
Covered Mall						
New	75 (23)	100 (30)	20 (6.1)	50 (15)	100 (30)	400 (120)[j]
Existing	75 (23)	100 (30)	50 (15)	50 (15)	150 (45)	400 (120)[j]
Business						
New	75 (23)[k]	100 (30)[k]	20 (6.1)	50 (15)	200 (60)	300 (91)
Existing	75 (23)[k]	100 (30)[k]	50 (15)	50 (15)	200 (60)	300 (91)
Industrial						
General	50 (15)	100 (30)	50 (15)	50 (15)	200 (60)[n]	250 (75)[l]
Special purpose	50 (15)	100 (30)	50 (15)	50 (15)	300 (91)	400 (122)
High hazard	0 (0)	0 (0)	0 (0)	0 (0)	75 (23)	75 (23)
Aircraft servicing hangars, ground floor	50 (15)[m]	50 (15)[m]	50 (15)[m]	50 (15)[m]	note n	note n

FIGURE 7.29 (*continued*) Table A.7.6.1. (*Source: NFPA, 101, Life Safety Code, 2000*) †

7.34

Type of Occupancy	Common Path Limit		Dead-End Limit		Travel Distance Limit	
	Unsprinklered ft (m)	Sprinklered ft (m)	Unsprinklered ft (m)	Sprinklered ft (m)	Unsprinklered ft (m)	Sprinklered ft (m)
Aircraft servicing hangars, mezzanine floor	50 (15)^m	50 (15)^m	50 (15)^m	50 (15)^m	75 (23)	75 (23)
Storage						
Low hazard	NR	NR	NR	NR	NR	NR
Ordinary hazard	50 (15)	100 (30)	50 (15)	100 (30)	200 (60)	400 (122)
High hazard	0 (0)	0 (0)	0 (0)	0 (0)	75 (23)	75 (23)
Parking garages, open	50 (15)	50 (15)	50 (15)	50 (15)	200 (60)	300 (91)
Parking garages, enclosed	50 (15)	50 (15)	50 (15)	50 (15)	150 (45)	200 (60)
Aircraft storage hangars, ground floor	50 (15)^m	100 (30)^m	50 (15)^m	50 (15)^m	note n	note n
Aircraft servicing hangars, mezzanine floor	50 (15)^m	75 (23)^m	50 (15)^m	50 (15)^m	75 (23)	75 (23)

FIGURE 7.29 *(continued)*   Table A.7.6.1. *(Source: NFPA, 101, Life Safety Code, 2000)*†

	Common Path Limit		Dead-End Limit		Travel Distance Limit	
Type of Occupancy	Unsprinklered ft (m)	Sprinklered ft (m)	Unsprinklered ft (m)	Sprinklered ft (m)	Unsprinklered ft (m)	Sprinklered ft (m)
Storage (*Continued*)						
Underground spaces in grain elevators	50 (15)[m]	100 (30)[m]	50 (15)[m]	100 (30)[m]	200 (60)	400 (122)

NA: Not applicable.
NR: No requirement.
[a]20 ft (6.1 m) for common path serving >50 persons; 75 ft (23 m) for common path serving ≤50 persons.
[b]Dead-end corridors not permitted; 20 ft (6.1 m) dead-end aisles permitted.
[c]See Chapters 12 and 13 for special considerations for smoke-protected assembly seating in arenas and stadia.
[d]This dimension is for the total travel distance, assuming incremental portions have fully utilized their permitted maximums. For travel distance within the room, and from the room exit access door to the exit, see the appropriate occupancy chapter.
[e]See business occupancies Chapters 38 and 39.
[f]See Chapter 23 for special considerations for existing common paths.
[g]This dimension is from the room/corridor or suite/corridor exit access door to the exit; thus, it applies to corridor common path.
[h]See appropriate occupancy chapter for special travel distance considerations for exterior ways of exit access.
[i]See appropriate occupancy chapter for requirement for second exit access based on room area.
[j]See Sections 36.4 and 37.4 for special travel distance considerations in covered malls considered pedestrian ways.
[k]See Chapters 38 and 39 for special common path considerations for single tenant spaces.
[l]See Chapter 40 for industrial occupancy special travel distance considerations.
[m]See Chapters 40 and 42 for special requirements if high hazard.

FIGURE 7.29 (*continued*) Table A.7.6.1. (*Source: NFPA, 101, Life Safety Code, 2000*)†

The figure below shows an example of a dead-end corridor. Here, an occupant leaves Room 2 and enters a corridor where visibility is limited by smoke or lighting malfunctions. The occupant may also be confused by the effects of toxic gases. Under these conditions, it is possible that he may mistakenly travel past Point A and on to Point B before he realizes that there is no exit. He now has no other option than to retrace his steps to Point A before he has a choice again. His actual travel distance has been increased by twice the distance from Point A to Point B. This backtracking can increase the occupant's confusion. In reality, not all dead ends can be practically eliminated. In recognition of this, the code allows dead ends of 20 feet or less. By placing a door at the location where the short corridor meets the main exit access corridor, Point C, the short corridor will not be classified as a dead end by the definition in 202. The door will alert the person that the corridor does not continue. (See definition of DEAD END in 202.)

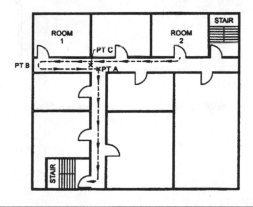

FIGURE 7.30   Dead-end corridors. *(Source: SBCCI, Standard Building Code Commentary, 1997)*

COMMON PATH OF TRAVEL

The common path of travel is that part of exit access traversed before two distinctly separate paths of travel are available to reach separate exits. It typically is limited to 75 ft in unsprinklered buildings and 100 ft in sprinklered buildings, with certain exceptions. Figure 7.31 is an example showing the common path of travel. The Life Safety Code allows business occupancies with an occupant load not more than 30 to have 100 ft of common path of travel. Other occupancies allowed 100-ft common path of travel are listed in Figure 7.32 from the International Building Code at 1004.2.5.

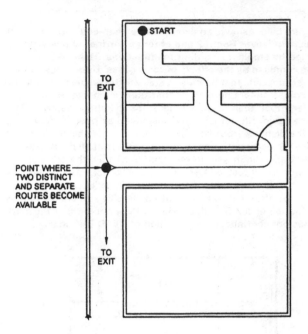

FIGURE 7.31   Common path of travel. *(Source: SBCCI, Standard Building Code Commentary, 1997)*

Exceptions:

1. The length of a common path of egress travel in an occupancy in Groups B, F and S shall not be more than 100 feet (30 480 mm), provided that the building is equipped throughout with an automatic sprinkler system installed in accordance with Section 903.3.1.1.

2. Where a tenant space in an occupancy in Groups B, S and U has an occupant load of not more than 30, the length of a common path of egress travel shall not be more than 100 feet (30 480 mm).

3. The length of a common path of egress travel in occupancies in Group I-3 shall not be more than 100 feet (30 480 mm).

FIGURE 7.32   Table 1004.2.5 exceptions. *(Source: ICC, International Building Code, 2000)*

TOTAL TRAVEL DISTANCE

One of the most important areas where the Life Safety Code and the International Building Code diverge is on the total travel distance allowed. The International Building Code provides Table 1004.2.4 with the maximum travel distances allowed, included here as Figure 7.33. As discussed earlier, the Life Safety Code provides one table summarizing all travel distance limitations. The International Building Code provides tables listing most, but not all, of the limits of total travel distance. Some limitations are within other parts of the code. IBC Section 402.4.4 limits travel distance in malls to 200 ft. IBC Section 404.9 limits travel distance from upper levels through an atrium to 150 ft.

IBC AND LSC TRAVEL DISTANCE VARIATIONS

While the allowable distances for dead ends and common path of travel are the same in both the IBC and the LSC, allowable travel distances vary greatly. The following list describes some of the occupancies relating to interior design and construction that have different values in the IBC and LSC. Obviously, when a project is governed by *both* codes, a careful analysis of allowable maximum travel distance is warranted [1, 2].

Occupancy	IBC travel distance	LSC travel distance
Assembly	200	150
Educational	150	150
Day care	200	150
Residential	200	175 (where required)
Mercantile	200	100
Malls	200	100
Industrial	150	200 (general type)

Note: All distances are measured in feet.

All values shown are for new buildings that are not sprinklered. Both codes allow greater travel distances for sprinklered buildings, because the safety of occupants is enhanced by a fire-protection system.

MEASUREMENT OF TRAVEL DISTANCE— GENERAL

Maximum travel distance is measured from the *most remote* point in the building or space subject to occupancy to the exit or entrance to an exit (IBC 1004.2.4). Calculations of travel distance to egress must provide a reasonable

TABLE 1004.2.4
EXIT ACCESS TRAVEL DISTANCE[a]

OCCUPANCY	WITHOUT SPRINKLER SYSTEM (feet)	WITH SPRINKLER SYSTEM (feet)
A, E, F-1, I-1, M, R, S-1	200	250[b]
B	200	300[c]
F-2, S-2, U	300	400[b]
H-1	Not Permitted	75[c]
H-2	Not Permitted	100[c]
H-3	Not Permitted	150[c]
H-4	Not Permitted	175[c]
H-5	Not Permitted	200[c]
I-2, I-3, I-4	150	200[c]

For SI: 1 foot = 304.8 mm.

a. See the following sections for modifications to exit access travel distance requirements:
   Section 402: For the distance limitation in malls.
   Section 404: For the distance limitation through an atrium space.
   Section 1004.2.4.1: For increased limitation in Groups F-1 and S-1.
   Section 1008.6: For increased limitation in assembly seating.
   Section 1008.6: For increased limitation for assembly open-air seating.
   Section 1005.2.2: For buildings with one exit.
   Chapter 31: For the limitation in temporary structures.
b. Buildings equipped throughout with an automatic sprinkler system in accordance with Section 903.3.1.1 or 903.3.1.2. See Section 903 for occupancies where sprinkler systems according to Section 903.3.1.2 are permitted.
c. Buildings equipped throughout with an automatic sprinkler system in accordance with Section 903.3.1.1.

FIGURE 7.33 Total travel distance. *(Source: ICC, International Building Code, 2000)* allowance for furnishings, equipment, and other fixed obstructions. A sample plan and travel distance calculation are provided in Figure 7.34. Travel distance can be greatly increased by the allowance for furniture, as illustrated by Figure 7.35, which shows sample plans and travel distance calculations with and without furnishings.

Figure 7.35 shows a curving path of egress, as required by the Life Safety Code, at Section 7.6. This way of measuring travel distance is easy to understand, but more difficult to calculate than the IBC method, since a radius and tangent points must be calculated for each turn.

MEASUREMENT OF TRAVEL DISTANCE— STAIRS

Stairs that are part of the travel distance pathway usually are open (not enclosed and not fire rated) and within a single-tenant space. Remember that a fire barrier must enclose stairs that are part of an exit and have all of the other protections discussed in Chapter 6, *Fire Resistance Rated Construction.* This protection is why we measure to the entrance to an exit, because it is assumed that the exit is a safe place during a fire or other emergency. Stairs are measured on the diagonal from the first stair riser nosing to the last, illustrated in Figure 7.36. This diagonal measurement can make a difference in whether or not the allowable travel distance is exceeded, as illustrated in Figure 7.37.

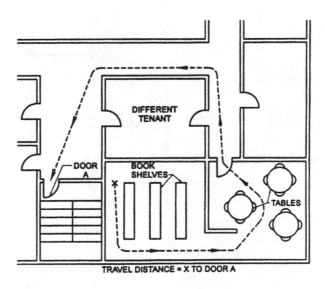

FIGURE 7.34 Travel distance. *(Source: SBCCI, Standard Building Code Commentary, 1997)*

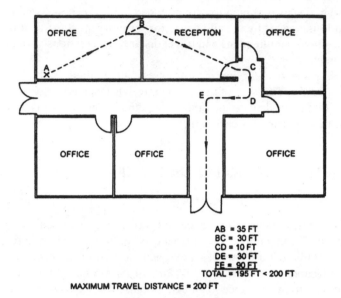

AB = 35 FT
BC = 30 FT
CD = 10 FT
DE = 30 FT
FE = 90 FT
TOTAL = 195 FT < 200 FT

MAXIMUM TRAVEL DISTANCE = 200 FT

**FIGURE 1004.1.1B
TRAVEL DISTANCE
UNSPRINKLERED BUSINESS OCCUPANCY**

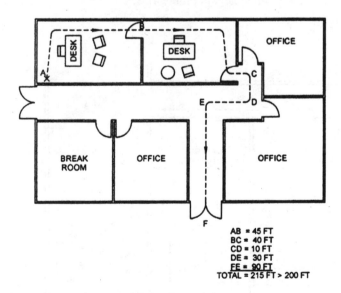

AB = 45 FT
BC = 40 FT
CD = 10 FT
DE = 30 FT
FE = 90 FT
TOTAL = 215 FT > 200 FT

FIGURE 7.35   Travel distance. *(Source: SBCCI, Standard Building Code Commentary, 1997)*

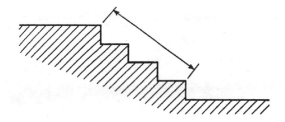

FIGURE 7.36 Method for measuring travel distance on stairs. Travel distance on stairs is measured in the plane of the tread nosings, not along each riser and tread. *(Source: NFPA, Life Safety Code Handbook, 1997)*††

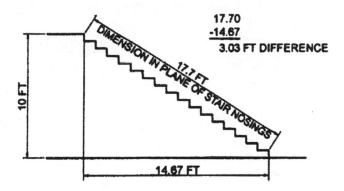

FIGURE 7.37 Travel distance for open stairs. *(Source: SBCCI, Standard Building Code Commentary, 1997)*

NUMBER OF EXITS—TRAVEL DISTANCE AND OCCUPANT LOAD

We have discussed the requirements for other components of means of egress in this chapter and examined the situations in which only one exit is required. It is always necessary to analyze interconnected rooms and multi-room tenant spaces for *both* common path of travel and occupant load. Some spaces may have fewer than 50 occupants but still require two exits based on a common path of travel distance, as shown in Figure 7.38.

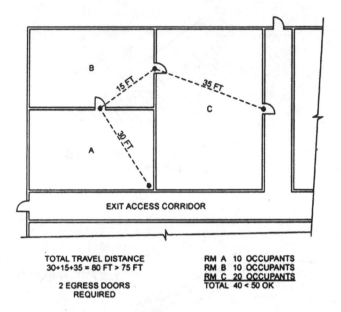

TOTAL TRAVEL DISTANCE
30+15+35 = 80 FT > 75 FT

2 EGRESS DOORS
REQUIRED

RM A   10 OCCUPANTS
RM B   10 OCCUPANTS
RM C   20 OCCUPANTS
TOTAL 40 < 50 OK

FIGURE 7.38   Number of exits required. *(Source: SBCCI, Standard Building Code Commentary, 1997)*

MINIMUM CEILING HEIGHT IN EGRESS COMPONENTS

The LSC requires ceiling heights within a means of egress to be not less than 7 ft 6 in., which basically applies to all normally occupied rooms and spaces, since exit access (a means of egress component) includes almost the entire building area (see Figure 7.2). The IBC allows 7 ft 10 in., and rooms with sloped ceilings may have a 7-ft height in no less than half the area. Projections from the ceiling may not reach below 6 ft 8 in. Stairways are allowed to have a minimum ceiling height of 80 in. or 6 ft 8 in. The means of measuring headroom in a stairway is described in Figure 7.39 [1, 2].

MINIMUM CORRIDOR WIDTH

Both codes arrive at minimum corridor width by dividing the total occupant load into the number of exits. The corridor leading to an exit must accommodate the required exit width, however static minimum values are specified. The Life Safety Code requires a minimum corridor width of 36 in, and also allows projections into required corridor width for furniture and movable partitions. The International Building Code requires a minimum corridor width of 44 in., with certain exceptions. The exceptions at IBC Section 1004.3.2.2 are listed in Figure 7.40 [1, 2].

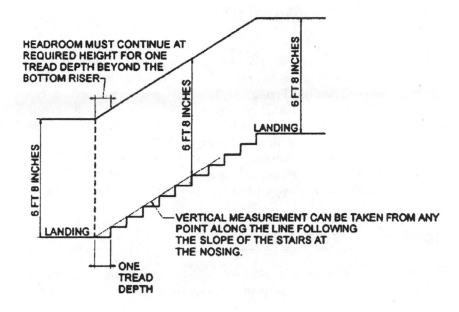

FIGURE 7.39   Headroom measurement. *(Source: SBCCI, Standard Building Code Commentary, 1997)*

Exceptions:

1. Twenty-four inches (610 mm)—For access to and utilization of electrical, mechanical, or plumbing systems or equipment.

2. Thirty-six inches (914 mm)—With a required occupant capacity of 50 or less.

3. Thirty-six inches (914 mm)—Within a dwelling unit.

4. Seventy-two inches (1829 mm)—In Group E with a corridor having a required capacity of 100 or more.

5. Seventy-two inches (1829 mm)—In corridors serving surgical Group I, health-care centers for ambulatory patients receiving outpatient medical care, which causes the patient to be not capable of self-preservation.

FIGURE 7.40   Minimum corridor width exceptions. *(Source: ICC, International Building Code, 2000)*

REDUCTIONS IN CORRIDOR WIDTH

Doors opening 90° directly into an exit access corridor may not reduce the corridor by more than half the required width minus 7 in. Doors opening 180° or 90° from a door alcove may not project more than 7 in. into the corridor. These concepts are illustrated clearly in Figure 7.41. Handrails, and other projections below a handrail, may project 3½ inches into the required exit width, as illustrated in Figure 7.42. Door jambs, including casing and trim, may project no more than 1 in. into the required width, as illustrated in Figure 7.43 [1, 2].

Horizontal projections, including wall-mounted items, are restricted to those shown in Figure 7.44. This restriction conforms to ICC (CABO) / ANSI A117.1 Standard on Accessible Buildings, which is covered in greater detail in Chapter 8.

CORRIDOR FIRE RATINGS

Corridors required for access to exits are required to have a one-hour fire-resistance rating, in most cases. Exceptions provide for no rating in corridors which

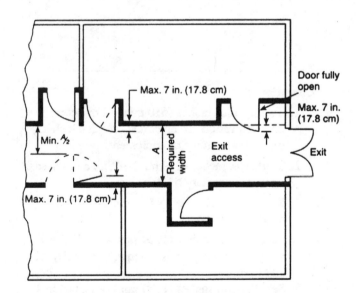

FIGURE 7.41 Door swing into a corridor. Doors that swing within a recessed pocket of the corridor so as not to protrude into the required corridor width provide the best arrangement for clear passage through an exit access corridor. Doors that swing 180° to come to rest against a wall and do not extend into more than 7 in. (17.8 cm) of required corridor width provide an acceptable arrangement. A door swinging 90° to come to rest in the path of travel is not encroaching excessively on the exit access corridor width if not more than 7 in. (17.8 cm) of the required width of the corridor remains obstructed. Any door swinging into the corridor must leave at least one-half of the required corridor width unobstructed during its entire swing. *(Source: NFPA, Life Safety Code Handbook, 1997)*††

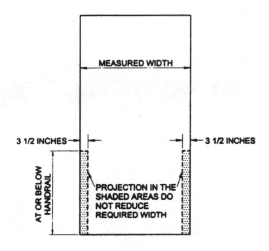

FIGURE 7.42 Handrail projection. *(Source: SBCCI, Standard Building Code Commentary, 1997)*

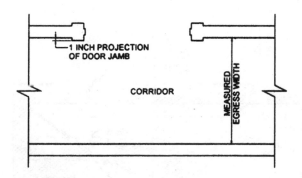

FIGURE 7.43 Door jamb projection. *(Source: SBCCI, Standard Building Code Commentary, 1997)*

form an exit for less than 30 occupants, buildings with approved fire sprinkler systems, and certain other situations. The IBC provides a summary of required corridor fire ratings in Table 1004.3.2.1, included here as Figure 7.45. The LSC provides specific requirements for corridor fire ratings in each occupancy chapter (11-40). Most of the requirements in the LSC occupancy chapters match those in the table from the IBC below. Certain requirements conflict, so it is imperative that the LSC requirements for corridor fire ratings specified in the applicable occupancy chapter be closely compared to the IBC requirements shown in Figure 7.45. When both codes apply, the most restrictive requirements must be observed.

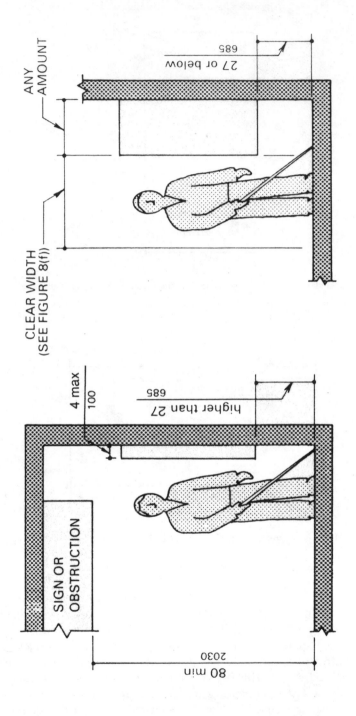

FIGURE 7.44 . Wall-mounted items. *(Source: CABO, ANSI A117.1 – 1992)*

CORRIDOR FIRE-RESISTANCE RATING

OCCUPANCY	OCCUPANT LOAD SERVED BY CORRIDOR	REQUIRED FIRE-RESISTANCE RATING (hours)	
		Without sprinkler system	With sprinkler system[c]
H-1, H-2, H-3	All	1	1
H-4, H-5	Greater than 30	1	1
A, B, E, F, M, S, U	Greater than 30	1	0
R	Greater than 10	1	1
I-2[a], I-4	All	Not Permitted	0
I-1, I-3	All	Not Permitted	1[b]

a. For requirements for occupancies in Group I-2, see Section 407.3.
b. For a reduction in the fire-resistance rating for occupancies in Group I-3, see Section 408.7.
c. Buildings equipped throughout with an automatic sprinkler system in accordance with Section 903.3.1.1 or 903.3.1.2.

FIGURE 7.45 Corridor fire ratings. *(Source: ICC, International Building Code, 2000)*

EXIT DISCHARGE

Exits must discharge directly to the building exterior, at grade level or to an outside area with direct access to grade level. Exterior courtyards or similar enclosed exterior spaces must have required exit capacity with direct access to a *public way*. Not more than half of the required exit capacity may discharge into an exit passageway, vestibule, lobby, or other area on the level of exit discharge, provided that certain conditions are met. Exceptions are granted for small buildings (less than 50 occupants), detention facilities, and others. The code also allows exit discharge to an open stairway when certain conditions are met.

EXIT PASSAGEWAY

An exit passageway is, simply, an extension of the exit enclosure. The exit passageway must be separated from the rest of the building with a fire barrier. All the other protections for openings, penetrations, ducts, and other requirements discussed in Chapter 6 apply to exit passageways. An exit passageway may extend the exit enclosure to the exterior, as illustrated in Figure 7.46. An exit passageway also may extend the exit enclosure into the area requiring exit access and reducing the total travel distance, as illustrated in Figure 7.47.

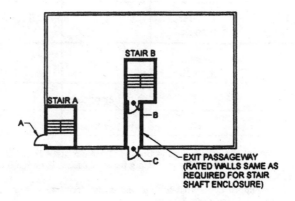

FIGURE 7.46   Exit passageway. *(Source: SBCCI, Standard Building Code Commentary, 1997)*

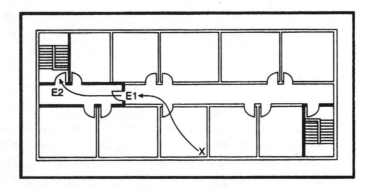

FIGURE 7.47   Exit passageway used to keep travel distance from becoming excessive. Travel distance measurement ends at entrance E1 to exit passageway. Distance from X to E2 exceeds allowed travel distance; distance from X to E1 is within allowed travel distance. *(Source: NFPA, Life Safety Code Handbook, 1997)*††

VESTIBULES

A vestibule is a special concept created by the code to allow exit discharge into an area that provides a level of protection for occupants similar to that provided in exits. A vestibule may not be more than 10 ft deep and 30 ft wide, must be sprinklered, must be separated from other parts of the building by a fire rating equal to wire glass in steel frames, and must be used for nothing other than egress. These concepts are illustrated in Figure 7.48.

LOBBIES

Lobbies are qualified as exit discharges if certain conditions are met. The egress point from the lobby must be readily identifiable from the exit enclosure termination point. The discharge area must be sprinklered and separated from the rest of the building by a fire rating equal to the exit enclosure or, if not separated, the entire level of exit discharge must be sprinklered. These options are illustrated in Figure 7.49.

HORIZONTAL EXITS

A horizontal exit provides passage into a separate fire compartment, replacing up to half the required exits leading to the exterior. A horizontal exit must pass through a two-hour fire-rated fire barrier, and have all the required protection for openings, penetrations, and continuity. The floor area inside the fire compartment

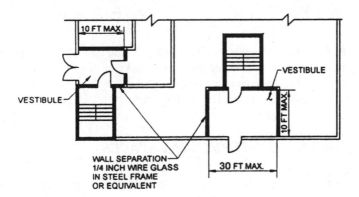

FIGURE 7.48   Vestibules. *(Source: SBCCI, Standard Building Code Commentary, 1997)*

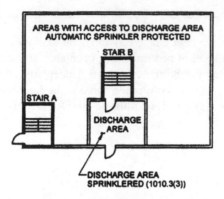

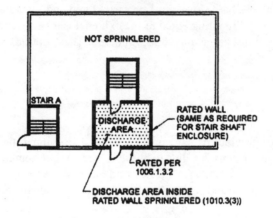

FIGURE 7.49   Exit discharge. *(Source: SBCCI, Standard Building Code Commentary, 1997)*

created by a horizontal exit must be sufficient to allow at least 3 sq ft per occupant, including both the original occupant load and that of occupants who must use the horizontal exit. The concepts and requirements are essentially the same in both the LSC at 7.2.4.2 and in the IBC at 1005.3.5.

EGRESS THROUGH INTERVENING SPACES

No path of egress may pass through a commercial kitchen, storeroom, closet, or any space subject to being locked. The LSC provides an exception that allows not more than one-half the required exits in mercantile occupancies to travel through a storeroom. The intent of this provision is that almost all normally occupied spaces should have direct access to an exit or exit access corridor.

These provisions are located at IBC 1004.2.3, Egress through Intervening Spaces, and at LSC 7.5.2, Impediments to Exit.

FLOORS AND CHANGES IN LEVEL

This book covers accessibility in Chapter 8 and floor finish fire resistance in Chapter 9. Please refer to those chapters for floor issues not covered here. Since basically all new construction should be accessible, the requirements for accessibility in floor surfaces should be observed [1, 2].

The IBC at 1003.2.6 Floor Surface requires the walking surfaces of any means of egress to be slip-resistant and securely attached, and at 1003.2.7 to be level. Changes in level less than 12 in. must be sloped, and changes in level less than 6 in. must be sloped and of contrasting material. No floor surface may slope more than 5 percent (1 in 20). Any greater slope constitutes a *ramp*, for which there are provisions covered later in this chapter under stairways and ramps.

The LSC at 7.2.1.3 requires that elevations on both sides of a door be level, with no difference in height greater than 0.5 in. In existing buildings, and one- and two-family dwellings, exterior doors may have the exterior walking surface one step below the interior, not to exceed 8 in.

The IBC at 1003.3.1.5 requires landings to be not less than the width of the door or stairway, and not less than 44 in. long. Landings in certain residential and utility occupancies may be 36 in. long.

DOORS AND DOOR HARDWARE

Doors in a means of egress must have a clear opening dimension not less than 32 in. (2 ft 8 in.), according to IBC 1003.3.1.1 and LSC 7.2.1.2.3. This also applies to at least one leaf in a pair of doors. Door opening width is measured when the door is at the 90° open position, as shown in Figure 7.50. Based on this measurement, a 36-in. door leaf is the minimum for all doors in a means of egress. The codes allow for projection of door hardware into the minimum width, as shown in Figures 7.51 and 7.52. Door height must be at least 80 in. (6 ft 8 in.).

DOOR SWING

Doors that serve an occupant load of more than 50 are required to open in the direction of travel, and be of the side-swing type. Exceptions in the codes also allow for balanced doors (with minimum clear openings), power-assisted doors,

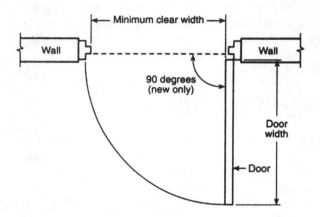

FIGURE 7.50   Minimum clear width. *(Source: NFPA, 101, Life Safety Code, 2000)*†

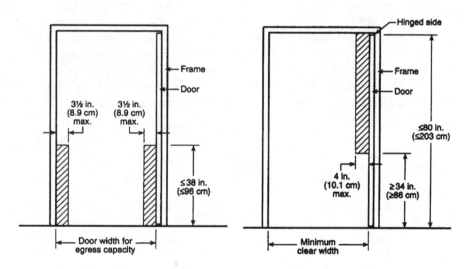

FIGURE   7.51 Minimum   clear   width.
(Source: NFPA, 101, Life Safety Code, 2000)†

FIGURE   7.52 Minimum   clear   width.
(Source: NFPA, 101, Life Safety Code, 2000)†

sliding doors, revolving doors, rolling grills, and other types of doors in certain circumstances and with qualifications to allow safe egress in an emergency. Power-operated and access-controlled doors must be fail-safe, meaning they must allow egress during an emergency. This is accomplished normally by connecting the door access controls to a fire-alarm system.

DOOR OPENING FORCE

Interior doors must open with a force of no more than 5 lbs applied at the latch strike side. Exterior doors are allowed to open with a 15-lb latch release force, 30 lbs to set the door in motion, and 15 lbs to swing full open. These provisions are identical at IBC 1003.3.1.2 and LSC 7.2.1.4.5. All hardware used for normal door operation must be mounted between 34 in. (2 ft 10 in. and 48 in. (4 ft) above floor level.

Door thresholds in the path of egress are allowed to be no more than 0.5 in. high, except residential sliding doors, which may be 0.75 in. high. Door thresholds higher than 0.25 in. must be beveled at a slope of not more than 1 in 2. This requirement matches that for accessible door thresholds, and is illustrated by Figure 7.53. An approved threshold profile is shown in Figure 7.54.

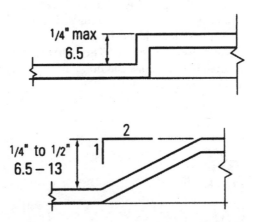

FIGURE 7.53 Approved threshold. *(Source: "Specifying Accessible Openings," Door and Hardware Institute May 2000)*

FIGURE 7.54 Approved threshold. *(Source: "Specifying Accessible Openings," Door and Hardware Institute May 2000)*

EXIT DEVICES

An exit device called panic hardware is required on all doors that are part of a means of egress for an occupant load of more than 100 in assembly and educational occupancies. The LSC also requires panic hardware in day-care facilities. Panic hardware operates the door latch with a force (maximum 15 lbs) applied in the direction of egress. Figure 7.55 shows two types of approved panic hardware: the traditional push bar and the more contemporary push pad. A paddle-type exit device, allowed on balanced doors only, is shown in Figure 7.56.

STAIRWAYS—AN ACCIDENT WAITING TO HAPPEN?

Stairways are the location of many falls resulting in injury every year. Stairways must be used by all kinds of people with differing heights, experience, and impairments, such as poor vision and artificial limbs. The act of negotiating stairs is a very complicated task, although many of us take well-known stairways for granted. Stair users establish a rhythm or repeating stride that anticipates a uniformity of dimensions. Many stair accidents have been traced to missteps resulting from irregular tread and riser dimensions. The stairway in Figure 7.57 is the type of stairway with variable dimensions and non-uniform walking surfaces the code requirements are intended to prevent [1].

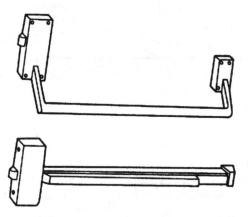

FIGURE 7.55 Pushpad and traditional panic hardware. This figure illustrates the difference between traditional panic hardware (top illustration) and pushpad panic hardware (bottom illustration). *(Source: NFPA, Life Safety Code Handbook, 1997)*††

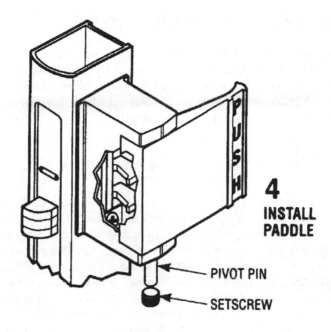

FIGURE 7.56 Paddle exit device. *(Source: Adams Rite Manufacturing Co.)*

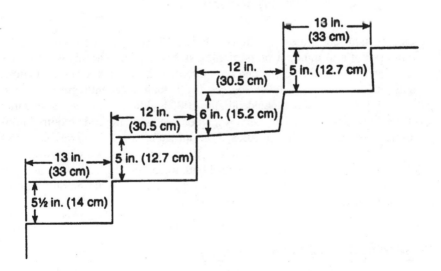

FIGURE 7.57 Variations in tread and riser dimensions. In this arrangement, the variations are excessive, invite accidents, and violate code provisions so as to warrant replacement. *(Source: NFPA, Life Safety Code Handbook, 1997)*††

STAIRWAYS—MINIMUM DIMENSIONS

Both the IBC at 1003.3.3 and the LSC at 7.2.2 require that stairways be at least 44 in. (3 ft 8 in.) wide, except stairways serving less than an occupant load of 50 which may be 36 in. (3 ft) wide. Stair risers' heights must be between 7 in. maximum and 4 in. minimum. Stair tread depth must be at least 11 in. Figure 7.58 illustrates these critical dimensions graphically.

STAIRWAYS—CONSTRUCTION AND DETAILS

Stair risers and treads must be of uniform height within ⅜ in. for any flight of stairs. The Life Safety Code also requires that no adjacent treads or risers may vary more than 3/16 in. Figure 7.59 illustrates how tread and riser dimensions are measured, with the nosing excluded. The leading edge of the tread may not protrude more than 1¼ in. (at IBC 1003.3.3.3.2) or 1½ in. (at LSC 7.2.2.3.3) beyond the tread below. Risers must be solid, with certain exceptions for open risers. Walking surfaces must be firm, stable and slip-resistant, not perforated, with no projections or tripping hazards, and level (with not more than 2 percent slope). Stair coverings must be attached firmly to provide solid footing to the outside edge of the tread surface.

STAIRWAYS—PROPORTIONING

Research conducted in the late 17th century by Charles Blondel resulted in the development of a formula for proportioning stairways. The formula is 2 risers + 1 tread equal not less than 24 in. and not more than 25 in. This formula has been used by model codes and other sources for a long time with great success. Although this formula is not included in the 2000 building codes, we believe that it is the best way to proportion stairways, when used with the code required minimum tread and riser dimensions. Based on our experience, a stairway is easiest to use when the tread is between 11 in. and 12 in. and the risers are between 6 in. and 7 in. We normally lay out stairs with 11-in. treads and 7-in. risers, or as close to 7 in. as the overall height will allow. A sample stairway design and proportioning calculation are shown in Figure 7.60.

STAIRWAYS—LANDINGS

Stairways must have level landings top and bottom at least as long (measured in the direction of travel) as the stairway is wide. However, no landing is required to be longer than 48 in. Measurement of landings in straight-run and reversing

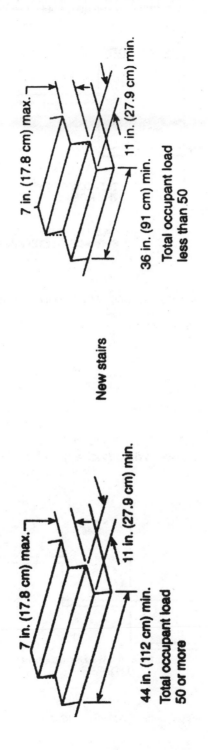

FIGURE 7.58 Stair specifications. (*Source: NFPA, Life Safety Code Handbook, 1997*)††

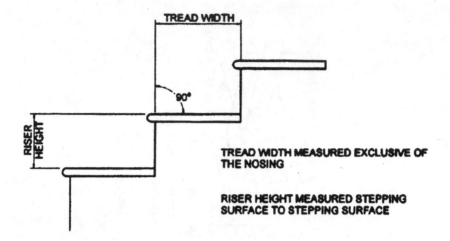

FIGURE 7.59   Treads and risers. *(Source: SBCCI, Standard Building Code Commentary, 1997)*

$$24 \leq 2R + T \leq 25$$
Where:
   R = Riser Height (inches)
   T = Tread Width (inches)

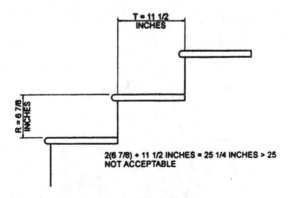

FIGURE 7.60 Treads and risers proportioning. *(Source: SBCCI, Standard Building Code Commentary, 1997)*

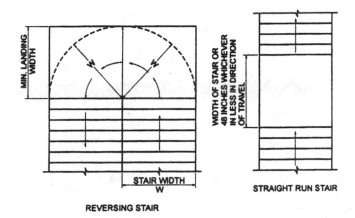

FIGURE 7.61 Landing dimensions. *(Source: SBCCI, Standard Building Code Commentary, 1997)*

stairs is illustrated by Figure 7.61. Landings are required at intermediate levels so that no flight of stairs exceeds 12 ft vertically, This feature allows recovery from a fall, and is found at IBC 1003.3.3.6.

STAIRWAYS—ALTERNATE DESIGNS

Circular Stairs

Circular, or curving, stairs are recognized by the codes as a reasonable alternative to straight stairs and reversing stairs in means of egress. Circular stairs designed according with Figure 7.62 are a perfectly acceptable alternate design. All other requirements for circular stairs are the same as other egress stairs.

Winders and Spiral Stairs

Except in very limited circumstances, spiral stairs and stair winders are not allowed. These stairs are hard to negotiate and are not suitable for use as a means of egress. Stair winders are only allowed within a dwelling, and only within the code-specified dimensions shown in Figure 7.63. Spiral stairs are allowed only in residences or spaces of less than 250 sq ft that serve fewer than 5 occupants. A code-complying spiral stair is described in Figure 7.64.

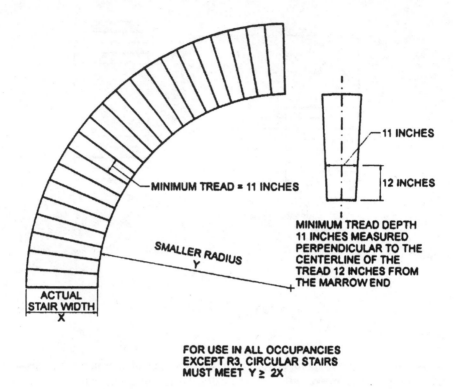

FIGURE 7.62   Circular stairs. *(Source: SBCCI, Standard Building Code Commentary, 1997)*

Other Stair Types

Other stair types, including ship ladders and alternating-tread stairs, are recognized and described by the code. Use of these stairs is limited primarily to use as access to roofs, mezzanines, and equipment platforms in occupancy groups F, H, and S, and not as a means of egress for multiple occupants. Scissors, or stacking, stairs may meet egress width requirements, but may not qualify as remotely located unless a rated corridor separates the stair entrances. A scissors stair is shown in Figure 7.65.

EGRESS STAIRS—NO OTHER USE ALLOWED

The codes do not allow exit enclosure (stairs) to be used for any other purpose. Egress stairs must be separated clearly from the building by a fire barrier in order to provide a safe haven and means of escape in a fire. This concept assumes there is no fire hazard within the exit enclosure that might block egress or cause a

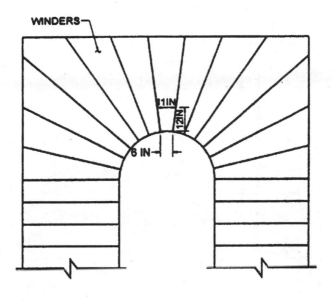

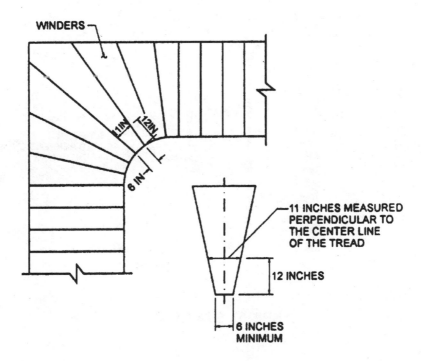

FIGURE 7.63 Winders. *(Source: SBCCI, Standard Building Code Commentary, 1997)*

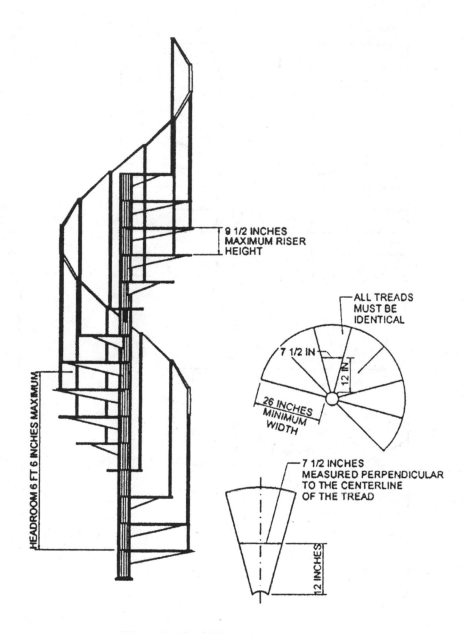

9 1/2 INCHES
MAXIMUM RISER
HEIGHT

ALL TREADS
MUST BE
IDENTICAL

7 1/2 IN

12 IN

26 INCHES
MINIMUM
WIDTH

HEADROOM 6 FT 6 INCHES MAXIMUM

7 1/2 INCHES
MEASURED PERPENDICULAR
TO THE CENTERLINE
OF THE TREAD

12 INCHES

SPIRAL STAIRWAY

FIGURE 7.64   Spiral stairs. *(Source: SBCCI, Standard Building Code Commentary, 1997)*

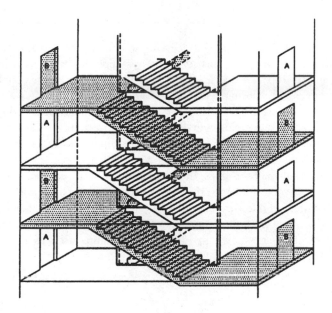

FIGURE 7.65 Scissor stairs. *(Source: SBCCI, Standard Building Code Commentary, 1997)*

threat. If the exit enclosure is used for storage, or any other use, the safe haven may be negated. For these reasons, the codes do not allow use of the exit enclosure for any reason other than egress. Many owners and designers see the space under a stair as wasted space, and want to use it for storage or some other reason. This can only be accomplished by enclosing the under-stair areas with a fire barrier that has a rating equal to the enclosure required for the stair, as illustrated in Figure 7.66.

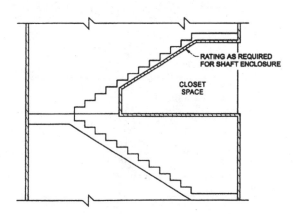

FIGURE 7.66 Space under stair. *(Source: SBCCI, Standard Building Code Commentary, 1997)*

RAMPS

A ramp is defined as a walking surface with a slope of more than 1 in 20, or 5 percent. Most of the requirements for stairways apply to ramps used for egress, as shown at IBC 1003.3.4 and LSC 7.2.5. LSC minimum dimensional requirements for ramps are summarized in Figure 7.67. The IBC allows a minimum ramp width of 36 in., and allows door openings to reduce the clear width to 42 in. Landings are required at changes in direction, door openings, and every 30 ft, as required by maximum vertical rise. Landings are required to be a minimum of 60 in. long and as wide as the ramp. Ramps with a vertical rise greater than 6 in. must have handrails on both sides. Edge protection also is required when there is a vertical drop beyond the ramp edge. Edge protection consists of a ramp extension, solid barrier, an intermediate rail 17 in. to 19 in. below the handrail, and a curb or barrier rail at the bottom, or a guard, as described below. Several options for edge protection are shown in Figure 7.68. Ramps used as exits must be enclosed and protected as required for stairs [1, 2].

HANDRAILS

Handrails are required on both sides of all stairs and qualifying ramps. Handrails are required to be continuous along the entire stairway or ramp, including the inside turn of reversing stairs and ramps. Handrail extensions are required at the top and bottom of stairways, as shown in Figure 7.69. Handrails must be mounted between 34 in. and 38 in. above the floor and be supported securely (required by IBC 1607.7.1 to be 50 lbs per linear foot and 250 lbs at any point). Open landings must be protected by 42 in. high guards as described below. Handrail height and guard heights are illustrated in Figure 7.70. Handrail ends must return to the wall or floor, or loop back to the handrail to prevent clothing or other items from catching on them. Handrail supports must also meet code requirements, so it is best to use approved support bracket shapes [1, 2].

Table 7.2.5.2(a) New Ramps

Minimum width clear of all obstructions, except projections not more than $3^1/_2$ in. (8.9 cm) at or below handrail height on each side	44 in. (112 cm)
Maximum slope	1 in 12
Maximum cross slope	1 in 48
Maximum rise for a single ramp run	30 in. (76 cm)

FIGURE 7.67   Table 7.2.5.2a New ramps. *(Source: NFPA, 101, Life Safety Code, 2000)*†

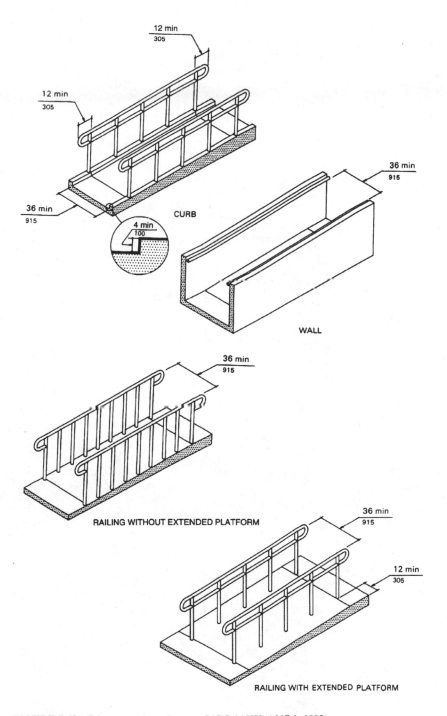

FIGURE 7.68   Edge protection. *(Source: CABO / ANSI, A117.1, 1992)*

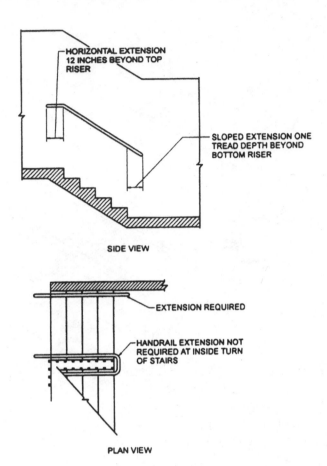

FIGURE 7.69   Handrail extensions. *(Source: SBCCI, Standard Building Code Commentary, 1997)*

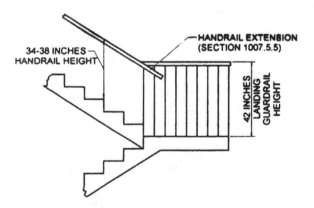

FIGURE 7.70   Handrail height. *(Source: SBCCI, Standard Building Code Commentary, 1997)*

Intermediate handrails also are required (at IBC Section 1003.3.3.11.1) so that all portions of the stairway width are within 30 in. of a handrail. This means that egress stairs wider than 67 in. must have an intermediate handrail, and handrails are required not more than 60 in. apart on wide stairs and ramps.

Many types of handrail shapes have been used through the years. Most of the *historically correct* and *designer* handrail shapes used in the past do not qualify as having *handrail graspability* under the 2000 building codes. We believe the new restrictions on handrail shape and size should be viewed as a challenge to the designer, rather than as an encumbrance.

New handrails are limited in size and shape to those shown in Figure 7.71. The LSC at Section 7.2.2.4.5 requires a handrail outside diameter of between 1¼ and 2 in. The IBC at Section 1003.3.3.11.3 allows 1½ to 2 in. Using both codes limits handrail sections to between 1½ to 2 in. in diameter. Handrails also may not project into the required egress width more than 3½ inches. This clearance, along with an analysis of three handrail designs, is shown in Figure 7.71a. Handrails are required at locations that also require guards. The discussion of guards below considers the incorporation of handrails and guards in a single design.

GUARDS (GUARDRAILS-BARRIER RAILS)

When a means of egress is more than 30 in. (2 ft 6 in.) above the floor or grade below, the codes require a guard, previously called a guardrail or barrier rail. A guard must be at least 42 in. (3 ft 6 in.) high. The guard must reject passage of a 4-in. sphere up to a height of 34 in. and reject passage of an 8-in. sphere above

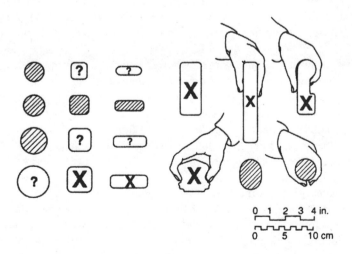

FIGURE 7.71 Acceptable, unacceptable, and marginal handrail sections. *(Source: NFPA, 101, Life Safety Code Handbook, 1997)*

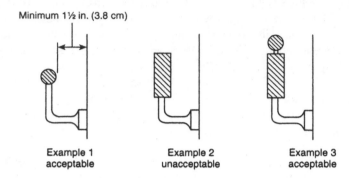

FIGURE 7.71a   Handrail sections. *(Source: NFPA, Life Safety Code Handbook, 1997)*††

34 in. The space between the walking surface and the bottom of the guard must reject passage of a 2-in. sphere. A compliant barrier is shown in Figure 7.72. The IBC allows an exception for the triangular space between stair tread, riser, and the bottom of the guard to reject a 6-in. sphere. The requirements for guards are found at LSC 7.2.2.4.6 and at IBC 1003.2.12.

EXIT SIGNAGE AND EMERGENCY LIGHTING

Exit signs or markings must mark access to exits so that the direction of egress is readily apparent from any direction. Signs must be placed so that no point in an exit access corridor is more than 100 ft from an exit sign. A suggested location of exit signage in three types of corridor/exit arrangements is shown in Figure 7.73.

Exit signs must have an emergency power source, such as batteries or standby power system. Some exit signs are *self-luminous* using an internal illumination source not requiring electricity. Externally illuminated exit markings can substitute for exit signs when they meet code requirements for size and emergency power illumination. Certain occupancies are required by the LSC to have exit signs near the floor, so that the signs are visible when smoke is present. Any door not leading to an exit that might be mistaken for an exit access must be so marked "NO EXIT."

All means of egress must be provided with emergency lighting equal to at least one foot-candle measured at the floor. Spaces requiring emergency lighting include corridors, stairs, rooms or spaces requiring two exits, exits, and exit discharge. Emergency lighting must operate automatically upon loss of power by activation of an internal power source (batteries) or standby power system.

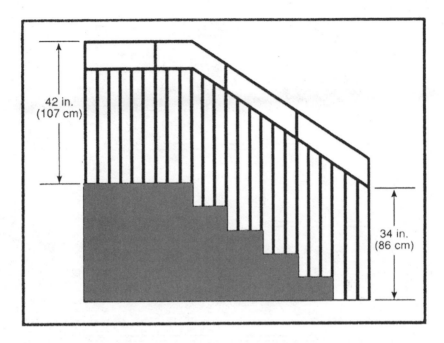

FIGURE 7.72 Height extension for application of 4 in. (10.1 cm) diameter sphere criterion. The space in the guard above 34 in. (86 cm) in height does not need to prevent the passage of a 4 in. (10.1 cm)-diameter sphere. *(Source: NFPA, Life Safety Code Handbook, 1997)*††

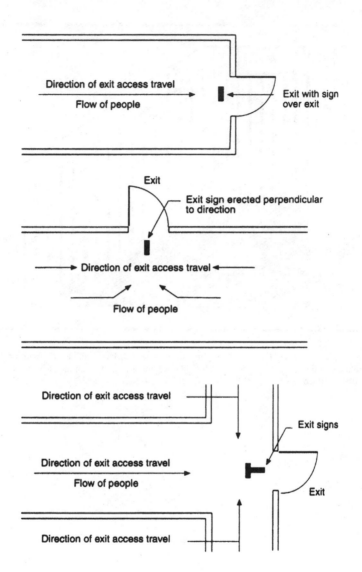

FIGURE 7.73   Location of exit signs. *(Source: NFPA, 101, Life Safety Code, 2000)*†

REFERENCES

1. ICC, 2000 Edition. 2000 International Building Code, International Code Council, Falls Church, VA
2. NFPA, 2000 Edition. NFPA, 101, Life Safety Code, National Fire Protection Association. Quincy, MA

CHAPTER 8
ACCESSIBILITY

HISTORY OF ACCESSIBILITY

The issue of accessibility gained importance during the last part of the 20th century. Many facilities in the past were designed with no consideration for individuals with limitations in sight, mobility, or hearing, which excluded those individuals from many activities. Improvements in lifestyle and medical technology have extended life expectancy and enabled individuals who previously might have been restricted to their homes to become more active and mobile. With encouragement from interest groups for people with disabilities, governments and design industry organizations have developed standards and laws intended to allow equal access to buildings and facilities for those with physical disabilities.

IBC AND ANSI A117.1

The American National Standards Institute (ANSI) adopted the first national criteria for accessibility in 1961 as A 117.1, Accessible and Usable Buildings and Facilities. This document was developed from research done at the University of Illinois under a grant from the National Easter Seal Society. ANSI A117.1 was revised and reissued in 1971, 1974, 1980, 1986, 1992 and 1996. The Congress of American Building Officials (CABO) was named secretariat for revisions to the document, and the 1992 revision is titled CABO/ANSI A117.1. CABO is now the International Code Council (ICC), and the document referred to in the 2000 IBC is ICC/ANSI A117.1-1998 [1]. The existing model building codes (UBC, BOCA, and SBC) and the 2000 International Building Code reference ICC/ANSI A117.1 are used as the standard for accessibility. This chapter is based on ICC/ANSI A117.1-1998; IBC Chapter 11, Accessibility; and the Americans with Disabilities Act Architectural Guidelines (ADAAG).

ADA AND ADAAG

In 1968, Congress created the Architectural Barriers Act, which requires that buildings funded by the federal government be made accessible to people with disabilities. Congress established accessibility as a civil right in the Americans with Disabilities Act (ADA) of 1990 requiring *all* new buildings and spaces to be made "readily accessible and usable" by people with disabilities. The Americans with Disabilities Act Architectural Guidelines (ADAAG) is a manual for design of accessible facilities published in 1991 by the United States Architectural and Transportation Barriers Compliance Board (Access Board). The ADAAG was largely adapted from ICC/ANSI A117.1, and the revised ADAAG follows the same numbering system. The Access Board also publishes recommendations for children's facilities and recreation facilities, and is developing other standards. Churches, private clubs, and single-family homes arc exempt from the ADA. These facilities, however, must meet the building codes and must be made accessible according to ICC/ANSI A117.1 [2].

UNIVERSAL ACCESSIBILITY— A DESIRABLE STANDARD

The IBC at 1103.1 requires that *all* buildings, sites, and facilities described in the code (including temporary facilities such as reviewing stands and portable bleachers) are to be made accessible to individuals with physical disabilities. If universal accessibility is planned in all new and renovated facilities, it is possible to eliminate barriers to access by anyone. This is the only way to ensure that persons with physical disabilities are not excluded from any space or activity.

BUILDING BLOCKS

Planning for accessibility is based largely on the requirements of an adult in a wheelchair. Allowable "reach" ranges determine how to locate work and storage elements, as well as the controls for building services operating equipment. The spatial demands of wheelchair maneuverability determine minimum passageways and floor areas. Minimum overhead clearance and limited protruding objects address detection of obstructions for persons using canes. These building blocks are discussed in detail below. This book does not address the ADAAG for Accessible Children's Facilities, which are issued by the Access Board.

Wheelchair Size and Clearance

The critical dimensions of an adult in a wheelchair are shown in Figure 8.1. The clear floor area required for a single wheelchair is 30 in. wide by 48 in. long, as illustrated in Figure 8.1a. The clear width required for a wheelchair in an accessible passageway is 36 in., with 32 in. allowed at reductions in width, such as columns or portals, for a distance of not more than 24 in. Reductions in width must be separated by 48 in. of passageway length that has the minimum 36 in. clear, as shown in Figure 8.2.

The required width for passage of a wheelchair and a person walking to pass is 48 in., as shown in Figure 8.3. Even this dimension requires the walking person to turn sideways slightly, and should be used only in passageways with limited traffic. The width required for two wheelchairs to pass is 60 in., as shown in Figure 8.4. Accessible alcoves must include maneuvering space, as shown in Figure 8.4a. The clear floor areas required for wheelchair seating in series, front and rear, or side approach are shown in Figure 8.4b.

Reach Ranges—Unobstructed

The codes prescribe ranges for both forward reach and side reach, with and without obstructions. The unobstructed forward and side reach from a wheelchair is 48 in. maximum, and 15 in. minimum, as shown in Figures 8.5 and 8.6. This means that any unobstructed wall-mounted items requiring access (e.g., lighting and air controls, fire extinguishers, fire alarm pull-stations) must be mounted between 15 in. and 48 in. from the floor.

Reach Ranges—Obstructed

The rules for obstructed reach are more complex, with lower maximum reach distance allowed over deeper obstructions. The high forward reach over an obstruction up to 20 in. deep is 48 in. When the obstruction is between 20 and 25 in. (the maximum depth for forward reach obstructions), the forward reach is reduced to 44 in. These concepts are illustrated in Figure 8.7.

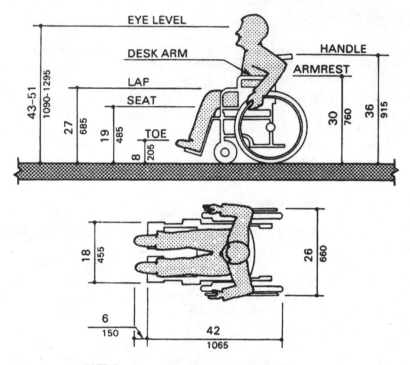

NOTE: Footrests may extend further for very large people.

FIGURE 8.1   Dimensions of adult sized wheelchair. *(Source: CABO, ANSI A117.1, 1992)*

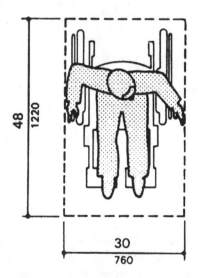

FIGURE 8.1a   Clear floor space for wheelchairs. *(Source: CABO, ANSI A117.1, 1992)*

Segment Length	Minimum Segment Width
≤ 24 inches (610 mm)	32 inches (815 mm)[1]
> 24 inches (610 mm)	36 inches (915 mm)

[1]Consecutive segments of 32 inches (815 mm) wide must be separated by a route segment 48 inches (1220 mm) long minimum and 36 inches (915 mm) wide minimum.

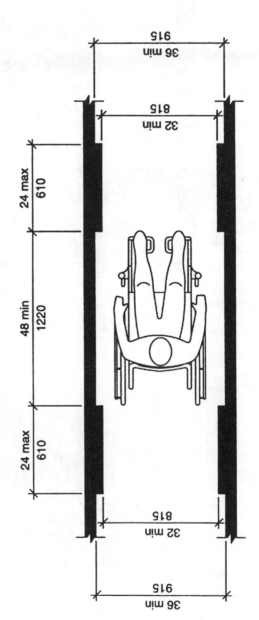

FIGURE 8.2 Clear width of an accessible route. *(Source: ICC/ANSI A117.1, 1998)*

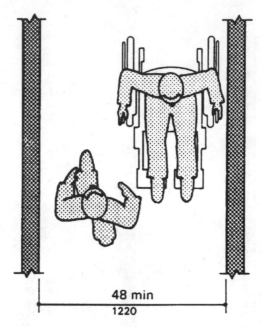

FIGURE 8.3   Minimum passage width for one wheelchair and one ambulatory person. *(Source: ICC/ANSI A117.1, 1992)*

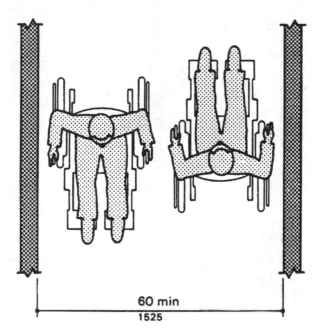

FIGURE 8.4   Minimum clear width for two wheelchairs. *(Source: ICC/ANSI A117.1, 1992)*

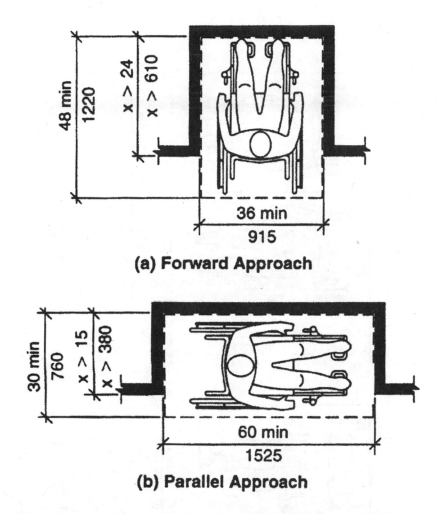

FIGURE 8.4a   Maneuvering clearance in an alcove. *(Source: ICC/ANSI A117.1, 1998)*

Clear floor space under forward reach obstructions must extend at least as deep as the obstruction. Obstructed side high reach is 48 in. maximum over an obstruction no deeper than 10 in. When the obstruction depth is between 10 in. and 24 in. (the maximum depth for side reach obstructions), side high reach is reduced to 46 in. These concepts are illustrated in Figure 8.8. No side reach obstruction may be higher than 34 in.

These reach range dimensions greatly affect designs for accessible kitchens, work stations, storage rooms, and other elements. It is indispensable to have these illustrations close at hand when designing accessible spaces.

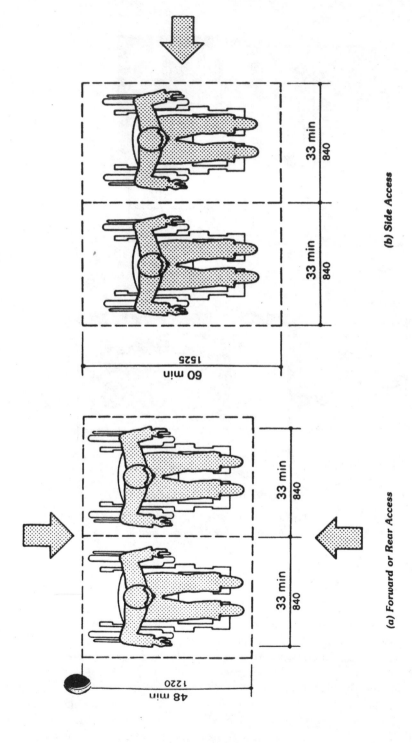

(b) Side Access

(a) Forward or Rear Access

FIGURE 8.4b Space requirements for wheelchair seating spaces in a series. (*Source: CABO, ANSI A117.1, 1992*)

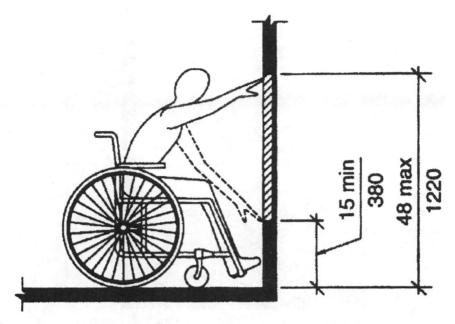

FIGURE 8.5   Unobstructed high forward reach. *(Source: ICC/ANSI A117.1, 1998)*

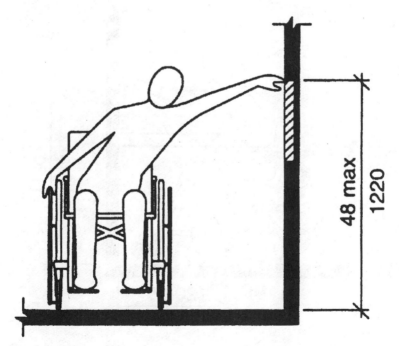

FIGURE 8.6   Unobstructed high side reach. *(Source: ICC/ANSI A117.1, 1998)*

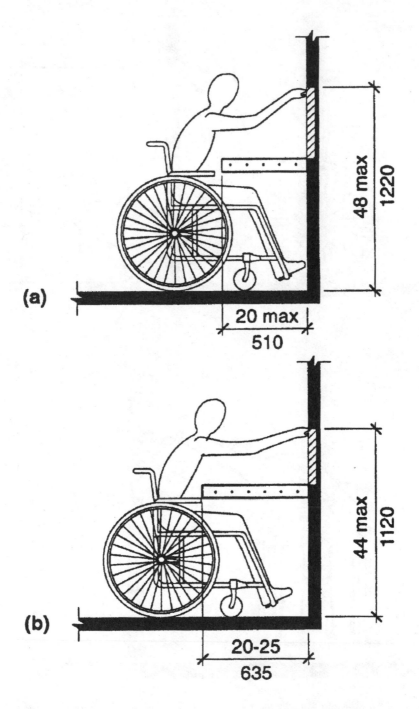

FIGURE 8.7   Obstructed high forward reach. *(Source: CABO, ANSI A117.1, 1998)*

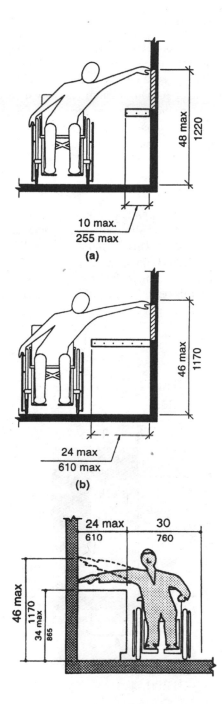

FIGURE 8.8 Obstructed high side reach. *(Source: ICC/ANSI A117.1, 1998)*

Knee and Toe Clearance

Knee and toe clearances are both 30 in. wide minimum. Minimum knee clearance is 8 in. deep at 27 in. minimum height, and 11 in. deep at 9 in. minimum height, as shown in Figure 8.8a. Toe clearance is 17 in. deep minimum and 25 in. deep maximum, with a height of 9 in. minimum, as shown in Figure 8.8b. These dimensions are critical in the design of drinking fountains, workstations, kitchens, accessible furnishings, and any other items that require the wheelchair to pull under a horizontal projection.

Operable Parts

Accessible controls and operable parts of building service equipment and appliances must be mounted within the allowable reach range, and the minimum clear floor space must be provided. This includes air conditioning controls, light switches, electrical outlets, intercoms, and appliances. Accessible controls may not require tight grasping, pinching, or twisting of the wrist to operate. One test that is used: Can the controls be operated with a closed fist? If yes, then they are probably accessible [1].

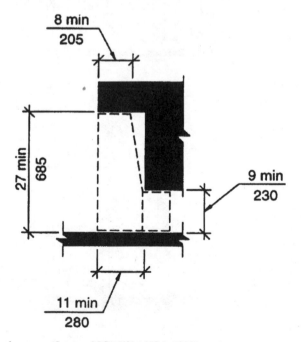

FIGURE 8.8a   Knee clearance. *(Source: ICC/ANSI A117.1, 1998)*

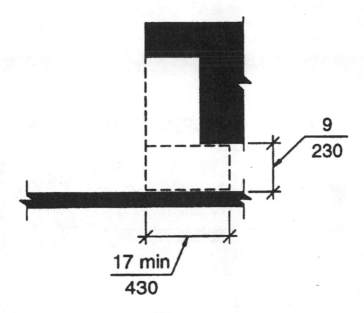

FIGURE 8.8b   Toe clearance. *(Source: ICC/ANSI A117.1, 1998)*

ACCESSIBLE ROUTE

At least one accessible route must connect all accessible elements and spaces, as specified in IBC 1104.2, and all accessible levels, including mezzanines, in multi-story buildings. The accessible route must coincide with the circulation path for the general population, and the year 2000 codes have been written so that many of the requirements for means of egress coincide with those for accessible routes. All of the elements that comprise an accessible route must meet the requirements for clearance and reach ranges, floor surfaces, protruding objects, ramps and stairs, elevators and wheelchair lifts, doors, and the other elements specified.

The accessible route may not pass through kitchens or storage rooms, since these rooms can be sources of hazards. The accessible route inside a dwelling unit, however, may pass through the kitchen. When a floor or level is less than 3000 sq ft in area and does not contain health-care provider facilities, IBC Group Business or Institutional, an accessible route is not required. Any floor or level in IBC Groups Assembly, Institutional, Residential, or Storage that does not contain the facilities *required* to be accessible need not have an accessible route [3].

Minimum Width

The minimum width of accessible routes is 36 in., except at doors and other conditions as described above under clearances. An example of a corridor clear width at turns is shown in Figure 8.9. Spaces allowing two wheelchairs to pass must be located at not more than 200 ft along the accessible route. Passing spaces must be 60 sq in. or as required for a T-turn. These requirements are found at ICC/ANSI A117.1, Section 4.3.

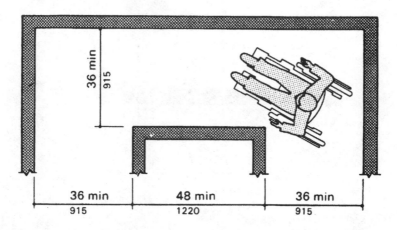

(a) Width of Accessible Route for 90° Turn

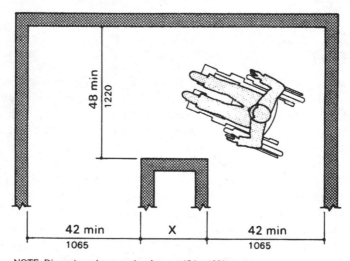

NOTE: Dimensions shown apply when $x < 48$ in (1220 mm).

*(b) Width of Accessible Route for Turns
around an Obstruction*

FIGURE 8.9   Accessible route width for turns. *(Source: CABO, ANSI A117.1, 1992)*

Maneuvering Area

The codes allow for a wheelchair to turn (change directions) in the following three ways: with a pivot turn, smooth turn, or T-turn. The pivot turn is most commonly used, requiring an open floor area with a radius of 60 in. (5 ft), as shown in Figure 8.10. Many wheelchair users find it difficult to perform the pivot turn in one motion, requiring several attempts while striking surrounding objects.

The smooth turn shown in Figure 8.11 is easier and is the preferred design criterion. The smooth turn requires 60 in. by 72 in. of clear floor area.

The overall dimension of a T-turn is 60 in., but the legs of the T need only be 36 in. wide (the minimum passageway width). The T-turn, illustrated in Figure 8.12, is a good solution in areas with limited space. A T-turn can be accomplished easily at the intersection of two 36 in. wide passageways.

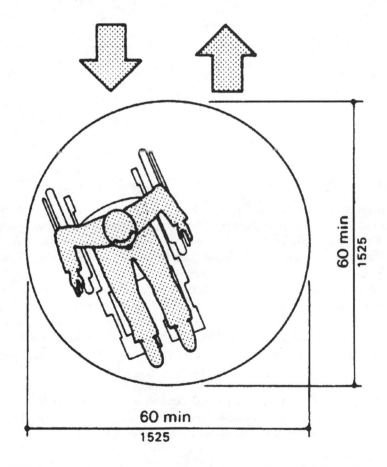

FIGURE 8.10   Wheelchair turning space, pivot turn. *(Source: CABO, ANSI A117.1, 1992)*

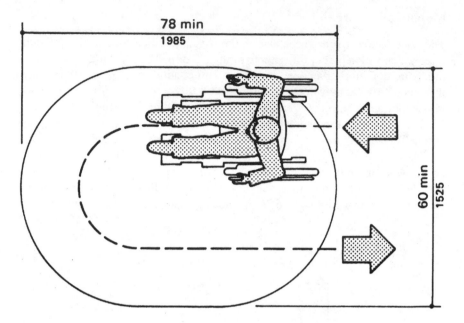

FIGURE 8.11   Wheelchair turning space, smooth turn. *(Source: CABO, ANSI A117.1, 1992)*

Floor Surfaces

The requirements for floor surfaces are found in ICC/ANSI A117.1, Section 4.5. Floor surfaces in accessible rooms and routes must be stable, firm, and slip-resistant. Since no specific definition is provided for the term *slip-resistant*, flooring materials with a coefficient of friction greater than 0.5 are preferred. Manufacturers of flooring materials usually can provide this information.

Carpet or carpet tiles must be attached securely and have a firm pad or no pad. Carpet thickness, with pad included, may not exceed ½ in., as shown in Figure 8.13. Exposed carpet edges must be attached firmly with trim along the entire edge of the carpet. Edge trim must be beveled to comply with the provisions for changes in level described below. These provisions are intended to allow wheelchairs to roll easily.

Gratings must have less than ½ in. spaces in the direction of travel, as shown in Figure 8.14. Gratings with *close-mesh* bearing bars, which may have gaps as small as ⅛ in., may be specified. The elongated openings must be placed perpendicular to the direction of travel, as shown in Figures 8.15 and 8.15a.

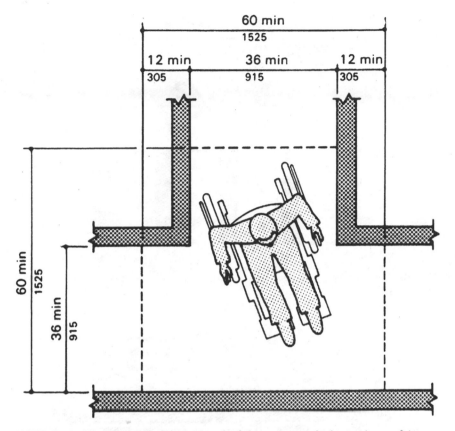

NOTE: Dashed lines indicate minimum length of clear space required on each arm of the T-shaped space in order to complete the turn.

FIGURE 8.12   Wheelchair turning space, T turn. *(Source: CABO, ANSI A117.1, 1992)*

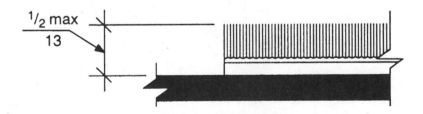

FIGURE 8.13   Carpet on floor surfaces. *(Source: ICC/ANSI A117.1, 1998)*

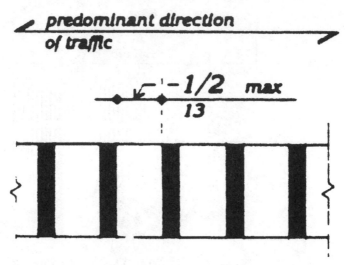

FIGURE 8.14   Gratings, bar spacing and direction. *(Source: Federal Register, ADA Accessibility Guidelines, 1991)*

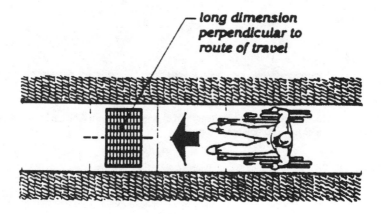

FIGURE 8.15   Grating orientation in an accessible path. *(Source: Federal Register, ADA Accessibility Guidelines, 1991)*

Changes in Level

Changes in floor level in accessible routes must be level, not to exceed 1 in 48 (about 2 percent). Changes in level not exceeding ¼ in. can be vertical. Changes in level not exceeding ½ in. must be beveled at a slope not more than 1 in 2. These requirements are illustrated in Figure 8.16. Changes in level more than ½ in. high and any slope steeper than 1 in 48 (2 percent) are considered ramps and must comply with the provisions for ramps discussed in the following sections.

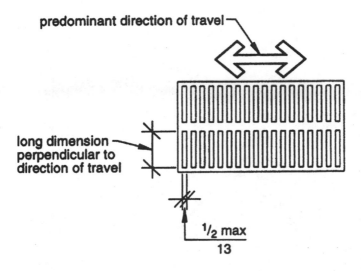

FIGURE 8.15a Grating orientation in accessible path. *(Source: ICC/ANSI A117.1, 1998)*

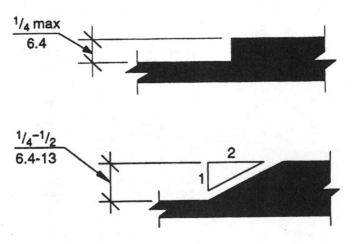

FIGURE 8.16 Changes in level in accessible path without a ramp. *(Source: ICC/ANSI A117.1, 1998)*

Protruding Objects

The restrictions placed on objects that protrude into the accessible route are primarily for the protection of sight-impaired individuals using a cane. The usual caning technique and the critical dimensions for detection of obstructions is demonstrated in Figure 8.17.

Objects with leading edges higher than 27 in. above the floor may project no more than 4 in. into the accessible route, as shown in Figure 8.18.

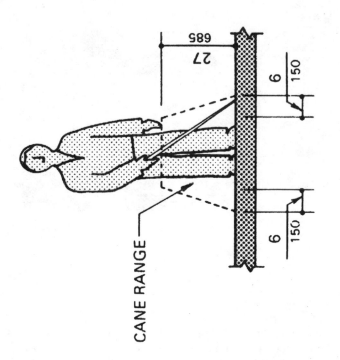

FIGURE 8.17 Caning technique. (*Source: CABO, ANSI A117.1, 1992*)

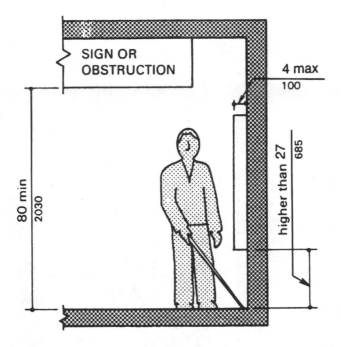

FIGURE 8.18   Protruding objects in accessible path. *(Source: CABO, ANSI A117.1, 1992)*

Objects with leading edges lower than 27 in. above the floor may project no more than 12 in. into the accessible route, as shown in Figure 8.19. The portion of protruding objects that cannot be approached from the accessible route may not project more than 12 in., as shown in Figure 8.20.

Protruding objects on walls in the accessible route should be mounted in accessible alcoves or protected with wing walls. Figure 8.20 shows a suggested design for protective wing walls at a corridor with wall-mounted protruding objects, along with dimensions indicating minimum width. These requirements are found in ICC/ANSI A117.1, Section 4.4.

Freestanding objects mounted on posts (e.g., signs) more than 12 in. apart must have an edge not more than 27 in. high or the bottom must be mounted above 80 in. These requirements are shown in Figure 8.21. Freestanding objects mounted on a single post with the bottom edge more than 27 in. may not project more than 12 in., as shown in Figure 8.21a.

Obstructions projecting lower than 80 in. above the floor must be protected with a barrier or railing not more than 27 in. high. This requirement allows detection of overhead obstructions by normal caning techniques. Figure 8.22 illustrates this protection where required under an open stairway.

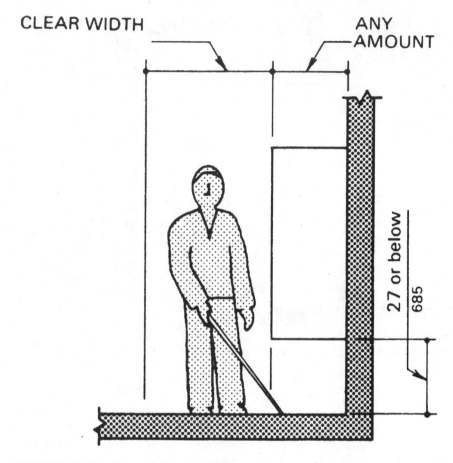

FIGURE 8.19   Protruding objects in accessible path. *(Source: CABO, ANSI A117.1, 1992)*

ACCESSIBLE MEANS OF EGRESS

The International Building Code at 1003.2.3 and Life Safety Code at 7.5.4 require two means of accessible egress. One means of accessible egress is allowed if the travel distance does not exceed the allowable common path of travel. An accessible means of egress includes an area of refuge at a stair or elevator that leads to a public way. The distance to an area of refuge may not exceed the total allowable travel distance. Figure 8.23 shows the measurement of travel distance when the area of refuge is part of the means of egress. Figure 8.23a shows the measurement of travel distance when the area of refuge is not part of the means of egress.

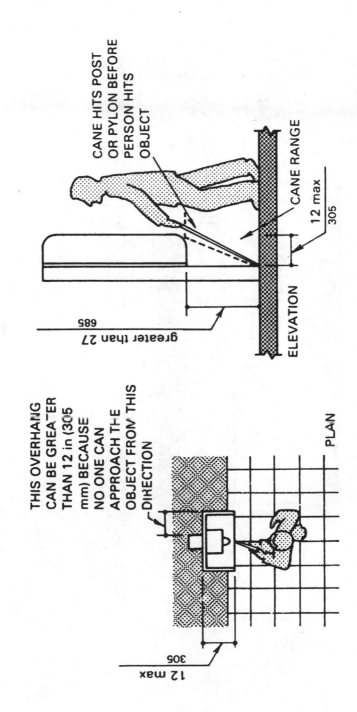

CANE HITS POST
OR PYLON BEFORE
PERSON HITS
OBJECT

CANE RANGE

12 max
305

ELEVATION

greater than 27
685

THIS OVERHANG
CAN BE GREATER
THAN 12 in (305
mm) BECAUSE
NO ONE CAN
APPROACH THE
OBJECT FROM THIS
DIRECTION

PLAN

12 max
305

FIGURE 8.20 Protruding objects in accessible path. (*Source: CABO, ANSI A117.1, 1992*)

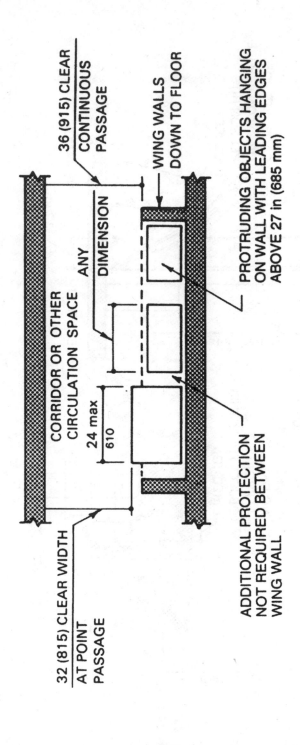

FIGURE 8.20 (*continued*) Protruding objects in accessible path. (*Source: CABO, ANSI A117.1, 1992*)

8.24

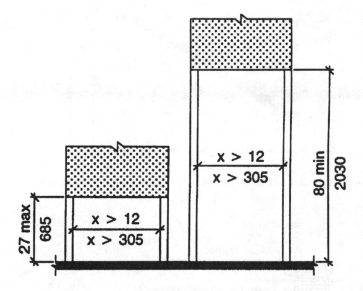

FIGURE 8.21 Post mounted protruding objects in accessible path. *(Source: ICC/ANSI A117.1, 1998)*

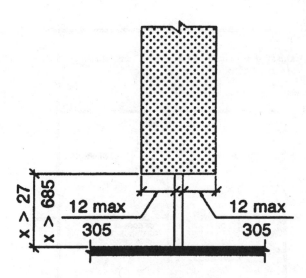

FIGURE 8.21a Post mounted protruding objects in accessible path. *(Source: ICC/ANSI A117.1, 1998)*

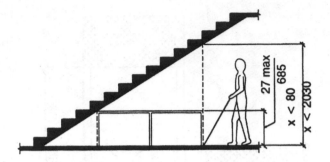

FIGURE 8.22   Protection for overhead obstructions in accessible path. *(Source: ICC/ANSI A117.1, 1998)*

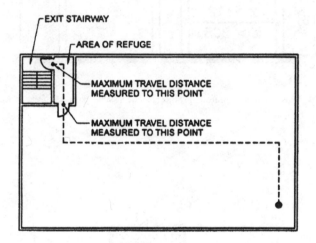

FIGURE 8.23   Maximum travel distance to an exit and area of refuge. *(Source: SBCC, Standard Building Code Commentary, 1997)*

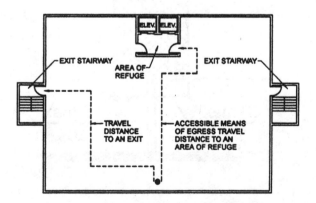

FIGURE 8.23a   Separate travel distance to an exit and an area of refuge. *(Source: SBCC, Standard Building Code Commentary, 1997)*

AREA OF REFUGE

The requirement for areas of refuge, once part of ANSI A117.1 and ADAAG, now are written into the building codes. The requirements for areas of refuge are identical at IBC 1003.2.13.5 and at LSC 7.12.2. Areas of refuge are provided at stairways and elevators to protect wheelchair users until they are rescued by emergency personnel or until the emergency is mitigated. Areas of refuge must accommodate one wheelchair space (30 in. by 48 in.) for each 200 occupants. The area of refuge may not obstruct the required egress width. An area of refuge must be protected by fire and smoke barriers and provide two-way communications with emergency personnel.

The area of refuge is created most easily by including it within the exit stair enclosure as shown in Figures 8.23b and 8.23c. Although an area of refuge located in the exit enclosure provides the necessary protection, a separate enclosure may provide the required area of refuge enclosure. Any areas of refuge larger than 1000 sq ft must prevent smoke accumulation. All areas of refuge must be marked with accessible signage.

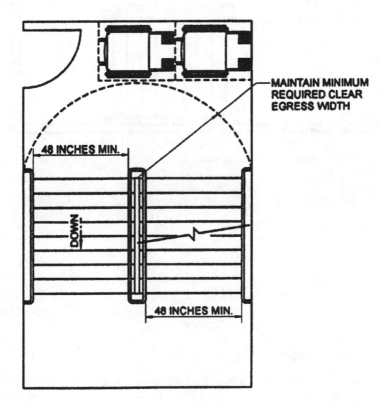

FIGURE 8.23b Area of refuge at stair landing. *(Source: SBCC, Standard Building Code Commentary, 1997)*

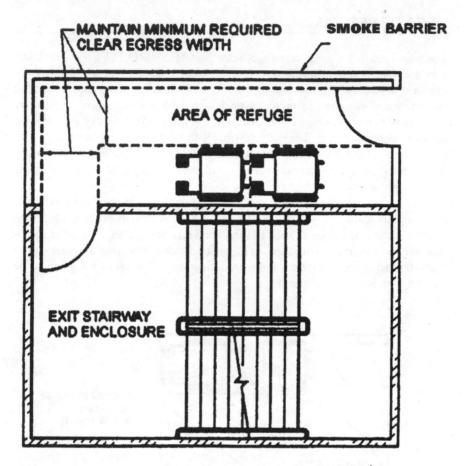

FIGURE 8.23c   Area of refuge at stain landing. *(Source: SBCC, Standard Building Code Commentary, 1997)*

ACCESSIBLE RAMPS AND STAIRS

The requirements for ramps and stairs in accessible routes parallel the requirements for ramps in means of egress (see Chapter 7, Means of Egress). This is because the IBC and the LSC have written their codes to coincide with ICC/ANSI A117.1, in order to achieve universal standards for accessibility.

Accessible Ramps

Ramp requirements and minimum dimensions are found in ICC/ANSI A117.1, Section 4.8. Ramps may not exceed 1 in 12 slope, except in existing buildings where steeper slopes are allowed with a vertical rise of no more than 6 in., as shown in Figure 8.24. Ramps must be 36 in. wide minimum with level landings at the top, the bottom, and at door openings. Ramps may rise no more than 30 in. without an intermediate landing. Landings must be as wide as the ramp and 60 in. long. Landings requiring a change in direction must be at least 60 sq in. These concepts are illustrated in Figure 8.24a. Ramps must be provided with edge protection to prevent wheelchairs from rolling off the ramp. The protection may be achieved with a ramp extension, curb, or barrier, as shown in Figure 8.24b. This requirement is the same as that specified by the IBC for ramps. Several types of ramps and means of edge protection are shown in Chapter 7, Figure 7.77.

Accessible Stairs

Stairs must have uniform tread and riser height, with risers from 4 in. to 7 in. high and treads not less than 11 in. deep. Treads and risers must be designed with tread nosings, as shown in Figure 8.25. Open risers are not permitted in an accessible stair. Please refer to the discussion about stairs in Chapter 7, Means of Egress, for other features of stair design. Since the details required for an accessible stair are nearly the same as those for stairs as means of egress, it makes sense to design all stairs to be accessible and to comply with the details shown. These requirements are found in ICC/ANSI A117.1, Section 4.9.

Accessible Handrails

Handrails are required on both sides of stairs and ramps, and must be continuous within the full length of each run or flight. The top surface of the handrail must be mounted 34 to 38 in. above the floor, as shown in Figure 8.25a. Handrails must be from 1½ to 2 in. outside diameter and easily grasped. Other shapes are allowed if the largest dimension is 2¼ in. and the outside perimeter is 6¼ in. maximum. The critical dimensions for handrails are illustrated in Figure 8.25b. There must be at least 1½ in. clearance between the handrail and the wall, as shown in Figure 8.25c. Handrails must not have abrasive or sharp parts, and may not have any inside radius diameters less than ⅛ in. Handrails must meet the structural requirements specified in the building code (see Chapter 7, Means of Egress), and may not rotate in their fittings.

Handrail extensions must be provided at the top and the bottom of accessible stairs and ramps. Figure 8.26 shows a suggested design and the critical dimensions for handrail extensions. The handrail extension may return to a wall or guard, or may continue to the handrail of another ramp or stair. These requirements are found in ICC/ANSI A117.1, Sections 4.3.10 and 4.3.11.

Slope[1]	Maximum Rise	
Steeper than 1:10 but not steeper than 1:8	3 in	75 mm
Steeper than 1:12 but not steeper than 1:10	6 in	150 mm

[1] A slope steeper than 1:8 shall not be permitted.

FIGURE 8.24 · Table 4.8.2. (*Source: CABO, ANSI A117.1, 1992*)

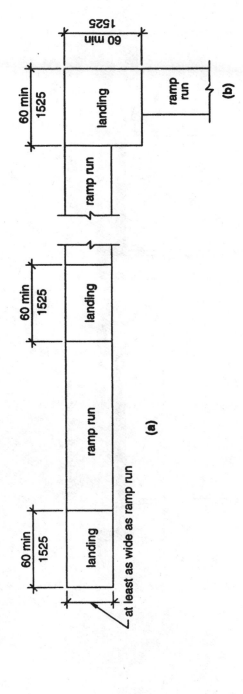

FIGURE 8.24a Ramp landing layouts. *(Source: CABO, ANSI A117.1, 1992)*

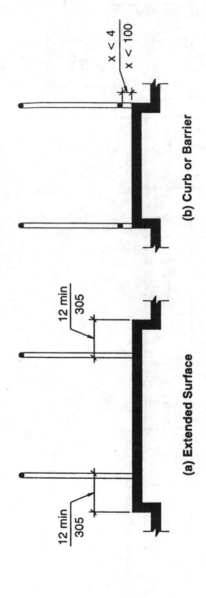

FIGURE 8.24b Ramp edge protection. (*Source: ICC/ANSI A117.1, 1998*)

8.32

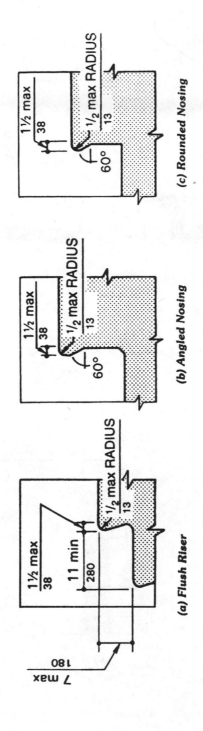

FIGURE 8.25 Acceptable stair tread and riser dimensions and nosings. (*Source: CABO, ANSI A117.1, 1992*)

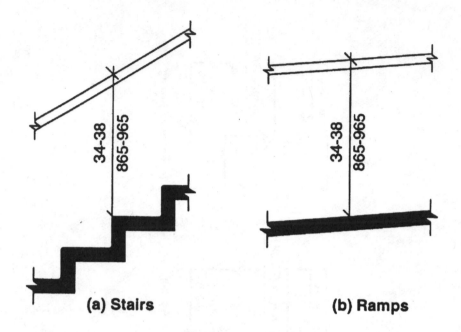

(a) Stairs   **(b) Ramps**

FIGURE 8.25a   Handrail height. *(Source: ICC/ANSI A117.1, 1998)*

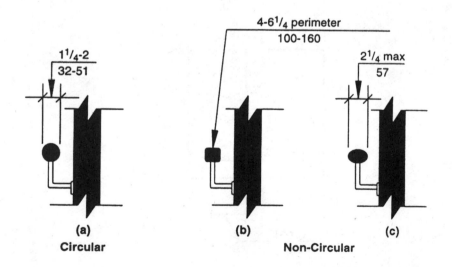

FIGURE 8.25b   Handrail cross section. *(Source: ICC/ANSI A117.1, 1998)*

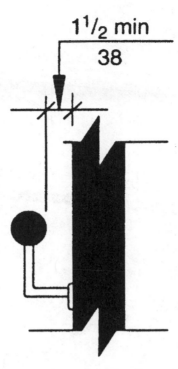

FIGURE 8.25c Handrail clearance at wall. *(Source: ICC/ANSI A117.1, 1998)*

ACCESSIBLE DOORS

Making doors accessible can be tricky, but following several basic rules can help. It is possible, with some design effort, to make every door accessible (universal accessibility). The minimum clear width of any accessible doorway is 32 in. for any type of door, as illustrated in Figure 8.27. ICC/ANSI A117.1 at 404 provides minimum clearances for each type of door approach, operation, and hardware condition. Layouts and dimensions for each type of swinging door are included in Figure 8.28. Layouts and dimensions for folding and sliding doors are included in Figure 8.29.

The bottom 12 in. of accessible swinging doors (without power operators) must have a smooth surface extending across the door-width to allow the door to be opened with a wheelchair footrest. Kick plates installed on bottom door rails less than 12 in. high must be capped, as shown in Figure 8.29a. View lights in doors must have the bottom edge not more than 43 in. above the floor, as shown in Figure 8.29b. Doors in series must have 48 in. minimum clearance, as shown in Figure 8.30. This means that accessible vestibules, in most instances, must be at least 7 ft long.

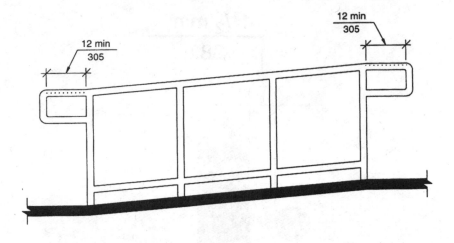

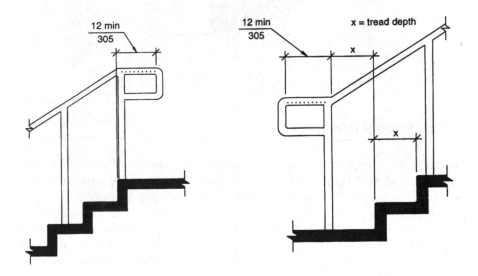

FIGURE 8.26   Handrail extensions. *(Source: ICC/ANSI A117.1, 1998)*

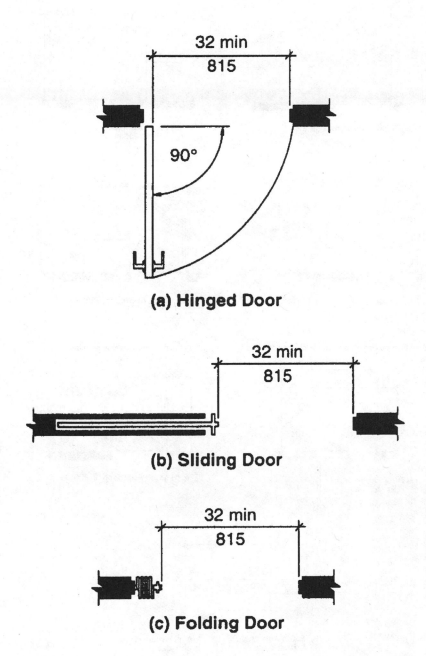

(a) Hinged Door

(b) Sliding Door

(c) Folding Door

FIGURE 8.27 Required clear width of swinging doors. *(Source: ICC/ANSI A117.1, 1998)*

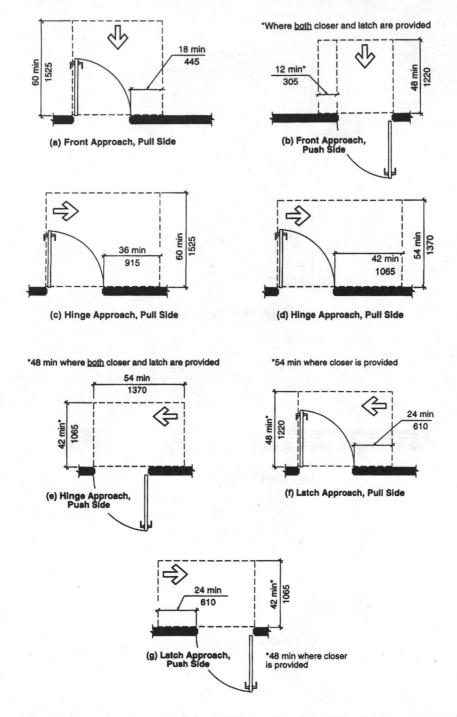

FIGURE 8.28 Required maneuvering clearance at swinging doors. *(Source: ICC/ANSI A117.1, 1998)*

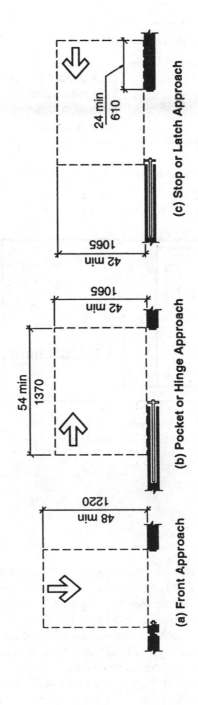

FIGURE 8.29 Required maneuvering clearance at sliding doors. *(Source: ICC/ANSI A117.1, 1998)*

8.39

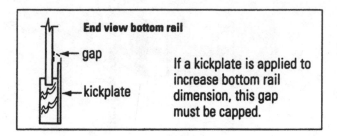

FIGURE 8.29a   Accessible entrance bottom rail. *(Source: Doors and Hardware Institute, May 2000 issue)*

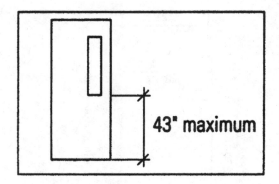

FIGURE 8.29b   Accessible view light mounting height. *(Source: Doors and Hardware Institute, May 2000 issue)*

DOOR HARDWARE

Door operating hardware must not require tight grasping, pinching, or twisting of the wrist to be accessible. This is typically achieved with lever-style hardware on swinging doors; several styles are shown in Figure 8.31.

Figure 8.32 shows the required range for location of door operating hardware and limitations on projections into the door. The door opening force for non-fire-rated doors may not be more than 5 lb. The door opening force for fire-rated doors may comply with the requirements for any door as a means of egress, that is, 15 lb. Thresholds may not be more than ½ in. high, and must be beveled as shown in Figure 8.33. Door closers and power-assisted operators are specified, along with other requirements for doors in ICC/ANSI A117.1, Section 4.13 [1, 2].

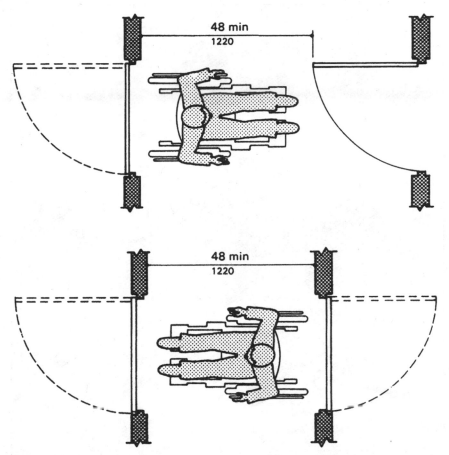

FIGURE 8.30   Clearance required at two hinged doors in series. *(Source: CABO, ANSI A117.1, 1992)*

PLUMBING ELEMENTS AND FACILITIES

The IBC at 1108.2 and ICC/ANSI A 117.1 at 601 require accessible toilet and bathing facilities to have minimum clearances for wheelchair maneuvering. All plumbing elements required to be accessible must comply with the requirements shown below. The number of plumbing elements and facilities required to be accessible is discussed in this chapter in Accessibility Scoping.

Drinking Fountains

Drinking fountains may be designed for forward or parallel approach. The minimum clear floor space of 30 in. by 48 in., centered on the fixture, must be pro-

FIGURE 8.31   Accessible door lever handles. *(Source: Schlage Lock Company, Architectural Guide, 1993)*

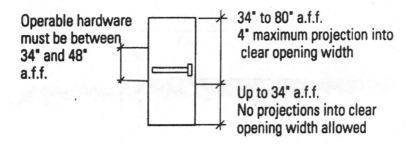

FIGURE 8.32 Accessible door hardware mounting height. *(Source: Doors and Hardware Institute, May 2000 issue)*

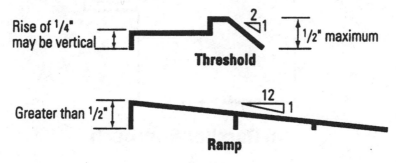

FIGURE 8.33 Accessible threshold designs. *(Source: Doors and Hardware Institute, May 2000 issue)*

vided. The waterspout must be at least 4 in. high (to allow use of a cup), and be located as shown in Figure 8.34. Knee and toe clearances must be provided at the front approach drinking fountain, as illustrated in Figure 8.34a. Both the front approach and parallel approach fountains should be installed in an alcove or within side walls to avoid creating a protruding object in an accessible route. A suggested design for a front approach fountain in an alcove is shown in Figure 8.34b. Remember, if the drinking fountain is located in an alcove more than 24 in. deep, the alcove must be at least 36 in. wide, as shown in Figure 8.4a.

Water Closets

Wheelchair users have two types of toilet transfer moves; front transfer is shown in Figure 8.35 and side front transfer is shown in Figure 8.35a. Not all wheelchair users can perform the front transfer, so the standard is based on the side transfer, which requires 60 in. clear floor width, as shown in Figure 8.36.

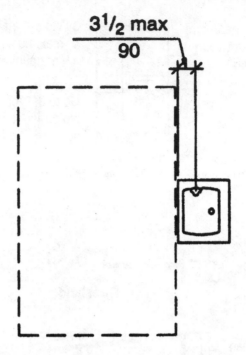

(a) Parallel Approach

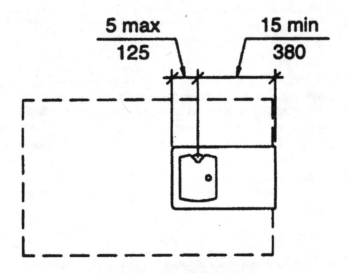

(b) Forward Approach

FIGURE 8.34   Drinking fountain clear floor area and water spout locations. *(Source: ICC/ANSI A117.1, 1998)*

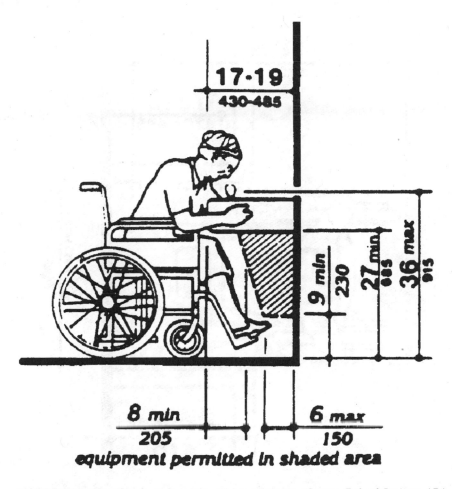

FIGURE 8.34a Drinking fountain height and knee clearance. *(Source: Federal Register, ADA Accessibility Guidelines, 1991)*

The centerline of the toilet may be located 16 in. to 18 in. from the side wall, as shown in Figure 8.37. Accessible toilet seats may be from 17 in. to 19 in. high, as shown in Figure 8.38. Grab bars must be located on the side and back walls as shown in Figure 8.38a. Toilet paper dispensers must be located as shown in Figure 8.38b, with 1½ in. clear beneath and 12 in. clear above the grab bar. Toilet paper dispensers must have controlled delivery.

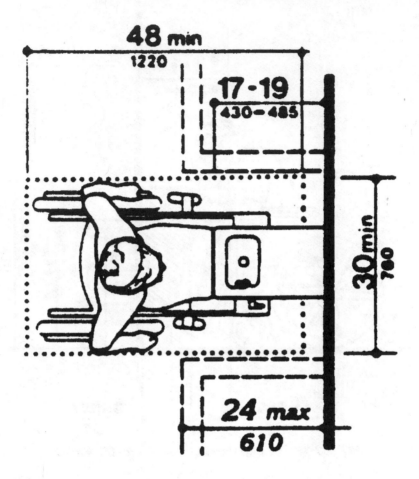

FIGURE 8.34b   Drinking fountain clear floor space. *(Source: Federal Register, ADA Accessibility Guidelines, 1991)*

Toilet Compartments

Wheelchair accessible toilet compartments must have clearance for maneuvering and transfer and the required clearances for doors, as discussed previously. Figure 8.38c shows accessible layouts for compartments with outswing and inswing doors. Compartment doors must be hinged not more than 4 in. from the corner as shown, and doors must have at least 32 in. clearance. In compartments less than 62 in. deep with a wall-hung toilet or 65 in. deep with a floor-mount toilet, a toe clearance must extend 6 in. past the front and one side of the compartment, as shown in Figure 8.38d.

Walk-in (ambulatory) accessible toilet compartments are 36 in. wide, as shown in Figure 8.38e. This design assumes a front transfer.

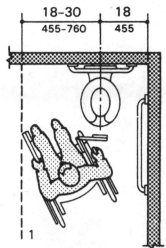

1

TAKES TRANSFER
POSITION, SWINGS
FOOTREST OUT OF
THE WAY, SETS
BRAKES

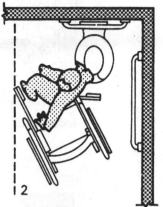

2

REMOVES
ARMREST,
TRANSFERS

3

MOVES
WHEELCHAIR OUT
OF THE WAY,
CHANGES
POSITION (SOME
PEOPLE FOLD
CHAIR OR PIVOT IT

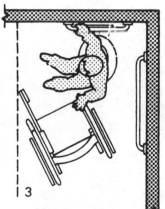

4

POSITIONS ON
TOILET, RELEASES
BRAKE

FIGURE 8.35   Front wheelchair transfer onto water closet. *(Source: CABO, ANSI A117.1, 1992)*

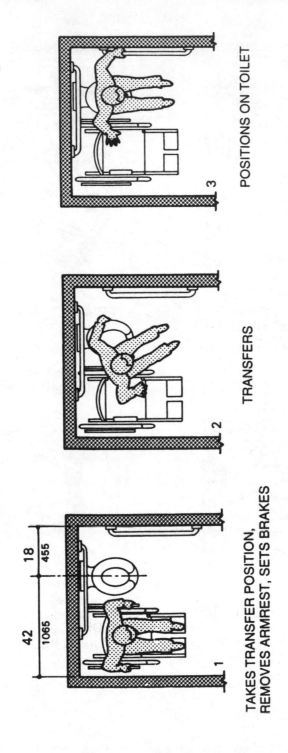

FIGURE 8.35a Side wheelchair transfer onto water closet. (*Source: CABO, ANSI A117.1, 1992*)

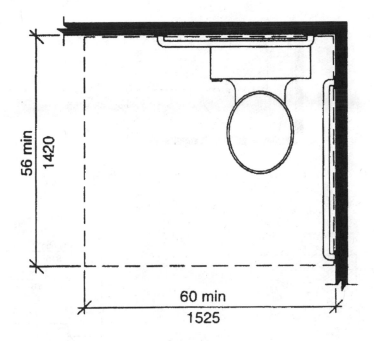

FIGURE 8.36   Water closet clear floor area. *(Source: ICC/ANSI A117.1, 1998)*

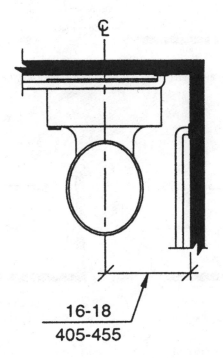

FIGURE 8.37   Water closet location. *(Source: ICC/ANSI A117.1, 1998)*

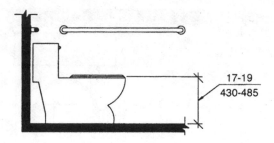

FIGURE 8.38   Water closet height. *(Source: ICC/ANSI A117.1, 1998)*

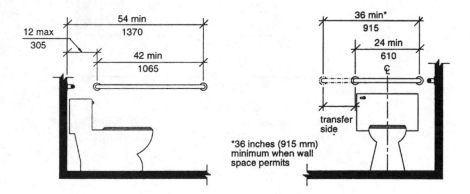

FIGURE 8.38a   Water closet grab bar at side wall. *(Source: ICC/ANSI A117.1, 1998)*

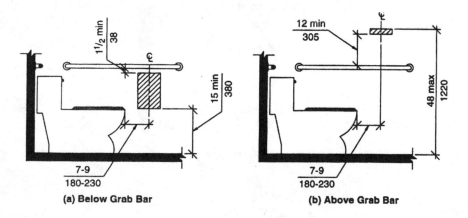

FIGURE 8.38b   Toilet tissue dispenser location and grab bar clearances. *(Source: ICC/ANSI A117.1, 1998)*

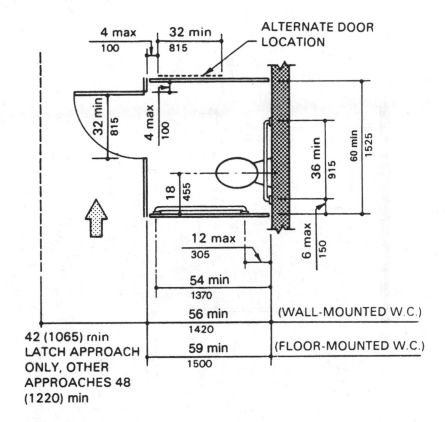

4 max
100

32 min
815

ALTERNATE DOOR LOCATION

32 min
815

4 max
100

36 min
915

60 min
1525

18
455

12 max
305

6 max
150

54 min
1370

56 min
1420
(WALL-MOUNTED W.C.)

42 (1065) min
LATCH APPROACH
ONLY, OTHER
APPROACHES 48
(1220) min

59 min
1500
(FLOOR-MOUNTED W.C.)

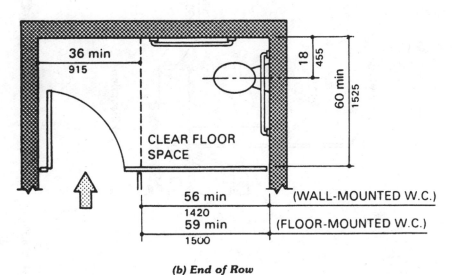

36 min
915

18
455

60 min
1525

CLEAR FLOOR
SPACE

56 min
1420
(WALL-MOUNTED W.C.)

59 min
1500
(FLOOR-MOUNTED W.C.)

(b) End of Row

FIGURE 8.38c   Wheelchair accessible toilet compartment with door swinging out and in. *(Source: CABO, ANSI A117.1, 1992)*

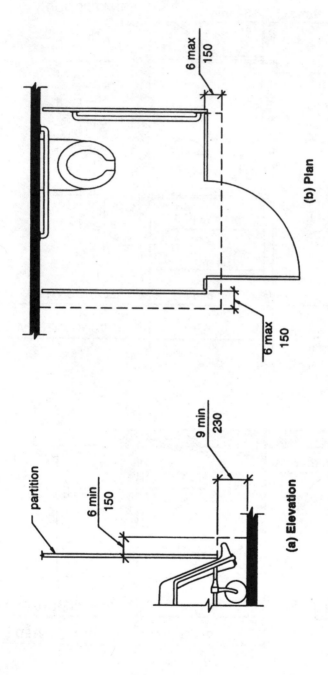

FIGURE 8.38d Toilet compartment toe clearance. *(Source: ICC/ANSI A117.1, 1998)*

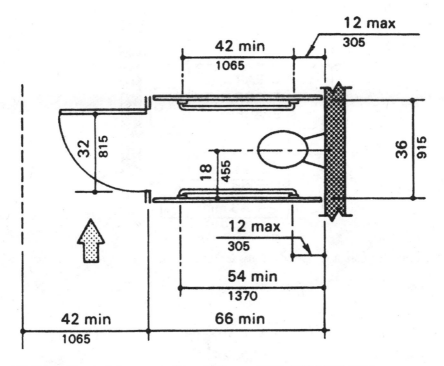

FIGURE 8.38e Ambulatory accessible stall. *(Source: CABO, ANSI A117.1, 1992)*

Lavatories

A clear floor space 30 in. wide by 48 in. long must be centered under the lavatory and extend under the lavatory, as shown in Figure 8.39. Accessible fixtures must extend at least 17 in. from the wall and have the clearances for knee and toe space, as shown in Figure 8.39a. Sinks must be 6½ in. deep maximum. Exposed piping must be insulated or covered. Lavatory controls must be within allowable reach ranges and not require tight grasping, pinching, or twisting of the wrist to operate [2]. This can be accomplished with a variety of faucet handle designs or with electric eye faucets.

Urinals

Accessible urinals must have a rim height of 17 in. maximum above the floor. A minimum clear floor area of 30 in. wide by 48 in. long must be provided, centered under the urinal. This clearance also applies to urinal screens. Toilet flush controls must be mounted within accessible reach ranges.

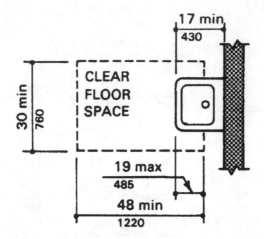

FIGURE 8.39   Clear floor space at lavatories and sinks. *(Source: CABO, ANSI A117.1, 1992)*

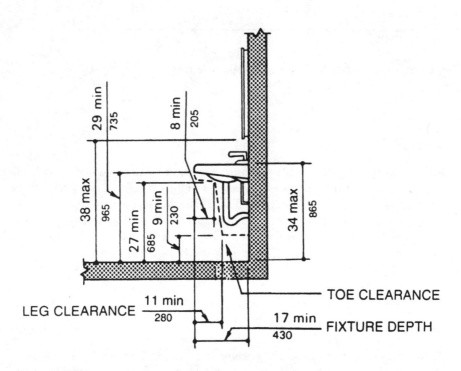

NOTE: Dashed line indicates dimensional clearance of optional under fixture enclosure.

FIGURE 8.39a   Lavatory mounting height, knee and toe clearances. *(Source: CABO, ANSI A117.1, 1992)*

Showers

There are two types of accessible showers: transfer type and roll-in type. Both types must have a beveled threshold no more than ½ in. high. All accessible showers are required to have an adjustable shower head, either of the sliding rod type or with a flexible hose at least 59 in. long.

One kind of transfer type shower, 36 in. wide and 36 in. deep, has a transfer seat mounted opposite the showerhead and the controls. Grab bars and maneuvering clearance must be provided as shown in Figure 8.40. The controls and showerhead must be mounted where shown in Figure 8.40a. Seat size and shape are shown in Figure 8.40b.

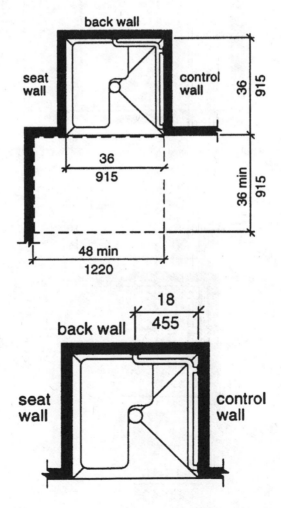

FIGURE 8.40 Transfer-type shower compartment. *(Source: ICC/ANSI A117.1, 1998)*

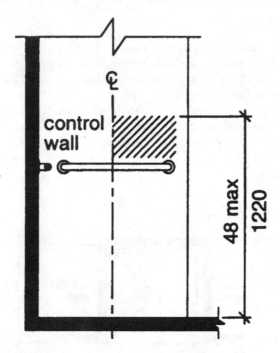

FIGURE 8.40a Controls in transfer-type showers. *(Source: ICC/ANSI A117.1, 1998)*

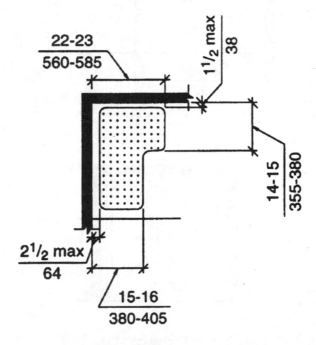

FIGURE 8.40b L-shaped shower compartment seat. *(Source: ICC/ANSI A117.1, 1998)*

The three types of accessible roll-in showers are shown in Figure 8.41. Roll-in showers must have the minimum dimensions and maneuvering room shown in Figure 8.41a. Grab bars must be provided around three sides, except where a seat is provided. The showerhead and controls may be mounted on the side or back walls where shown in Figure 8.41b. The shower seat must be the shape and size shown in Figure 8.41c.

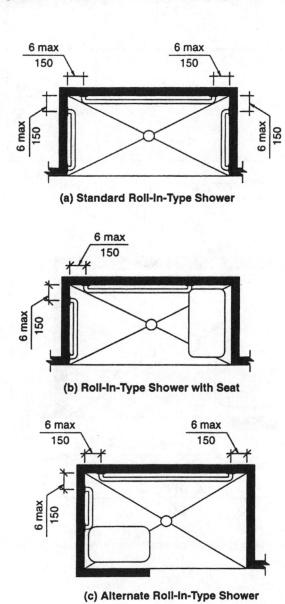

(a) Standard Roll-In-Type Shower

(b) Roll-In-Type Shower with Seat

(c) Alternate Roll-In-Type Shower

FIGURE 8.41   Grab bars in roll-in-type showers. *(Source: ICC/ANSI A117.1, 1998)*

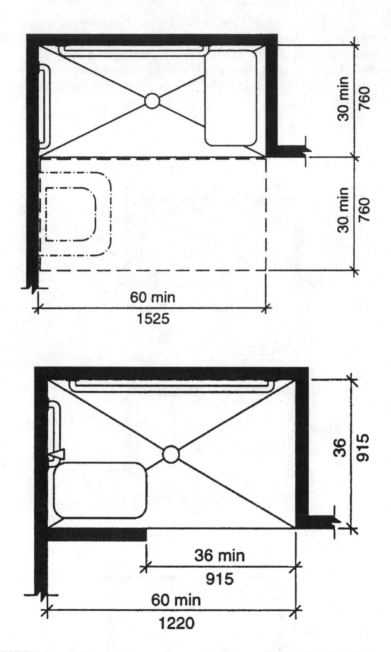

FIGURE 8.41a   Roll-in-type shower compartments. *(Source: ICC/ANSI A117.1, 1998)*

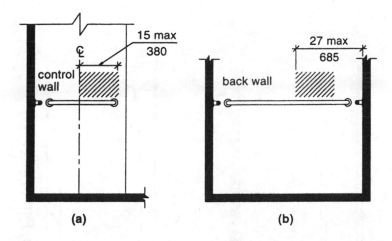

FIGURE 8.41b Location of shower spray unit. *(Source: CABO, ANSI A117.1, 1998)*

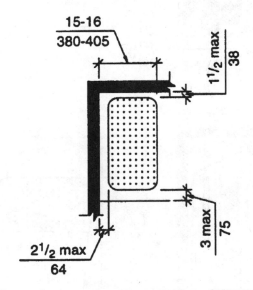

FIGURE 8.41c Rectangular shower compartment seat. *(Source: ICC/ANSI A117.1, 1998)*

Bathtubs

Accessible bathtubs must have a fixed or removable seat as shown in Figure 8.42. Maneuvering room must be provided as shown in Figure 8.43. A fixed or movable seat must be provided. Grab bars must be provided as shown in Figure 8.44. Bathtub enclosures must not obstruct controls or transfer from a wheelchair and may not have a track mounted on the bathtub rim.

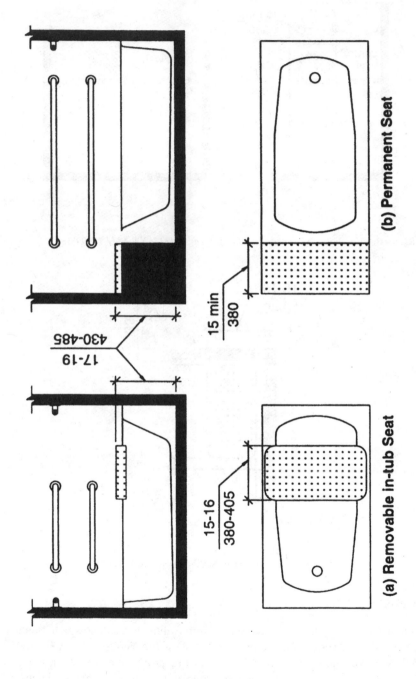

(a) Removable in-tub Seat

(b) Permanent Seat

FIGURE 8.42 Bathtub seat. (*Source: ICC/ANSI A117.1, 1998*)

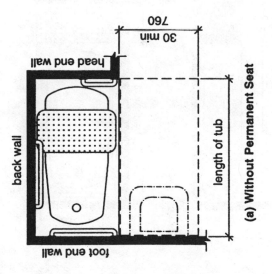

FIGURE 8.43 Clearance for bathtubs. (*Source: ICC/ANSI A117.1, 1998*)

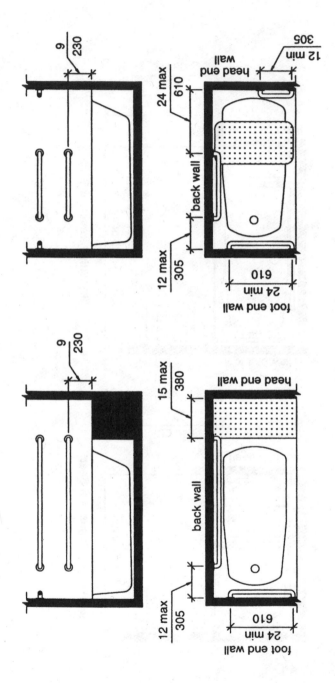

FIGURE 8.44 Grab bars for bathtubs with and without permanent seats. *(Source: ICC/ANSI A117.1, 1998)*

Grab Bars

Grab bars may be circular or non-circular in cross section, but must be within the minimum and maximum dimensions shown in Figure 8.45. They must be mounted 1½ in. from the wall and 15 in. minimum clearance must be maintained above, as shown in Figure 8.46, and be able to withstand 250 lb of force applied to any part, as specified in ICC/ANSI A 117.1 at 903.5.

Mirrors

Accessible mirrors above lavatories must be mounted not more than 40 in. above the floor to the bottom of the mirror. No requirement exists for the size of mirrors, but full-length mirrors are preferred since downward tilted mirrors typically don't permit viewing of the feet and legs.

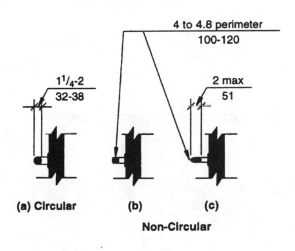

FIGURE 8.45   Size of grab bars. *(Source: ICC/ANSI A117.1, 1998)*

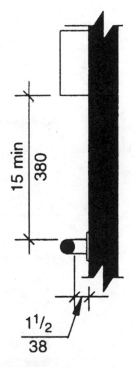

FIGURE 8.46 Spacing of grab bars. *(Source: ICC/ANSI A117.1, 1998)*

KITCHENS

Accessible kitchens must contain all of the elements of any kitchen, but special care must be taken to locate the functional components and operating controls within allowable reach ranges. All required tables, counters, and work surfaces must be mounted between 28 in. and 34 in. high. One work surface must at least 30 in. wide to allow forward approach and required knee and toe clearance, as shown in Figure 8.47. A similar area must be provided for the sink, as shown in Figure 8.48.

   The minimum distance between cabinets in a galley-style layout is 40 in. When cabinets are located on three contiguous sides in a U-shape, the minimum dimension is 60 in. Within any accessible kitchen, the floor area must accommodate a wheelchair turning space, pivot turn, or T-turn. The minimum 30 in. by 48 in. clear floor area is required at each appliance, including when the dishwasher door is open.

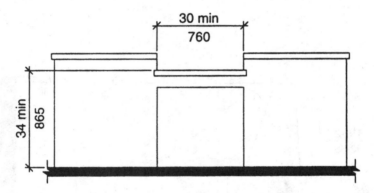

FIGURE 8.47   Work surface in kitchen. *(Source: ICC/ANSI A117.1, 1998)*

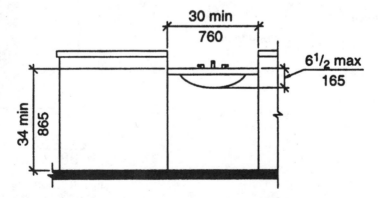

FIGURE 8.48   Accessible kitchen sink. *(Source: ICC/ANSI A117.1, 1998)*

Ranges and ovens must have an adjacent countertop, as shown in Figure 8.49. Wall or countertop mounted ovens are preferred, since the operating parts can be located within allowable reach ranges. Cooktops with front approach must have required knee and toe clearance, and the knee space must be insulated from shock or burns. Combination refrigerator/freezers must have at least half of the freezer space within 54 in. of the floor. Most side-by-side models achieve this standard.

DRESSING, FITTING, AND LOCKER ROOMS

Accessible dressing, fitting, and locker rooms must have wheelchair turning space into which the door does not swing. The size required for an accessible dressing room is similar to the size required for an accessible toilet compartment. A bench, 20 in. to 24 in. wide and at least 42 in. long and attached to the wall on one of its long sides, must be provided within the room or compartment. Coat hooks must be located within allowable reach range, not higher than 48 in. When a folding shelf is provided, it must be mounted at 40 in. to 48 in.

STORAGE FACILITIES

Wheelchair turning space must be provided. The height of storage shelves or hangers must comply with at least one of the reach ranges (i.e., shelves may extend above 48 in. but must start at 15 in.). Hanging rods should not be mounted above 48 in. These concepts are illustrated in Figure 8.50. Operating controls of mechanical storage systems must be within accessible reach ranges.

TABLES, COUNTERS, AND WORK SURFACES

Wheelchair maneuvering and turning space must be provided, along with required knee and toe clearances. All surfaces must be located from 28 in. to 34 in. above the floor. Figure 8.51 shows accessible seating at a dining table. Food and drink counters must be at least 60 in. long.

CHECKOUT AND SERVICE COUNTERS

Wheelchair maneuvering and turning space must be provided, with required knee and toe clearances. Checkout counters may not be higher than 38 in., and the counter edge may not be higher than 2 in. above the counter, as shown in Figure 8.52. Sales or service counters must have at least one portion with a 36 in. wide minimum that is not higher than 36 in.

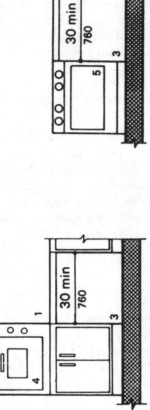

(c) Range Oven

30 min
760

SYMBOL KEY
1. Countertop or wall-mounted oven
2. Pull-out board preferred with side-opening door
3. Clear open space
4. Bottom-hinged door
5. Range oven

(b) Bottom-Hinged Door

30 min
760

(a) Side-Hinged Door

30 min
760

FIGURE 8.49 Accessible oven and workspace design. *(Source: CABO, ANSI A117.1, 1992)*

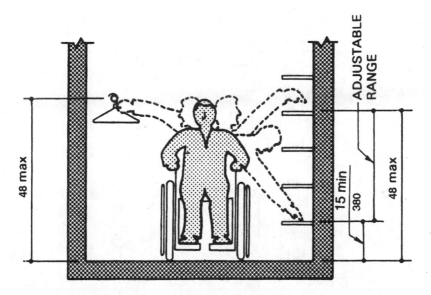

FIGURE 8.50 Accessible storage shelves and closets. *(Source: CABO, ANSI A117.1, 1992)*

DWELLING UNITS

While most of the accessibility standards discussed earlier in this chapter apply to accessible dwelling units, ICC/ANSI A117.1, Chapter 10 contains a number of special requirements and exceptions. Special standards and exceptions for certain elements include floor surfaces, doors, elevators, toilet and bathing facilities, kitchens, and other elements.

Separate standards are written for Class A and Class B dwellings, with a higher level of accessibility for Class A dwellings. The Class B standard was developed to comply with the Federal Fair Housing Amendments Act Accessibility Guidelines [1]. Type B dwellings are adaptable, with exceptions involving items that can be modified easily. The code allows the authority in charge of adoption to determine which standard is used.

At least one accessible route must be maintained through accessible dwellings, and turning space must be provided in every room. Class B dwellings may have sunken or raised floor areas that are not part of the accessible route and may have loose, thick, or irregular floor surfaces. Only the minimum width of the accessible route must be maintained.

Exceptions for dwellings allowing certain operable parts to be located outside allowable reach range are shown Figure 8.53. Class B dwellings also may have appliance controls located out of reach range.

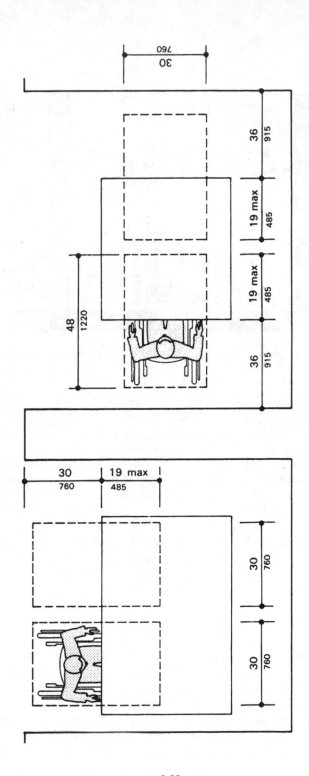

FIGURE 8.51 Accessible seating at dining tables. *(Source: CABO, ANSI A117.1, 1992)*

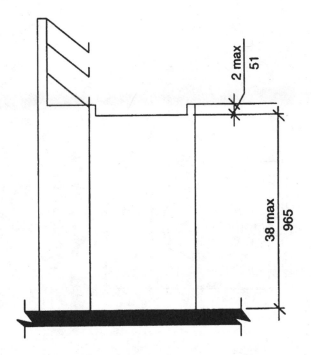

FIGURE 8.52 Allowable height for checkout counters. *(Source: ICC/ANSI A117.1, 1998)*

EXCEPTIONS:

1. Electrical receptacles serving a dedicated use.

2. A single outlet where all of the following conditions are met:
   (a) the outlet is above a length of countertop that is uninterrupted by a sink or appliance; and
   (b) at least one receptacle complying with Section 1002.9 is provided for that length of countertop; and
   (c) all other receptacles provided for that length of countertop comply with Section 1002.9.

3. Floor electrical receptacles.

4. HVAC diffusers.

5. Controls mounted on range hoods if accessible redundant controls are provided.

6. Controls mounted on ceiling fans.

FIGURE 8.53 Exceptions for operable parts *not* in reach range. *(Source: ICC/ANSI A117.1, 1998)*

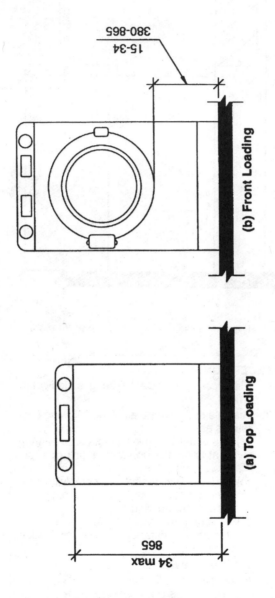

FIGURE 8.54 Design of accessible laundry equipment. (*Source: ICC/ANSI A117.1, 1998*)

Clear floor space requirements apply at all kitchen and laundry appliances. Accessible laundry equipment is shown in Figure 8.54.

Figure 8.55 shows the critical dimensions for the design of a Class A accessible dwelling toilet. Note that this design allows the lavatory to overlap the clear floor space at the water closet. The design for Class B is similar, with the exception that only grab bar reinforcements are required. Class B contains an Option A (requiring all fixtures to be accessible), and Option B (requiring only one of each type of accessible fixture).

COMMUNICATIONS ELEMENTS

ICC/ANSI A 117.1, Chapter 7 contains standards for alarms, signs, telephones, assistive listening systems, automatic teller machines, and automatic fare machines. Only the requirements for accessible signs and telephones are covered in this book.

SIGNS

Accessible signs must have both tactile and visual characters or letters and be duplicated in Braille. Tactile characters must be raised $\frac{1}{32}$ in. above the background, contrast with the background, and have non-glare surfaces. Character height, thickness, and spacing are specified in detail in ICC/ANSI A 117.1 at 703, shown in Figure 8.56.

Accessible signs must be mounted from 48 in. to 60 in. high alongside the door on the latch side, with an 18 in. by 18 in. clear floor space centered in front of the sign, as shown in Figure 8.57. At double doors, the sign must be located on the right unless there is no room beside the door, in which case the sign may be mounted on the nearest adjacent wall. The clear floor space must be located outside of any door swing. Door signs may be mounted on the push side of doors with closers and no hold-open. Where pictograms are used, they must be duplicated in tactile characters and in Braille, and be of the size indicated in Figure 8.58.

ICC/ANSI A 117.1 at 703.7.2 also specifies several symbols such as the International Symbol of Accessibility (ISA), which is used to mark accessible routes and elements. The ISA, shown in Figure 8.59, is required to identify exit stairways, accessible toilet and bathing facilities, dressing rooms, checkout aisles, and other elements when all are not accessible [1, 2].

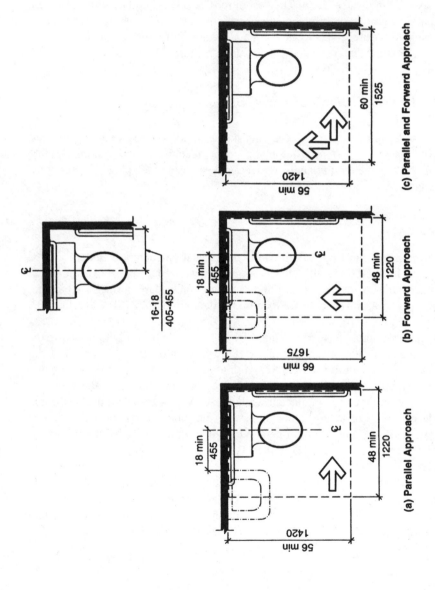

(a) Parallel Approach

(b) Forward Approach

(c) Parallel and Forward Approach

FIGURE 8.55 Water closet clearance in Type A dwelling units. *(Source: ICC/ANSI A117.1, 1998)*

8.72

Height above Floor or Ground to Top of Character	Minimum Viewing Distance	Minimum Character Height	Notes
40 inches - ≤70 inches (1015 mm - 1780 mm)	≤6 feet (1830 mm)	$5/8$ inch (16 mm)	Except elevators
40 inches - ≤70 inches (1015 mm - 1780 mm)	>6 feet (1830 mm)	$5/8$ inch (16 mm), plus $1/8$ inch per foot (3.2 mm per 305 mm) of viewing distance beyond 6 feet (1830 mm)	Except elevators
>70 inches - ≤120 inches (1780 mm - 3050 mm)	≤15 feet (4570 mm)	2 inches (51 mm)	
>70 inches - ≤120 inches (1780 mm - 3050 mm)	>15 feet (4570 mm)	2 inches (51 mm), plus $1/8$ inch per foot (3.2 mm per 305 mm) of viewing distance beyond 15 feet (4570 mm)	
> 120 inches (3050 mm)	≤21 feet (6400 mm)	3 inches (75 mm)	
> 120 inches (3050 mm)	>21 feet (6400 mm)	3 inches (75 mm), plus $1/8$ inch per foot (3.2 mm per 305 mm) of viewing distance beyond 21 feet (6400 mm)	

FIGURE 8.56 Table 703.4.2.4. Minimum sign character heights. (*Source: ICC/ANSI A117.1, 1998*)

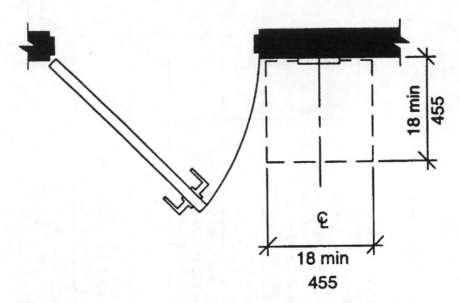

FIGURE 8.57   Sign mounting location and clear floor space at doors. *(Source: ICC/ANSI A117.1, 1998)*

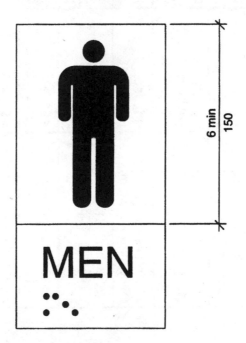

FIGURE 8.58   Accessible pictogram sign dimensions. *(Source: ICC/ANSI A117.1, 1998)*

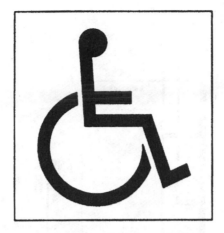

FIGURE 8.59 International symbol of accessibility. *(Source: ICC/ANSI A117.1, 1998)*

Telephones

A front or parallel approach is allowed at accessible telephones, requiring the minimum clear floor space of 30 in. by 48 in. When the telephone is mounted in a front approach enclosure deeper than 24 in., the clear floor space required is 36 in. by 48 in. The required dimensions for an accessible telephone enclosure are shown in Figure 8.60.

ACCESSIBILITY SCOPING—HOW MANY MUST BE ACCESSIBLE?

How are the minimum number of accessible spaces and elements determined? Which parts of a space or how many of the elements (e.g., toilets, motel rooms, and classrooms) must be designed for accessibility? Scoping requirements are contained in the International Building Code, ICC/ANSI A 117.1, and the ADAAG. Minimum percentages are specified for each type of element required to be accessible, but at least one accessible element must be provided.

ACCESSIBLE ROUTE

The ADAAG requires at least one accessible route in all buildings leading to the required accessible facilities and elements. If the building is multi-story, each level must have an accessible route connected by an accessible elevator. Levels less than 3000 sq ft are not required to have an elevator, except for shopping centers or medical care providers.

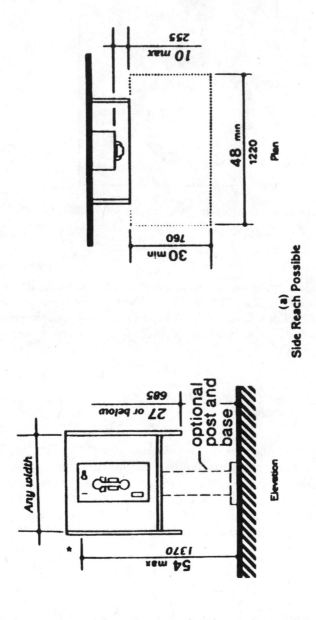

FIGURE 8.60 Mounting heights and clearances for telephones. (*Source: Federal Register, ADA Accessibility Guidelines, 1991*)

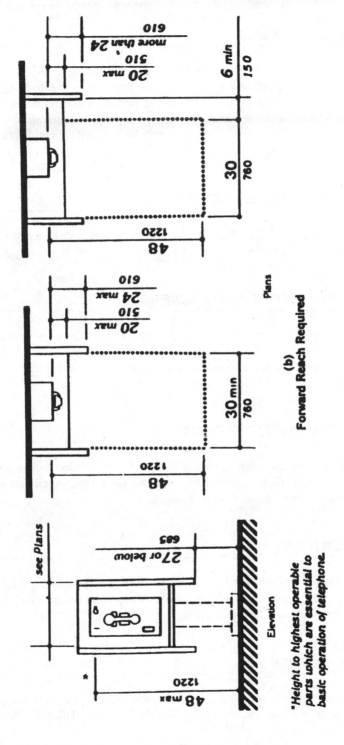

FIGURE 8.60 (*continued*) Mounting heights and clearances for telephones. (*Source: Federal Register, ADA Accessibility Guidelines, 1991*)

DRINKING FOUNTAINS

At least one, but not less than half of the drinking fountains on any level must be accessible. The ADAAG at 4.1.3(10) requires that at least one drinking fountain also be located at a height to accommodate persons who cannot bend. This is described as a high/low drinking fountain arrangement. Equivalent facilitation, such as a cup dispenser and an appropriately designed fountain spout also may qualify.

TOILET AND BATHING FACILITIES

At least one, but not less than 5 percent of toilet and bathing elements must be accessible.

STORAGE FACILITIES AND LOCKERS

Where built-in storage elements such as cabinets, shelves, closets, or drawers are provided, at least one of each type of storage element must be accessible. At least 5 percent of lockers must be accessible, a requirement that can be achieved with double-tier lockers.

DRESSING AND FITTING ROOMS

At least one, and not less than 5 percent of dressing and fitting rooms must be accessible and each must be equipped with the same type of clothes-hooks, shelves, and other elements as in other rooms.

CARE FACILITIES

The IBC at 1107.4 requires care facilities to be entirely accessible. Care facilities include Assembly Group A-3 (including the uses shown in Figure 8.61), Educational, Day Care, and R-3 (assisted living).

DINING FACILITIES

The entire floor of dining areas must be accessible, with 5 percent of the seating accessible. A plan of accessible dining seating accommodation is shown in

---

A-3 Assembly uses intended for worship, recreation or amusement and other assembly uses not classified elsewhere in Group A, including, but not limited to:

> Amusement arcades
> Art galleries
> Auditoriums
> Bowling alleys
> Churches
> Community halls
> Courtrooms
> Dance halls
> Exhibition halls
> Funeral parlors
> Gymnasiums
> Indoor swimming pools
> Indoor tennis courts
> Lecture halls
> Libraries
> Museums
> Passenger stations (waiting area)
> Pool and billiard parlors

FIGURE 8.61 Care facilities. *(Source: ICC, International Building Code, 2000)*

Figure 8.51. A mezzanine in a dining facility need not be accessible if it does not exceed 25 percent of the total dining area. Dining counters more than 34 in. high must include at least one accessible section not less than 60 in. wide.

SLEEPING ACCOMMODATIONS

Accessible sleeping facilities and accessible rooms with roll-in showers must be provided in the proportions shown in Figure 8.62.

CHECKOUT AISLES

Accessible checkout aisles must be provided in the proportions shown in Figure 8.63.

TOTAL NUMBER OF SLEEPING ACCOMMODATIONS PROVIDED	MINIMUM REQUIRED NUMBER OF ACCESSIBLE SLEEPING ACCOMMODATIONS ASSOCIATED WITH ROLL-IN SHOWERS	TOTAL NUMBER OF REQUIRED ACCESSIBLE SLEEPING ACCOMMODATIONS
1 to 25	0	1
26 to 50	0	2
51 to 75	1	4
76 to 100	1	5
101 to 150	2	7
151 to 200	2	8
201 to 300	3	10
301 to 400	4	12
401 to 500	4	13
501 to 1,000	1% of total	3% of total
Over 1,000	10 plus 1 for each 100 over 1,000	30 plus 2 for each 100 over 1,000

FIGURE 8.62   Table 1107.5.1. (*Source: ICC, International Building Code, 2000*)

ACCESSIBLE CHECK-OUT AISLES

TOTAL CHECK-OUT AISLES OF EACH FUNCTION	MINIMUM NUMBER OF ACCESSIBLE CHECK-OUT AISLES EACH FUNCTION
1 to 4	1
5 to 8	2
9 to 15	3
Over 15	3, plus 20% of additional aisles

FIGURE 8.63   Table 1108.12.2. (*Source: ICC, International Building Code, 2000*)

EXEMPTIONS

Exemptions from requirements for accessibility are provided for the following uses and spaces: individual employee work stations, detached one- and two-family dwellings, utility and agricultural buildings, construction sites, raised areas used for security or safety (e.g., guard towers, fire towers, lifeguard stands), limited-access spaces (e.g., ladders, catwalks, service tunnels, crawl spaces), mechanical and electrical equipment rooms, single-occupant buildings such as tollbooths, boarding houses, or motels with less than five rooms for rent.

REFERENCES

1. ICC/ANSI. 1998 Edition. *Accessible and Usable Buildings and Facilities ICC/ANSI A117.1-1998.* International Code Council and American National Standards Institute. Falls Church, VA
2. ATBCB. 1991 Edition. *Americans with Disabilities Act Accessibility Guidelines for Buildings and Facilities.* Architectural and Transportation Barriers Compliance Board, Federal Register July 1991. Washington, D.C.
3. ANSI A 117.1 101

CHAPTER 9
INTERIOR FINISHES

The following narrative from the 1997 Life Safety Code Commentary demonstrates the serious potential threat from fire involving interior finish materials:

> In the 1981 Las Vegas Hilton Hotel fire, combustible carpeting on the walls and ceilings of elevator lobbies contributed to horizontal fire spread on the floor of origin and vertical spread involving 22 floors. Eight people died in this fire.
>
> In a 1978 Holiday Inn fire that killed 10 people, "lightweight plywood paneling in stairway did not meet Life Safety Code, was involved early in fire, and produced rapid growth and spread." In a 1979 Holiday Inn fire that also killed 10 people, "carpeting and some wall covering in corridors had excessively high flame-spread properties."
>
> In a 1972 Springfield, Illinois convalescent nursing home fire that killed 10 of the 41 patients, "the wood-panel finish accelerated fire spread. Combustible interior finish—especially interior finish such as the wood paneling in this facility—should not be allowed where infirm people are housed. The paneling on the stairway had completely burned away, permitting fire spread into the first floor through holes in the plaster [1]."

RESTRICTIONS ON INTERIOR FINISHES

One of the most important fire protection strategies in the building codes is the regulation of interior finishes. The development and spread of fire is closely related to the surface burning characteristics of the floors, walls, and ceilings. By regulating the finish of these surfaces, fire development and spread can be controlled to some extent [1].

MATERIALS REGULATED AS INTERIOR FINISH

The IBC at 802 defines interior floor finish as *the exposed floor surfaces of buildings, including coverings applied over a finish floor or stair, including risers.* Interior wall and ceiling finishes are defined as *the exposed interior surfaces of buildings including, but not limited to, fixed or movable walls and partitions, columns, ceilings, and interior wainscoting, paneling, or other finish applied structurally or for decoration, acoustical correction, surface insulation, structural fire resistance or similar purposes, but not including trim* [2].

The Life Safety Code (LSC) definition is more concise, but means the same: any combustible material used on the exposed interior surfaces of walls, ceilings and floors is regulated as an interior finish. This includes movable office compartments, built-in cabinetry and furnishings, window treatment, decorations, and even furniture, in certain occupancies. The following narrative from the 1997 LSC Commentary describes other items the code official may regulate:

> Interior finishes are the interior surfaces of a building that are generally secured in place. Thus, wall, ceiling, and column coverings are considered interior wall and ceiling finishes. The surfaces of movable walls or folding partitions would also be treated as interior wall and ceiling finishes. However, this section uses the expression "but not limited to," which allows the authority having jurisdiction to exercise judgment in determining what constitutes interior finish. For example, a tapestry would not normally be considered as interior finish. However, a large tapestry that is secured to and covers a major portion of a wall could promote the rapid growth of fire and might warrant regulation.
>
> Furnishings (including high-backed, plastic-upholstered restaurant booths) are not normally considered as interior finish, even in cases where the furnishings are fixed in place. However, if the furnishings are judged to represent a hazard, they could be regulated as interior finish by the authority having jurisdiction [1].

Materials that are not combustible, i.e., metal, are not regulated under the code provisions for interior finishes. Materials less than 0.036 (¹⁄₂₈) in. thick that are cemented or applied directly to an interior surface, such as paint or wallpaper, are not regulated as an interior finish unless they have a flame spread more than plain paper under the same conditions [2]. The 1997 LSC Commentary includes narrative regarding this exception, as follows:

> *The [Code] recognizes that thin coverings [those less than ⅟₂₈ in. (0.09 cm) in thickness] with surface burning characteristics no greater than paper will not significantly affect the performance of the basic wall or ceiling material. Thermally thin coverings such as paint and wallpaper coverings, where secured to a noncombustible substrate, will not significantly alter the performance of the substrate during a fire.* However, thicker coverings, such as multiple layers of wallpaper, can and have contributed to rapid fire growth in actual fires. For example, multiple layers of wall coverings contributed to rapid fire growth in the multiple-death fire in the Holiday Inn in Cambridge, Ohio, which occurred on July 31, 1979. The exception requires any wall or ceiling covering ⅟₂₈ in. (0.09 cm) or more in thickness to be treated as interior finish [1].

Baseboards, chair rails, crown moldings, door and window casings, and other architectural ornamentation not comprising more than 10 percent of the wall area are considered trim. Decorations and furnishings which do not comprise more than 10 percent of the wall area are regulated under the 2000 LSC at 10.3 as Contents and Furnishings. Trim contents and furnishings are covered later in this chapter [1, 2].

FLAME AND SMOKE CLASSIFICATIONS AND TESTS

The IBC classifies wall and ceiling finishes according to ASTM E 84, Standard Test of Surface Burning Characteristics of Building Materials. This test, often called the *tunnel test* or *Steiner tunnel test*, results in a classification for smoke and flame development. The codes classify interior finishes according to the following scale:

Class A:	Flame Spread Index 0-25	Smoke Developed Index 0-450
Class B:	Flame Spread Index 26-75	Smoke Developed Index 0-450
Class C:	Flame Spread Index 76-200	Smoke Developed Index 0-450

The LSC refers to NFPA 255, Standard Test of Surface Burning Characteristics of Building Materials. This test is identical to ASTM E 84 and also to UL 723, Surface Burning Characteristics of Building Materials. The LSC also recognizes several other tests for textile wall coverings, hanging fabrics, upholstered furnishings, and other items discussed later in this chapter. NFPA recommends use of the most recent and closely applicable standard in the evaluation of the flame and smoke characteristics of finish materials [1].

No material that has a flame spread rating of more than 200 and a smoke development rating of more than 450 may be used as an interior finish. Older building codes allowed flame spread ratings of Class D and E that had ratings higher than the current maximum. The LSC exempts existing buildings from the smoke development index, since no standard for smoke development was included in the code before 1976 [6].

OLDER MODEL BUILDING CODES

Class A, B, and C designations used by the IBC and the LSC correspond directly with the designations used by the Standard Building Code and also correspond directly with the Class I, II, and III designations used by the Uniform Building Code and the BOCA Standard Building Code [3, 4, 5].

FLAME AND SMOKE RATINGS BASED ON OCCUPANT CONDITION

The IBC and the LSC both regulate the type of interior finishes allowed based on the occupancy classification of a building or space. In uses such as Institutional or Health Care, where the ability of occupants to respond in an emergency might be impaired, the codes are more restrictive. In uses such as Office or Factory, where the occupants are assumed to be alert and capable of self-preservation, the codes are not as restrictive. The following narrative from the 1997 LSC Commentary addresses this concern:

> *Occupancies used by those who are mobility-impaired have stricter interior finish requirements than occupancies used by fully ambulatory occupants. For example, although both hospitals and hotels provide sleeping accommodations, the interior finish requirements are more stringent for hospitals because hospital patients are less capable of self-preservation.*

FLAME AND SMOKE RATINGS BASED ON AREA OF USE

Flame and smoke ratings are highest in exits and exit access corridors, that is, areas that must be traversed to exit in an emergency. The following from the 1997 LSC Commentary gives a more detailed explanation of the thinking behind this strategy.

The Code requires the use of specific classes of interior wall and ceiling finish materials, which are differentiated by their allowable flame spread rating, based on consideration of their installed location within the building, the building's egress paths, and the occupancy in question. Different classes of interior finish materials are specified for an office area, for example, as opposed to an exit stair enclosure or exit access corridor. The different classes recognize that when escaping a building people must move away from the flames while traveling through the means of egress toward an exit. The classes of interior finishes that are considered acceptable within an open office, therefore, are different from those that are required for exit enclosures.

The IBC at Table 803.4 Exception (c) allows the finish classification to be established based on the use of each individual space or room, regardless of the overall building occupancy classification. Figure 9.1 (pages 9.6-9.7) gives the table used under the IBC to determine the required rating according to occupancy and area of use [2].

The LSC has specific requirements for interior finishes contained in each occupancy (Chapters 12-40) used to determine the required finish rating. The 2000 LSC Annex at A10.2.2 includes a tabular compilation of the requirements for interior finish based on occupancy and area of use, shown in Figure 9.2 (pages 9.8-9.10) [1].

IBC AND NFPA CONFLICTS

As discussed in Chapter 3, *Use and Occupancy*, the definitions and categories used by the IBC and LSC do not always correspond. The requirements of each code must be compared. Where the codes conflict, a determination from the code enforcement authority with jurisdiction is recommended [1, 2].

FLAME AND SMOKE RATINGS BASED ON SPRINKLERS

The codes recognize the effectiveness of sprinklers in preventing the development of fires. The IBC, as shown in Figure 9.1, organizes the chart describing required flame and smoke rating based on buildings being sprinkled or unsprinkled. The LSC at 10.2.8 simply states that, when the building is sprinkled according to NFPA 13, the required flame and smoke rating may be reduced by one rating classification [1, 2].

TABLE 803.4
INTERIOR WALL AND CEILING FINISH REQUIREMENTS BY OCCUPANCY^k

GROUP	SPRINKLERED[l]			UNSPRINKLERED		
	Vertical exits and exit passageways[a,b]	Exit access corridors and other exitways	Rooms and enclosed spaces[c]	Vertical exits and exit passageways[a,b]	Exit access corridors and other exitways	Rooms and enclosed spaces[c]
A-1 & A-2	B	B	C	A	A[d]	B[e]
A-3[f], A-4, A-5	B	B	C	A	A[d]	C
B, E, M, R-1, R-4	B	C	C	A	B	C
F	C	C	C	B	C	C
H	B	B	C[g]	A	A	B
I-1	B	C	C	A	B	B
I-2	B	B	B[h,i]	A	A	B
I-3	A	A[j]	C	A	A	B
I-4	B	B	B[h,j]	A	A	B
R-2	C	C	C	B	B	C
R-3	C	C	C	C	C	C
S	C	C	C	B	B	C
U	No restrictions			No restrictions		

FIGURE 9.1 IBC Table 803.4 Interior wall and ceiling finish requirements by occupancy. (*Source: ICC, International Building Code, 2000*)

For SI: 1 inch = 25.4 mm, 1 square foot = 0.0929 m².

a. Class C interior finish materials shall be permitted for wainscoting or paneling of not more than 1,000 square feet of applied surface area in the grade lobby where applied directly to a noncombustible base or over furring strips applied to a noncombustible base and fireblocked as required by Section 803.3.1.

b. In vertical exits of buildings less than three stories in height of other than Group I-3, Class B interior finish for unsprinklered buildings and Class C interior finish for sprinklered buildings shall be permitted.

c. Requirements for rooms and enclosed spaces shall be based upon spaces enclosed by partitions. Where a fire-resistance rating is required for structural elements, the enclosing partitions shall extend from the floor to the ceiling. Partitions that do not comply with this shall be considered enclosing spaces and the rooms or spaces on both sides shall be considered one. In determining the applicable requirements for rooms and enclosed spaces, the specific occupancy thereof shall be the governing factor regardless of the group classification of the building or structure.

d. Lobby areas in A-1, A-2 and A-3 occupancies shall not be less than Class B materials.

e. Class C interior finish materials shall be permitted in places of assembly with an occupant load of 300 persons or less.

f. For churches and places of worship, wood used for ornamental purposes, trusses, paneling or chancel furnishing shall be permitted.

g. Class B material required where building exceeds two stories.

h. Class C interior finish materials shall be permitted in administrative spaces.

i. Class C interior finish materials shall be permitted in rooms with a capacity of four persons or less.

j. Class B materials shall be permitted as wainscoting extending not more than 48 inches above the finished floor in exit access corridors.

k. Finish materials as provided for in other sections of this code.

l. Applies when the vertical exits, exit passageways, exit access corridors or exitways, or rooms and spaces are protected by a sprinkler system installed in accordance with Section 903.3.1.1 or Section 903.3.1.2.

FIGURE 9.1 (continued) IBC Table 803.4 Interior wall and ceiling finish requirements by occupancy. (Source: ICC, International Building Code, 2000)

Table A.10.2.2 Interior Finish Classification Limitations

Occupancy	Exits	Access to Exits	Other Spaces
Assembly — New			
>300 occupant load	A	A or B	A or B
≤300 occupant load	A	A or B	A, B, or C
Assembly — Existing			
>300 occupant load	A	A or B	A or B
≤300 occupant load	A	A or B	A, B, or C
Educational — New	A	A or B	A or B, C on low partitions†
Educational — Existing	A	A or B	A, B, or C
Day-Care Centers — New	A I or II	A I or II	A or B NR
Day-Care Centers — Existing	A or B	A or B	A or B
Group Day-Care Homes — New	A or B	A or B	A, B, or C
Group Day-Care Homes — Existing	A or B	A, B, or C	A, B, or C
Family Day-Care Homes	A or B	A, B, or C	A, B, or C

FIGURE 9.2 Table A.10.2.2 LSC interior finish classification limitations. *(Source: NFPA, 101, Life Safety Code, 2000)*†

INTERIOR WALL AND CEILING FINISHES— CONSTRUCTION AND APPLICATION

Direct Application and Furred Construction

The IBC at 803.3.1 requires fire-rated and noncombustible walls and ceilings to have the interior finish applied directly against the surface or furred-out not more than 1.75 in. When furring is used, the open space behind the finish material must be filled with Class A material and fireblocked at 8 ft or less.

Set-Out Construction

Finishes which are set-out or furred more than 1.75 in from the fire resistant or noncombustible surface are required to be Class A rated materials, supported by noncombustible furring and supports, or sprinkled on both sides. This requirement also applies to acoustical ceilings, which are discussed later in this chapter. In construction Type III or V, fire-retardant treated wood may be used as furring

Table A.10.2.2 Interior Finish Classification Limitations *(Continued)*

Occupancy	Exits	Access to Exits	Other Spaces
Health Care — New (sprinklers mandatory)	A or B	A or B C on lower potion of corridor wall[†]	A or B C in small individual rooms[†]
Health Care — Existing	A or B	A or B	A or B
Detention and Correctional — New	A[†] I	A[†] I	A, B, or C
Detention and Correctional — Existing	A or B[†] I or II	A or B[†] I or II	A, B, or C
1- and 2-Family Dwellings, Lodging or Rooming Houses	A, B, or C	A, B, or C	A, B, or C
Hotels and Dormitories — New	A I or II	A or B I or II	A, B, or C
Hotels and Dormitories — Existing	A or B I or II[†]	A or B I or II[†]	A, B, or C
Apartment Buildings — New	A I or II[†]	A or B I or II[†]	A, B, or C
Apartment Buildings — Existing	A or B I or II[†]	A or B I or II[†]	A, B, or C
Residential, Board and Care — *(See Chapters 32 and 33.)*			
Mercantile — New	A or B	A or B	A or B

FIGURE 9.2 *(continued)*   Table A.10.2.2 LSC interior finish classification limitations. *(Source: NFPA, 101, Life Safety Code, 2000)*[†]

or supports. Any finish material that is less than ¼ in. thick must be applied directly to a noncombustible backing or be Class A fire rated.

The IBC at 803.3.4 requires any material not more than ¼ in. thick to be "applied directly against a solid noncombustible backing." The only exceptions are for Class A materials and materials which have been tested furred-out or suspended.

INTERIOR WALL AND CEILING FINISHES— SPECIFIC MATERIALS

Certain wall and ceiling finishes have been shown to contribute to the development and spread of fires. In response to this potential hazard, separate requirements are specified in the codes for textile wall and ceiling finishes, expanded vinyl wall covering, and foam plastics.

Table A.10.2.2 Interior Finish Classification Limitations *(Continued)*

Occupancy	Exits	Access to Exits	Other Spaces
Mercantile — Existing Class A or Class B	A or B	A or B	Ceilings — A or B, walls — A, B, or C
Mercantile — Existing Class C	A, B, or C	A, B, or C	A, B, or C
Business and Ambulatory Health Care — New	A or B I or II	A or B I or II	A, B, or C
Business and Ambulatory Health Care — Existing	A or B	A or B	A, B, or C
Industrial	A or B	A, B, or C	A, B, or C
Storage	A or B	A, B, or C	A, B, or C

NR: No requirement.
Notes:
1. Class A interior wall and ceiling finish — flame spread 0–25, (new) smoke developed 0–450.
2. Class B interior wall and ceiling finish — flame spread 26–75, (new) smoke developed 0–450.
3. Class C interior wall and ceiling finish — flame spread 76–200, (new) smoke developed 0–450.
4. Class I interior floor finish — critical radiant flux, not less than 0.45 W/cm^2.
5. Class II interior floor finish — critical radiant flux, not less than 0.22 W/cm^2 but less than 0.45 W/cm^2.
6. Automatic sprinklers — where a complete standard system of automatic sprinklers is installed, interior wall and ceiling finish with flame spread rating not exceeding Class C is permitted to be used in any location where Class B is required and with rating of Class B in any location where Class A is required; similarly, Class II interior floor finish is permitted to be used in any location where Class I is required, and no critical radiant flux rating is required where Class II is required. These provisions do not apply to new health care facilities.
7. Exposed portions of structural members complying with the requirements for heavy timber construction are permitted.
†See corresponding chapters for details.

FIGURE 9.2 *(continued)*   Table A.10.2.2 LSC interior finish classification limitations. *(Source: NFPA, 101, Life Safety Code, 2000)*†

Textile Wall Coverings

Textile wall coverings include any tufted carpet-like materials. In sprinkled buildings, textile wall coverings complying with NFPA 255 Class A may be used. Sprinkling is required in addition to the Class A rating because of the inadequacy of NFPA 255 to predict the performance of textile wall coverings in a fire. Textile wall coverings used in unsprinkled buildings must be tested according to NFPA 265. The background of this test is discussed in an excerpt from the 1997 LSC at A-6-5.3 as follows:

Previous editions of the Code have regulated textile materials on walls and ceilings using NFPA 255, Standard Method of Test of Surface Burning Characteristics of Building Materials. Full-scale room/corner fire test research has shown that flame spread indices produced by NFPA 255 may not reliably predict all aspects of the fire behavior of textile wall and ceiling coverings.

Testing by NFPA 265, Standard Methods of Fire Tests for Evaluating Room Fire Growth Contribution of Textile Wall Coverings, uses a reasonably sized ignition source to show that the material will not spread fire to involve objects remote from the area of origin, and that the textile product will not generate sufficient energy to cause the room of origin to flashover. Acceptance of textile wall covering materials should be contingent upon qualification tests in which a specific textile/adhesive pair has been evaluated.

Although NFPA 265, Standard Methods of Fire Tests for Evaluating Room Fire Growth Contribution of Textile Wall Coverings, was developed for assessing the performance of textile wall coverings, the method can be, and has been, used to evaluate other types of wall finish. As long as a wall finish is tested using a mounting system, substrate, and adhesive (if appropriate) representative of actual use, NFPA 265 provides an evaluation of a product's flammability behavior. Manufacturers, installers, and specifiers should be encouraged to use NFPA 265 because it has the ability to characterize actual product behavior. This is in contrast to NFPA 255 data that only allows comparisons of one product's performance with another. If a manufacturer or installer chooses to test a wall finish in accordance with NFPA 265, additional testing in accordance with NFPA 255 is not necessary.

The LSC also recognizes NFPA 286, Standard Methods of Fire Tests for Evaluating Contribution of Interior Wall and Ceiling Interior Finish to Room Fire Growth. This recently developed test qualifies textile wall and ceiling coverings for use in buildings with no sprinkler protection. NFPA encourages the use of the newest and most appropriate test for the classification of finish materials, especially wall and ceiling finishes. Although not specifically mentioned by the IBC, it is reasonable to expect code officials to approve materials qualified according to NFPA 286. The 2000 LSC at A.10.2.4.1.5 contains the following narrative about the relationship of NFPA 265 and NFPA 286:

NFPA 286, Standard Methods of Fire Test for Evaluating Contribution of Wall and Ceiling Interior Finish Room Fire Growth, has now been developed to evaluate other interior finish materials. Manufacturers, installers, and specifiers should be encouraged to use NFPA 265 or NFPA 286, as appropriate—but not both—because each of these standard fire tests has the ability to characterize actual product behavior, as opposed to data generated by tests using NFPA 255, which only allows comparisons of one product's performance with another. If a manufacturer or installer chooses to test a wall finish in accordance with NFPA 265 or NFPA 286, as appropriate, additional testing in accordance with NFPA 255 is not necessary.

Expanded Vinyl Wall Covering

Both the LSC and the IBC have special sections regulating expanded vinyl wall covering. This wall covering is made of expanded vinyl that is blown onto a fabric backing and covered with a thin vinyl skin. The resulting material is textured to simulate string, cloth, or other textures. Expanded vinyl wall covering is treated like textile wall covering and must be Class A rated in sprinkled buildings. In sprinkled buildings, expanded vinyl wall covering must be rated according to NFPA 265 or 286 [1, 2].

Fabric Upholstered Wall Finishes

Fabric used as an upholstered wall finish must be attached to a noncombustible backing, be Class A rated, sprinkled, or tested according to NFPA 701, Standard Method of Fire Tests for Flame Propagation of Textiles and Films. This is the same test used for the evaluation of draperies. The 2000 LSC at A-6.5.5.1 contains a narrative on this subject, as follows:

> It has been shown that the method of mounting interior finish materials may affect actual performance. Where materials are tested in intimate contact with a substrate to determine a classification, such materials should be installed in intimate contact with a similar substrate. Such details are especially important for "thermally thin" materials.
>
> Some interior wall and ceiling finish materials, such as fabrics not applied to a solid backing, may not lend themselves to a test made in accordance with NFPA 255, Standard Method of Test of Surface Burning Characteristics of Building Materials. In these cases, the large-scale test outlined in NFPA 701, Standard Methods of Fire Tests for Flame Resistant Textiles and Films, may be used.

Ceiling Finishes

The IBC at 803.5.2 allows "carpet or similar textiles" used as ceiling finish only in sprinkled buildings and only when they are Class A rated according to ASTM E 84 (NFPA 255/UL 723). While NFPA 286 does allow for testing of walls and ceilings, the IBC makes no provision for use of any test for ceilings other than NFPA 255. It is reasonable to expect code officials to approve materials tested according to NFPA or other established testing sources.

Acoustical Ceilings

The IBC references ASTM C 635, which covers materials, and ASTM C 638, which covers installation of suspended acoustical ceilings. ASTM C 635 classifies suspended acoustical ceilings as light, intermediate, or heavy duty. Light duty ceilings support tiles only; intermediate duty is required for ceilings that support light fixtures and air diffusers [2].

Foamed Plastics

Cellular or foamed plastic may not be used as a finish material on walls or floors unless it has been certified by full-scale fire tests. The IBC allows no imitation leather finishes, including pyroxylin plastic, in any Group Assembly occupancy. A discussion of foam plastics from the 1997 LSC Commentary follows:

> The prohibition on the use of foamed plastics within buildings is based upon actual fire experience in which foamed plastics have contributed to very rapid fire development. It is also acknowledged that tunnel testing per NFPA 255/ASTM E84 (see 6-5.4.1) may not accurately assess the potential hazard of plastics in general. Therefore, if cellular or foamed plastics are to be used within a building, their use should be substantiated on the basis of full-scale fire tests or fire testing that simulates conditions of actual use.

TRIM

The codes recognize the minimal amount of fire load contributed by trim and allow a Class C flame and smoke rating in any area, when it comprises less than 10 percent of wall and ceiling areas. Class C is the rating typically achieved by untreated wood, and any other material used as trim must also achieve this rating. The 2000 LSC at A-6-5.7, contains the following narrative on trim:

> [The code allows] the use of wood trim around doors and windows as a decoration or as functional molding (such as chair rails). Wood trim must meet the criteria for Class C materials. Where such trim is used in rooms or spaces requiring the use of Class A or B materials, the trim may constitute not more than 10 percent of the aggregate wall or ceiling area. The intent of the 10 percent area limit is that the trim will be more or less uniformly distributed throughout the room or space. If the trim is concentrated in one sizable, continuous pattern (for example, on one wall of a room) the materials could contribute to rapid fire growth, and application of this paragraph as substantiation for such a practice would be in error.

The IBC contains detailed requirements for dimensions and flame ratings of plastic trim at 2604; the LSC provisions at 10.2.4.3(2) are nearly identical, with the exception that the LSC limits width to 4 in. The 1997 LSC Commentary on plastic trim follows:

Limiting plastic trim to Class A or B materials, in combination with the 10 percent area limit for walls and ceilings imposes a greater restriction than would be applicable to wood. This limitation ensures that the performance of the plastic trim will be equivalent or superior to that of more traditional materials.

In establishing the 10 percent limit, it is intended that the trim will be used around doors and windows or at the junction of walls and ceilings. Therefore, the trim will be uniformly distributed throughout the room. There would be a significant difference in the probable performance of wall and ceiling finish if the 10 percent were concentrated in one area, and this exception intends to prohibit such a situation.

FIRE-RETARDANT COATINGS

Many types of fire-retardant paints, coatings, and penetrants that improve the performance of combustible finish materials are available on the market today. One of the most important limitations of fire-retardant coatings is that the material is so thin and exposed to degradation. The LSC does recognize fire-retardant coatings when they meet the requirements of NFPA 703, and when they are maintained to the standards tested. The 1997 LSC Commentary contains the following discussion on fire-retardants:

> *Fire-retardant paints, coatings, and penetrants are sometimes used to improve the flame-spread ratings of materials or assemblies used as interior finishes within buildings. Fire-retardant treatments may be used to satisfy the flame spread requirements only for existing interior finish materials within existing buildings.*
>
> *Fire-retardants are generally a surface treatment that, through intumescence or other chemical reaction, will delay ignition of a material and slow the flame spread. The basic nature of the material to which the treatment has been applied is not changed. Fire exposures of sufficient duration or intensity can ultimately cause a treated material to burn. Therefore, as a rule, materials with favorable intrinsic performance characteristics are preferred over those that achieve a satisfactory level of performance through the use of externally applied treatments. However, external treatments, where properly applied and maintained, can be effective in achieving reasonable fire performance.*
>
> *Fire-retardant paints, coatings, and penetrants must be applied in strict accordance with the manufacturer's instructions and in conformance with the results of fire tests performed on appropriate specimens. Most fire-retardant paints and coatings require an application rate three- to four-times greater than that of ordinary paints. Application is usually done by brush, spray, immersion, or pressure treatment. The treatment should be reapplied or renewed at periodic intervals. Treatments that may be removed by regular maintenance, washing, or cleaning procedures will require periodic examination and reapplication to maintain the required level of performance.*

FLOOR FINISHES—CONSTRUCTION AND APPLICATION

The requirements for combustible interior floor finishes at IBC 8037 apply to buildings of Type I and Type II construction (see Chapter 5: Height, Area, and Types of Construction). Combustible interior floor finishes must be applied directly against the noncombustible floor, or when installed on floor sleepers or nailer blocks, the open space between combustible supports must be filled with noncombustible materials or fireblocked. Fireblocking must be installed under all permanent partitions and at 8 ft centers elsewhere, according to IBC Section 716. A diagram of fire blocking at partitions is shown in Figure 9.3.

Combustible insulating boards not more than ½ in. thick can be attached directly to noncombustible floor construction or above a wood subfloor with sleepers fireblocked, and covered with an approved finish material.

FLOOR FINISHES—MATERIALS

Traditional floor finishes such as wood, resilient tile, hard tile, terrazzo, and other finishes "not containing fibers" are exempt from the IBC provisions for rating of floor finishes. The LSC also contains an exemption at 10.2.2.2.4(2) requiring regulation of floor finishes only where required in the individual occupancy chapter, or where a special hazard is presented. This means that the code requirements for ratings really apply to only carpets, rugs, and other *fibered* or *hazardous* floor coverings. Narratives about traditional floor finishes contained in the 1997 LSC Commentary follow:

> Experience and full-scale fire test data have shown that floor coverings of modest resistance to flame spread are unlikely to become involved in the early growth of a fire. Regulation of flooring materials based upon flammability considerations should, therefore, only be undertaken where required by the Code or where a need is clearly recognized. Regulation of flooring materials in general use areas of a building is usually not warranted, except where they are judged to represent an unusual hazard.
>
> *Experience has shown that traditional floor coverings, such as wood flooring and resilient tile, do not contribute to the early growth of fire. [The Code] acknowledges the satisfactory performance of traditional floor coverings and exempts such materials from the restrictions that would otherwise be applicable. However, the authority having jurisdiction can require substantiation of the performance of any unfamiliar floor covering. For example, "plastic" imitation wood floors, artificial turf, artificial surfaces of athletic fields, and carpeting are types of products that might merit substantiation.*

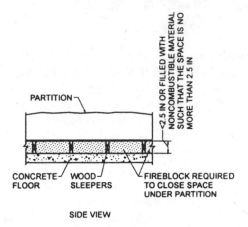

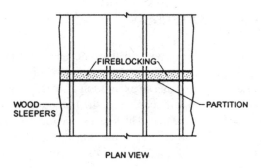

FIGURE 9.3   Fireblocking at partitions in wood floor with sleepers. *(Source: SBCCI, Standard Building Code Commentary, 1997)*

The requirements for floor finish rating based on occupancy are indicated in Figure 9.2. Regulated floor finishes are rated Class I or Class II based on their performance under NFPA 253, which only applies to exits and access to exits (corridors). Traditional floor finishes and carpet not tested under NFPA 253 may be used in other spaces. A narrative on the reasoning behind this follows:

Fire tests have been conducted by the National Bureau of Standards (now the National Institute of Standards and Technology; see NBSIR 76-1013, Flame Spread of Carpet Systems Involved in Room Fires) demonstrating that carpet that passes the Federal Flammability Standard FF1-70 Pill Test is not likely to become involved in a fire until a room reaches or approaches flash over. Since all carpet manufactured for sale in the United States has been required since April 1971 to meet the Pill Test, no further regulation is necessary for carpet located within rooms.

On the other hand, it has been shown that floor coverings may propagate flame under the influence of a sizable exposure fire. For example, it has been shown that carpet located in a corridor might spread flame when subjected to the energy emanating from the doorway of a room fully developed in fire. The fire discharges flame and hot gases into the corridor, causing a radiant heat exposure to the floor. It has been shown that the level of energy radiating onto the floor is a significant factor in determining whether or not progressive flaming will occur. NFPA 253, Standard Method of Test for Critical Radiant Flux of Floor Covering Systems Using a Radiant Heat Energy Source, measures the minimum energy required on the floor covering to sustain flame, measured in W/cm^2. This minimum value is termed the critical radiant flux. The Flooring Radiant Panel Test, therefore, measures a floor covering's tendency to spread flames where located in a corridor and exposed to the flame and hot gases from a room fire.

In summary, the Flooring Radiant Panel Test is to be used as a basis for estimating the fire performance of a floor covering installed in a building corridor or exit. Floor coverings in open building spaces and in rooms within buildings merit no further regulation, provided the floor covering is at least as resistant to flame spread as material that meets the Federal Flammability Standard FF1-70 Pill Test.

DECORATIONS, CONTENTS, AND FURNISHINGS

According to both the IBC and the LSC, draperies, curtains, and other loosely hanging decorations must be tested according to NFPA 701. The IBC does not regulate furnishings. The LSC includes requirements for flame ratings of draperies, curtains, and other furnishings at LSC 10.3, Contents and Furnishings. This section contains a menu of potential requirements that are applied according to the various requirements of each occupancy chapter (LSC 11–40). In required occupancies, upholstered furniture and mattresses must pass NFPA 260, 261, 266, ASTM E 1537 and FAR 1632 to ensure resistance to flame ignition and spread. In required occupancies, furnishings with foam plastics must meet UL 1925. A complete list of NFPA referenced documents is included in Appendix B. A narrative on furniture testing from the 1997 LSC Commentary follows:

NFPA 260 tests individual components of upholstered furniture such as cover fabric, interior fabric, welt cord, filling-padding decking materials, and barrier materials. Specimens of the component to be tested are assembled with specimens of standardized materials to create a miniature horizontal base panel and vertical panel tester, a mocked-up arrangement that simulates the junction and surrounding area of a seat cushion and back cushion in a piece of upholstered furniture. Standardizing all the components of the mocked-up tester except the component being tested allows the test to measure the ignition resistance of that component. Components that meet the test criteria are designated as Class I materials. Components that do not meet the test criteria are designated as Class II materials. Upholstered furniture constructed from components that individually received a Class I designation is judged to be resistant to cigarette ignition without the need to test the actual combination of materials. Cigarette ignition-resistant upholstered furniture can also be constructed using Class II cover fabric materials over conventional polyurethane foam cushions, if a Class I barrier material is used between the Class II fabric and the conventional foam cushion.

NFPA 261 tests a mocked-up assembly consisting of all the actual components that will be used to construct the piece of upholstered furniture, rather than testing the components individually. The test procedure specifies that a char length be measured and reported. There are no pass/fail criteria within the document, so 6-6.2(b) specifies that the char length not exceed 1.5 in. (3.8 cm) if the mocked-up assembly is to be considered resistant to cigarette ignition.

NFPA 260 and 261 address the cigarette ignition resistance of upholstered furniture; 16 CFR 1632 addresses cigarette ignition resistance of mattresses. For this test method, 6-6.2(c) establishes that a char length of 2 in. (5.1 cm) qualifies the mattress as resistant to cigarette ignition.

REFERENCES

1. NFPA. 1997 Edition. *NFPA 101 Life Safety Code Commentary,* National Fire Protection Association. Quincy, MA

2. IBC 2000 Edition. International Building Code, International Code Council, Falls Church, VA

3. SBCCI. 1997. Edition. *An Illustrated Commentary to the 1997 Standard Building Code*, Southern Building Code Congress International, Inc. Birmingham, AL

4. BOCA/NBC. 1997 Edition. BOCA National Building Code, Building Officials and Code Administrators International, Country Club Hill, IL

5. UBC. 1997 Edition. Uniform Building Code, International Conference of Building Officials, Whittier, CA

CHAPTER 10
OTHER ISSUES

INTERIOR ENVIRONMENT

In Chapter 12, *Interior Environment*, the 2000 International Building Code at contains minimum requirements for ventilation, temperature, lighting, interior dimensions, and sound transmission in dwelling units. These requirements apply to the interior spaces of buildings.

VENTILATION

The 2000 IBC at 1202.1 requires that buildings be provided with natural ventilation according to Section 1202.4, or be mechanically ventilated according to the International Mechanical Code (IMC). Most buildings are mechanically ventilated, but the code does establish minimum standards for natural ventilation. Openings to the outside totaling not less than 4 percent of the floor area served must be provided. Interior rooms may be ventilated through adjoining exterior rooms, through unobstructed openings totaling not less than 8 percent of the floor area served and not less than 25 square ft in any case [9].

CONTAMINANTS MECHANICALLY REMOVED

Contaminant sources in naturally ventilated buildings must be removed mechanically according to the IMC. Although *contaminant* source is not defined in the IBC, it can be construed to mean cooking fumes and toilet gases. Rooms with bathtubs, showers, spas, and similar bathing fixtures are specifically required to be mechanically ventilated. Mechanical ventilation also is required for other occupancies and operations that produce contaminant sources [9].

TEMPERATURE CONTROL

Interior spaces intended for human occupancy must be provided with space-heating systems to maintain a minimum temperature of 68°F (20°C) measured at 3 ft above the floor. An exception is provided for spaces not associated with human comfort [9].

NATURAL LIGHTING

Every space intended for human occupancy must be provided with natural or artificial lighting. Natural lighting is accomplished with glazed openings to the outside totaling not less than 8 percent of the floor area served. An adjacent interior room may be lighted naturally where one-half of the dividing wall is open and unobstructed, and provides an opening equal to at least 10 percent of the floor area served and not less than 25 square feet in any case [9].

ARTIFICIAL LIGHTING

Illumination, measured in footcandles (fc), is measured easily with hand-held instruments. Artificial lighting must provide an average of 10 fc measured at 30 in. off the floor in rooms intended for human occupancy. By way of reference, a typical office might require 50 fc and a drafting room 100 fc. Interior stairways must have 10 fc, measured at *each* tread nosing. Accomplishing this requires careful planning of stairway lighting, especially the consideration of minimum height, width, and restrictions on protruding objects in the means of egress [9].

SOUND TRANSMISSION

The requirements for sound transmission at IBC Section 1206 apply to common interior walls, partitions, and to floor/ceiling assemblies between dwelling units, as well as between dwelling units and service or common spaces. These assemblies are required to have an airborne sound transmission class (STC) of 50 (45 when field tested) in accordance with ASTM E 90 and an impact insulation class (IIC) of 50 (45 when field tested) in accordance with ASTM E 492. These values ensure that a minimum amount of sound transmission insulation will be present in dwelling units larger than two-family dwellings.

INTERIOR SPACE DIMENSIONS

Habitable spaces, other than kitchens, must not be less than 7 ft in any plan dimension. According to the IBC, habitable space is a space in a building for living, sleeping, eating, or cooking. Bathrooms, toilet rooms, closets, halls, storage or utility spaces, and similar areas are not considered habitable spaces.

Kitchens are required to have a minimum clear passageway at appliances and counter fronts of 3 ft.

Ceilings in "occupiable spaces, habitable spaces, and corridors" must have a minimum ceiling height of 7 ft, 6 in. The IBC considers occupiable space to be a room or enclosed space designed for human occupancy in which individuals congregate for amusement, education, or similar purposes, or in which occupants are engaged in labor.

This provision seems to contradict or supersede the requirement found at IBC 1003.2.4, which allows a minimum ceiling height in a means of egress of 7 ft. Since means of egress also includes "occupiable spaces, habitable spaces, and corridors," the minimum of 7 ft, 6 in. must be observed in almost every space. Bathrooms, toilet rooms, kitchens, storage rooms, and laundry rooms, however, are expressly allowed to have a ceiling height of 7 ft.

Rooms with furred ceilings must have the minimum ceiling height in two-thirds of the area, and must not be lower than 7 ft in any area. Sloped ceilings must maintain the minimum height in at least one-half of the room area, and any area with a ceiling of less than 5 ft cannot count in the room area or dimension calculations. The diagram in Figure 10.1 shows a room with a sloped ceiling, and how to calculate the room areas.

EFFICIENCY DWELLING UNITS

IBC Section 1207.4 contains minimum space requirements for efficiency dwelling units. The living room must be at least 220 square feet for two occupants, plus 100 square ft for each additional occupant. A separate bathroom and closet must be provided. A kitchen must provide, at minimum, a sink, cooking appliance, and refrigerator, all with at least 30 in. clear in front.

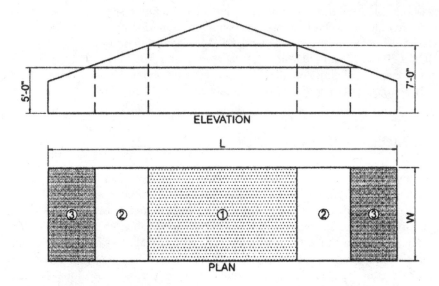

FIGURE 10.1 Ceiling height and room area calculations. *(Source: SBCCI, Standard Building Code Commentary, 1997)*

ACCESS TO UNOCCUPIED SPACES

Crawl spaces, attics, mechanical rooms, and similar unoccupied spaces must have access provided according to minimum sizes and use. Crawl spaces must have an 18 in. by 24 in. access opening, attics must have a 20 in. by 30 in. access opening and 30 in. headroom above the access opening. Access to mechanical equipment is specified in the International Mechanical Code (IMC) and International Residential Code (IRC). These codes typically require working access to all operating and replaceable parts of heating and ventilating equipment and other built-in equipment that will require service or replacement.

SURROUNDING MATERIALS

Walls within 2 ft of water closets and urinals must be smooth, hard, nonabsorbent, and resistant to moisture damage to a height of 4 ft above the floor. A return wall or toilet compartment, if within 2 ft of a toilet, also must meet this requirement. Floors in toilet and bathing rooms also must meet these requirements and have a similar base material at least 6 in. high. Extreme caution is advised in the selection of floor finishes in wet areas. Materials with manufacturer-certified slip-resistant surfaces are advisable. The intent of the code in this instance is to prevent structural damage due to prolonged exposure to water from plumbing fixtures. (Please refer to the discussion on floor finish slip resistance in Chapter 7.) While we are not aware of published standards relating directly to slip-resistance in wet-floor building areas, it is best to use a material with as high a wet coefficient-of-friction as possible, that is, 0.80 or 0.90. This can be achieved with certain tile, terrazzo, concrete, or poured epoxy floors.

MATERIALS—CONCRETE

The 2000 IBC contains detailed provisions for structural concrete in Chapter 19, which specifically references requirements contained in the American Concrete Institute ACI 318, as amended in the code. ACI 318 is a detailed specification for the design and construction of reinforced concrete that has been written for adoption as a building code [1].

SLABS ON GRADE

Concrete slabs-on-grade that do not transmit vertical or lateral (structural) loads from other parts of the building are exempt from the requirements of IBC Chapter 19, except for the requirements of Section 1904 and Section 1911. Durability Requirements, Section 1904, specifies the water-cement ratio and admixture proportions for exterior concrete subject to weathering and does not typically apply to interior concrete work. Section 1911, Minimum Slab Provisions, requires a minimum floor-slab thickness of 3.5 in. and 6 mil vapor barrier in heated spaces. No minimum reinforcing is required for slabs-on-grade when no forces are transmitted from other parts of the structure, since floor loads are transmitted directly to the sub-grade soils supporting the slab. Wire reinforcing or fiber reinforcing may be used to control shrinkage-cracking during concrete setting, but are not sufficient to span weaknesses in the sub-grade. Adequate support of an unreinforced slab-on-grade depends on a well-compacted subgrade.

REINFORCED GYPSUM CONCRETE

IBC Section 1915 addresses reinforced gypsum concrete, which is often used as part of an interior floor system. The reinforced gypsum concrete material is required to comply with ASTM C 317 and ASTM C 956. Minimum thickness is 2 in.; thickness of 1.5 in. is allowed when the following conditions are met:

1. The overall thickness, including the formboard, is not less than 2 in.

2. The clear span of the gypsum concrete between supports does not exceed 33 in.

3. Diaphragm action is not required.

4. The design live load does not exceed 40 lb/ft^2.

MASONRY MATERIALS

IBC Chapter 21 covers requirements for "materials, design, construction, and quality" of all masonry-type materials, including adobe, concrete block and brick, structural clay tile, brick, stone, glass block, ceramic tile, terra cotta, and mortar. Most of IBC Chapter 21 pertains to the structural design of masonry construction, seismic design, weatherproofing for exterior walls, fireplaces, and other issues beyond the scope of this book. This text includes specifications and construction requirements for masonry-type materials typically encountered in the design and construction of interiors—concrete block, brick, glass block, and tile.

MASONRY CONSTRUCTION—GENERAL

Most of the building code requirements for masonry construction relate to temperature limitations and protection of work for exterior conditions infrequently encountered in interior construction. Since masonry mortar must have water for hydration during and after construction, conditions that prevent freezing or removal of the water must be maintained. Special procedures are specified for cold weather (below 40°F) and for hot weather (above 100°F or 90°F with an 8 mph wind) at IBC 2104.3 and 2103.4.

Hollow unit masonry corbelling cannot exceed one-half the wall thickness. Solid unit masonry corbelling cannot exceed one-half the unit height nor one-third the thickness for solid units. Brick that has a high rate of absorption (more than 30 g per 30 in^2 per minute), must be wetted when laid to prevent the brick from removing the moisture from the mortar. Brick manufacturers usually are aware of brick that requires wetting and can advise about this when brick selection is made. For the same reason, concrete block may require wetting before construction and, when exposed to hot weather (as described above), must be wetted three times daily for three days after laying. Some of these requirements may apply occasionally to interior construction.

CONCRETE BLOCK

Concrete block can be made with various aggregates with varying weight, insulation value, and fire resistance properties. A table from the IBC regarding calculated fire resistance of concrete block is included in Chapter 6, *Fire Resistance Rated Construction*. All load-bearing concrete block is required to meet ASTM C 90 or ASTM C 477 for prefaced units. No requirement is specified for non-load-bearing block, but it is advisable to use either one of the recognized standards described above, even in non-load-bearing construction. Concrete block is manufactured in many different shapes and sizes and most are based on a nominal dimension of 8 in. horizontal or vertical. Blocks usually are manufactured with an allowance for a ⅜ in. thick mortar joint. Some typical concrete block shapes are shown in Figure 10.2 on the following pages.

Construction of concrete block must meet the requirements specified in ACI 530/ASCE 6/TMS 602. This is a detailed specification for construction of concrete masonry written jointly by the American Concrete Institute [2], the American Society of Civil Engineers, and The Masonry Society. The height or thickness of an unreinforced interior concrete block wall can be up to 36 times the thickness, as shown in Figure 10.3. Using this table from IBC Section 2109,

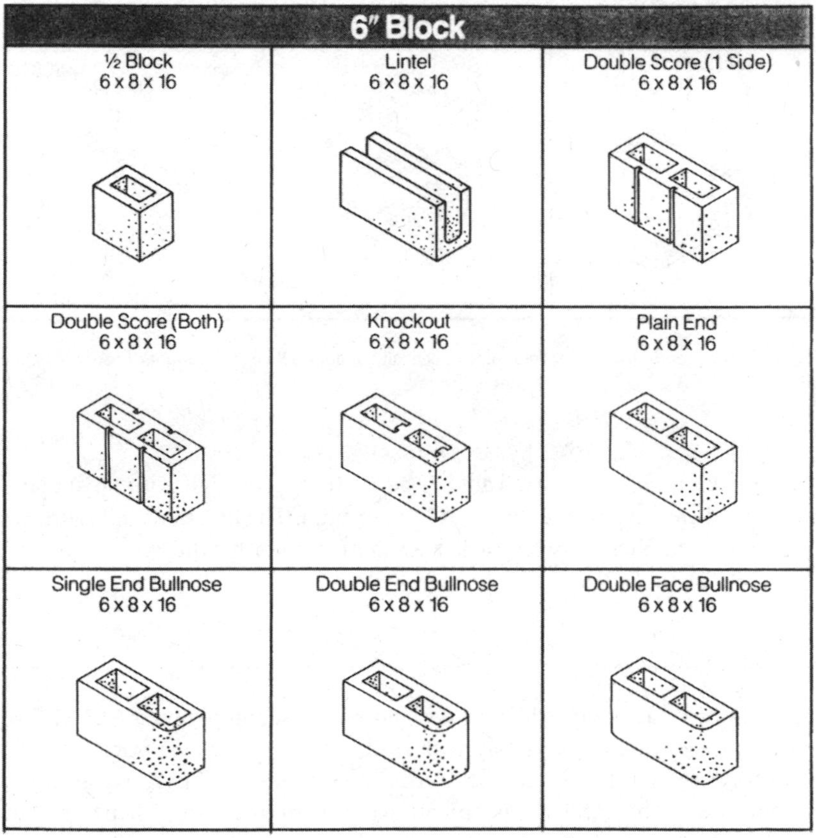

FIGURE 10.2 Concrete block sizes and shapes. *(Source: Alabama Masonry Institute, a division of ACIA)*

4″ Block		
Regular 4 x 8 x 16	½ Block 4 x 8 x 16	Lintel 4 x 8 x 16
Split Face 4 x 8 x 16	Split Face (4 Rib) 4 x 8 x 16	Split Face (8 Rib) 4 x 8 x 16
Split Face Solid 4 x 4 x 16	Split Face Solid 4 x 8 x 16	Split Face Return Corner 4 x 8 x 12

FIGURE 10.2 *(continued)*   Concrete block sizes and shapes. *(Source: Alabama Masonry Institute, a division of ACIA)*

a 6 in. thick interior masonry wall can be 18 ft long or high with no support or bracing, and an 8 in. wall can be 24 ft long or high. The diagrams in Figure 10.3a illustrate how to measure wall thickness, and length or height.

BRICK

Typical hollow-face brick (the type with holes) must comply with ASTM C 652. Solid common brick must comply with ASTM C 62; solid face brick must comply with ASTM C 216. Other brick types seldom are produced, except for special purposes. The ASTM specifications govern the size, shape, material,

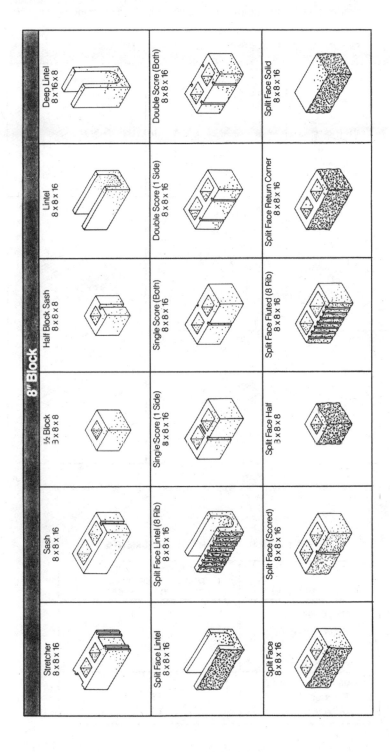

8" Block

Stretcher 8 x 8 x 16	Sash 8 x 8 x 16	½ Block 3 x 8 x 8	Half Block Sash 8 x 8 x 8	Lintel 8 x 8 x 16	Deep Lintel 8 x 16 x 8
Split Face Lintel 8 x 8 x 16	Split Face Lintel (8 Rib) 8 x 8 x 16	Single Score (1 Side) 8 x 8 x 16	Single Score (Both) 8 x 8 x 16	Double Score (1 Side) 8 x 8 x 16	Double Score (Both) 8 x 8 x 16
Split Face 8 x 8 x 16	Split Face (Scored) 8 x 8 x 16	Split Face Half 3 x 8 x 8	Split Face Fluted (8 Rib) 8 x 8 x 16	Split Face Return Corner 8 x 8 x 16	Split Face Solid 8 x 8 x 16

FIGURE 10.2 (*continued*)   Concrete block sizes and shapes. (*Source: Alabama Masonry Institute, a division of ACIA*)

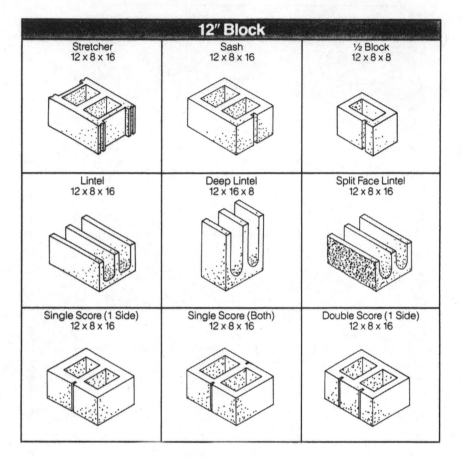

FIGURE 10.2 *(continued)*   Concrete block sizes and shapes. *(Source: Alabama Masonry Institute, a division of ACIA)*

WALL LATERAL SUPPORT REQUIREMENTS

CONSTRUCTION	MAXIMUM WALL LENGTH TO THICKNESS OR WALL HEIGHT TO THICKNESS
Bearing walls	
Solid units or fully grouted	20
All others	18
Nonbearing walls	
Exterior	18
Interior	36

FIGURE 10.3   IBC Table 2109.4.1 Masonry wall lateral support requirements. *(Source: ICC, International Building Code, 2000)*

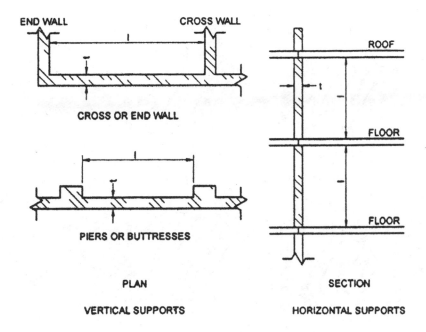

FIGURE 10.3a Masonry wall lateral support conditions. *(Source: SBCCI, Standard Building Code Commentary, 1997)*

manufacture, compressive strength, and other critical aspects of brick These standards have been accepted in the industry and referred to by building codes for many years. Brick masonry walls may be unreinforced and unbraced according to the values derived from Figure 10.3. Some of the most popular brick shapes are shown in Figure 10.4. Modular brick is the most commonly used; these units are made with an allowance for mortar joints so that three courses is exactly 8 in. high.

MASONRY MORTAR

Masonry mortar is made from portland cement blended with aggregate (sand), lime, and water. Lime gives mortar more workability and moisture retention than concrete alone, making it suitable for shaping and furrowing. The IBC at 2103.7 requires all masonry mortar to comply with ASTM C 270, and be proportioned according to Figure 10.5. Mortar types are specified M, N, S, or O, with O the type that gets the most severe exposure and M the type that gets the least severe exposure. Interior non-load-bearing construction may be Type M, which is the most workable. Mortar often becomes stiff after mixing and not being used expeditiously. It may be retempered by adding water. The code allows retempering, but requires mortar that is not used within $2\frac{1}{2}$ hours to be discarded.

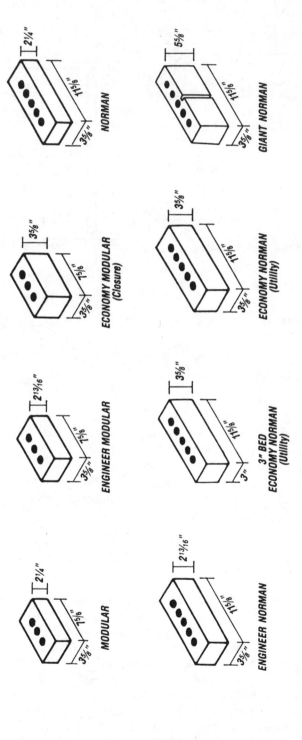

FIGURE 10.4 Brick sizes and shapes. (*Source: Endicott Clay Products Company*)

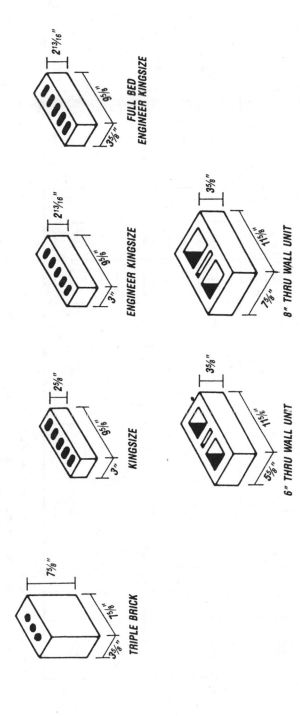

FIGURE 10.4 (*continued*)   Brick sizes and shapes. (*Source: Endicatt Clay Products Company*)

10.13

MORTAR PROPORTIONS

MORTAR	TYPE	Portland cement or blended cement[b]	Masonry cement[c] M	S	N	Mortar cement[d] M	S	N	HYDRATED LIME OR LIME PUTTY	AGGREGATE MEASURED IN A DAMP, LOOSE CONDITION
Cement-lime	M	1	—	—	—	—	—	—	1/4	Not less than 2 1/4 and not more than 3 times the sum of the separate volumes of cementitious materials
	S	1	—	—	—	—	—	—	over 1/4 to 1/2	
	N	1	—	—	—	—	—	—	over 1/2 to 1 1/4	
	O	1	—	—	—	—	—	—	over 1 1/4 to 2 1/2	
Mortar cement	M	1	—	—	—	—	—	1	—	
	M	—	—	—	—	1	—	—	—	
	S	1/2	—	—	—	—	—	1	—	
	S	—	—	—	—	—	1	—	—	
	N	—	—	—	—	—	—	1	—	
	O	—	—	—	—	—	—	1	—	
Masonry cement	M	1	—	—	1	—	—	—	—	
	M	—	1	—	—	—	—	—	—	
	S	1/2	—	—	1	—	—	—	—	
	S	—	—	1	—	—	—	—	—	
	N	—	—	—	1	—	—	—	—	
	O	—	—	—	1	—	—	—	—	

a. Portland cement conforming to the requirements of ASTM C 150.
b. Blended cement conforming to the requirements of ASTM C 595.
c. Masonry cement conforming to the requirements of ASTM C 91.
d. Mortar cement conforming to the requirements of ASTM C 1329.

FIGURE 10.5 Table 2103.7(1) Mortar proportions. *(Source: ICC, International Building Code, 2000)*

GLASS BLOCK

Glass block, when hollow units are used, must have a minimum face shell thickness of $\frac{3}{16}$ in. Glass block surfaces in contact with mortar must be coated with latex paint or polyvinyl butyral. Reclaimed glass block units may be used. The IBC at 2103.7 contains detailed requirements for glass block mortar. Type S or N mortar is required, adjusted for lower water. Glass block mortar may not be retempered, and must be discarded within 1½ hours if not used. A higher quality mortar is required for glass block since there is lower bond (adhesion) between the mortar and the masonry units than in other types of unit masonry. Glass block units are made with an allowance for ¼ in. thick mortar joints, and may come in 6, 8, or 12 in. modular sizes. Glass block is available with fire ratings of up to 90 minutes in certain applications, as shown in Figure 10.6. Glass block is sometimes used in stairs and walkways, and is also available in prefabricated wall and window panels.

CERAMIC TILE

Ceramic tile includes all types of hard manufactured tile. The IBC requires ceramic tile materials to comply with the American National Standards Institute ANSI A 137.1. Mortar for ceramic tile must comply with ANSI A 108 and be of the composition shown in Figure 10.7. ANSI A 108 contains detailed specifications for many types of mortar and grout materials for use with tile, and for all kinds of tile installations. The 2000 IBC at 2103.9.1–8 references each type of ceramic tile setting material and a corresponding ANSI specification for each type—dry-set, electrically conductive dry-set, latex-modified portland cement, epoxy, furan (chemical resistant), modified epoxy emulsion, organic adhesive, and portland cement. The number of types of mortar and grout materials for tile is indicative of the amount of technology developed in the tile industry. A comprehensive manual with all of the ANSI standards for tile installation is available from The Tile Council of America [3]

STEEL CONSTRUCTION

The design, fabrication, and construction of structural (hot-rolled) steel is required by the IBC at 2204.1 to comply with the American Institute of Steel Construction (AISC) manuals [4]. The AISC manuals contain tables with the sizes and structural properties of steel shapes made by members of the AISC, connection details, and structural design methods used for sizing structural steel members. Light-gage metal studs are the most commonly encountered steel materials in the design and construction of interiors. Metal studs are referred to in the building code as cold-

Premiere Series Glass Block Products Fire Ratings

Pattern	Size[1] Nominal/ Actual (mm)	Weight (lbs/kg)		■ 45 Min ▲ 60 Min ● 90 Min	Masonry Wall Construction		Non-Masonry Wall Construction		Channel Framing/ Panel Anchor Framing
					Max Area /Panel (ft²)	Max Ht or Width (ft)	Max Area /Panel (ft²)	Max Ht or Width (ft)	
Standard *Premiere Series* Block (4 3⅞ 98mm thick)									
ARGUS®	6"x 6"/5¾" (146mm)	3.5/1.57		■	120	12	94	10.75	■
	8"x 8"/7¾" (197mm)	6/2.72		■	120	12	94	10.75	■
	12"x 12"/11¾" (299mm)	15.3/6.93							
ARGUS® Parallel Fluted	8"x 8"/7¾" (197mm)	6/2.72		■	120	12	94	10.75	■
DECORA®	6"x 6"/5¾" (146mm)	3.5/1.57		■	120	12	94	10.75	■
	8"x 8"/7¾" (197mm)	6/2.72		■	120	12	94	10.75	■
	12"x 12"/11¾" (299mm)	15.3/6.93							
	4"x 8"/3¾"x 7¾" (95 x 197mm)	3.5/1.59		■	120	12	94	10.75	■
	6"x 8"/5¾"x 7¾" (146 x 197mm)	4.5/2.03		■	120	12	94	10.75	■
ESSEX® AA	8"x 8"/7¾" (197mm)	6/2.72		■	120	12	94	10.75	■
IceScapes™	8"x 8"/7¾" (197mm)	6/2.72							
SPYRA®	8"x 8"/7¾" (197mm)	6/2.72		■	120	12	94	10.75	■
VUE®	6"x 6"/5¾" (146mm)	3.5/1.57		■	120	12	94	10.75	■
	8"x 8"/7¾" (197mm)	6/2.72		■	120	12	94	10.75	■
	12"x 12"/11¾" (299mm)	15.3/6.93							
	4"x 8"/3¾"x 7¾" (95 x 197mm)	3.5/1.59		■	120	12	94	10.75	■
	6"x 8"/5¾"x 7¾" (146 x 197mm)	4.5/2.03		■	120	12	94	10.75	■
DECORA® "LX" Filter	6"x 6"/5¾" (146mm)	3.5/1.57		■	120	12	94	10.75	■
	8"x 8"/7¾" (197mm)	6/2.72		■	120	12	94	10.75	■
	12"x 12"/11¾" (299mm)	15.3/6.93							
	4"x 8"/3¾"x 7¾" (95 x 197mm)	3.5/1.59		■	120	12	94	10.75	■
	6"x 8"/5¾"x 7¾" (146 x 197mm)	4.5/2.03		■	120	12	94	10.75	■
THICKSET Block (4 3⅞ 98mm thick)									
THICKSET® Block — DECORA® & VUE®	6"x 6"/5¾" (146mm)	5.75/2.60		■ ▲ ●	100	10	94 ■ ▲	10.75	■ ▲ ●[8]
	8"x 8"/7¾" (197mm)	10/4.56		■ ▲ ●	100	10	94 ■ ▲	10.75	■ ▲ ●[8]
ENDURA™	8"x 8"/7¾" (197mm)	10/4.56		■ ▲ ●	100	10	94 ■ ▲	10.76	■ ▲ ●[8]
VISTABRIK Solid Glass Block (3 76mm thick 1½ 38mm thick)									
VISTABRIK® Solid Glass Block	8"x 8"x 3"/7⅝", 3" (194mm, 76mm)	15/6.80		■ ▲ ●	100	10	94 ■ ▲	10.75	■ ▲ ●[8]
	3"x 8"x 3"/3"x 7⅝"x 3" (194 x 76, 76mm)	6/2.72		■ ▲ ●	100	10	94 ■ ▲	10.75	■ ▲ ●[8]
	8"x 8"x 1½"/7⅝", 1½" (194mm, 38mm)	7.5/3.4							
STIPPLE Finish	8"x 8"x 3"/7⅝", 3" (194mm, 76mm)	15/6.80		■ ▲ ●	100	10	94 ■ ▲	10.75	■ ▲ ●[8]
Thinline Series Block (3 3⅛ 79mm thick)									
DECORA®	8"x 8"/7¾" (197mm)	5/2.27		■	120	12	94	10.75	■
	6"x 8"/5¾"x 7¾" (146 x 197mm)	4.1/1.86		■	120	12	94	10.75	■
MISTIQUE®	8"x 8"/7¾" (197mm)	5/2.27		■	120	12	94	10.75	■
	6"x 8"/5¾"x 7¾" (146 x 197mm)	4.1/1.86		■	120	12	94	10.75	■

FIGURE 10.6 Glass block fire resistance chart. *(Source: Pittsburgh Corning Corporation)*

CERAMIC TILE MORTAR COMPOSITIONS

LOCATION	MORTAR	COMPOSITION
Walls	Scratchcoat	1 cement; $1/5$ hydrated lime; 4 dry or 5 damp sand
	Setting bed and leveling coat	1 cement; $1/2$ hydrated lime; 5 damp sand to 1 cement 1 hydrated lime, 7 damp sand
Floors	Setting bed	1 cement; $1/10$ hydrated lime 5 dry or 6 damp sand; or 1 cement; 5 dry or 6 damp sand
Ceilings	Scratchcoat and sand bed	1 cement; $1/2$ hydrated lime; $2 1/2$ dry sand or 3 damp sand

FIGURE 10.7   IBC Table 2103.9 ceramic tile mortar compositions. *(Source: ICC, International Building Code, 2000)*

formed metal framing. The cold-formed steel industry association is the American Iron and Steel Institute, which publishes the SG-671 [5], Specification for Design of Cold-Formed Steel Members, referenced by the IBC at 2205. The specification used for non-load-bearing metal studs with gypsum board is ASTM C 645.

Even interior metal framing is subject to lateral forces from doors, built-in shelving, and wall-mounted cabinets. The strength of a metal stud wall is derived from the number of studs in the same plane and, to a great extent, from the coverings on each side (such as gypsum board). An individual 25-gage stud, the type typically used for interiors, has very little strength by itself. Metal stud manufacturers typically provide guidelines for the size and thickness of metal studs in various interior applications, normally in combination with gypsum board. Some details for light gage walls and doorframes are shown in Figure 10.8.

LIGHT FRAME WOOD CONSTRUCTION

The 2000 IBC regulates wood construction for interiors and all other light-frame wood construction at Section 2304, General Construction Requirements, and Section 2308, Conventional Light Frame Construction. Most of Section 2308 covers wood framing, sheathing, fastening, weather, and termite proofing for exterior structural walls and roofs, but also it contains requirements for interior wood-stud walls and floors. Detailed tables at IBC 2304.7 limit allowable spans for wood floor-sheathing of all types, included as Appendix M. The IBC contains span tables for floor joists, ceiling joists, and rafters of common wood species at Sections 2308.8 and 2808.10. Part of these span tables are shown in Figure 10.8a; the complete tables are given in Appendix O.

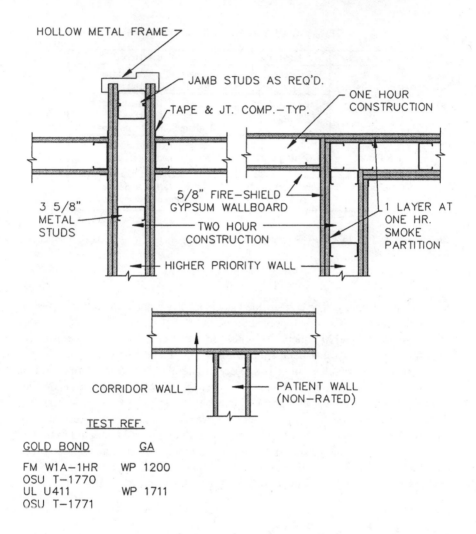

FIGURE 10.8   Gypsum and metal stud construction details. *(Source: National Gypsum Company, Architect and Technical Manual)*

Span tables for wood joists and rafters under many more loading and service conditions are available from the American Wood Council [6] and from regional industry organizations including: the Southern Forest Products Association [7], the Western Wood Products Association, and the Canadian Wood Council. The span tables shown in Figure 10.9, provided by the Southern Pine Council, demonstrate the higher structural values of southern pine when compared to other wood species.

Framing around floor openings is specified at IBC 2308.8.3 and requires doubling of joist headers at openings larger than 4 ft. Headers for openings larger than 6 ft require metal. These concepts are illustrated in Figure 10.10.

JOIST SPACING (inches)	SPECIES AND GRADE		DEAD LOAD = 10 psf				DEAD LOAD = 20 psf			
			2x6	2x8	2x10	2x12	2x6	2x8	2x10	2x12
						Maximum floor joist spans				
			(ft. - in.)	(ft. - in.)	(ft. - in.)	(ft. - in.)	(ft. - in.)	(ft. - in.)	(ft. - in.)	(ft. - in.)
12	Douglas Fir-Larch	SS	11-4	15-0	19-1	23-3	11-4	15-0	19-1	23-3
	Douglas Fir-Larch	#1	10-11	14-5	18-5	22-0	10-11	14-2	17-4	20-1
	Douglas Fir-Larch	#2	10-9	14-2	17-9	20-7	10-6	13-3	16-3	18-10
	Douglas Fir-Larch	#3	8-8	11-0	13-5	15-7	7-11	10-0	12-3	14-3
	Hem-Fir	SS	10-9	14-2	18-0	21-11	10-9	14-2	18-0	21-11
	Hem-Fir	#1	10-6	13-10	17-8	21-6	10-6	13-10	16-11	19-7
	Hem-Fir	#2	10-0	13-2	16-10	20-4	10-0	13-1	16-0	18-6
	Hem-Fir	#3	8-8	11-0	13-5	15-7	7-11	10-0	12-3	14-3
	Southern Pine	SS	11-2	14-8	18-9	22-10	11-2	14-8	18-9	22-10
	Southern Pine	#1	10-11	14-5	18-5	22-5	10-11	14-5	18-5	22-5
	Southern Pine	#2	10-9	14-2	18-0	21-9	10-9	14-2	16-11	19-10
	Southern Pine	#3	9-4	11-11	14-0	16-8	8-6	10-10	12-10	15-3
	Spruce-Pine-Fir	SS	10-6	13-10	17-8	21-6	10-6	13-10	17-8	21-6
	Spruce-Pine-Fir	#1	10-3	13-6	17-3	20-7	10-3	13-3	16-3	18-10
	Spruce-Pine-Fir	#2	10-3	13-6	17-3	20-7	10-3	13-3	16-3	18-10
	Spruce-Pine-Fir	#3	8-8	11-0	13-5	15-7	7-11	10-0	12-3	14-3
16	Douglas Fir-Larch	SS	10-4	13-7	17-4	21-1	10-4	13-7	17-4	21-0
	Douglas Fir-Larch	#1	9-11	13-1	16-5	19-1	9-8	12-4	15-0	17-5
	Douglas Fir-Larch	#2	9-9	12-7	15-5	17-10	9-1	11-6	14-1	16-3
	Douglas Fir-Larch	#3	7-6	9-6	11-8	13-6	6-10	8-8	10-7	12-4
	Hem-Fir	SS	9-9	12-10	16-5	19-11	9-9	12-10	16-5	19-11
	Hem-Fir	#1	9-6	12-7	16-0	18-7	9-6	12-0	14-8	17-0
	Hem-Fir	#2	9-1	12-0	15-2	17-7	8-11	11-4	13-10	16-1
	Hem-Fir	#3	7-6	9-6	11-8	13-6	6-10	8-8	10-7	12-4
	Southern Pine	SS	10-2	13-4	17-0	20-9	10-2	13-4	17-0	20-9
	Southern Pine	#1	9-11	13-1	16-9	20-4	9-11	13-1	16-4	19-6
	Southern Pine	#2	9-9	12-10	16-1	18-10	9-6	12-4	14-8	17-2
	Southern Pine	#3	8-1	10-3	12-2	14-6	7-4	9-5	11-1	13-2
	Spruce-Pine-Fir	SS	9-6	12-7	16-0	19-6	9-6	12-7	16-0	19-6
	Spruce-Pine-Fir	#1	9-4	12-3	15-5	17-10	9-1	11-6	14-1	16-3
	Spruce-Pine-Fir	#2	9-4	12-3	15-5	17-10	9-1	11-6	14-1	16-3
	Spruce-Pine-Fir	#3	7-6	9-6	11-8	13-6	6-10	8-8	10-7	12-4

FIGURE 10.8a IBC Table 2308.8(2) Floor joist spans for common lumber species. (*Source: ICC, International Building Code, 2000*)

FLOOR JOIST SPANS FOR COMMON LUMBER SPECIES (Residential Living Areas, Live Load = 40 psf, L/Δ = 360)

Spacing	Species	Grade								
19.2	Douglas Fir-Larch	SS	9-8	12-10	16-4	19-10	9-8	12-10	16-4	19-2
	Douglas Fir-Larch	#1	9-4	12-4	15-0	17-5	8-10	11-3	13-8	15-11
	Douglas Fir-Larch	#2	9-1	11-6	14-1	16-3	8-3	10-6	12-10	14-10
	Douglas Fir-Larch	#3	6-10	8-8	10-7	12-4	6-3	7-11	9-8	11-3
	Hem-Fir	SS	9-2	12-1	15-5	18-9	9-2	12-1	15-5	18-9
	Hem-Fir	#1	9-0	11-10	14-8	17-0	8-8	10-11	13-4	15-6
	Hem-Fir	#2	8-7	11-3	13-10	16-1	8-2	10-4	12-8	14-8
	Hem-Fir	#3	6-10	8-8	10-7	12-4	6-3	7-11	9-8	11-3
	Southern Pine	SS	9-6	12-7	16-0	19-6	9-6	12-7	16-0	19-6
	Southern Pine	#1	9-4	12-4	15-9	19-2	9-4	12-4	14-11	17-9
	Southern Pine	#2	9-2	12-1	14-8	17-2	8-8	11-3	13-5	15-8
	Southern Pine	#3	7-4	9-5	11-1	13-2	6-9	8-7	10-1	12-1
	Spruce-Pine-Fir	SS	9-0	11-10	15-1	18-4	9-0	11-10	15-1	17-9
	Spruce-Pine-Fir	#1	8-9	11-6	14-1	16-3	8-3	10-6	12-10	14-10
	Spruce-Pine-Fir	#2	8-9	11-6	14-1	16-3	8-3	10-6	12-10	14-10
	Spruce-Pine-Fir	#3	6-10	8-8	10-7	12-4	6-3	7-11	9-8	11-3
24	Douglas Fir-Larch	SS	9-0	11-11	15-2	18-5	9-0	11-11	14-9	17-1
	Douglas Fir-Larch	#1	8-8	11-0	13-5	15-7	7-11	10-0	12-3	14-3
	Douglas Fir-Larch	#2	8-1	10-3	12-7	14-7	7-5	9-5	11-6	13-4
	Douglas Fir-Larch	#3	6-2	7-9	9-6	11-0	5-7	7-1	8-8	10-1
	Hem-Fir	SS	8-6	11-3	14-4	17-5	8-6	11-3	14-4	16-10a
	Hem-Fir	#1	8-4	10-9	13-1	15-2	7-9	9-9	11-11	13-10
	Hem-Fir	#2	7-11	10-2	12-5	14-4	7-4	9-3	11-4	13-1
	Hem-Fir	#3	6-2	7-9	9-6	11-0	5-7	7-1	8-8	10-1
	Southern Pine	SS	8-10	11-8	14-11	18-1	8-10	11-8	14-11	18-1
	Southern Pine	#1	8-8	11-5	14-7	17-5	8-8	11-3	13-4	15-11
	Southern Pine	#2	8-6	11-0	13-1	15-5	7-9	10-0	12-0	14-0
	Southern Pine	#3	6-7	8-5	9-11	11-10	6-0	7-8	9-1	10-9
	Spruce-Pine-Fir	SS	8-4	11-0	14-0	17-0	8-4	11-0	13-8	15-11
	Spruce-Pine-Fir	#1	8-1	10-3	12-7	14-7	7-5	9-5	11-6	13-4
	Spruce-Pine-Fir	#2	8-1	10-3	12-7	14-7	7-5	9-5	11-6	13-4
	Spruce-Pine-Fir	#3	6-2	7-9	9-6	11-0	5-7	7-1	8-8	10-1

Check sources for availability of lumber in lengths greater than 20 feet.

For SI: 1 inch = 25.4 mm, 1 foot = 304.8 mm, 1 pound per square foot = 47.8 N/m^2.

a. End bearing length shall be increased to 2 inches.

FIGURE 10.8a (continued)   IBC Table 2308.8(2) Floor joist spans for common lumber species.
(Source: ICC, International Building Code, 2000)

Species and Grade	40 psf live load, 10 psf dead load, ℓ/360				30 psf live load, 10 psf dead load, ℓ/360			
	2x10		2x12		2x10		2x12	
	16" o.c.	24" o.c.	16" o.c.	24" o.c.	16" o.c.	24" o.c.	16" o.c.	24" o.c.
SP No. 1	16'-9"	14'-7"	20'-4"	17'-5"	18'-5"	16'-1"	22'-5"	19'-6"
DFL No. 1	16'-5"	13'-5"	19'-1"	15'-7"	18'-5"	15'-0"	21'-4"	17'-5"
SP No. 2	16'-1"	13'-2"	18'-10"	15'-4"	18'-0"	14'-8"	21'-1"	17'-2"
HF No. 1	16'-0"	13'-1"	18'-7"	15'-2"	17'-8"	14'-8"	20'-10"	17'-0"
SPF Nos. 1 & 2	15'-4"	12'-7"	17'-10"	14'-7"	17'-2"	14'-0"	19'-11"	16'-3"
DFL No. 2	15'-4"	12'-7"	17'-10"	14'-7"	17'-2"	14'-0"	19'-11"	16'-3"
HF No. 2	15'-2"	12'-5"	17'-7"	14'-5"	16'-10"	13'-10"	19'-8"	16'-1"
SP No. 3	12'-2"	9'-11"	14'-5"	11'-10"	13'-7"	11'-1"	16'-2"	13'-2"
DFL No. 3	11'-8"	9'-6"	13'-6"	11'-0"	13'-0"	10'-8"	15'-1"	12'-4"
HF No. 3	11'-8"	9'-6"	13'-6"	11'-0"	13'-0"	10'-8"	15'-1"	12'-4"
SPF No. 3	11'-8"	9'-6"	13'-6"	11'-0"	13'-0"	10'-8"	15'-1"	12'-4"

Note: These spans were calculated using published design values and are for comparison purposes only. They include the repetitive member factor, C_r=1.15, but do not include composite action of adhesive and sheathing. Spans may be slightly different than other published spans due to rounding. SP=Southern Pine, DFL=Douglas Fir–Larch, HF=Hem–Fir, SPF=Spruce–Pine–Fir.

FIGURE 10.9 Maximum span comparisons for joists. (*Source: Southern Forest Products Association, Construction Guide: Southern Pine Joists & Rafters*)

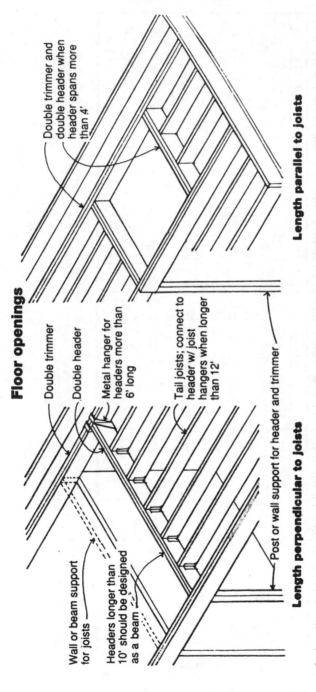

Floor openings

Double trimmer and double header when header spans more than 4'

Double trimmer

Double header

Metal hanger for headers more than 6' long

Tail joists; connect to header w/ joist hangers when longer than 12'

Wall or beam support for joists

Headers longer than 10' should be designed as a beam

Post or wall support for header and trimmer

Length parallel to joists

Length perpendicular to joists

Stairwell and chimney openings are also easily framed. The versatility of joist construction even allows some of these changes to be made when construction is in progress for maximum design flexibility.

FIGURE 10.10 Framing details for wood floor headers and beams. *(Source: Southern Forest Products Association, Construction Guide: Southern Pine Joists & Rafters)*

10.22

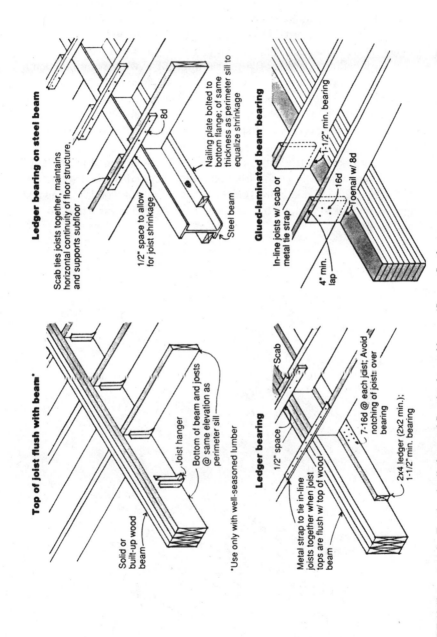

Ledger bearing on steel beam

Scab ties joists together, maintains horizontal continuity of floor structure, and supports subfloor

8d

1/2" space to allow for joist shrinkage

Nailing plate bolted to bottom flange; of same thickness as perimeter sill to equalize shrinkage

Steel beam

Glued-laminated beam bearing

In-line joists w/ scab or metal tie strap

1-1/2" min. bearing

16d

Toenail w/ 8d

4" min. lap

Top of joist flush with beam*

Joist hanger

Bottom of beam and joists @ same elevation as perimeter sill

Solid or built-up wood beam

*Use only with well-seasoned lumber

Ledger bearing

Scab

1/2" space

Metal strap to tie in-line joists together when joist tops are flush w/ top of wood beam

7-16d @ each joist; Avoid notching of joist over bearing

2x4 ledger (2x2 min.); 1-1/2" min. bearing

FIGURE 10.10 (*continued*) Framing details for wood floor headers and beams. (*Source: Southern Forest Products Association, Construction Guide: Southern Pine Joists & Rafters*)

Lateral support must be provided for floor or ceiling joists to prevent joist rotation under load. This is because the strength of a wood structure largely depends on a number of joists or studs in plane, with sheathing on one or both faces to hold the member in the structurally correct orientation. Lateral support is provided by holding one or both faces of the joist in line and by *bridging* or *blocking*. This is typically accomplished with sheathing at the top or the bottom of the joists with ceiling boards or floor sheathing. Joists with a nominal depth to thickness ratio of more than 1:5 (for example, a 2 × 10) must be supported on at least one side. Joists with a nominal depth to thickness ratio of more than 1:6 (for example, a 2 × 12) must be supported on one side and have one row of bridging or blocking for every 8 ft of span. Bridging and blocking are shown in Figure 10.11.

It is possible to attain fire ratings with wood construction. Figure 10.12 (pages 10.24-10.34) shows floor construction with described fire and sound ratings. IBC Section 720.6 regulates the fire resistance ratings of wood framing and sheathing. Please refer to Chapter 6, Fire Resistance Rated Construction, for the related discussion.

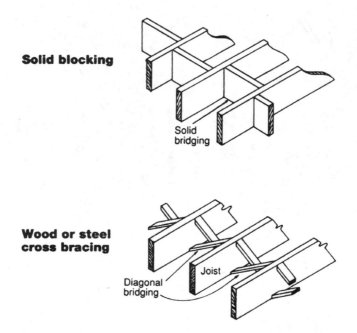

Solid blocking

Solid
bridging

**Wood or steel
cross bracing**

Joist

Diagonal
bridging

FIGURE 10.11   Wood joist lateral support. *(Source: Southern Forest Products Association, Construction Guide: Southern Pine Joists & Rafters)*

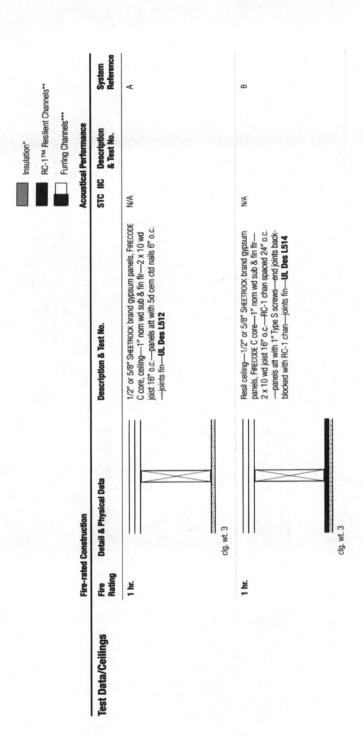

FIGURE 10.12 Fire and sound rated wood wood floor construction details. (*Source: United States Gypsum Company*)

	Fire-rated Construction			Acoustical Performance		
Fire Rating	**Detail & Physical Data**	**Description & Test No.**	**STC**	**IIC**	**Description & Test No.**	**System Reference**
1 hr.	12⅝" clg. wt. 3	Resil ceiling—5/8" SHEETROCK brand gypsum panels, FIRECODE C core—1-5/8" perlite-sand conc over 5/8" plywd sub-floor—2 x 10 wd joist 16" o.c.—RC-1 chan spaced 24" o.c.—panels att with 1" Type S screws—end joints back-blocked with RC-1 chan—joints fin—**UL Des L516**	59 47 65		Based on 3" THERMAFIBER SAFB, 3/4" gypsum concrete and 1/2" SHEETROCK brand gypsum panels, FIRECODE C core—**USG 740704** Based on 3" THERMAFIBER SAFB, vinyl tile atop flooring—**USG 740703** Based on 3" THERMAFIBER SAFB, 44 oz. carpet & 40 oz. pad atop flooring—**USG 740705**	C
1 hr. est	clg. wt. 3	Resil ceiling—1/2" or 5/8" SHEETROCK brand gypsum panels, FIRECODE core—1-1/4" nom wd sub & fin flr—2 x 10 wd joist 16" o.c.—RC-1 chan spaced 24" o.c.—panels att with 1" Type S screws—end joints back-blocked with RC-1 chan—joints fin—est. fire rating based on UL Des L514	47 47	39 37	Based on 1/2" SHEETROCK brand gypsum panels, FIRECODE C core—**CK-6512-6** Based on 5/8" SHEETROCK brand gypsum panels, FIRECODE core—**CK-6412-10**	D
1 hr. est		Resil ceiling—1/2" or 5/8" SHEETROCK brand gypsum panels, FIRECODE core—1-1/4" nom wd sub & fin flr—44 oz carpet & 40 oz pad atop flr—2 x 10 wd joist 16" o.c.—RC-1 chan spaced 24" o.c.—panels att with 1" Type S screws—end joints back-blocked with RC-1 chan—joints fin—est. fire rating based on UL Des L514	47 48	67 66	Based on 1/2" SHEETROCK brand gypsum panels, FIRECODE C core—**CK-6512-7** Based on 5/8" SHEETROCK brand gypsum panels, FIRECODE core—**CK-6412-9**	E

FIGURE 10.12 (*continued*) Fire and sound rated wood wood floor construction details. (*Source: United States Gypsum Company*)

Test Data/Ceilings

Fire-rated Construction

Fire Rating	Detail & Physical Data	Description & Test No.	STC	IIC	Description & Test No.	System Reference
					Acoustical Performance	
1 hr. est		Resil ceiling—1/2" or 5/8" SHEETROCK brand gypsum panels, FIRECODE core—1-1/4" nom wd sub & fin flr—2 x 10 wd joist 16" o.c.—3" THERMAFIBER SAFB betw joists—RC-1 chan spaced 24" o.c.—panels att with 1" Type S screws—end joints back-blocked with RC-1 chan—joints fin—est. fire rating based on UL Des L514	51	46	Based on 1/2" SHEET-ROCK brand gypsum panels, FIRECODE C core—**CK-6512-9**	F
			50	46	Based on 5/8" SHEETROCK brand gypsum panels, FIRECODE core—**CK-6412-3**	
1 hr. est	clg. wt. 3	Resil ceiling—1/2" or 5/8" SHEETROCK brand gypsum panels, FIRECODE core—1-1/4" nom wd sub & fin flr—44 oz carpet & 40 oz pad atop flr—2 x 10 wd joist 16" o.c.—3" THERMAFIBER SAFB betw joists—RC-1 chan spaced 24"o.c.—panels att with 1" Type S screws—end joints back-blocked with RC-1 chan—joints fin—est. fire rating based on UL Des L514	52	71	Based on 1/2" SHEETROCK brand gypsum panels, FIRECODE C core—**CK-6512-8**	G
			51	70	Based on 5/8" SHEETROCK brand gypsum panels, FIRECODE core—**CK-6412-4**	

FIGURE 10.12 (*continued*) Fire and sound rated wood wood floor construction details.
(*Source: United States Gypsum Company*)

10.27

Test Data/Ceilings

	Fire-rated Construction			Acoustical Performance			
	Fire Rating	Detail & Physical Data	Description & Test No.	STC	IIC	Description & Test No.	System Reference
	1 hr.	clg. wt. 3	5/8″ SHEETROCK brand gypsum panels, FIRECODE core, ceiling—single 4 x 10 or double 2 x 10 wd joist 48″ o.c.—met fur chan spaced 24″ o.c.—panels att with 1″ Type S screws—joints fin—**UL Des L508**	N/A			H
	1 hr.	clg. wt. 3	5/8″ SHEETROCK brand gypsum panels, FIRECODE core, 1″ nom wd sub & fin flr—2 x 10 wd joist 16″ o.c.—panels att with 6d nails 6″ o.c.—joints fin—**UL Des L501**	38	32	Based on 1-1/4″ nom wd flr —**CK-6412-7**	I
				39	56	Based on 1-1/4″ nom wd flr, 44 oz carpet & 40-oz pad atop flooring —**CK-6412-8**	

FIGURE 10.12 (*continued*)   Fire and sound rated wood wood floor construction details. (*Source: United States Gypsum Company*)

Test Data/Ceilings

	Fire-rated Construction			Acoustical Performance			
	Fire Rating	Detail & Physical Data	Description & Test No.	STC	IIC	Description & Test No.	System Reference
	1 hr. est	 clg. wt. 3	5/8″ SHEETROCK brand gypsum panels, FIRECODE core, ceiling—1″ nom wd sub & fin flr—2 x 10 wd joist 16″ o.c. —3″ THERMAFIBER SAFB betw joists—panels att with 6d nails 6″ o.c.—joints fin—est. fire rating based on UL Des L501	41 40	32 58	Based on 1-1/4″ nom wd flr—**CK-6412-6** Based on 1-1/4″ nom wd flr, 44 oz carpet 40 oz pad atop flooring —**CK-6412-5**	J
	1 hr.	 clg. wt. 3	1/2″ or 5/8″ SHEETROCK brand gypsum panels, FIRECODE C core, ceiling—1″ nom wd sub & fin flr—2 x 10 wd joist 16″ o.c.—susp grid with main run 48 o.c. and cross tees 24″ o.c.—panels screw-att below grid—joints fin— **UL Des L525**	N/A			K
	1 hr.	 clg. wt. 3	5/8″ SHEETROCK brand gypsum panels, FIRECODE C core, ceiling—2 x 12 wd truss of 2 x 4 lbr secured with steel truss plates—trusses 24″ o.c.—3/4″ nom plywd flr—met fur chan 24″ o.c.wire-tied to trusses—panels att with 1″ Type S screws 12″ o.c.—joints fin—**UL Des L528**	N/A			L

FIGURE 10.12 *(continued)* Fire and sound rated wood wood floor construction details. *(Source: United States Gypsum Company)*

| Test Data/Ceilings | Fire-rated Construction | | | Acoustical Performance | | | |
	Fire Rating	Detail & Physical Data	Description & Test No.	STC	IIC	Description & Test No.	System Reference
	1 hr.	20⅛" clg. wt. 3	5/8" SHEETROCK brand gypsum panels, FIRECODE C core, ceiling—2 x 12 wd truss of 2 x 4 lbr secured with steel truss plates—trusses 24" o.c.—3/4" nom plywd flr— susp grid with main run 48" o.c.and cross tees 24" o.c.— panels att with 1" Type S-12 screws12" o.c.—joints fin— **UL Des L529**	N/A			M
	1½ hr. and 2 hr.	13½" clg. wt. 4/5	Resil ceiling—1-1/2 hr. sys with 2 layers 1/2" SHEETROCK brand gypsum panels, FIRECODE C core— 1" nom wd sub & fin flr—2 x 10 wd joist 16" o.c.— RC-1 chan spaced 24" o.c. screw-att over base layer panels—face layer screw att to chan 12" o.c.— joints fin—**UL Des L510**—2 hr. sys. with 5/8" SHEETROCK brand gypsum panels, FIRECODE C core— **UL Des L511**	N/A		Assembly not recommended when sound control is a major consideration	N

FIGURE 10.12 *(continued)* Fire and sound rated wood wood floor construction details. *(Source: United States Gypsum Company)*

Test Data/Ceilings

	Fire-rated Construction			Acoustical Performance			
	Fire Rating	**Detail & Physical Data**	**Description & Test No.**	**STC**	**IIC**	**Description & Test No.**	**System Reference**
	2 hr.	13¼"	Floor/ceiling—floor of 8" x 8" ceramic tile, 1/2" DUROCK exterior cement board, 1" SHEETROCK brand gypsum liner panels, 1/2" plywood—2 x 10 wd joist 16" o.c.—3" THERMAFIBER SAFB—ceiling of 2 layers 5/8" SHEETROCK brand gypsum panels, FIRECODE C core, over RC-1 chan 16" o.c.—**UL Des L541**	60	52	**RAL-TL89-141** (54 MTC)— **RAL-IN89-5**	0
				58	51	Based on vinyl tile over oriented strand board in place of ceramic tile and cement board —**RAL-TL89-145** (53 MTC)—**RAL-IN89-7**	
				59	62	Based on carpet/pad over oriented strand board in place of ceramic tile and cement board —**RAL-TL89-146** (54 MTC)—**RAL-IN89-8**	

FIGURE 10.12 (*continued*) Fire and sound rated wood wood floor construction details.
(*Source: United States Gypsum Company*)

10.31

Fire-rated Construction

Test Data/Ceilings	Fire Rating	Detail & Physical Data	Description & Test No.	Acoustical Performance		
				STC	IIC	Description & Test No.
	2 hr.	13"	Floor/ceiling—floor of carpet/pad, 1-1/2" Type F flooring, 1/2" plywood—2 x 10 wd joist 16" o.c.—3" THERMAFIBER SAFB—ceiling of 2 layers 5/8" SHEETROCK brand gypsum panels, FIRECODE C core, over RC-1 chan 16" o.c.—**UL Des L541**	59	69	**RAL-TL90-40** (54 MTC)— **RAL-IN90-5**	P
				59	37	Based on vinyl tile in place of carpet/ pad—**RAL-TL90-40** (54 MTC)—**RAL-IN90-6**	

*Where thermal insulation is shown in assembly drawings, the specific product is required in the assembly to achieve the stated fire rating. Fiberglass insulation cannot be substituted for THERMAFIBER Insulation.

**Use RC-1 Resilient Channels or equivalent.

FIGURE 10.12 (*continued*) Fire and sound rated wood wood floor construction details. (*Source: United States Gypsum Company*)

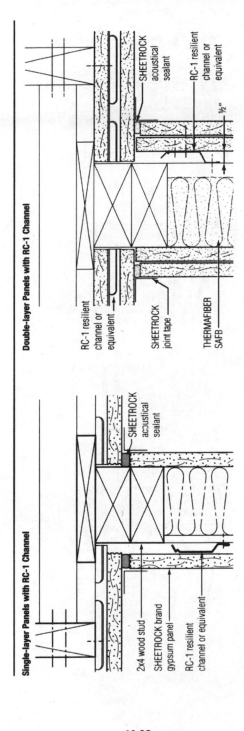

FIGURE 10.12 (*continued*) Fire and sound rated wood wood floor construction details. (*Source: United States Gypsum Company*)

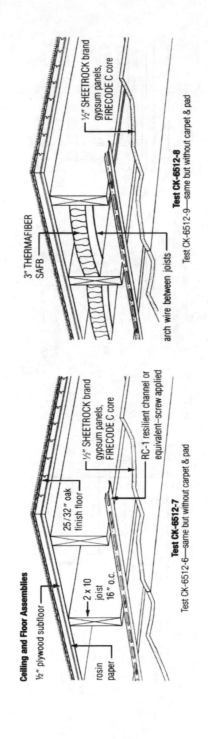

Ceiling and Floor Assemblies

½" plywood subfloor

25/32" oak finish floor

2 × 10 joist 16" o.c.

rosin paper

½" SHEETROCK brand gypsum panels, FIRECODE C core

RC-1 resilient channel or equivalent–screw applied

Test CK-6512-7

Test CK-6512-6—same but without carpet & pad

3" THERMAFIBER SAFB

½" SHEETROCK brand gypsum panels, FIRECODE C core

arch wire between joists

Test CK-6512-8

Test CK-6512-9—same but without carpet & pad

FIGURE 10.12 (*continued*) Fire and sound rated wood wood floor construction details. (*Source: United States Gypsum Company*)

10.34

Interior non-load-bearing partitions may be spaced not more than 28 in. on center and may be set *flat*, with the long dimension parallel to the wall. While this design may meet code, it also may result in a wall with excessive deflection. Top stud plates must be continuous, with reinforcing or splices at joints, at changes in wall height and at intersections with other walls. All wall studs must be supported by a bottom stud plate of 2 in. nominal thickness at a minimum. The table in Figure 10.13 shows limits in allowable size, height, and spacing of wood studs, even in non-load-bearing applications. This table assumes the use of #2 grade lumber. Studs or utility-grade studs may not be longer than 10 ft, even for interior non-load-bearing applications.

Contractors often need to cut or notch wood joists or studs to run plumbing, mechanical, or electrical work. This is acceptable, within limits. Wood joists and studs may be cut in areas and sizes so that the structural integrity is not compromised. The diagram in Figure 10.14 shows limitations on cutting floor joists. Figure 10.15 shows limitations on cutting wood studs. Headers or beams may not be notched or cut in any case.

Wood may not be used to support concrete or masonry, with certain exceptions. Masonry floor surfacing less than 4 in. thick may be supported by wood joists. Interior masonry veneers may be supported on wood floor framing when sized to support the load. Glass block may be supported by wood when designed to limit deflection (sagging) and shrinkage to $L/600$, where L = length, as described at IBC 2304.12 Exception 4.

GLASS AND GLAZING

The IBC regulates the use of glass and glazing in Chapter 24. Most of the requirements are written for wind and snow loads, skylights and sloped glazing, and other issues not encountered in the design and construction of interiors. All sides of glass panes must be supported firmly, or designed and detailed by a design professional. In glazing designs with unsupported glass edges (butt glazed), the required engineering and details usually are provided by the glazing system manufacturer and contractor. The criteria for *firmly supported* glass pane sides are established as limiting deflection to not more than $1/175$ of the glass edge length, but not more than ¾ in. Interior glazing adjacent to a walking surface (floor) is limited to deflection of not more than the glass thickness when subjected to the load specified at IBC 2403.4. Glass louvers or jalousies must be at least ³⁄₁₆ in. thick, not more than 48 in. long, and have smooth edges. Glass sloped more than 15 percent vertically is considered sloped glazing (usually required for skylights and roofs) and is beyond the scope of this book. Interior walls classified as sloped glazing, however, must meet the requirements in IBC Section 2405, *Sloped Glazing and Skylights*.

SIZE, HEIGHT AND SPACING OF WOOD STUDS

STUD SIZE (inches)	BEARING WALLS				NONBEARING WALLS	
	Laterally unsupported stud height[a] (feet)	Spacing (inches)			Laterally unsupported stud height[a] (feet)	Spacing (inches)
		Supporting roof and ceiling only	Supporting one floor, roof and ceiling	Supporting two floors, roof and ceiling		
2 × 3[b]	—	—	—	—	10	16
2 × 4	10	24	16	—	14	24
3 × 4	10	24	24	16	14	24
2 × 5	10	24	24	—	16	24
2 × 6	10	24	24	16	20	24

For SI: 1 inch = 25.4 mm, 1 foot = 304.8 mm.

a. Listed heights are distances between points of lateral support placed perpendicular to the plane of the wall. Increases in unsupported height are permitted where justified by an analysis.

b. Shall not be used in exterior walls.

FIGURE 10.13 IBC Table 2308.9.1 Required size, height and spacing of wood studs.
(*Source: ICC, International Building Code, 2000*)

Notching of bending members should be avoided whenever possible, especially on the tension side of the member. When necessary, however, cutting and notching of joists is allowed to accommodate electrical, plumbing and other small lines.

The figure and table below provide guidelines for cutting holes and notches into joists. They were summarized from the *National Design Specification*® *for Wood Construction* published by NFPA[1], and from model building code requirements. The building code references for wood or floor construction are: SBCCI[2] *Standard Building Code*, Chapter 17; BOCA[3] *National Building Code*, Article 17; ICBO[4] *Uniform Building Code*, Chapter 25; and CABO[5] *One and Two Family Dwelling Code*, Chapter 6.

[1]National Forest Products Association, now known as the American Forest & Paper Association (AFPA). [2] Southern Building Code Congress International. [3] Building Officials and Code Administrators International. [4] International Conference of Building Officials. [5] Council of American Building Officials.

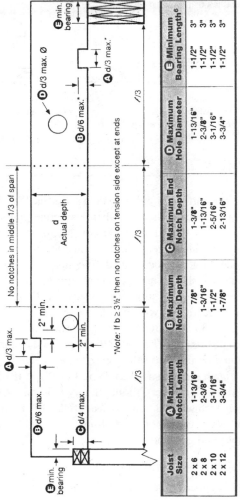

Joist Size	Ⓐ Maximum Notch Length	Ⓑ Maximum Notch Depth	Ⓒ Maximum End Notch Depth	Ⓓ Maximum Hole Diameter	Ⓔ Minimum Bearing Length[6]	
2 x 6	1-13/16"	7/8"	1-3/8"	1-13/16"	1-1/2"	3"
2 x 8	2-3/8"	1-3/16"	1-13/16"	2-3/8"	1-1/2"	3"
2 x 10	3-1/16"	1-1/2"	2-5/16"	3-1/16"	1-1/2"	3"
2 x 12	3-3/4"	1-7/8"	2-13/16"	3-3/4"	1-1/2"	3"

6 Minimum bearing: 1-1/2" on wood or steel; 3" on masonry.

FIGURE 10.14 Allowable size and location of wood floor Joist holes and notches. (*Source: Southern Forest Products Association, Construction Guide: Southern Pine Joists & Rafters*)

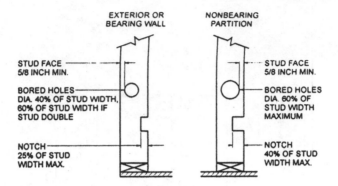

FIGURE 10.15   Allowable size and location of wood stud holes and notches. *(Source: SBCCI, Standard Building Code Commentary, 1997)*

SAFETY GLAZING

Glass used in locations in buildings classified at IBC 2406.2 as hazardous (subject to human impact loads, e.g., where someone might fall or hit the glass) must be composed of safety glazing. Safety glazing is manufactured by laminating glass to a plastic inter-layer, which is intended to reinforce and hold the glass in place if broken. Interior locations defined as hazardous glazing include all kinds of doors; bath and shower enclosures; glazing within 24 in. of a door and less than 60 in. above the walking surface, as shown in Figure 10.16; and glazing panels larger than 9 square feet with bottom edge less than 18 in. above the floor, top edge more than 36 in. above the floor, and within 36 in. of a walking surface, as shown in Figure 10.16a. The code allows protective bars in front of the hazardous glazing as an alternative to safety glazing, as shown in Figure 10.17.

Safety glazing is classified as Type I or Type II based on size and location, according to the Consumer Product Safety Commission Regulation 1201, Safety Standard for Architectural Glazing Materials [8], as shown in Figure 10.18.

The following exceptions are allowed at IBC 2406.2.1 for certain products and uses not required to be safety glass:

1. Openings in doors through which a 3 in. (76 mm) sphere is unable to pass.
2. Decorative glass in Section 2406.2, Item 1, 6, or 7.
3. Glazing materials used as curved glazed panels in revolving doors.
4. Commercial refrigerated cabinet glazed doors.
5. Glass block panels complying with Section 2101.2.4.
6. Louvered windows and jalousies complying with the requirements of Section 2403.5.
7. Mirrors and other glass panels mounted or hung on a surface that provides a continuous backing support.

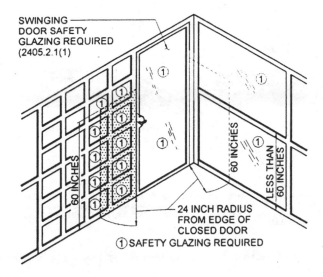

FIGURE 10.16 Hazardous locations requiring safety glazing. *(Source: SBCCI, Standard Building Code Commentary, 1997)*

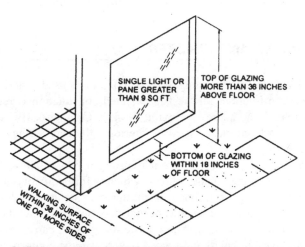

GLAZING WHICH MEETS ALL FOUR OF THE CRITERIA IS CONSIDERED TO BE A HAZARDOUS LOCATION AND THEREFORE MUST BE SAFETY GLAZED. IF THE PANEL (PANE OR LIGHT) DOES NOT MEET ANY ONE OF THE FOUR CRITERIA, THAN PANEL IS NOT CONSIDERED A HAZARDOUS LOCATION AND THEREFORE IS NOT REQUIRED TO BE SAFETY GLAZED.

FIGURE 10.16a Hazardous locations requiring safety glazing. *(Source: SBCCI, Standard Building Code Commentary, 1997)*

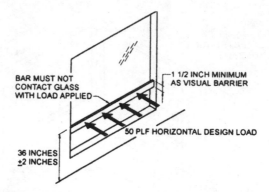

BAR MUST NOT
CONTACT GLASS
WITH LOAD APPLIED

1 1/2 INCH MINIMUM
AS VISUAL BARRIER

50 PLF HORIZONTAL DESIGN LOAD

36 INCHES
±2 INCHES

A PANEL OF GLASS WHICH IS CONSIDERED TO BE A HAZARDOUS LOCATION BY
2405.2.1(4) MUST BE SAFETY GLAZED. IN LIEU OF SAFETY GLAZING A HORIZONTAL
PROTECTIVE BAR MEETING THE CRITERIA OF 2405.2.2(7) AS ILLUSTRATED MAY
BE INSTALLED.

FIGURE 10.17   Horizontal rail used in lieu of safety glazing. *(Source: SBCCI, Standard Building Code Commentary, 1997)*

Other materials allowed by the IBC as alternatives to safety glazing include wire glass or plastic glazing meeting ANSI Z97.1, glass block, and louvers or jalousies. Glazing in handrails and guards, floors, and racquetball or squash courts are regulated by the requirements at IBC Sections 2407-2409. Glazing for these applications should be designed by a qualified individual.

GYPSUM BOARD AND PLASTER

Gypsum board and plaster are among the most commonly used materials for fire-resistance rated construction. Fire-resistance rated construction is regulated by the IBC at Chapter 7 and addressed by this book in Chapter 6. IBC Chapter 25 covers gypsum board and plaster used in interior walls and ceilings, as well as exterior applications.

Gypsum board is manufactured from gypsum, a non-combustible mineral derived from natural or man-made sources, which is formed between paper facings. Wood framing for gypsum board or plaster must be at least 2 in. nominal size in minimum dimension (2×), except that material 1 in. thick (1×) can be used as furring over solid backing. Solid plaster or gypsum partitions must be at least 2 in. thick. Gypsum board and related materials must conform to the standards shown in Figure 10.19; gypsum board and related construction must conform to the standards shown in Figure 10.19a.

MINIMUM CATEGORY CLASSIFICATION OF GLAZING

EXPOSED SURFACE AREA OF ONE SIDE OF ONE LITE	GLAZING IN STORM OR COMBINATION DOORS (Category class)	GLAZING IN DOORS (Category class)	GLAZED PANELS REGULATED BY ITEM 7 OF SECTION 2406.2 (Category class)	GLAZED PANELS REGULATED BY ITEM 6 OF SECTION 2406.2 (Category class)	DOORS AND ENCLOSURES REGULATED BY ITEM 5 OF SECTION 2406.2 (Category class)	SLIDING GLASS DOORS PATIO TYPE (Category class)
9 square feet or less	I	I	No requirement	I	II	II
More than 9 square feet	II	II	II	II	II	II

For SI: 1 square foot = 0.0929m².

FIGURE 10.18 IBC Table 2406.1 Safety glazing classifications. (*Source: ICC, International Building Code, 2000*)

GYPSUM BOARD MATERIALS AND ACCESSORIES

MATERIAL	STANDARD
Accessories for gypsum board	ASTM C 1047
Gypsum sheathing	ASTM C 79
Gypsum wallboard	ASTM C 36
Joint reinforcing tape and compound	ASTM C 474; C 475
Nails for gypsum boards	ASTM C 514, F 547, F 1667
Steel screws	ASTM C 954; C 1002
Steel studs, nonload bearing	ASTM C 645
Steel studs, load bearing	ASTM C 955
Water-resistant gypsum backing board	ASTM C 630
Exterior soffit board	ASTM C 931
Fiber-reinforced gypsum panels	ASTM C 1278
Gypsum backing board	ASTM C 442
Gypsum ceiling board	ASTM C 1395
Predecorated gypsum board	ASTM C 960
Adhesives for fastening gypsum wallboard	ASTM C 557
Testing gypsum and gypsum products	ASTM C 22; C 472; C 473
Glass mat gypsum substrate	ASTM C 1177
Glass mat gypsum backing panel	ASTM C 1178

FIGURE 10.19   IBC Table 2506.2 Specifications for gypsum board materials and accessories. *(Source: ICC, International Building Code, 2000)*

INSTALLATION OF GYPSUM CONSTRUCTION

MATERIAL	STANDARD
Gypsum sheathing	ASTM C 1280
Gypsum veneer base	ASTM C 844
Gypsum board	GA-216; ASTM C 840
Interior lathing and furring	ASTM C 841
Steel framing for gypsum boards	ASTM C 754; C 1007

FIGURE 10.19a   IBC Table 2508.1 Specifications for lath, plastering materials and accessories. *(Source: ICC, International Building Code, 2000)*

Gypsum absorbs moisture and is of limited use in areas subject to continuous moisture. For this reason, gypsum board must be installed in areas protected from weather. When gypsum board is used in wet areas, such as bathrooms or toilet areas, and as backing for hard tile, it must be of the moisture-resistant type. Moisture-resistant gypsum board has a moisture-resistance treated paper facer that is typically tinted green to indicate these special properties. Even moisture-resistant gypsum board cannot be used in continuously wet areas such as saunas, showers, or pools. Moisture-resistant gypsum board used in ceilings must be at least ½ in. thick with supports spaced at 12 in. maximum, and ¾ in. thick with supports spaced at 16 in. maximum.

Materials for lath and plaster must meet the specifications found at IBC section 2507, shown in Figure 10.20. Construction of lath and plaster must meet the standards shown in Figure 10.21. All materials used in plaster construction must be corrosion-resistant materials, typically galvanized steel or other coated ferrous or non-ferrous materials. Since plaster is a cement-based material, proper environmental conditions must be maintained during and after construction, so that the material can cure. Plaster may be used in wet areas, but must be installed over an approved moisture barrier and over wood studs.

PLASTIC

The IBC regulates plastic at Chapter 26, including foam plastic insulation, glazing, veneer, and trim. Most of the requirements for plastic glazing are beyond the scope of this book, since they deal with skylights or exterior roof and wall material.

FOAM PLASTIC INSULATION AND TRIM

Foam plastic insulation is a source of potential fire hazard, not only because it is combustible, but also because it generates deadly gases when burned. The Life Safety Code (LSC) prohibits use of foam plastic as an interior finish, except where full-scale fire tests prove that the material has acceptable fire and smoke ratings. A discussion about this topic from the 1997 LSC Commentary at 6-5.3.1.5.2 follows:

> The prohibition on the use of foamed plastics within buildings is based upon actual fire experience in which foamed plastics have contributed to very rapid fire development. It is also acknowledged that tunnel testing per NFPA 255/ASTM E84 (see 6-5.4.1) may not accurately assess the potential hazard of plastics in general. Therefore, if cellular or foamed plastics are to be used within a building, their use should be substantiated on the basis of full-scale fire tests or fire testing that simulates conditions of actual use.

LATH, PLASTERING MATERIALS AND ACCESSORIES

MATERIAL	STANDARD
Accessories for gypsum veneer base	ASTM C 1047
Exterior plaster bonding compounds	ASTM C 932
Gypsum base for veneer plasters	ASTM C 588
Gypsum casting and molding plaster	ASTM C 59
Gypsum Keene's cement	ASTM C 61
Gypsum lath	ASTM C 37
Gypsum plaster	ASTM C 28
Gypsum veneer plaster	ASTM C 587
Interior bonding compounds, gypsum	ASTM C 631
Lime plasters	ASTM C 5; C 206
Masonry cement	ASTM C 91
Metal lath	ASTM C 847
Plaster aggregates Sand	ASTM C 35; C 897
Perlite	ASTM C 35
Vermiculite	ASTM C 35
Plastic cement	ASTM C 1328
Blended cement	ASTM C 595
Portland cement	ASTM C 150
Steel studs and track	ASTM C 645; C 955
Steel screws	ASTM C 1002; C 954
Welded wire lath	ASTM C 933
Woven wire plaster base	ASTM C 1032

FIGURE 10.20   IBC Table 2507.2 Specifications for materials and accessories for gypsum construction. *(Source: ICC, International Building Code, 2000)*

The IBC at Section 2603 requires that foam plastic insulation used anywhere in a building must have at least a Class C rating (75 flame spread index and 450 smoke development index) when tested according to ASTM E 84. Class C foam plastic trim may be used when it is limited in size and thickness, as discussed in this book in Chapter 9, Interior Finishes.

INSTALLATION OF PLASTER CONSTRUCTION

MATERIAL	STANDARD
Gypsum plaster	ASTM C 842
Gypsum veneer plaster	ASTM C 843
Interior lathing and furring (gypsum plaster)	ASTM C 841
Lathing and furring (cement plaster)	ASTM C 1063
Portland cement plaster	ASTM C 926
Steel framing	ASTM C 754; C 1007

2511.1.1 Installation. Installation of lathing and plaster materials shall conform with Table 2511.1 and Section 2508.

FIGURE 10.21 IBC Table 2511.1 Specifications for installation of plaster construction. *(Source: ICC, International Building Code, 2000)*

PLASTIC GLAZING (LIGHT-TRANSMITTING PLASTIC)

Plastic materials used in glazing or light-transmitting applications include acrylic (Plexiglas), polycarbonate (Lexan), fiberglass, and others. As discussed earlier in this chapter, plastic glazing can be used as a substitute for safety glazing in certain applications. Plastic glazing, however, is not included in any fire rated applications, since it is combustible. The IBC at Section 2606 requires plastic glazing to have a Class C flame and smoke rating and an ignition temperature of 650°F minimum.

The IBC also regulates light diffusing systems. These systems are defined as: construction consisting in whole or in part of lenses, panels, grids or baffles made with light transmitting plastics positioned below independently mounted electrical light sources, skylights or light-transmitting plastic roof panels. Lenses, panels, grids, and baffles that are part of an electrical fixture shall not be considered as a light-diffusing system.

Light diffusing systems may not be used in exit passageways and stairways, group I-2 and I-3 occupancies, theaters with a working stage with more than 700 occupants, or assembly occupancies with more 1000 occupants unless the building is sprinkled. The area above the light diffusing system also must be sprinkled, unless tested otherwise. The code also regulates support, installation, and allowable size of light diffusing systems.

Plastic glazing used in interior signs must meet the flame, smoke, and ignition temperature requirements discussed above, may not exceed 20 percent of the wall area, and may not be larger than 24 square feet in any case. Signs in covered mall buildings are discussed in Chapter 5, *Special Use and Occupancy.*

BUILDING INFRASTRUCTURE

Most building infrastructure is designed by a design professional other than the interior designer or is already present in the space to be designed or constructed. The IBC has limited sections on mechanical, plumbing, electrical infrastructure, and elevators because these areas are regulated by other codes. This book touches briefly on the areas of building infrastructure regulated by the IBC that are relevant to the design and construction of interiors.

ELECTRICAL

The IBC regulates electrical work at Chapter 27 and refers to the ICC Electrical Code for the design and construction of electrical components, equipment, and systems. The International Electrical Code (IEC), maintained and owned by NFPA, is a separate document referenced by most of the current model codes.

The IBC at Section 2702 requires emergency and standby power systems in several applications. Voice (evacuation) communication systems, smoke control systems, exit signs, lighting in means of egress, elevators, sliding security grills, malls, high-rise buildings, hospitals, and similar group I-3 occupancies, among others, are required to have emergency or standby power.

MECHANICAL

Mechanical equipment is required by the IBC in Chapter 28 to meet the provisions of the International Mechanical Code and the International Fuel Gas Code. Masonry chimneys, fireplaces, heaters, and barbecue grills are regulated in IBC Chapter 21, Masonry.

PLUMBING

Plumbing equipment and systems must comply with the International Plumbing Code, as specified in IBC Chapter 29. This chapter specifies the minimum number of plumbing fixtures based on occupancy, as shown in the chart in Figure 10.22.

MINIMUM NUMBER OF PLUMBING FACILTIES[a]

	OCCUPANCY	WATER CLOSETS (see Section 419.2 of the International Plumbing Code for urinals)		LAVATORIES	BATHTUBS/ SHOWERS	DRINKING FOUNTAINS (See Section 410.1 of the International Plumbing Code)	OTHERS
		Male	Female				
	Nightclubs	1 per 40	1 per 40	1 per 75	—	1 per 500	1 service sink
	Restaurants	1 per 75	1 per 75	1 per 200	—	1 per 500	1 service sink
	Theaters, halls, museums, etc.	1 per 125	1 per 65	1 per 200	—	1 per 500	1 service sink
A S S E M B L Y	Coliseums, arenas (less than 3,000 seats)	1 per 75	1 per 40	1 per 150	—	1 per 1,000	1 service sink
	Coliseums, arenas (3,000 seats or greater)	1 per 120	1 per 60	Male 1 per 200 Female 1 per 150	—	1 per 1,000	1 service sink
	Churches[b]	1 per 150	1 per 75	1 per 200	—	1 per 1,000	1 service sink
	Stadiums (less than 3,000 seats), pools, etc.	1 per 100	1 per 50	1 per 150	—	1 per 1,000	1 service sink
	Stadiums (3,000 seats or greater	1 per 150	1 per 75	Male 1 per 200 Female 1 per 150	—	1 per 1,000	1 service sink

FIGURE 10.22 IBC Table 2902.1 Minimum number of plumbing fixtures. *(Source: ICC, International Building Code, 2000)*

MINIMUM NUMBER OF PLUMBING FACILITIES[a]

OCCUPANCY	WATER CLOSETS (see Section 419.2 of the International Plumbing Code for urinals)		LAVATORIES	BATHTUBS/ SHOWERS	DRINKING FOUNTAINS (See Section 410.1 of the International Plumbing Code)	OTHERS
	Male	Female				
Mercantile (see Sections 2902.2, 2902.5, 2902.6)	1 per 500		1 per 750	—	1 per 1,000	1 service sink
Business (see Sections 2902.2, 2902.4, 2902.4.1)	1 per 50		1 per 80	—	1 per 100	1 service sink
Educational	1 per 50		1 per 50	—	1 per 100	1 service sink
Factory and industrial	1 per 100		1 per 100	See Section 411 of the International Plumbing Code	1 per 400	1 service sink
Passenger terminals and transportation facilities	1 per 500		1 per 750	—	1 per 1,000	1 service sink

FIGURE 10.22 (continued)   IBC Table 2902.1 Minimum number of plumbing fixtures.
(Source: ICC, International Building Code, 2000)

MINIMUM NUMBER OF PLUMBING FACILITIES[a]

OCCUPANCY	WATER CLOSETS (see Section 419.2 of the International Plumbing Code for urinals) Male	Female	LAVATORIES	BATHTUBS/ SHOWERS	DRINKING FOUNTAINS (See Section 410.1 of the International Plumbing Code)	OTHERS
I N S T I T U T Residential care	1 per 10	1 per 10	1 per 10	1 per 8	1 per 100	1 service sink
I O N A L Hospitals, ambulatory nursing home patients[c]	1 per room[d]	1 per room[d]	1 per room[d]	1 per 15	1 per 100	1 service sink per floor
Day nurseries, sanitariums, non-ambulatory nursing home patients, etc.[c]	1 per 15	1 per 15	1 per 15	1 per 15[e]	1 per 100	1 service sink
Employees, other than residential care[c]	1 per 25	1 per 25	1 per 35	—	1 per 100	—
Visitors, other than residential care	1 per 75	1 per 75	1 per 100	—	1 per 500	—
Prisons[c]	1 per cell	1 per cell	1 per cell	1 per 15	1 per 100	1 service sink
Asylums, reformatories, etc.[c]	1 per 15	1 per 15	1 per 15	1 per 15	1 per 100	1 service sink

FIGURE 10.22 (continued) IBC Table 2902.1 Minimum number of plumbing fixtures. (Source: ICC, International Building Code, 2000)

MINIMUM NUMBER OF PLUMBING FACILITIES[a]

OCCUPANCY	WATER CLOSETS (see Section 419.2 of the International Plumbing Code for urinals)		LAVATORIES	BATHTUBS/SHOWERS	DRINKING FOUNTAINS (see Section 410.1 of the International Plumbing Code)	OTHERS
	Male	Female				
Hotels, motels	1 per guestroom		1 per guestroom	1 per guestroom	—	1 service sink
Lodges	1 per 10	1 per 10	1 per 10	1 per 8	1 per 100	1 service sink
Multiple family	1 per dwelling unit		1 per dwelling unit	1 per dwelling unit	—	1 kitchen sink per dwelling unit; 1 automatic clothes washer connection per 20 dwelling units
Dormitories	1 per 10	1 per 10	1 per 10	1 per 8	1 per 100	1 service sink
One- and two-family dwellings	1 per dwelling unit		1 per dwelling unit	1 per dwelling unit	—	1 kitchen sink per dwelling unit; 1 automatic clothes washer connection per dwelling unit[f]
Storage (See Sections 2902.2 and 2902.4)	1 per 100		1 per 100	(See Section 411 of the International Plumbing Code)	1 per 1,000	1 service sink

(The rows from Hotels/motels through One- and two-family dwellings are grouped under RESIDENTIAL.)

a. The fixtures shown are based on one fixture being the minimum required for the number of persons indicated or any fraction of the number of persons indicated. The number of occupants shall be determined by this code.

b. Fixtures located in adjacent buildings under the ownership or control of the church shall be made available during periods the church is occupied.

c. Toilet facilities for employees shall be separate from facilities for inmates or patients.

d. A single-occupant toilet room with one water closet and one lavatory serving not more than two adjacent patient rooms shall be permitted where such room is provided with direct access from each patient room and with provisions for privacy.

e. For day nurseries, a maximum of one bathtub shall be required.

FIGURE 10.22 (continued) IBC Table 2902.1 Minimum number of plumbing fixtures.
(Source: ICC, International Building Code, 2000)

Separate toilet facilities must be provided for men and women except in private facilities, occupancies with less than 15 employees, or spaces with a total occupant load of 15 or less. Plumbing fixtures must be allocated equally between the sexes, unless information supporting a different occupant distribution is approved by the building official.

Employee toilet facilities must be located within the same building as the employee workspace, not more than one story above or below, and within a 500 foot travel distance. Factory and industrial occupancies may exceed the 500 ft travel distance with building official approval. Employee toilets may be combined with public toilets.

Public toilet facilities must be provided in assembly, mercantile, or similar occupancies with "customers, patrons, and visitors." Public toilet facilities must be located not more than one story above or below and within the 500 ft travel distance. Public toilet facilities in covered malls must be located within a 300 foot travel distance. Access to some public toilets must be free of charge, although pay toilets may be provided after the required minimum of free toilets is met.

ELEVATORS

The most widely recognized standard for elevators, referenced at IBC Chapter 30, *Elevators and Conveying Systems*, is the American Society of Mechanical Engineers ASME A 17.1, Safety Code for Elevators and Escalators. This standard regulates the design, construction, operation, and maintenance of elevators. Elevators required to be accessible (in an accessible means of egress) also must meet ICC/ANSI A 177.1. This standard regulates the features of hallway call-stations, indicator lamps, elevator car controls, and thresholds to assist individuals with physical disabilities in using elevators.

Elevator hoistway enclosures and openings must be of fire resistance rated construction. Please refer to the sections on opening-protectives and vertical shaft enclosures in Chapter 7, *Fire Resistance Rated Construction*. Not more than four elevators can be located in a single hoistway, and when four or more elevators serve the same floors, they must be located in at least two separate hoistway enclosures. Elevators may not occupy the same enclosure as an exit stairway. Elevator machine rooms must be enclosed, with fire resistance rated construction equal to that required for the hoistway enclosure. In sprinkled buildings, a shunt-trip breaker must automatically disconnect the main power to the elevator equipment upon application of water.

Elevators that are not part of an accessible means of egress must have signs warning occupants to use stairs during an emergency. In buildings with more than four floors and certain other facilities, at least one elevator must accommodate an ambulance stretcher and be identified as such. The minimum elevator dimensions that will accommodate a stretcher are shown in Figure 10.23.

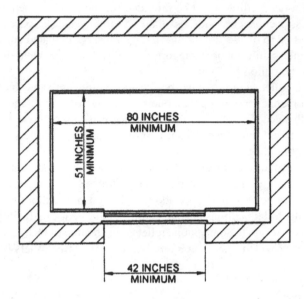

FIGURE 10.23   Minimum elevator size to accommodate ambulance stretchers. *(Source: SBCCI, Standard Building Code Commentary, 1997)*

STRUCTURAL

IBC Chapter 16, *Structural Design*, contains structural design requirements for live and dead loads and calculation methods for roofs and exterior walls, which are beyond the scope of this book. Certain types of floors, however, may be encountered during the design and construction of interiors, and, although another design professional may perform the engineering, it is helpful to understand the loads and concepts involved.

Live loads are those imposed on the structure by wind, snow, floodwater, and earthquakes, as well as people, furniture, and movable objects. Live loads change over time, so maximum anticipated live loads are specified in the code. Live loads are assumed to be evenly distributed over the entire structure or major parts of it. Concentrated loads are point loads, such as heavy equipment or furniture. Figure 10.24 gives the table included in the code for live loads and concentrated loads based on various uses. These values have been developed over many years of experience and engineering calculations. Dead loads are those imposed by the weight of the structure itself, and may be calculated based on the known weight of material tables. Dead loads do not typically change over time unless remodeling occurs.

Where the design live load exceeds 50 pounds per square ft (psf) in industrial or commercial buildings, the load must be posted. In office buildings with movable partitions, 20 psf must be included in the live load when the design floor load is less than 80 psf.

MINIMUM UNIFORMLY DISTRIBUTED LIVE LOADS AND MINIMUM CONCENTRATED LIVE LOADS[g]

OCCUPANCY OR USE	UNIFORM (psf)	CONCENTRATED (lbs.)
1. Apartments (see residential)		
2. Access floor systems		
Office use	50	2,000
Computer use	100	2,000
3. Armories and drill rooms	150	—
4. Assembly areas and theaters		—
Fixed seats (fastened to floor)	60	
Lobbies	100	
Movable seats	100	
Stages and platforms	125	
Follow spot, projection and control rooms	50	
Catwalks	40	
5. Balconies (exterior)	100	—
On one- and two-family residences only, and not exceeding 100 ft.[2]	60	
6. Decks	Same as occupancy served[h]	
7. Bowling alleys	75	—
8. Cornices	60	—
9. Corridors, except as otherwise indicated	100	—
10. Dance halls and ballrooms	100	—
11. Dining rooms and restaurants	100	—
12. Dwellings (see residential)	—	—
13. Elevator machine room grating (on area of 4 in.[2])	—	300
14. Finish light floor plate construction (on area of 1 in.[2])	—	200
15. Fire escapes	100	—
On single-family dwellings only	40	
16. Garages (passenger cars only)	50	Note a
Trucks and buses	See Section 1607.6	
17. Grandstands (see stadium and arena bleachers)	—	—
18. Gymnasiums, main floors and balconies	100	—
19. Handrails, guards and grab bars	See Section 1607.7	
20. Hospitals		
Operating rooms, laboratories	60	1,000
Private rooms	40	1,000
Wards	40	1,000
Corridors above first floor	80	1,000
21. Hotels (see residential)	—	—
22. Libraries		
Reading rooms	60	1,000
Stack rooms	150[b]	1,000
Corridors above first floor	80	1,000
23. Manufacturing		
Light	125	2,000
Heavy	250	3,000
24. Marquees and canopies	75	—

FIGURE 10.24 IBC Table 1607.1 Minimum live load and concentrated floor loads. (*Source: ICC, International Building Code, 2000*)

MINIMUM UNIFORMLY DISTRIBUTED LIVE LOADS AND MINIMUM CONCENTRATED LIVE LOADS[g]

OCCUPANCY OR USE	UNIFORM (psf)	CONCENTRATED (lbs.)
25. Office buildings		
File and computer rooms shall be designed for heavier loads based on anticipated occupancy		
Lobbies and first floor corridors	100	2,000
Offices	50	2,000
Corridors above first floor	80	2,000
26. Penal Institutions		
Cell blocks	40	—
Corridors	100	
27. Residential		—
Group R-3 as applicable in Section 101.2		
Uninhabitable attics without storage	10	
Uninhabitable attics with storage	20	
Habitable attics and sleeping areas	30	
All other areas except balconies and decks	40	
Hotels and multifamily dwellings		
Private rooms	40	
Public rooms and corridors serving them	100	
28. Reviewing stands, grandstands and bleachers	100[c]	—
29. Roofs	See Section 1607.11	
30. Schools		
Classrooms	40	1,000
Corridors above first floor	80	1,000
First floor corridors	100	1,000
31. Scuttles, skylight ribs, and accessible ceilings	—	200
32. Sidewalks, vehicular driveways and yards, subject to trucking	250[d]	8,000[e]
33. Skating rinks	100	—
34. Stadiums and arenas		
Bleachers	100[c]	
Fixed seats (fastened to floor)	60[c]	
35. Stairs and exits	100	Note f
One- and two-family dwellings	40	
All other	100	
36. Storage warehouses (shall be designed for heavier loads if required for anticipated storage)		
Light	125	
Heavy	250	
37. Stores		
Retail		
First floor	100	1,000
Upper floors	75	1,000
Wholesale, all floors	125	1,000
38. Vehicle barriers	See Section 1607.7	
39. Walkways and elevated platforms (other than exitways)	60	—
40. Yards and terraces, pedestrians	100	—

FIGURE 10.24 (*continued*)   IBC Table 1607.1 Minimum live load and concentrated floor loads. (*Source: ICC, International Building Code, 2000*)

Handrails and guards must withstand a force of 50 lb per linear ft, applied at the top. Handrails, guards, and any mounting attachment must withstand a concentrated load of 200 lb applied in a single direction. Intermediate rails must withstand a 50 lb force applied over any square-foot area. Grab bars, shower seats, and bench seats in dressing rooms must resist a concentrated load of 250 lb applied in a single direction.

EARTHQUAKE RESISTANT DESIGN AND CONSTRUCTION

Suspended ceilings and other architectural components, mechanical and electrical equipment, and supports for these building elements must resist earthquake loads in many areas. The amount of ground movement experienced during recorded earthquakes has been mapped and included in the code. A simple map of ground movement velocity, showing the continental United States only, is included here as Figure 10.25 The amount of ground movement is used to determine the required lateral resistance of structures and architectural components. The western portion of the United States is most likely to experience earthquakes, although major earthquakes have been experienced near Charleston, South Carolina, and near the confluence of the Ohio and Mississippi rivers. It is important to determine the earthquake zone for any project and determine what level of earthquake resistance is required, if any. A structural engineer or building official in the project area may be the best source for this information.

FIRE PROTECTION SYSTEMS

Fire protection systems design and construction are specified in the International Fire Code referenced in IBC Chapter 9. This chapter includes requirements for automatic sprinkler systems, standpipe systems, portable fire extinguishers, fire alarm and detection systems, emergency alarm systems, smoke control systems, smoke and heat vents, and fire command centers. Many of these provisions duplicate or contradict requirements found in the NFPA Life Safety Code. The LSC requires that automatic sprinkler systems comply with NFPA 13, Standard for the Installation of Sprinkler Systems. The IBC also requires sprinkler systems to meet NFPA 13. Both codes allow use of a residential sprinkler system, as defined by NFPA 13R, in certain applications. The IBC recognizes limited-area sprinkler systems of up to 20 heads.

As with other portions of the codes that conflict, it is necessary to consult with building officials to determine which code will be enforced. If both codes apply, the more restrictive or conservative provisions should be observed.

One major conflict between the IBC and the LSC is in fire protection system monitoring. The LSC in Section 9.7.2 requires all sprinkler systems to be monitored according to NFPA 72, National Fire Alarm Code, by an "approved super-

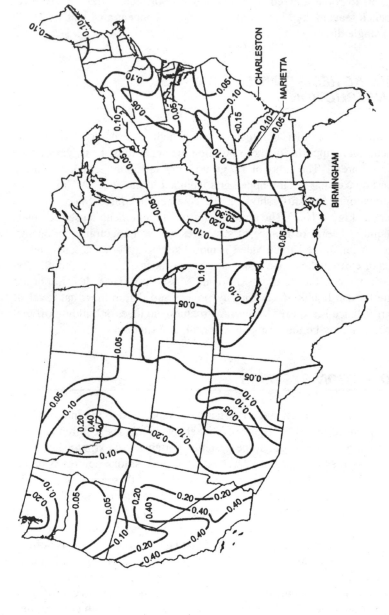

CONTOUR MAP OF EFFECTIVE PEAK VELOCITY-RELATED ACCELERATION COEFFICIENT, Av

FIGURE 10.25 Seismic map of expected ground movement in earthquakes.
(*Source: SBCCI, Standard Building Code Commentary, 1997*)

vising station." An approved supervising station is typically the fire department, but it also can be a private alarm company staffed 24 hours per day. The IBC also requires monitoring according to NFPA 72, but does not require the monitoring of limited-area systems or one- and two-family dwellings [10].

The IBC at Section 903 requires automatic sprinklers to be located in buildings of certain use and size. Assembly group A-1 (theaters and auditoriums) must be sprinkled when it consists of more than 12,000 square feet or 300 occupants, has fire areas on floors other than the level of exit discharge, or is a multi-theater complex. Assembly group A-2 (restaurants and bars) must be sprinkled when it consists of more than 5000 square feet or 300 occupants, or has fire areas on floors other than the level of exit discharge. Assembly groups A-3 (places of worship, recreation, or amusement) and A-4 (indoor sports arenas) must be sprinkled under the same conditions as Assembly group A-1, except for areas used exclusively for participant sports when on the level of exit discharge. Assembly group A-5 (outdoor sports arenas) must be sprinkled only in press boxes, concession stands, retail areas, and similar enclosed spaces.

Group E (schools) must be sprinkled when they consist of more than 20,000 square feet, unless each classroom has a ground level exit door. Group F-1 (moderate hazard factories), M (mercantile), and S (storage) must be sprinkled when the fire area containing that use exceeds 12,000 square feet, the building is more than 3 stories in height, or 24,000 square feet total area. Woodworking operations that use or generate "finely divided combustible materials" in an area larger than 2,500 square feet must be sprinkled. Group R-1 (hotels and boarding houses) must be sprinkled except when less than three stories high and exterior exits are provided from each room. Other residential occupancies (R-2, R-3, and R-4) also must be sprinkled when certain conditions exist. This is also true of basements and other stories without openings. Buildings with an occupant load of 30 or more located more than 55 ft above fire department access must be sprinkled. Commercial cooking operations must have an automatic extinguishing system installed in the kitchen exhaust hood.

Installation of sprinklers in areas with sensitive electrical or mechanical equipment has long been a problem. The IBC at 903.3.1.1.1 has addressed this problem by exempting certain areas from sprinklers, as follows:

1. Any room where the application of water, or flame and water, constitutes a serious life or fire hazard.

2. Any room or space where sprinklers are considered undesirable because of the nature of the contents, when approved by the building official.

3. Generator and transformer rooms separated from the remainder of the building by walls and floor/ceiling or roof/ceiling assemblies having a fire-resistance rating of not less than two hours.

4. Spaces or areas in telecommunications buildings used exclusively for telecommunications equipment, associated electrical power distribution equipment, batter-

ies, and standby engines, provided those spaces or areas are equipped throughout with an automatic fire alarm system and are separated from the remainder of the building by a wall with a fire-resistance rating of not less than one hour and a floor/ceiling assembly with a fire-resistance rating of not less than two hours.

5. In rooms or areas that are of noncombustible construction with wholly noncombustible contents.

Other fire suppression systems are required in other parts of the code as shown in Figure 10.26.

Alarm, supervisory, and trouble signals must be transmitted to the supervising station or to an approved 24-hour attended location. All sprinkler systems must have an audible flow alarm mounted outside the building which is activated by water flow in any part of the system. When a fire alarm is present, activation of the sprinkler system shall actuate the fire alarm.

STANDPIPE SYSTEMS

Standpipes are water distribution systems used by firefighting personnel inside the building. Since parts of some buildings are located beyond the reach of fire department hoses, standpipes may provide the only water source for fighting a

ADDITIONAL REQUIRED SUPPRESSION SYSTEMS

SECTION	SUBJECT
402.8	Covered malls
403.2,403.3	High-rise buildings
404.3	Atriums
405.3	Underground structures
407.5	Group I-2
410.6	Stages
411.4	Special amusement buildings
412.2.5, 412.2.6	Aircraft hangers
415.7.2.4	Group H-2
416.4	Flammable finishes
417.4	Drying rooms
507	Unlimited area buildings
IFC	Sprinkler requirements as set forth in Section 903.2.15 of the *International Fire Code*

FIGURE 10.26   IBC Table 903.2.15 Fire suppression systems required in special situations and occupancies. *(Source: ICC, International Building Code, 2000)*

fire. The IBC references NFPA 14, Standard for the Installation of Standpipe, Private Hydrant, and Hose Systems. Standpipes must be installed in all buildings having occupied spaces more than 30 ft above or below the level of fire department access. Standpipes must be installed in buildings exceeding 10,000 square feet per floor, where any part of the building is more than 200 ft from the nearest point of fire department access. These building are not required to have standpipes when they are sprinkled. Standpipes must be installed in Group A facilities with occupant loads of more than 1000; covered mall buildings; stages larger than 1000 square feet; and underground buildings.

PORTABLE FIRE EXTINGUISHERS

The IBC requires portable fire extinguishers in all buildings as required by the International Fire Code. Where required by the Life Safety Code occupancy chapters (11–40), portable fire extinguishers must comply with NFPA 10, Standard for Portable Fire Extinguishers. In situations where both codes apply, the more restrictive or conservative provisions should be observed. Both codes require portable fire extinguishers to be located according to a specified maximum travel distance from any occupied space. The extinguishers must be a minimum size and type requirements of extinguishing material. The standpipe connection, tools, and portable fire extinguishers often are located in a common cabinet [9, 10].

FIRE ALARM AND DETECTION SYSTEMS

The IBC regulates fire alarm and detection systems at Section 907, and it requires these systems to comply with NFPA 72, National Fire Alarm Code. Fire alarm and detection systems must be provided with emergency power. Fire alarm systems are required in Group A (assembly) facilities with occupant loads of more than 300, except where the buildings are sprinkled. Group A facilities with occupant loads of more than 1000 also must have a pre-recorded voice notification. Fire alarm systems are required in Group B (business) and M (mercantile) facilities with occupant loads of more than 500, or with occupant loads of more than 100 above or below the lowest level of exit discharge. Group M also must have a voice emergency notification system. Group E (educational) facilities with occupant loads of more than 50 are required to have fire alarm systems. Manual fire alarm boxes (pull stations) are not required in Group E when the fire detection and alarm systems meet stated conditions. Group F (factory/industrial) facilities are required to have fire alarm systems only when two or more stories contain more than 500 occupants above or below the level of exit discharge. Fire alarm and detection systems are required in Group H (hazardous) and Group I (institutional). All residential (Group R) occupancies are required to have fire alarms. Group R-1 (hotel or transient boarding house) facilities are not required to have fire alarm systems when stated conditions are met. As discussed in

Chapter 4, *Special Use and Occupancy*, all high-rise, atria, and covered mall buildings must have fire alarm and detection systems. Covered malls exceeding 50,000 square feet also must have a voice emergency notification system [9].

Manual fire alarm boxes must be located within 5 ft of each building exit and be red in color. The alarm system must be zoned not to exceed 22,500 square feet, with a zoning indicator panel. Duct smoke detectors must be connected to the fire alarm system. Alarm notification must be audible (bells or horns) and visible (flashing lights). The codes also regulate the type, size, intensity, and location of required alarm notification appliances.

CONSTRUCTION SAFEGUARDS— FIRE PROTECTION AND EXITS DURING CONSTRUCTION

The IBC regulates construction safeguards at Chapter 33. All structures under construction must have portable fire extinguishers located at each stair, at other locations where combustible materials collect, and in every construction storage trailer or shed. The building official may require other extinguishers where special hazards exist. Construction materials cannot be stored so as to prevent access to fire extinguishers or standpipes. Required exits must be maintained at all times. This means that if a required exit cannot be used during construction, a replacement exit must be provided. When a building is more than 50 ft high, a lighted exit stairway must be maintained at all times. Buildings higher than four stories must have at least one working standpipe available for fire department use. The construction standpipe must be present, with required connections and water, before the building reaches 40 ft above the lowest level of fire department access. Automatic sprinkler systems must be operational and tested before any part of a building is occupied.

EXISTING STRUCTURES

IBC Chapter 34, Existing Structures, covers alteration, repair, addition, or change of occupancy. When any of these conditions are met, the new construction must comply with the IBC and the other referenced ICC codes. This chapter contains Section 3409, Compliance Alternatives, a method for determining the code compliance of existing structures based on fire safety, means of egress, and general safety. Section 3409, along with the scorecard used to assign a total value, is included in Appendix P. Table 3409.8 establishes a minimum score based on the size of the occupancy group. This score is subtracted from the building score, and if the result is zero or more, the building is in compliance with Section 3409. This method, however, cannot be used to establish code compliance for occupancy groups H (hazardous) or I (institutional).

ALTERATIONS AND REPAIRS

Alterations and repairs not affecting structural or required fire-resistance rated building elements may be constructed of the same materials as the original building. Existing stairways need not be upgraded to new stairway proportions when the existing space and construction will not allow a reduction in pitch or slope. Glass replacement must be in accordance with provisions for new construction.

CHANGE OF OCCUPANCY

No change in occupancy or occupancy group is allowed unless the facility complies with the code requirements for the intended occupancy. The building official may approve a change to a less restrictive occupancy in existing buildings without requiring compliance with the IBC. A certificate of occupancy must be issued for the new use.

HISTORIC BUILDINGS

Historic buildings may be exempted from the provisions of Chapter 34 when it is determined that no distinct hazard to life safety exists.

ACCESSIBILITY

Provisions for accessibility in new structures apply to additions and building alterations, unless technically unfeasible. Facilities undergoing a change of group or occupancy must include the following accessibility features [9]:

1. At least one accessible entrance.
2. At least one accessible route from an accessible entrance to primary function areas.
3. Signage complying with Section 1109.
4. Accessible parking, where parking is being provided.
5. At least one accessible passenger loading-zone, where loading-zones are provided.

When alterations affect the major function of a facility, the route to that area must be accessible and must include toilets and drinking fountains. This provision mirrors requirements from the ADAAG (enforced since 1992). The following exceptions are allowed:

1. The cost of providing the accessible route is not required to exceed 20 percent of the cost of the alterations affecting the area of primary function.

2. This provision does not apply to alterations limited solely to windows, hardware, operating controls, electrical outlets, and signs.

3. This provision does not apply to alterations limited solely to mechanical systems, electrical systems, installation or alteration of fire-protection systems, and abatement of hazardous materials.

4. This provision does not apply to alterations undertaken for the primary purpose of increasing the accessibility of an existing building, facility, or element.

When it is technically unfeasible to make toilet or bath facilities accessible, an accessible unisex facility may be provided. Platform lifts complying with ICC/ANSI A117.1 are specifically allowed in existing buildings. The maximum height of door thresholds is allowed to be ¾ in., with beveled edges on each side.

REFERENCES

1. ACI. 1999 Edition. *Building Code Requirements for Structural Concrete and Commentary*, American Concrete Institute. Farmington Hills, MI

2. ACI. 1999 Edition. *1999 Building Code Requirements for Masonry Structures, Specifications for Masonry Structures and Related Commentaries*, American Concrete Institute. Farmington Hills, MI

3. TCA. 2000 Edition. *2000 Handbook for Ceramic Tile Installation.* Tile Council of America. Anderson, SC

4. AISC. 1989. *ASD Manuals of Steel Construction, 9th Edition.* American Institute of Steel Construction. Chicago, IL

5. AISI. 1989. *American Iron and Steel Institute, 1986 Edition with 1989 Commentary.* Washington, D.C.

6. American Forest & Paper Association, American Wood Council Web site: http://www.forestprod.org/awc/

7. SPC. 1997. *Maximum Span—Southern Pine Joists & Rafters*, Southern Pine Council. Kenner, LA

8. CPSC. 1980. *Code of Federal Regulations, Title 16—Commercial Practices, Part 1201—Safety Standard for Architectural Glazing Materials.* Washington, D.C.

9. ICC. 2000 Edition. *2000 International Building Code.* International Code Council. Falls Church, VA

10. NFPA, 2000 Edition. *2000 Life Safety Code.* National Fire Protection Association, Quincy, MA

ntion Codes cover:
ional, maintenance, and use of buildings
lers and alarms
d tanks and piping, compressed gas or Liquid
e Gas (LPG)
d storage of hazardous materials

Codes cover:
and electrical distribution
cal equipment installation
l hazards

des cover:
nt of insulation required
and glazing
iltration
y efficiency in equipment design

lity Codes cover:
er-free access to buildings—Ramps, access and
s, door widths and door hardware, and plumbing
es

y Codes® cover:
to life from fire in buildings and structures
epartment access

Who Publishes the Codes?

CA publishes the National Building Codes

BO publishes the Uniform Building Codes

CCI publishes the Standard Building Codes

C publishes the family of International Codes

FPA publishes the Life Safety Code®, National
ectrical Code®, and numerous fire standards

UD publishes the Manufactured Housing Standard

PMO publishes the Uniform Plumbing Code and
PMO Uniform Mechanical Codes

AP
WHAT'

Source: NCSBCS,

Wh

Codes safeguard the
occupants by regulati
building components a
such intangibles as ai

Building Codes cove
- **Use group, occup**
  educational, factor
  mercantile, resider
- **Interior light and**
- **Means of egress -**
  exit, corridor and d
- **Fire-resistive con**
  roofs, ceilings, and
- **Fire protection** -- s
  other aspects of fire
- **Structural loads** --
  and dead loads
- **Foundation and fo**
- **Acceptable materi**
- **Construction asse**
  floors, and exterior
- **Special uses** -- gar
  buildings, and interi
- **Other building sys**
  chimneys, electrical
  energy conservation
- **Accessibility**

Mechanical Codes cov
- **Air distribution and**
- **Heating and coolin**
- **Hydronic piping an**
- **Kitchen exhaust ec**
- **Fossil fuel equipme**
  incinerators, chimney
- **Air conditioning an**

Plumbing Codes cover:
- **Water supply, drain**

Fire Preve
- **Opera**
- **Sprin**

- **Fuel**
  Propa
- **Use a**

Electrical
- **Wirin**

- **Elect**
- **Spec**

Energy C
- **Amo**
- **Glass**
- **Air in**
- **Energ**

Accessib
- **Barri**
  egres
  facilit

Life Safe
- **Safe**
- **Fire**

B
IC
S
I
N
E

APPENDIX B
BUILDING CODES TIMELINE

Source: NCSBCS, Introduction to Building Codes 2000

Building Codes Timeline

BC

3500 | City of Ur - markings on bricks and hinges

2000 | Code of Hammurabi mandates death to son of builder if building collapses and kills son of owner

500

100 | Roman building laws

AD

1189 | Henry Fitz-Elwyne's Assize of Buildings—forerunner of modern building code

1666 | Great Fire of London -- first codes are adopted

Building Codes Timeline, Continued

1850	New York City adopts its first city building code
1896	The National Fire Protection Association **(NFPA)** is founded
1905	National Board of Fire Underwriters publishes model building construction regulations
1914	The state of Wisconsin adopts its first mandatory statewide building code
1915	Building Officials and Code Administrators International **(BOCA)** is established, publishes code in 1930
1922	The International Conference of Building Officials **(ICBO)** is established
1927	**ICBO** publishes codes
1940	The Southern Building Code Congress International **(SBCCI)** is established, publishes code same year
1967	The National Conference of States on Building Codes and Standards, Inc. **(NCSBCS)** is established
1972	The Council of American Building Officials **(CABO)** is established
1974	Congress passes the Federal Mobile Home Construction and Safety Standards Act
1977	**NCSBCS** and **CABO** write the Model Energy Code
1980	Congress preempts state regulation of manufactured homes and establishes Federal Manufactured Home Standard
1992	The European community's initiative affects construction products and technologies
	More states adopt statewide building codes based on model codes with no or few amendments
1994	The International Code Council **(ICC)** is established
1995	First ICC Codes made available for adoption
2000	**ICC** "Family of Codes" is published

APPENDIX C

DEFINITION OF GENERAL TERMS

Source: NCSBCS, Introduction to Building Codes 2000

Definition of General Terms:

Codes

are performance and prescriptive requirements for building construction established and enforced by a state or local agency for the protection of public health, safety and welfare.

Model codes

are documents generated by organizations comprised of individuals from the public and private sector. Among these organizations are the International Code Council (ICC), Building Officials and Code Administrators International (BOCA), International Conference of Building Officials (ICBO), Southern Building Code Congress International (SBCCI), the National Fire Protection Association (NFPA), the Western Fire Chiefs Association (WFCA), and the International Association of Plumbing and Mechanical Officials (IAPMO). Model codes include requirements for building, mechanical, plumbing, and fire prevention, and often form the basis for state and local building regulations and laws.

Standards

prescribe a level of acceptability or an approved model to be used in building construction as a basis for comparison. **Test Standards** prescribe test methods and the minimum acceptable results. **Rating Standards** establish a method of measurement to ensure that all similar products can be compared on the same basis. **Design Standards** are minimum criteria that are applied to particular aspects of a building and/or system design.

Regulations

are laws or rules prescribed by an authority to regulate conduct. State, local, or Federal construction regulations incorporate codes and referenced standards.

Building Codes Timeline, Continued

1850	New York City adopts its first city building code
1896	The National Fire Protection Association **(NFPA)** is founded
1905	National Board of Fire Underwriters publishes model building construction regulations
1914	The state of Wisconsin adopts its first mandatory statewide building code
1915	Building Officials and Code Administrators International **(BOCA)** is established, publishes code in 1930
1922	The International Conference of Building Officials **(ICBO)** is established
1927	**ICBO** publishes codes
1940	The Southern Building Code Congress International **(SBCCI)** is established, publishes code same year
1967	The National Conference of States on Building Codes and Standards, Inc. **(NCSBCS)** is established
1972	The Council of American Building Officials **(CABO)** is established
1974	Congress passes the Federal Mobile Home Construction and Safety Standards Act
1977	**NCSBCS** and **CABO** write the Model Energy Code
1980	Congress preempts state regulation of manufactured homes and establishes Federal Manufactured Home Standard
1992	The European community's initiative affects construction products and technologies
	More states adopt statewide building codes based on model codes with no or few amendments
1994	The International Code Council **(ICC)** is established
1995	First ICC Codes made available for adoption
2000	**ICC** "Family of Codes" is published

APPENDIX B
BUILDING CODES TIMELINE

Source: NCSBCS, Introduction to Building Codes 2000

Building Codes Timeline

BC

3500 | City of Ur - markings on bricks and hinges

2000 | Code of Hammurabi mandates death to son of builder if building collapses and kills son of owner

500

100 | Roman building laws

AD

1189 | Henry Fitz-Elwyne's Assize of Buildings—forerunner of modern building code

1666 | Great Fire of London -- first codes are adopted

APPENDIX A
WHAT'S IN A CODE

Source: NCSBCS, Introduction to Building Codes 2000

What's In A Code?

Codes safeguard the health, life safety, and welfare of building occupants by regulating building construction, as well as the building components and materials used. Codes also address such intangibles as air quality and energy consumption.

Building Codes cover:

- **Use group, occupancy type** -- assembly, business, educational, factory and industrial, hazardous, institutional, mercantile, residential, storage, and utility occupancies
- **Interior light and ventilation**
- **Means of egress** -- number of exits, travel distance to an exit, corridor and door widths
- **Fire-resistive construction** -- types of materials for walls, roofs, ceilings, and floors
- **Fire protection** -- sprinklers, fire alarms, standpipes, and other aspects of fire and smoke control
- **Structural loads** -- wind, snow, flood, seismic, and live and dead loads
- **Foundation and footings**
- **Acceptable materials for use in construction**
- **Construction assemblies and fasteners** -- roofs, ceilings, floors, and exterior walls and how they are assembled
- **Special uses** -- garages, atriums, mezzanines, high rise buildings, and interior spaces
- **Other building systems** -- elevators, escalators, fireplaces, chimneys, electrical wiring, mechanical, plumbing, and energy conservation
- **Accessibility**

Mechanical Codes cover:
- **Air distribution and duct system**
- **Heating and cooling equipment**
- **Hydronic piping and fuel oil piping**
- **Kitchen exhaust equipment**
- **Fossil fuel equipment** -- fireplaces, woodstoves, incinerators, chimneys, ventilation, air quality
- **Air conditioning and refrigeration**

Plumbing Codes cover:
- **Water supply, drainage, sewage, and materials**

Fire Prevention Codes cover:
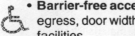
- Operational, maintenance, and use of buildings
- Sprinklers and alarms
- Fuel oil tanks and piping, compressed gas or Liquid Propane Gas (LPG)
- Use and storage of hazardous materials

Electrical Codes cover:
- Wiring and electrical distribution
- Electrical equipment installation
- Special hazards

Energy Codes cover:
- Amount of insulation required
- Glass and glazing
- Air infiltration
- Energy efficiency in equipment design

Accessibility Codes cover:
- Barrier-free access to buildings—Ramps, access and egress, door widths and door hardware, and plumbing facilities

Life Safety Codes® cover:
- Safety to life from fire in buildings and structures
- Fire department access

Who Publishes the Codes?

BOCA publishes the National Building Codes

ICBO publishes the Uniform Building Codes

SBCCI publishes the Standard Building Codes

ICC publishes the family of International Codes

NFPA publishes the Life Safety Code®, National Electrical Code®, and numerous fire standards

HUD publishes the Manufactured Housing Standard

IAPMO publishes the Uniform Plumbing Code and IAPMO Uniform Mechanical Codes

APPENDIX D

MODEL CODES AND STANDARDS RELATED ORGANIZATIONS AND ASSOCIATIONS

Source: NCSBCS, Introduction to Building Codes 2000

Model Codes and Standards Related Organizations and Associations

Many organizations are involved in the development of the model codes and standards that form the basis for many building construction regulations throughout the United States. A partial list is provided below.

Building Officials and Code Administrators International (BOCA)
4051 West Flossmoor Road
Country Club Hills, IL 60478-5795
(708) 799-2300, Fax: (708) 799-4981
Internet: www.bocai.org
Publishes the National Codes series

International Conference of Building Officials (ICBO)
5360 South Workman Mill Road
Whittier, CA 90601
(562) 699-0541, Fax: (562) 692-3853
Internet: www.icbo.org
Publishes the Uniform Codes series

Southern Building Code Congress International (SBCCI)
900 Montclair Road
Birmingham, AL 35213-1206
(205) 591-1853, Fax: (205) 592-7001
Internet: www.sbcci.org
Publishes the Standard Codes series

International Code Council (ICC)
5203 Leesburg Pike, Suite 709
Falls Church, VA 22041
(703) 931-4533, Fax (703) 379-1546
Internet: www.intlcode.org
Publishes the International Code series including the CABO
One-and Two-Family Dwelling Code and Model Energy Code

Air Conditioning and Refrigeration Institute (ARI)
4301 North Fairfax Drive., Suite 425
Arlington, VA 22203
(703) 524-8800, Fax: (703) 528-3816
Internet: www.ari.org

American National Standards Institute (ANSI)
11 West 42nd Street, 13th Floor
New York, NY 10036
(212) 642-4900, Fax (212) 398-0023
Internet: www.ansi.org

American Society of Heating, Refrigerating, and Air Conditioning Engineers (ASHRAE)
1791 Tullie Circle, NE
Atlanta, GA 30329
(404) 636-8400, Fax (404) 321-5478
Internet: www.ashrae.org

American Society of Mechanical Engineers (ASME)
3 Park Avenue
New York, NY 10016
(212) 591-7722, Fax: (212) 591-7674
Internet: www.asme.org

American Society of Testing and Materials (ASTM)
100 Barr Harbor Drive
West Conshocken, PA 19428-2956
(610) 832-9500, Fax: (610) 832-9555
Internet: www.astm.org

Association of Major City Building Officials (AMCBO)
505 Huntmar Park Drive, Suite 210
Herndon, VA 20170
(703) 437-0100, Fax: (703) 481-3596

Industrialized Buildings Commission (IBC)
505 Huntmar Park Drive, Suite 210
Herndon, VA 20170
(703) 481-2022, Fax (703) 481-3596

International Association of Plumbing and Mechanical Officials (IAPMO)
20001 Walnut Drive, South
Walnut, CA 91789-2825
(909) 595-8449, Fax: (909) 594-1537
Internet: www.iapmo.org
(IAPMO publishes the Uniform Plumbing Code)

National Conference of States on Building Codes and Standards, Inc. (NCSBCS)
505 Huntmar Park Drive, Suite 210
Herndon, VA 20170
(703) 437-0100, Fax (703) 481-3596
Internet: www.ncsbcs.org

National Fire Protection Association (NFPA)
One Batterymarch Park
Quincy, MA 02269-9101
(617) 770-3000, Fax (617) 770-0700
Internet: www.nfpa.org
(NFPA publishes Life Safety Codes®, National Electrical Code®, and numerous other fire standards)

Plumbing-Heating-Cooling Contractors National Association (PHCC)
180 South Washington Street
P.O. Box 6808
Falls Church, VA 22040
(800) 533-7694, Fax: (703) 237-7442
Internet: www.naphcc.org

Underwriters Laboratories (UL)
333 Pfingsten Road
Northbrook, IL 60062
(847) 272-8800, Fax: (847) 272-8129
Internet: www.ul.com

Western Fire Chiefs Association (WFCA)
300 N. Main St. #25
Fallbrook, CA 92028
Phone: 760-723-6911
Fax: 760-723-6912
Internet: www.wfca.com

APPENDIX E

SAMPLE MODEL CODES AND STANDARDS

Source: AIA Handbook. American Institute of Architects

SAMPLE MODEL CODES AND STANDARDS

Building codes	BOCA National Building Code	BOCA
	Standard Building Code	SBCCI
	Uniform Building Code	ICBO
	One- and Two-Family Dwelling Code	CABO
Mechanical codes	National Mechanical Code	BOCA
	Standard Mechanical Code	SBCCI
	Uniform Mechanical Code	ICBO
Plumbing codes	National Plumbing Code	BOCA
	Standard Plumbing Code	SBCCI
	ICBO Plumbing Code	ICBO
	Uniform Plumbing Code	IAMPO
Fire codes	National Fire Prevention Code	BOCA
	Standard Fire Prevention Code	SBCCI
	Uniform Fire Code	ICBO
	Fire Prevention Code	NFPA
	National Fire Codes	NFPA

SAMPLE MODEL CODES AND STANDARDS

Energy conservation code	Model Energy Code	CABO
Electrical code	National Electrical Code	NFPA
Gas codes	National Fuel Gas Codes	NFPA
	Standard Gas Code	SBCCI
Sign codes	Uniform Sign Code	ICBO
One-and	Model One- and	
Two-family dwellings	Two-Family Dwelling Code	CABO

Miscellaneous standards

	ANSI Standards Catalogue	ANSI
	ASTM Standards Catalogue	ASTM
	NFPA Codes and Standards Catalogue	NFPA
	Life Safety Code (NFPA 101)	NFPA
	Standard Building Code Book of Standards	SBCCI
	Uniform Building Code Book of Standards	ICBO

SAMPLE MODEL CODES AND STANDARDS

ANSI	American National Standards Institute
ASTM	American Society for Testing and Materials
BOCA	Building Officials and Code Administrators, Inc.
CABO	Council of American Building Officials
ICBO	International Conference of Building Officials
IAMPO	International Association of Plumbing and Mechanical Officials
NFPA	National Fire Protection Association
SBCCI	Southern Building Code Congress International

APPENDIX F
SBCCI PUBLICATIONS

Source: SBCCI Web site, www.sbcci.org

SBCCI PUBLICATIONS

Southern Building Code Congress International, Inc.
900 Montclair Road
Birmingham, Alabama 35213-1206
205-591-1853

1994 Standard Building Code

1997 Standard Building Code

1999 Standard Building Code

1999 Standard Fire Prevention Code

1994 Standard Gas Code

1997 Standard Gas Code

1999 Standard Gas Code

1994 Standard Mechanical Code

1997 Standard Mechanical Code

1994 Standard Plumbing Code

1997 Standard Plumbing Code

1994 Standard Fire Prevention Code

1997 Standard Fire Prevention Code

1997 Standard Existing Building Code

1994 Standard Swimming Pool Code

1996 National Electrical Code, (NFPA 70-96)

1999 National Electrical Code, (NFPA 70-99)

1995 ICABO Model Energy Code

1995 ICABO 1 & 2 Family Dwelling Code

International Codes

1998 International One- and Two-Family Dwelling Code

2000 International Building Code

1998 International Energy Conservation Code

2000 International Energy Conservation Code

2000 International Fire Code

1998 International Fuel Gas Code

2000 International Fuel Gas Code

1998 International Mechanical Code

2000 International Mechanical Code

1999 Private Sewage Disposal Code

1997 International Plumbing Code

2000 International Plumbing Code

1998 International Property Maintenance Code

2000 International Property Maintenance Code

2000 International Residential Code

2000 International Zoning Code

1997 International Plumbing Code and International Private Sewage Disposal Code

1997 International Private Sewage Disposal Code

1997 International Property Maintenance Code, 1998

Code Revisions and Supplements

1998 Standard Building Code Revisions

1997 Standard Plumbing Code Revisions

1996 Standard Plumbing Code Revisions

1996 Standard Gas Code Revisions

Standard Fire Prevention Code Revisions

1996 Standard Mechanical Code Revisions

1996 Building Code Revisions

1996/97 ICABO 1 & 2 Family Dwelling Code Revisions

1999 ICC Accumulative Supplement

1998 Supplement to the International Private Sewage Disposal Code

1996 Supplement to the International Plumbing Code and International Sewage Disposal Code 1997 Supplement to the International Mechanical Code

Commentaries

1997 Standard Building Code Commentary

1997 Standard Gas Code Commentary

1997 Mechanical Code Commentary

1995 Commentary to CABO 1 & 2 Family Dwelling Code

1995 Commentary to CABO Model Energy Code

1997 International Plumbing Code Commentary

1996 International Mechanical Code Commentary

APPENDIX G
BOCA PUBLICATIONS

Source: BOCA Web site, www.bocai.org

BOCA PUBLICATIONS

Building Officials Code Administration International, Inc.
4051 West Flossmoor Road
Country Club Hills, IL 50478
708-799-2300

2000 International Building Code

2000 International Residential Code

1996 BOCA National Building Code

1999 BOCA National Building Code

1993 BOCA National Building Code Commentary

1996 BOCA National Building Code Commentary

1999 BOCA National Building Code Commentary

1993 BOCA National Mechanical Code

1996 BOCA National Fire Prevention Code

1999 BOCA National Fire Prevention Code

1990 BOCA National Plumbing Code

1993 BOCA National Plumbing Code

1996 BOCA National Property Maintenance Code

1998 International One- and Two-Family Dwelling Code

1995 International Plumbing Code

1997 International Plumbing Code

1996 International Mechanical Code

1998 International Mechanical Code

1998 International Property Maintenance Code

1997 International Fuel Gas Code

1998 International Zoning Code

1998 International Energy Conservation Code

1995 International Private Sewage Disposal Code

1997 International Private Sewage Disposal Code

1995 CABO One- and Two-Family Dwelling Code

1995 CABO Model Energy Code

1992 CABO/ANSI Al 17.1 Standard for Accessible & Usable Building & Facilities

1998 ICC/ANSI Al 17.1 Standard for Accessible & Usable Building & Facilities

1998 ICC/ANSI 2.0 Manufactured Housing Construction and Safety Standard

1999 ASTM Building Code Standards

2000 ADA & Building Transportation Handbook

1997 Kentucky Building Code

1998 Ohio Building Code with Ohio Elevator Code

1998 Ohio Fire Code with Selected Ohio Laws

1998 Ohio Mechanical Code with Pressure Piping and Boiler Code

1998 Ohio Plumbing Code

1996 OBOA One-, Two-, and Three-Family Dwelling Code

APPENDIX H
ICBO PUBLICATIONS

Source: ICBO Web site, www.icbo.org

ICBO PUBLICATIONS

International Conference of Building Officials
5360 Workman Mill Road
Whittier, CA 90601-2298
800-284-4406
562-699-0541

1998 International Energy Conservation Code

1998 International Zoning Code

1998 International Property Maintenance Code

1997 International Fuel Gas Code

1996 International Mechanical Code

1997 International Mechanical Code Supplement

1998 International Mechanical Code

1995 International Private Sewage Disposal Code

1997 International Private Sewage Disposal Code

1994 Uniform Building Code, Volumes 1, 2, & 3

1997 Uniform Building Code, Volumes 1, 2, & 3

1997 Uniform Swimming Pool, Spa, and Hot Tub Code

1997 Dwelling Requirements under the Uniform Plumbing Code

1991 Uniform Building Code

1988 UBC Standards

1991 UBC Standards

1988 Uniform Mechanical Code

1991 Uniform Mechanical Code

1994 Uniform Mechanical Code

1997 Uniform Mechanical Code

1991 Uniform Housing Code

1994 Uniform Housing Code

1997 Uniform Housing Code

1991 Uniform Code for the Abatement of Dangerous Buildings

1994 Uniform Code for the Abatement of Dangerous Buildings

1997 Uniform Code for the Abatement of Dangerous Buildings

1991 Uniform Sign Code

1994 Uniform Sign Code

1997 Uniform Sign Code

1991 Dwelling Construction under the Uniform Mechanical Code

1994 Dwelling Construction under the Uniform Mechanical Code

1997 Dwelling Construction under the Uniform Mechanical Code

1991 Dwelling Construction under the Uniform Building Code

1994 Dwelling Construction under the Uniform Building Code

1997 Dwelling Construction under the Uniform Building Code

1991 Uniform Fire Code

1994 Uniform Fire Code, Volumes 1 & 2

1997 Uniform Fire Code, Volumes 1 & 2

1991 Analysis of Revisions to the 1991 Uniform Codes

1994 Analysis of Revisions to the 1994 Uniform Codes

1997 Analysis of Revisions to the 1997 Uniform Codes

1993 Accumulative Supplement to the Uniform Codes

1996 Accumulative Supplement to the Uniform Codes

1992 CABO One- and Two-Family Dwelling Code

1995 CABO One- and Two-Family Dwelling Code

1998 International One- and Two-Family Dwelling Code

1995 International Plumbing Code

1997 International Plumbing Code

1995 International Plumbing Code and International Private Sewage Disposal Code

1997 International Plumbing Code and International Private Sewage Disposal Code

1996 Supplement to the International Plumbing Code and International Private Sewage Disposal Code

1998 Supplement to the International Plumbing Code and International Private Sewage Disposal Code

1994 Uniform Plumbing Code

1997 Uniform Plumbing Code

1994 Uniform Solar Energy Code

1997 Uniform Solar Energy Code

1993 National Electrical Code

1996 National Electrical Code

1999 National Electrical Code

1993 Uniform Administrative Code Provisions for the NEC

1996 Uniform Administrative Code Provisions for the NEC

1991 Uniform Building Security Code

1994 Uniform Building Security Code

1997 Uniform Building Security Code

1991 Uniform Administrative Code

1994 Uniform Administrative Code

1997 Uniform Administrative Code

1991 UFC Standards

1994 Uniform Zoning Code

1997 Uniform Zoning Code

1993/1994 Amendments to the CABO One- and Two-Family Dwelling Code

1996/1997 Amendments to the CABO One- and Two-Family Dwelling Code

1992 CABO Model Energy Code

1993 CABO Model Energy Code

1995 CABO Model Energy Code

1991 Guidelines for Manufactured Housing Installations

1991 Uniform Code for Building Conservation

1994 Uniform Code for Building Conservation

1997 Uniform Code for Building Conservation

1997 Urban-Wildland Interface Code

1997 Uniform Swimming Pool, Spa, and Hot Tub Code

1995 CABO One- and Two-Family Dwelling Code

1998 International One- and Two-Family Dwelling Code

1997 Uniform Solar Energy Code

1996 National Electrical Code

1995 CABO Model Energy Code

1996 BOCA National Building Code

1999 BOCA National Building Code

1996 BOCA National Fire Code

1999 BOCA National Fire Code

1999 National Fire Code

1997 Standard Building Code

1999 Standard Building Code

1997 Standard Fire Code

1999 Standard Fire Code

1997 Standard Gas Code

1999 Standard Gas Code

1997 Standard Mechanical Code

2000 International Fuel Gas Code

2000 International Building Code

2000 International Mechanical Code

2000 International Fire Code

APPENDIX I
NFPA PUBLICATIONS

Source: NFPA Web site, www.nfpa.org

NFPA PUBLICATIONS

National Fire Protection Association
1 Batterymarch Park
Quincy, MA 02269
617-770-3000
800-344-3555

NFPA 1: Fire Prevention Code, 2000 Edition

NFPA Fire Prevention Code Handbook, 2000 Edition

NFPA 1: Fire Prevention Code, 1997 Edition

NFPA Fire Prevention Code Handbook, 1997 Edition

NFPA 10: Standard for Portable Fire Extinguishers, 1998 Edition

NFPA 10: Standard for Portable Fire Extinguishers, 1994 Edition

NFPA 11: Standard for Low Expansion Foam, 1998 Edition

NFPA 11A: Standard for Medium- and High-Expansion Foam Systems, 1999 Edition

NFPA 12: Standard on Carbon Dioxide Extinguishing Systems, 2000 Edition

NFPA 12: Standard on Carbon Dioxide Extinguishing Systems, 1998 Edition

NFPA 12A: Standard on Halon 1301 Fire Extinguishing Systems, 1997 Edition

NFPA 13: Installation of Sprinkler Systems, 1999 Edition

NFPA 13: Installation of Sprinkler Systems, 1994 Edition (Spanish)

NFPA 13D: Standard for the Installation of Sprinkler in One- and Two-Family Dwellings and Manufactured Homes, 1999 Edition

NFPA 13E: Guide for Fire Department Operations in Properties Protected by Sprinkler and Standpipe Systems, 2000 Edition

NFPA 13E: Guide for Fire Department Operations in Properties Protected by Sprinkler and Standpipe Systems, 1995 Edition

NFPA 13R: Standard for Installation of Sprinkler Systems in Residential Occupancies up to and Including Four Stories in Height, 1999 Edition

NFPA 14: Standard for the Installation of Standpipe, Private Hydrants, and Hose Systems, 2000 Edition

NFPA 14: Standard for the Installation of Standpipe and Hose Systems, 1996 Edition

NFPA 15: Standard for Water Spray Fixed Systems for Fire Protection, 1996 Edition

NFPA 16: Standard for the Installation of Foam-Water Sprinkler and Foam-Water Spray Systems, 1999 Edition

NFPA 16A: Standard for the Installation of Closed-Head Foam-Water Sprinkler Systems, 1994 Edition

NFPA 17: Standard for Dry Chemical Extinguishing Systems, 1998 Edition

NFPA 17A: Standard for Wet Chemical Extinguishing Systems, 1998 Edition

NFPA 18: Standard on Wetting Agents, 1995 Edition

NFPA 20: Standard for the Installation of Stationary Fire Pumps for Fire Protection, 1999 Edition

NFPA 20: Standard for the Installation of Centrifugal Fire Pumps, 1996 Edition

NFPA 22: Standard for Water Tanks for Private Fire Protection, 1998 Edition

NFPA 24: Installation of Private Fire Service Mains and Their Appurtenances, 1995 Edition

NFPA 25: Inspection, Testing, and Maintenance of Water-Based Fire Protection Systems, 1998 Edition

NFPA 30: Flammable & Combustible Liquids Code, 1996 Edition

NFPA 3OA: Automotive and Marine Service Stations Code, 1996 Edition

NFPA 3OA: Automotive and Marine Service Stations Code, 1996 Edition (Spanish)

NFPA 3OB: Code for the Manufacture and Storage of Aerosol Products, 1998 Edition

NFPA 31: Standard for the Installation of Oil Burning Equipment, 1997 Edition

NFPA 32: Standard for Dry-cleaning Plants, 1996 Edition

NFPA 33: Standard for Spray Application Using Flammable or Combustible Materials, 1995 Edition

NFPA 34: Standard for Dipping and Coating Processes Using Flammable or Combustible Liquids, 1995 Edition

NFPA 35: Standard for the Manufacture of Organic Coatings, 1999 Edition

NFPA 36: Standard for Solvent Extraction Plants, 1997 Edition

NFPA 37: Standard for the Installation and Use of Stationary Combustion Engines and Gas Turbines, 1998 Edition

NFPA 40: Standard for the Storage and Handling of Cellulose Nitrate Motion Picture Film, 1997 Edition

NFPA 42: Code for the Storage of Pyroxylin Plastic, 1997 Edition

NFPA 45: Standard on Fire Protection for Laboratories Using Chemicals, 1996 Edition

NFPA 49: Hazardous Chemicals Data, 1994 Edition

NFPA 50: Standard for Bulk Oxygen Systems at Consumer Sites, 1996 Edition

NFPA 5OA: Standard for Gaseous Hydrogen Systems at Consumer Sites, 1999 Edition

NFPA 5OB: Standard for Liquefied Hydrogen Systems at Consumer Sites, 1999 Edition

NFPA 51: Standard for the Design and Installation of Oxygen Fuel Gas Systems for Welding, Cutting, and Allied Processes, 1997 Edition

NFPA 51A: Standard for Acetylene Cylinder Charging Plants, 1996 Edition

NFPA 51B: Standard for Fire Prevention During Welding, Cutting, and Other Hotwork, 1999 Edition

NFPA 52: Compressed Natural Gas (CNG) Vehicular Fuel Systems Code, 1998 Edition

NFPA 53: Recommended Practice on Materials, Equipment, and Systems Used in Oxygen-Enriched Atmospheres, 1999 Edition

National Fuel Gas Code Handbook, 1999 Edition

NFPA 54: National Fuel Gas Code, 1999 Edition

NFPA 54: National Fuel Gas Code, 1996 Edition (Spanish)

NFPA 55: Standard for the Storage, Use, and Handling of Compressed and Liquefied Gases in Portable Cylinders, 1998 Edition

NFPA 57: Liquefied Natural Gas (LNG) Fuel Systems Code, 1999 Edition

NFPA 58: Liquefied Petroleum Gas Code 1998 Edition

NFPA 58: Liquefied Petroleum Gas Code, 1995 Edition (Spanish)

LP Gas Code and Handbook Set, 1998 Edition

NFPA 59: Standard for the Storage and Handling of Liquefied Petroleum Gases at Utility Gas Plant, 1998 Edition

NFPA 59A: Standard for the Production, Storage, and Handling of Liquefied Natural Gas (LNG), 1996 Edition

NFPA 61: Standard for the Prevention of Fires and Dust Explosions in Agricultural and Food Products Facilities, 1999 Edition

NFPA 68: Guide for Venting of Deflagrations, 1998 Edition

NFPA 69: Standard on Explosion Prevention Systems, 1997 Edition

NFPA 70: National Electrical Code, 1999 Edition

NFPA 70E: Standard for Electrical Safety Requirements for Employee Workplaces, 2000 Edition

NFPA 7OB: Recommended Practice for Electrical Equipment Maintenance, 1998 Edition

NFPA 70E: Standard for Electrical Safety Requirements for Employee Workplaces, 1995 Edition

NFPA 72: National Fire Alarm Code, 1999

NFPA 73: Residential Electrical Maintenance Code for One- and Two-Family Dwellings, 1996 Edition

NFPA 75: Standard for the Protection of Electronic Computer/Data Processing Equipment, 1999 Edition

NFPA 75: Standard for the Protection of Electronic Computer/Data Processing Equipment, 1992 Edition (Spanish)

NFPA 77: Recommended Practice on Static Electricity, 1993 Edition

NFPA 79: Electrical Standard for Industrial Machinery, 1997 Edition

NFPA 80: Standard for Fire Doors, Fire Windows, 1999 Edition

NFPA 8OA: Recommended Practice for Protection of Buildings from Exterior Fire, Exposures, 1996 Edition

NFPA 82: Standard on Incinerators and Waste and Linen Handling Systems and Equipment, 1999 Edition

NFPA 86: Standard for Ovens and Furnaces, 1999 Edition

NFPA 86C: Standard for Industrial Furnaces Using a Special Processing Atmosphere, 1999 Edition

NFPA 86D: Standard for Industrial Furnaces Using Vacuum as an Atmosphere, 1999 Edition

NFPA 88A: Standard for Parking Structures, 1998 Edition

NFPA 88B: Standard for Repair Garages, 1997 Edition

NFPA 9OA: Standard for the Installation of Air Conditioning and Ventilating Systems, 1999 Edition

NFPA 9OB: Standard for the Installation of Warm Air Heating and Air Conditioning Systems, 1999 Edition

NFPA 91: Standard for Exhaust Systems for Air Conveying of Vapors, Gases, Mists, and Noncombustible Particulate Solids, 1999 Edition

NFPA 92A: Recommended Practice for Smoke-Control Systems, 1996 Edition

NFPA 92B: Guide for Smoke Management Systems in Malls, Atria, and Large Areas, 1995 Edition

NFPA 96: Standard for Ventilation Control and Fire Protection of Commercial Cooking Operations, 1998 Edition

NFPA 97: Standard Glossary of Terms Relating to Chimneys, Vents, and Heat-Producing Appliances, 2000 Edition

NFPA 99: Standard for Health Care Facilities, 1999 Edition

NFPA 99B: Standard for Hypobaric Facility, 1999 Edition

NFPA 99C: Standard on Gas and Vacuum Systems, 1999 Edition

NFPA 101: Life Safety Code, 2000 Edition

NFPA 101: Life Safety Code, 1997 Edition

NFPA 101A: Guide on Alternative Approaches to Life Safety, 1998 Edition

NFPA 101 B: Code for Means of Egress for Buildings and Structures, 1999 Edition

NFPA 102: Standard for Grandstands, Folding and Telescopic Seating, Tents, and Membrane Structures, 1995 Edition

NFPA 105: Recommended Practice for the Installation of Smoke-Control Door Assemblies, 1999 Edition

NFPA 110: Standard for Emergency and Standby Power Systems, 1999 Edition

NFPA 111: Standard on Stored Electrical Energy Emergency and Standby Power Systems, 1996 Edition

NFPA 115: Recommended Practice on Laser Fire Protection, 1999 Edition

NFPA 120: Standard for Coal Preparation Plants, 1999 Edition

NFPA 121: Standard on Fire Protection for Self-Propelled and Mobile Surface Mining Equipment, 1996 Edition

NFPA 122: Standard for Fire Prevention and Control in Underground Metal and Nonmetal Mines, 1995 Edition

NFPA 123: Standard for Fire Prevention and Control in Underground Bituminous Coal Mines, 1999 Edition

NFPA 130: Standard for Fixed Guideway Transit and Passenger Rail Systems, 2000 Edition

NFPA 130: Standard for Fixed Guideway Transit Systems, 1997 Edition

NFPA 140: Standard on Motion Picture and Television Production Studio Soundstages and Approved Production Facilities, 1999 Edition

NFPA 150: Standard on Fire Safety in Racetrack Stables, 1995 Edition

NFPA 160: Standard for the Flame Effects Before an Audience, 1998 Edition

NFPA 170: Standard for Fire Safety Symbols, 1999 Edition

NFPA 203: Guide on Roof Coverings and Roof Deck Constructions, 1995 Edition

NFPA 204: Guide for Smoke and Heat Venting, 1998 Edition

NFPA 211: Standard for Chimneys, Fireplaces, Vents, and Solid Fuel-Burning Appliances, 2000 Edition

NFPA 211: Standard for Chimneys, Fireplaces, Vents, and Solid Fuel-Burning Appliances, 1996 Edition

NFPA 214: Standard on Water-Cooling Towers, 1996 Edition

NFPA 220: Standard on Types of Building Construction, 1999 Edition

NFPA 221: Standard for Fire Walls and Fire Barrier Walls, 1997 Edition

NFPA 230: Standard for the Fire Protection of Storage, 1999 Edition

NFPA 231D: Standard for Storage of Rubber Tires, 1998 Edition

NFPA 232: Standard for the Protection of Records, 1995 Edition

NFPA 232A: Guide for Fire Protection for Archives and Records Centers, 1995 Edition

NFPA 241: Standard for Safeguarding Construction, Alteration, and Demolition Operations, 1996 Edition

NFPA 251: Standard Methods of Tests of Fire Endurance of Building Construction and Materials, 1999 Edition

NFPA 252: Standard Methods of Fire Tests of Door Assemblies, 1999 Edition

NFPA 253: Standard Method of Test for Critical Radiant Flux for Floor Covering Systems Using a Radiant Heat Energy Source, 2000 Edition

NFPA 253: Standard Method of Test for Critical Radiant Flux for Floor Covering Systems Using a Radiant Heat Energy Source, 1995 Edition

NFPA 255: Standard Method of Test of Surface Burning Characteristics of Building Materials, 2000 Edition

NFPA 255: Standard Method of Test of Surface Burning Characteristics of Building Materials, 1996 Edition

NFPA 256: Standard Methods of Fire Tests of Roof Coverings, 1998 Edition

NFPA 257: Standard on Fire Test for Window and Glass Block Assemblies, 2000 Edition

NFPA 257: Standard for Fire Test for Window and Glass Block Assemblies, 1996 Edition

NFPA 258: Standard Research Test Method for Determining Smoke Generation of Solid Materials, 1997 Edition

NFPA 259: Standard Test Method for Potential Heat of Building Materials, 1998 Edition

NFPA 260: Standard Methods of Tests and Classification System for Cigarette Ignition Resistance of Components of Upholstered Furniture, 1998 Edition

NFPA 261: Standard Method of Test for Determining Resistance of Mock-Up Upholstered Furniture Material Assemblies to Ignition by Smoldering Cigarettes, 1998 Edition

NFPA 262: Standard Method of Test for Flame Travel and Smoke of Wires and Cables for Use in Air-Handling Spaces, 1999 Edition

NFPA 265: Standard Methods of Fire Tests for Evaluating Room Fire Growth Contribution of Textile Wallcoverings, 1998 Edition

NFPA 266: Standard Method of Test for Fire Characteristics of Upholstered Furniture Exposed to Flaming Ignition Source, 1998 Edition

NFPA 267: Standard Method of Test for Fire Characteristics of Mattresses and Bedding Assemblies Exposed to Flaming Ignition Source, 1998 Edition

NFPA 268: Standard Test Method for Determining Ignitability of Exterior Wall Assemblies Using a Radiant Heat Energy Source, 1996 Edition

NFPA 269: Standard Test Method for Developing Toxic Potency Data for Use in Fire Hazard Modeling, 2000 Edition

NFPA 269: Standard Test Method for Developing Toxic Potency Data for Use in Fire Hazard Modeling, 1996 Edition

NFPA 270: Standard Test Method for Measurement of Smoke Obscuration Using Conical Radiant Source in a Single Closed Chamber, 1998 Edition

NFPA 271: Standard Method of Test for Heat and Visible Release Rates for Materials and Products using an Oxygen Consumption Calorimeter, 1998 Edition

NFPA 272: Standard Method of Test for Heat and Visible Smoke Release Rates for Materials and Products Using an Oxygen Consumption Calorimeter, 1999 Edition

NFPA 285: Evaluation of Flammability Characteristics of Exterior Non-load-bearing Wall Assemblies Containing Components Using the Intermediate Scale Multi-Story Test Apparatus, 1998 Edition

NFPA 286: Standard Methods of Fire Tests for Evaluating Room Fire Growth Contribution of Wall and Ceiling Interior Finish, 2000 Edition

NFPA 295: Standard for Wildfire Control, 1998 Edition

NFPA 299: Standard for Protection of Life and Property from Wildfire, 1997 Edition

NFPA 301: Code for Safety to Life from Fire on Merchant Vessels, 1998 Edition

NFPA 302: Fire Protection Standard for Pleasure and Commercial Motor Craft, 1998 Edition

NFPA 303: Fire Protection Standard for Marinas and Boatyards, 1995 Edition

NFPA 306: Standard for the Control of Gas Hazards on Vessels, 1997 Edition

NFPA 307: Standard for the Construction and Fire Protection of Marine Terminals Piers, and Wharves, 1995 Edition

NFPA 312: Standard for Fire Protection of Vessels during Construction, Repair, and Lay-Up, 1995 Edition

NFPA 318: Standard for the Protection of Clean Rooms, 1998 Edition

NFPA 325: Guide to Fire Hazard Properties of Flammable Liquids, Gases, and Volatile Solids, 1994 Edition

NFPA 326: Standard for the Safeguarding of Tanks and Containers for Entry, Cleaning, or Repair, 1999 Edition

NFPA 329: Recommended Practice for Handling Releases of Flammable and Combustible Liquids and Gases, 1999 Edition

NFPA 385: Standard for Tank Vehicles for Flammable and Combustible Liquids, 2000 Edition

NFPA 385: Standard for Tank Vehicles for Flammable and Combustible Liquids, 1990 Edition

NFPA 395: Standard for the Storage of Flammable and Combustible Liquids at Farms and Isolated Sites, 1993 Edition

NFPA 402: Guide for Aircraft Rescue and Fire Fighting Operations, 1996 Edition

NFPA 402: Guide for Aircraft Rescue and Fire Fighting Operations, 1996 Edition (Spanish)

NFPA 403: Standard for Aircraft Rescue and Fire Fighting Services at Airports, 1998 Edition

NFPA 403: Standard for Aircraft Rescue and Fire Fighting Services at Airports, 1993 Edition

NFPA 405: Recommended Practice for the Recurring Proficiency Training of Aircraft Rescue and Fire Fighting Services, 1999 Edition

NFPA 407: Standard for Aircraft Fuel Servicing, 1996 Edition

NFPA 408: Standard for Aircraft Hand Portable Fire Extinguishers, 1999 Edition

NFPA 409: Standard on Aircraft Hangers, 1995 Edition

NFPA 410: Standard on Aircraft Maintenance, 1999 Edition

NFPA 412: Standard for Evaluating Aircraft Rescue and Fire Fighting Foam Equipment, 1998 Edition

NFPA 414: Standard for Aircraft Rescue and Fire Fighting Vehicles, 1995 Edition

NFPA 415: Standard on Airport Terminal Buildings, Fueling Ramp Drainage, and Loading Walkways, 1997 Edition

NFPA 415: Standard on Airport Terminal Buildings, Fueling Ramp Drainage, and Loading Walkways, 1997 Edition (Spanish)

NFPA 418: Standard for Heliports, 1995 Edition

NFPA 422: Guide for Aircraft Accident Response, 1999 Edition

NFPA 423: Standard for Construction and Protection of Aircraft Engine Test Facilities, 1999 Edition

NFPA 424: Guide for Airport Community Emergency Planning, 1996 Edition

NFPA 430: Code for the Storage of Liquid and Solid Oxidizers, 2000 Edition

NFPA 430: Code for the Storage of Liquid and Solid Oxidizers, 1995 Edition

NFPA 432: Code for the Storage of Organic Peroxide Formulations, 1997 Edition

NFPA 434: Code for the Storage of Pesticides (formerly 43D), 1998 Edition

NFPA 471: Recommended Practice for Responding to Hazardous Materials Incidents, 1997 Edition

NFPA 472: Standard for Professional Competence of Responders to Hazardous Materials Incidents, 1997 Edition

NFPA 473: Standard for Competencies for EMS Personnel Responding to Hazardous Materials Incidents, 1997 Edition

NFPA 480: Standard for the Storage, Handling, and Processing of Magnesium Solids and Powders, 1998 Edition

NFPA 481: Standard for the Production, Processing, Handling and Storage of Titanium, 1995 Edition

NFPA 482: Standard for the Production, Processing, Handling, and Storage of Zirconium, 1996 Edition

NFPA 485: Standard for the Storage, Handling, Processing, and Use of Lithium Metal, 1999 Edition

NFPA 490: Code for the Storage of Ammonium Nitrate, 1998 Edition

NFPA 495: Explosive Materials Code, 1996 Edition

NFPA 496: Standard for Purged and Pressurized Enclosures for Electrical Equipment, 1998 Edition

NFPA 497: Classification of Flammable Liquids, Gases, or Vapors and of Hazardous (Classified) Locations for Electrical Installations in Chemical Process Areas, 1997 Edition

NFPA 498: Standard for Safe Havens and Interchange Lots for Vehicles Transporting Explosives, 1996 Edition

NFPA 499: Classification of Combustible Dusts and of Hazardous (Classified) Locations for Electrical Installations in Chemical Process Areas, 1997 Edition

NFPA 501: Standard on Manufactured Housing, 1999 Edition

NFPA 501A: Standard for Fire Safety Criteria for Manufactured Home Installations, Sites, and Communities, 1999 Edition

NFPA 502: Standard for Road Tunnels, Bridges, and Other Limited Access Highways, 1998 Edition

NFPA 505: Fire Safety Standard for Powered Industrial Trucks Including Type Designations, Areas of Use, Conversions, Maintenance, and Operations, 1999 Edition

NFPA 513: Standard for Motor Freight Terminals, 1998 Edition

NFPA 520: Standard on Subterranean Spaces, 1999 Edition

NFPA 550: Guide to the Fire Safety Concepts Tree, 1995 Edition

NFPA 555: Guide on Methods for Evaluating Potential for Room Flashover, 1996 Edition

NFPA 560: Standard for the Storage, Handling, and Use of Ethylene Oxide for Sterilization and Fumigations, 1995 Edition

NFPA 600: Standard on Industrial Fire Brigades, 2000 Edition

NFPA 600: Standard on Industrial Fire Brigades, 1996 Edition

NFPA 601: Standard for Security Services in Fire Loss Prevention, 2000 Edition

NFPA 601: Standard for Security Services in Fire Loss Prevention, 1996 Edition

NFPA 650: Standard for Pneumatic Conveying Systems for Handling Combustible Particulate Solids, 1998 Edition

NFPA 651: Standard for the Machining and Finishing of Aluminum and the Production and Handling of Aluminum Products, 1998 Edition

NFPA 654: Standard for the Prevention of Fire and Dust Explosions from the Manufacturing, Processing, and Handling of Combustible Particulate Solids, 1997 Edition

NFPA 655: Standard for Prevention of Sulfur Fires and Explosions, 1993 Edition

NFPA 664: Standard for the Prevention of Fires and Explosions in Wood Processing and Woodworking Facilities, 1998 Edition

NFPA 701: Standard Methods of Fire Tests for Flame Propagation of Textiles and Films, 1999 Edition

NFPA 703: Standard for Fire Retardant Impregnated Wood and Fire Retardant Coatings for Building Materials, 1995 Edition

NFPA 704: Standard for the Identification of the Fire Hazards of Materials for Emergency Response, 1996 Edition

NFPA 705: Recommended Practice for a Field Flame Test for Textiles and Films, 1997 Edition

NFPA 720: Recommended Practice for the Installation of Household Carbon Monoxide (CO) Warning Equipment, 1998 Edition

NFPA 750: Standard on Water Mist Fire Protection Systems, 2000 Edition

NFPA 750: Standard on Water Mist Fire Protection Systems, 1996 Edition

NFPA 780: Standard for the Installation of Lightning Protection Systems, 1997 Edition

NFPA 801: Standard for Fire Protection for Facilities Handling Radioactive Materials, 1998 Edition

NFPA 803: Standard for Fire Protection for Light Water Nuclear Power Plants

NFPA 804: Standard for Fire Protection for Advanced Light Water Reactor Electric Generating Plants, 1995 Edition

NFPA 820: Standard for Fire Protection in Wastewater Treatment and Collection Facilities, 1999 Edition

NFPA 850: Recommended Practice for Fire Protection for Electric Generating Plants and High Voltage Direct Current Converter Stations, 2000 Edition

NFPA 850: Recommended Practice for Fire Protection for Electric Generating Plants and High Voltage Direct Current Converter Stations, 1996 Edition

NFPA 851: Recommended Practice for Fire Protection for Hydroelectric Generating Plants, 2000 Edition

NFPA 851: Recommended Practice for Fire Protection for Hydroelectric Generating Plants, 1996 Edition

NFPA 901: Standard Classifications for Incident Reporting and Fire Protection Data, 1995 Edition

NFPA 902: Fire Reporting Field Incident Guide, 1997 Edition

NFPA 903: Fire Reporting Property Survey Guide, 1996 Edition

NFPA 904: Incident Follow-up Report Guide, 1996 Edition

NFPA 906: Guide for Fire Incident Field Notes, 1998 Edition

NFPA 909: Standard for the Protection of Cultural Resources Including Museums, Libraries, Places of Worship, and Historic Properties, 1997 Edition

NFPA 914: Recommended Practice for Fire Protection in Historic Structures, 1994 Edition

NFPA 921: Guide for Fire and Explosion Investigations, 1998 Edition

NFPA 921: Guide for Fire and Explosion Investigations, 1995 Edition (Spanish)

NFPA 1000: Standard for Fire Service Professional Qualifications Accreditation and Certification Systems, 1994 Edition

NFPA 1001: Standard for Fire Fighter Professional Qualifications, 1997 Edition

NFPA 1002: Standard on Fire Apparatus Driver/Operator Professional Qualifications, 1998 Edition

NFPA 1003: Standard for Airport Fire Fighter Professional Qualifications, 2000 Edition

NFPA 1003: Standard for Airport Fire Fighter Professional Qualifications, 1994 Edition

NFPA 1006: Standard for Rescue Technician Professional Qualifications, 2000 Edition

NFPA 1021: Standard for Fire Officer Professional Qualifications, 1997 Edition

NFPA 1031: Standard for Professional Qualifications for Fire Inspector and Plan Examiner, 1998 Edition

NFPA 1033: Standard for Professional Qualifications for Fire Investigator, 1998 Edition

NFPA 1035: Standard for Professional Qualifications for Public Fire and Life Safety Educator, 2000 Edition

NFPA 1035: Standard for Professional Qualifications for Public Fire and Life Safety Educator, 1993 Edition

NFPA 1041: Standard for Fire Service Instructor Professional Qualifications, 1996 Edition

NFPA 1051: Standard on Wildland Fire Fighter Professional Qualifications, 1995 Edition

NFPA 1061: Standard for Professional Qualifications for Public Safety Telecommunicator, 1996 Edition

NFPA 1122: Model Rocketry, 1997 Edition

NFPA 1123: Code for Fireworks Display, 1995 Edition

NFPA 1124: Code for the Manufacture, Transportation, and Storage of Fireworks and Pyrotechnic Articles, 1998 Edition

NFPA 1125: Code for the Manufacture of Model Rocket and High Power Rocket Motors, 1995 Edition

NFPA 1126: Standard for the Use of Pyrotechnics Before a Proximate Audience, 1996 Edition

NFPA 1127: Code for High Power Rocketry, 1998 Edition

NFPA 1141: Standard for Fire Protection in Planned Building Groups, 1998 Edition

NFPA 1142: Standard on Water Supplies for Suburban and Rural Fire Fighting, 1999 Edition

NFPA 1150: Standard on Fire Fighting Foam Chemicals for Class A Fuels in Rural, Suburban, and Vegetated Areas, 1999 Edition

NFPA 1192: Standard on Recreational Vehicles, 1999 Edition

NFPA 1194: Standard for Recreational Vehicle Parks and Campgrounds, 1999 Edition

NFPA 1201: Standard for Developing Fire Protection Services for the Public, 2000 Edition

NFPA 1201: Standard for Developing Fire Protection Services for the Public, 1994 Edition

NFPA 1221: Standard for the Installation, Maintenance, and Use of Public Fire Service Communication Systems, 1999 Edition

NFPA 1250: Recommended Practice in Emergency Service Organization Risk Management, 2000 Edition

NFPA 1401: Recommended Practice for Fire Service Training Reports and Records, 1996 Edition

NFPA 1402: Guide to Building Fire Service Training Centers, 1997 Edition

NFPA 1403: Standard on Live Fire Training Evolutions, 1997 Edition

NFPA 1404: Standard for a Fire Department Self Contained Breathing Apparatus Program, 1996 Edition

NFPA 1405: Guide for Land-Based Fire Fighters Who Respond to Marine Vessel Fires, 1996 Edition

NFPA 1410: Standard on Training for Initial Emergency Scene Operations, 2000

NFPA 1410: Standard on Training for Initial Fire Attack, 1995 Edition

NFPA 1451: Standard for a Fire Service Vehicle Operations Training Program, 1997 Edition

NFPA 1452: Guide for Training Fire Service Personnel to Make Dwelling Fire Safety Surveys, 2000 Edition

NFPA 1452: Guide for Training Fire Service Personnel to Make Dwelling Fire Safety Surveys, 1993 Edition

NFPA 1470: Standard on Search and Rescue Training for Structural Collapse Incident, 1994 Edition

NFPA 1500 Standard on Fire Department Occupational Safety and Health Program, 1997 Edition

NFPA 1521: Standard for Fire Department Safety Officer, 1997 Edition

NFPA 1561: Standard on Fire Department Incident Management System, 2000 Edition

NFPA 1561: Standard on Fire Department Incident Management System, 1995 Edition

NFPA 1581: Standard on Fire Department Infection Control Program, 2000 Edition

NFPA 1581: Standard on Fire Department Infection Control Program, 1995 Edition

NFPA 1582: Standard on Medical Requirements for Fire Fighters, 2000 Edition

NFPA 1582: Standard on Medical Requirements for Fire Fighters, 1997 Edition

NFPA 1600: Standard for Disaster Emergency Management, 2000 Edition

NFPA 1600: Recommended Practice for Disaster Management, 1995 Edition

NFPA 1620: Recommended Practice for Pre-Incident Planning, 1998 Edition

NFPA 1670: Standard on Operations and Training for Technical Rescue Incidents, 1999 Edition

NFPA 1901: Standard for Automotive Fire Apparatus, 1999 Edition

NFPA 1906: Standard for Wildland Fire Apparatus, 1995 Edition

NFPA 1911: Standard for Service Tests of Fire Pump Systems on Fire Apparatus, 1997 Edition

NFPA 1914: Standard for Testing Fire Department Aerial Devices, 1997 Edition

NFPA 1925: Standard on Marine Fire Fighting Vessels, 1998 Edition

NFPA 1931: Standard on Design of and Design Verification Tests for Fire Department Ground Ladders, 1999 Edition

NFPA 1932: Standard on Use, Maintenance, and Service Testing of Fire Department Ground Ladders, 1999 Edition

NFPA 1936: Standard on Powered Rescue Tool Systems, 1999 Edition

NFPA 1961: Standard for Fire Hose, 1997 Edition

NFPA 1962: Standard for the Care, Use, and Service Testing of Fire Hose, Including Couplings and Nozzles, 1998 Edition

NFPA 1963: Standard for Fire Hose Connections, 1998 Edition

NFPA 1964: Standard for Spray Nozzles (Shutoff and Tip), 1998 Edition

NFPA 1971: Standard on Protective Ensemble for Structural Fire Fighting, 2000 Edition

NFPA 1971: Standard on Protective Ensemble for Structural Fire Fighting, 1997 Edition

NFPA 1975: Standard on Station Work Uniforms for Fire and Emergency Services, 1999 Edition

NFPA 1976: Standard on Protective Ensemble for Proximity Fire Fighting, 2000 Edition

NFPA 1976: Standard on Protective Clothing for Proximity Fire Fighting, 1992 Edition

NFPA 1977: Standard on Protective Clothing and Equipment for Wildland Fire Fighting, 1998 Edition

NFPA 1981: Standard on Open-Circuit Self-Contained Breathing Apparatus for the Fire Service, 1997 Edition

NFPA 1982: Standard on Personal Alert Safety Systems (PASS), 1998 Edition

NFPA 1983: Standard on Fire Service Life Safety Rope and System Components, 1995 Edition

NFPA 1991: Standard on Vapor-Protective Ensembles for Hazardous Materials Emergencies, 2000 Edition

NFPA 1991: Standard on Vapor-Protective Suits for Hazardous Chemical Emergencies, 1994 Edition

NFPA 1992: Standard on Liquid Splash-Protective Clothing for Hazardous Materials Emergencies, 2000 Edition

NFPA 1992: Standard on Liquid Splash-Protective Suits for Hazardous Chemical Emergencies, 1994 Edition

NFPA 1999: Standard on Protective Clothing for Emergency Medical Operations, 1997 Edition

NFPA 2001: Standard on Clean Agent Fire Extinguishing Systems, 2000 Edition

NFPA 8501: Standard for Single Burner Boiler Operation, 1997 Edition

NFPA 8502: Standard for the Prevention of Furnace Explosions/Implosions in Multiple Burner Boilers, 1999 Edition

NFPA 8503: Standard for Pulverized Fuel Systems, 1997 Edition

NFPA 8604: Standard on Atmospheric Fluidized-Bed Boiler Operation, 1996 Edition

NFPA 8505: Standard for Stoker Operation, 1998 Edition

NFPA 8506: Standard on Heat Recovery Steam Generator Systems, 1998 Edition

APPENDIX J
FIDER ACCREDITED PROGRAMS

This list of FIDER accredited programs is valid as of July 2000, when it was down-
loaded from the FIDER Web site (www.fider.org/dircc.htm). The list is updated
twice a year following FIDER Accreditation Commission meetings.

Source: FIDER Web site, www.fider.org

FIDER ACCREDITED PROGRAMS

Foundation for Interior Design Education Research
60 Monroe Center NW, Suite 300
Grand Rapids, MI 49503-2920
Phone: 616-458-0400

ALABAMA

Auburn University
Interior Environments Program
Department of Consumer Affairs
College of Human Sciences
160 Spidle Hall
Auburn, AL 36849
Phone: 334-844-1334
Fax: 334-844-1340
E-mail: readmar@aubum.edu
Marilyn Read, Coordinator
FIDER Professional Level Program (1998, 2001)
Bachelor of science, Interior Environments

Samford University
Interior Design Program
Department of Human Sciences and Design
School of Education and Professional Studies
800 Lakeshore Drive
Birmingham, AL 35229-2239
Phone: 205-726-2843
Fax: 205-726-2068
E-mail: jckrumdi@samford.edu
Jeannie Krumdieck, Program Coordinator
FIDER Professional Level Program (2000, 2003)
Bachelor of arts

University of Alabama
Interior Design Program
Clothing, Textiles, and Interior Design
Human Environmental Sciences
Box 870158
Tuscaloosa, AL 35487-0158
Phone: 205-348-6176
Fax: 205-348-3789
Carolyn Callis, Head
FIDER Professional Level Program (1994, 2000)
Bachelor of science in Human Environmental Sciences

ARIZONA

Arizona State University
Interior Design Program
School of Design
College of Architecture and Environmental Design
Tempe, AZ 85287-2105
Phone: 480-965-4135
Fax: 480-965-9717
E-mail: joni.escobedo@asu.edu
Jacques Giard, Director
FIDER Professional Level Program (1996, 2002)
Bachelor of science in Design

ARKANSAS

University of Arkansas
Interior Design Program
School of Human Environmental Sciences
118 HOEC Building
Fayetteville, AR 72701-1201
Phone: 501-575-2578
Fax: 501-575-7171
E-mail: mccurry@comp.uark.edu
Gary McCurry, Coordinator
FIDER Professional Level Program (1999, 2005)
Bachelor of interior design (BID)

CALIFORNIA

Academy of Art College
Interior Architecture and Design
79 New Montgomery Street, 6th Floor
San Francisco, CA 94105
Phone: 415-274-2209
Fax: 415-263-4171
Prospective Student Services
FIDER Professional Level Program (1995, 2001)
Bachelor of fine arts, Interior Design

American InterContinental University
Interior Design Department
12655 West Jefferson Boulevard
Los Angeles, CA 90066
Phone: 310-302-2323
Fax: 310-302-2407
E-mail: jgriffln@aiuniv.edu
Judith Griffin, Program Chair
FIDER Professional Level Program (1997, 2000)
Bachelor of fine arts

Brooks College
Interior Design Program
4825 East Pacific Coast Highway
Long Beach, CA 90804
Phone: 562-597-6611
Fax: 562-597-6209
Profull Gupta, Chair
FIDER Pre-Professional Assistant Level Program (1996, 2003)
Associate of arts in Interior Design

California College of Arts and Crafts
Interior Architecture Program
School of Architectural Studies
450 Irwin Street
San Francisco, CA 94107
Phone: 415-703-9568
Fax: 415-621-2396
Amy Eliot, Chairman
FIDER Professional Level Program (2000, 2003)
BFA in Interior Architecture

California State University, Fresno
Interior Design Program
Department of Art and Design
5225 North Backer Avenue, Mail Stop 65
Fresno, CA 93740-8001
Phone: 209-278-2516
Fax: 209-278-4706
Nancy Brian, Interior Design Coordinator
FIDER Professional Level Program (1996, 2002)
Bachelor of arts in Interior Design

California State University, Northridge
Family and Consumer Sciences
18111 Nordhoff Street
Northridge, CA 91330-8308
Phone: 818-677-3051
Fax: 818-677-4778
E-mail: alyce.blackmon@csun.edu
Alyce A. Blackmon, Chair
FIDER Professional Level Program (1998, 2004)
Bachelor of science

California State University, Sacramento
Interior Design
Department of Design
School of the Arts
6000 J Street
Sacramento, CA 95819
Phone: 916-278-6375
James R. Kenney, Coordinator
FIDER Professional Level Program (1998, 2004)
Bachelor of arts, Interior Design

Design Institute of San Diego
Interior Design Program
8555 Commerce Avenue
San Diego, CA 92121
Phone: 858-566-1200
Fax: 858-566-2711
E-mail: gloriarosenstein@hotmail.com
Gloria B. Rosenstein, Director
FIDER Professional Level Program (1998, 2004)
Bachelor of fine arts in Interior Design

The Fashion Institute of Design and Merchandising
Interior Design Program
919 South Grand Avenue
Los Angeles, CA 90015-1421
Phone: 213-624-1200
Fax: 213-624-9354
Dina Morgan, Chairperson
FIDER Pre-Professional Assistant Level Program (1999, 2003)
Associate of arts

Interior Designers Institute
Interior Design Program
1061 Camelback Road
Newport Beach, CA 92660
Phone: 949-675-4451
Fax: 949-759-0667
Judy Deaton, Executive Director
FIDER Professional Level Program (1999, 2001)
Bachelor of arts in Interior Design

San Diego Mesa College
Interior Design Program
Architecture and Environmental Design Department
7250 Mesa College Drive
San Diego, CA 92111
Phone: 858-627-2941
Fax: 858-627-2677
E-mail: mmoore@sdccd.net
Mimi Moore, Program Coordinator
FIDER Pre-Professional Assistant Level Program (1997, 2000)
Associate of science

UCLA Extension
Interior Design Program
Department of the Arts
10995 Le Conte Avenue #414
Los Angeles, CA 90024
Phone: 310-825-9061
Fax: 310-206-7382
Jeffrey Daniels, Program Director
FIDER Professional Level Program (1997, 2000)
Professional Designation in Interior Design

University of California, Berkeley Extension
Interior Design and Interior Architecture
Department of Arts, Letters, and Sciences
1995 University Avenue
Berkeley, CA 94720-7002
Phone: 510-643-6827
Fax: 510-643-0599
E-mail: mak@unx.berkeley.edu
Marsha Karr, Program Director
FIDER Professional Level Program (1997, 2003)
Certificate in Interior Design and Interior Arch.

West Valley College
Interior Design Department
14000 Fruitvale Avenue
Saratoga, CA 95070
Phone: 408-741-2406
Fax: 408-741-2145
E-mail: dianehurd@westvalley.edu
Diane Hurd, Department Chair
FIDER Professional Level Program (1994, 2000)
Advanced Certificate

Woodbury University
Department of Interior Architecture
School of Architecture and Design
7500 Glenoaks Boulevard
Burbank, CA 91510-7846
Phone: 818-767-0888
Fax: 818-504-9320
Linda Pollari, Chair
FIDER Professional Level Program (1999, 2001)
Bachelor of science

COLORADO

Colorado State University
Interior Design Program
Department of Design & Merchandising
College of Applied Human Sciences
154 Aylesworth SE
Fort Collins, CO 80523-1575
Phone: 970-491-7890
Fax: 970-491-4855
E-mail: kotsiop@cahs.colostate.edu
Antigone Kotsiopulos, Professor and Head
FIDER Professional Level Program (1999, 2002)
Bachelor of science

DISTRICT OF COLUMBIA

George Washington University at Mount Vernon College
Interior Design Program
2100 Foxhall Road NW
Washington, DC 20007
Phone: 202-625-4501
Fax: 202-338-5978
Nancy Blossom
FIDER Professional Level Program (1993, 2000)
Bachelor of fine arts

FLORIDA

Florida State University
Department of Interior Design
School of Visual Arts and Dance
105 Fine Arts Annex
Tallahassee, FL 32306-1130
Phone: 904-644-1436
Fax: 904-644-3112
E-mail: dbutler@mailer.fsu.edu
David Butler, Chairman
FIDER Professional Level Program (1996, 2002)
Bachelor of science and bachelor of arts in Interior Design

International Academy of Design, Tampa
Interior Design Program
5225 Memorial Highway
Tampa, FL 33634
Phone: 813-881-0007
Fax: 813-881-0008
E-mail: patj@academy.edu
Pat Johnston, Chairperson
FIDER Professional Level Program (1996, 2002)
Bachelor of fine arts in Interior Design

International Fine Arts College
Interior Design Department
1737 North Bayshore Drive
Miami, FL 33132
Phone: 305-995-5000
Fax: 305-374-5933
Gregory Hoffman, Chairman
FIDER Pre-Professional Assistant Level Program (1997, 2003)
Associate of arts in Interior Design

Ringling School of Art and Design
Interior Design Department
2700 North Tamiami Trail
Sarasota, FL 34234
Phone: 941-351-5100
Fax: 941-359-7517
E-mail: nhervieu@rsad.edu
Norman Hervieux, Department Head
FIDER Professional Level Program (1995, 2001)
Bachelor of fine arts, Interior Design

Seminole Community College
Interior Design Technology
Career Programs
100 Weldon Boulevard
Sanford, FL 32773
Phone: 407-328-2267
Fax: 407-328-2139
E-mail: smithj@mail.seminole.cc.fl.us
Jill D. Smith, Program Manager
FIDER Pre-Professional Assistant Level Program (1999, 2003)
Associate in science, Interior Design Technology

Southern College
Interior Design Program
Department of Interior Design
5600 Lake Underhill Road
Orlando, FL 32807
Phone: 407-273-1000
Fax: 407-273-0492
Mary Mueller, Department Head
FIDER Professional Level Program (1998, 2000)
Four-year Interior Design Associate in Science

University of Florida
Department of Interior Design
College of Architecture
P. O. Box 115705
Gainesville, FL 32611-5705
Phone: 352-392-0252
Fax: 352-392-7266
E-mail: nielson@ufl.edu
Jerry L. Nielson, Professor and Chairman
FIDER Professional Level Program (1998, 2004)
Bachelor of design

GEORGIA

American Intercontinental University
Interior Design Program
3330 Peachtree Road NE
Atlanta, GA 30326
Phone: 404-965-5816
Fax: 404-965-5705
Liset Robinson, Chair
FIDER Professional Level Program (1996, 2002)
Bachelor of fine arts in Interior Design

Art Institute of Atlanta
Interior Design Program
School of Design
6600 Peachtree Dunwoody Road
100 Embassy Row
Atlanta, GA 30328
Phone: 770-394-8300
Fax: 770-394-9800
Lori Rush, Program Chair
FIDER Professional Level Program (1997, 2003)
Bachelor of fine arts in Interior Design

Atlanta College of Art
Interior Design Program
1280 Peachtree Street NE
Atlanta, GA 30309
Phone: 404-733-5160
Fax: 404-733-5201
Allan M. Hing, Department Head
FIDER Professional Level Program (1998, 2001)
Bachelor of fine arts in Interior Design

Bauder College
Interior Design Department
3500 Peachtree Road NE
Atlanta, GA 30326
Phone: 404-237-7573
Fax: 404-237-1642
Deborah Maer Mas, Program Chair
FIDER Pre-Professional Assistant Level Program (1997, Aug. 31, 2000)
Associate of arts in Interior Design

Brenau University
Interior Design Program
Department of Art and Design
School of Fine Arts and Humanities
One Centennial Circle
Gainesville, GA 30501
Phone: 770-534-6240
Fax: 770-538-4599
E-mail: lmjones@lib.brenau.edu
Lynn M. Jones, Program Director/Chair of Art and Design
FIDER Professional Level Program (1997, 2000)
Bachelor of fine arts

University of Georgia
Interior Design Program
School of Art
Jackson Street
Athens, GA 30602
Phone: 706-542-1511
Fax: 706-542-0226
John A. Huff, Chairman
FIDER Professional Level Program (2000, 2006)
Bachelor of fine arts, Interior Design

IDAHO

Ricks College
Interior Design Program
Home Economics
Clarke Building 244
Rexburg, ID 83460-0615
Phone: 208-356-1340
E-mail: mcraetl@ricks.edu
T. L. McRae, Program Director
FIDER Professional Level Program (1995, 2001)
Three-year Professional Degree in Interior Design

ILLINOIS

Harrington Institute of Interior Design
410 South Michigan Avenue
Chicago, IL 60605-1496
Phone: 312-939-4975
Fax: 312-939-8005
E-mail: harringtoninstitute@interiordesign.edu
Patrick W. Comstock, President
FIDER Professional Level Program (1994, 2001)
Bachelor of fine arts in Interior Design

Illinois Institute of Art at Schaumburg
Interior Design Department
1000 Plaza Drive
Schaumburg, IL 60173-4913
Phone: 847-619-3450
Fax: 847-619-3064
John C. Becker, Acting Director
FIDER Professional Level Program (1998, 2001)
Bachelor of fine arts in Interior Design

International Academy of Merchandising and Design, Chicago
Interior Design Department
One North State Street, Suite 400
Chicago, IL 60602
Phone: 312-980-9236
Fax: 312-960-1449
E-mail: skirkman@iamd.edu
Sue Kirkman, Director
FIDER Professional Level Program (1997, 2003)
Bachelor of fine arts in Interior Design

Southern Illinois University at Carbondale
Interior Design Program
Department of Applied Arts
College of Applied Sciences and Arts
410 Quigley Hall
Carbondale, IL 62901-4337
Phone: 618-453-3734
Fax: 618-453-1129
E-mail: towens@siu.edu or jdavey@siu.edu
Terry A. Owens and Jon Daniel Davey, Chair and Program Representative
FIDER Professional Level Program (1998, 2000)
Bachelor of science in Interior Design

INDIANA

Indiana University
Interior Design Program
Apparel Merchandising & Interior Design
College of Arts & Sciences
232 Memorial Hall East
1021 East Third Street
Bloomington, IN 47405
Phone: 812-855-5071
Fax: 812-855-0362
E-mail: benhamou@indiana.edu
Reed Benhamou, Director
FIDER Professional Level Program (1998, 2004)
Bachelor of science in Interior Design

Purdue University
Interior Design Program
Department of Visual and Performing Arts
Division of Art and Design
1352 Creative Arts Building # 1
West Lafayette, IN 47907
Phone: 765-494-3058
Fax: 765-496-1198
Rosemary Kilmer, Area Representative
FIDER Professional Level Program (1997, 2000)
Bachelor of arts

IOWA

Iowa State University of Science and Technology
Interior Design Program
Department of Art and Design
158 College of Design
Ames, IA 50011-3092
Phone: 515-294-0677
Fax: 515-294-2725
E-mail: ssinger@iastate.edu
Shirlee Singer, Program Coordinator
FIDER Professional Level Program (1996, 2002)
Bachelor of fine arts in Interior Design

KANSAS

Kansas State University
Interior Design Program
Department of Apparel, Textiles, and Interior Design
College of Human Ecology
Justin Hall
Manhattan, KS 66506
Phone: 785-532-6993
Fax: 785-532-3796
E-mail: hubbell@humec.ksu.edu
Neal Hubbell, FIDER Coordinator
FIDER Professional Level Program (1997, 2003)
Bachelor of science in Interior Design

Kansas State University
Department of Interior Architecture
College of Architecture, Planning & Design
203 Seaton Hall
Manhattan, KS 66506-2912
Phone: 785-532-5992
Fax: 785-532-6722
E-mail: smurphy@ksu.edu
Stephen M. Murphy, Department Head
FIDER Professional Level Program (2000, 2006)
Bachelor of interior architecture

KENTUCKY

University of Kentucky
Interior Design Program
Department of Interior Design, Merchandising, and Textiles
College of Human Environmental Sciences
113 Funkhouser Building
Lexington, KY 40506-0054
Phone: 606-257-3106
Fax: 606-323-7799
Laura D. Jolly, Chair
FIDER Professional Level Program (1999, 2002)
Bachelor of arts in Interior Design

University of Louisville
Interior Design Program
The Hite Art Institute
College of Arts and Sciences
Schneider Hall
2301 South Third Street
Louisville, KY 40292
Phone: 502-852-6794
Fax: 502-852-6791
Stow Chapman and Moon-He Baik, Heads
FIDER Professional Level Program (1998, 2001)
Bachelor of science in Interior Design

LOUISIANA

Louisiana State University
Department of Interior Design
College of Design
402 Design Building
Baton Rouge, LA 70803-7030
Phone: 225-388-8422
Fax: 225-388-8457
E-mail: gwacho1@lsu.edu
George S. Wachob, Chair
FIDER Professional Level Program (1995, 2001)
Bachelor of interior design (B.I.D)

Louisiana Tech University
Interior Design Program
School of Architecture
P. O. Box 3175
Tech Station
Ruston, LA 71272
Phone: 318-257-2816
Fax: 318-257-4687
Jody Brotherston, Program Chair
FIDER Professional Level Program (1995, 2001)
Bachelor of interior design

University of Louisiana at Lafayette
Interior Design Program
School of Architecture
College of the Arts
P. O. Box 43850
Lafayette, LA 70504-3850
Phone: 337-482-6225
Fax: 337-482-5907
Charlotte Roberts, Coordinator
FIDER Professional Level Program (1998, 2004)
Bachelor of interior design

MARYLAND

Maryland Institute, College of Art
Interior Architecture & Design
1300 West Mount Royal Avenue
Baltimore, MD 21217
Phone: 410-225-2240
Fax: 410-225-2545
John Wilson, Interim Chair
FIDER Professional Level Program (1998, 2000)
Bachelor of fine arts

MASSACHUSETTS

Endicott College
Interior Design Program
Department of Interior Design
Art and Design Division
376 Hale Street
Beverly, MA 01915
Phone: 978-232-2202
Fax: 978-232-3100
E-mail: rschneid@endicott.edu
Richard Schneider, Chair
FIDER Professional Level Program (1997, 2000)
Bachelor of science in Interior Design

Mount Ida College
Interior Design Program
The Chamberlayne School of Design and Merchandising
777 Dedham Street
Newton, MA 02159
Phone: 617-928-4500
Fax: 617-928-4760
RoseMary Botti-Salitsky, Department Chair
FIDER Professional Level Program (1995, 2001)
Bachelor of science

Newbury College
Interior Design Program
School of Arts, Science, and Technology
129 Fisher Avenue
Brookline, MA 02445
Phone: 617-730-7068
Fax: 617-730-7182
Andrew J. Paraskos, Interior Design Program Coordinator
FIDER Pre-Professional Assistant Level Program (1999, 2003)
Associate of science

The New England School of Art & Design at Suffolk University
Interior Design Program
81 Arlington Street
Boston, MA 02116-3904
Phone: 617-536-0383
Fax: 617-536-0461
Karen J. A. Clarke, Program Director
FIDER Professional Level Program (1995, 2001)
Diploma and Bachelor of fine arts, Interior Design

University of Massachusetts/Amherst
Architectural Studies Option
Interior Design Option
Design Area
Fine Arts Centre 461
Amherst, MA 01003
Phone: 413-545-1902
Fax: 413-545-3929
E-mail: lugosch@art.umass.edu
Kathleen Lugosch, Program Director
FIDER Professional Level Program (2000, 2003)
Bachelor of fine arts

Wentworth Institute of Technology
Interior Design Program
Department of Design & Facilities
550 Huntington Avenue
Boston, MA 02115
Phone: 617-989-4051
Fax: 617-989-4172
E-mail: freminh@wit.edu
Herb Fremin, Program Coordinator
FIDER Professional Level Program (1998, 2004)
Bachelor of science, Interior Design

MICHIGAN

Eastern Michigan University
Interior Design Program
Department of Human Environmental and Consumer Resources
College of Health and Human Services
206 Roosevelt Hall
Ypsilanti, MI 48197
Phone: 734-487-5634
Fax: 734-487-7087
Keith Fineberg, Program Director
FIDER Professional Level Program (1998, 2004)
Bachelor of science in Interior Design

Kendall College of Art and Design
Interior Design Program
Design Studies
111 Division Avenue North
Grand Rapids, MI 49503
Phone: 616-451-2787
Fax: 616-451-9867
E-mail: lahammar@kcad.edu
Mary Laham, Program Head
FIDER Professional Level Program (1996, 2002)
Bachelor of fine arts in Interior Design

Lawrence Technological University
Interior Architecture/Design
Department of Art & Design
College of Architecture and Design
21000 West Ten Mile Road
Southfield, MI 48075
Phone: 248-204-2848
Fax: 248-204-2900
Virginia North, Chair
FIDER Professional Level Program (1999, 2001)
Bachelor of interior architecture

Michigan State University
Interior Design Program
Department of Human Environment & Design
College of Human Ecology
204 Human Ecology
East Lansing, MI 48824-1030
Phone: 517-355-7712
Fax: 517-432-1058
E-mail: dgstewa@msu.edu
Dana Stewart, Chairperson
FIDER Professional Level Program (1998, 2004)
Bachelor of arts

Western Michigan University
Interior Design Program
Family and Consumer Sciences
Kalamazoo, MI 49008
Phone: 616-387-3708
Fax: 616-387-3353
E-mail: patricia.viard@wmich.edu
Pat Viard, Program Coordinator
FIDER Professional Level Program (1997, 2003)
Bachelor of science

MINNESOTA

Alexandria Technical College
Interior Design Program
Marketing Education
1601 Jefferson Street
Alexandria, MN 56308-3799
Phone: 320-762-4497
Fax: 320-762-4501
E-mail: candyj@alx.tec.mn.us
Candace E. Johnson, Lead Instructor
FIDER Pre-Professional Assistant Level Program (1995, 2003)
Associate of applied science

Dakota County Technical College
Interior Design and Sales Program
1300 145th Street East
Rosemount, MN 55068
Phone: 651-423-8414
Fax: 651-423-8775
E-mail: karen.doyle@dctc.mnscu.edu
Karen Doyle, Program Head
FIDER Pre-Professional Assistant Level Program (1998, 2003)
Diploma

University of Minnesota
Interior Design Program
Department of Design, Housing, and Apparel
College of Human Ecology
240 McNeal Hall
1985 Buford Avenue
St. Paul, NM 55108
Phone: 612-624-9700
Fax: 612-624-2750
Dee Ginthner, Chair
FIDER Professional Level Program (1999, 2005)
Bachelor of science

MISSISSIPPI

Mississippi State University
Interior Design Program
School of Human Sciences
128 Lloyd-Ricks
P. O. Box 9745
Mississippi State, MS 39762
Phone: 662-325-2950
Fax: 662-325-8188
E-mail: brmiller@humansci.msstate.edu
Beth Miller, Program Director
FIDER Professional Level Program (1997, 2000)
Bachelor of science

University of Southern Mississippi
Interior Design Program
School of Family and Consumer Sciences
Box 5035
Hattiesburg, MS 39406-5035
Phone: 601-266-4679
Fax: 601-266-4680
Joan S. Traylor, Program Coordinator
FIDER Professional Level Program (1998, 2004)
Bachelor of science

MISSOURI

Maryville University of St. Louis
Interior Design Program
Art and Design Department
13550 Conway Road
St. Louis, MO 63141-7299
Phone: 314-529-9300
Fax: 314-529-9940
E-mail: trutta@maryville.edu
Leslie Armontrout, Program Director
FIDER Professional Level Program (2000, 2003)
Bachelor of fine arts in Interior Design

University of Missouri, Columbia
Interior Design Program
Department of Environmental Design
College of Human Environmental Sciences
137 Stanley Hall
Columbia, MO 65211
Phone: 573-882-7224
Fax: 573-884-6679
Ruth S. Brent, Chairperson
FIDER Professional Level Program (1999, 2005)
Bachelor of science

NEBRASKA

University of Nebraska
Interior Design Program
Department of Architecture
College of Architecture
232 Arch Hall
Lincoln, NE 68588-0107
Phone: 402-472-9245
Fax: 402-472-3806
Betsy S. Gabb, Program Director
FIDER Professional Level Program (1994, 2000)
Bachelor of science in Design

NEVADA

University of Nevada, Las Vegas
Interior Architecture and Design Program
School of Architecture
4505 Maryland Parkway
Las Vegas, NV 89154-4018
Phone: 702-895-3031
Fax: 702-895-1119
E-mail: attila@nevada.edu
Attila Lawrence, Coordinator
FIDER Professional Level Program (1998, 2001)
Bachelor of science in Interior Architecture

NEW JERSEY

Berkeley College/Bergen Campus
Interior Design Program
I 00 West Prospect Street
Waldwick, NJ 07463
Phone: 201-652-0388
Fax: 201-652-2366
Bonita Bavetta, Chairperson
FIDER Pre-Professional Assistant Level Program (2000, 2003)
Associate in applied science

Kean University
Interior Design Program
Department of Design
100 Morris Avenue
Union, NJ 07083
Phone: 908-527-3198
Linda S. Fisher, Assistant Chair
FIDER Professional Level Program (1999, 2005)
Bachelor of fine arts in Interior Design

NEW YORK

Cornell University
Interior Design Program
Department of Design and Environmental Analysis
College of Human Ecology
E106 Van Rensselaer Hall
Ithaca, NY 14853-4401
Phone: 607-255-2168
Fax: 607-255-0305
E-mail: fdb2@cornell.edu
Franklin D. Becker, Chairman
FIDER Professional Level Program (1995, 2002)
Bachelor of science

Fashion Institute of Technology State University of New York
Department of Interior Design D-314
Seventh Avenue at West 27th Street
New York, NY 10001-5992
Phone: 212-217-7800
Fax: 212-217-7102
E-mail: fitinfo@sfitva.cc.suny.edu
Frank Memoli, Chairperson
FIDER Professional Level Program (1997, Aug. 31, 2000)
Bachelor of fine arts
FIDER Pre-Professional Assistant Level Program (1997, 2000)
Associate in applied science

New York Institute of Technology - Old Westbury
Interior Design Department
School of Architecture and Design
Midge Karr Fine Arts and Design Center
P. O. Box 8000
Northern Boulevard
Old Westbury, NY 11568
Phone: 516-686-7786
Fax: 516-626-1268
E-mail: msiegel@iris.nyit.edu
Martha Siegel, Chair
FIDER Professional Level Program (1997, 2000)
Bachelor of fine arts in Interior Design

New York School of Interior Design
Interior Design Program
170 East 70th Street
New York, NY 10021-5110
Phone: 212-472-1500
Fax: 212-288-6577
Scott M. Ageloff, Dean
FIDER Professional Level Program (2000, 2006)
Bachelor of fine arts

Pratt Institute
Interior Design Department
School of Art and Design
200 Willoughby Avenue
Brooklyn, NY 11205
Phone: 718-636-3630
Fax: 718-399-4440
E-mail: mkarlen@pratt.edu
Mark Karlen, Chair
FIDER Professional Level Program (1 999, 2002)
Bachelor of fine arts, Interior Design

Rochester Institute of Technology
Professional Level Program
Department of Industrial and Interior Design
School of Design
College of Imaging Arts and Sciences
73 Lomb Memorial Drive
Rochester, NY 14623-6357
Phone: 716-475-6357
Fax: 716-475-7533
Charles Lewis, Chair
FIDER Professional Level Program (1997, 2000)
Bachelor of fine arts

School of Visual Arts
Interior Design Department
209 East 23rd Street
New York, NY 10010
Phone: 212-592-2572
Fax: 212-592-2573
Lovejoy Duryea, Chair
FIDER Professional Level Program (1998, 2004)
Bachelor of fine arts in Interior Design

Suffolk County Community College
Interior Design Program
121 Speonk Riverhead Road
Riverhead, NY 11901-3499
Phone: 631-548-2588
Fax: 631-548-3612
Laurette Lizak, Associate Professor
FIDER Pre-Professional Assistant Level Program (1997, 2000)
Associate of applied science

Syracuse University
Interior Design Program
School of Art and Design
College of Visual & Performing Arts
334 Smith Hall
Syracuse, NY 13244-1180
Phone: 315-443-2455
Fax: 315-443-9688
E-mail: design@vpa.syr.edu
Francis Morigi, Coordinator
FIDER Professional Level Program, (1996, 2002)
Bachelor of fine arts in Interior Design

Syracuse University
Environmental Design/Interiors
Environmental Arts, Consumer Studies, and Retailing
College for Human Development
224 Slocum Hall
Syracuse, NY 13244
Phone: 315-443-4275
Fax: 315-443-2562
Lara Turney, Contact
FIDER Professional Level Program (1997, 2000)
Bachelor of science in Environmental Design/Interiors

Villa Maria College of Buffalo
Interior Design Program
Art Department
240 Pine Ridge Road
Buffalo, NY 14225-3999
Phone: 716-896-0700
Fax: 716-896-0705
Edwin Smart, Program Coordinator
FIDER Pre-Professional Assistant Level Program (1997, 2000)
Associate in applied science

NORTH CAROLINA

East Carolina University
Interior Design Program
Department of Apparel, Merchandising, and Interior Design
Greenville, NC 27858

Phone: 252-328-6929
Fax: 252-328-4276
Katherine Warsco, Associate Professor
FIDER Professional Level Program (1999, 2002)
Bachelor of science

Meredith College
Interior Design Program
Department of Human Environmental Sciences
3800 Hillsborough Street
Raleigh, NC 27607-5298
Phone: 919-760-8395
Fax: 919-760-2819
Ellen B. Goode, Program Coordinator
FIDER Professional Level Program (1994, 2000)
Bachelor of science

University of North Carolina at Greensboro
Department of Housing and Interior Design
School of Human Environmental Sciences
259 Stone Building
P. O. Box 26170
Greensboro, NC 27402-6170
Phone: 336-334-5320
Fax: 336-334-5049
E-mail: HID@uncg.edu
Thomas Lambeth, Chair
FIDER Professional Level Program (2000, 2006)
Bachelor of science in Interior Design

Western Carolina University
Interior Design Program
College of Applied Sciences
Human Environmental Sciences
308F Belk Building
Cullowhee, NC 28723
Phone: 828-227-2155
Fax: 828-227-7705
E-mail: myops@wpopp.wcu.edu
Marc R. Yops, Coordinator
FIDER Professional Level Program (2000, 2002)
Bachelor of science

NORTH DAKOTA

North Dakota State University
Department of Apparel, Textiles, and Interior Design
College of Human Development & Education
EML 178
Fargo, ND 58105-5057
Phone: 701-231-8604
Fax: 701-231-7174
Susan Ray-Degges, Program Coordinator
FIDER Professional Level Program (1997, 2003)
Bachelor of arts or bachelor of science in Interior Design

OHIO

Columbus College Art & Design
Interior Design Program
107 North Ninth Street
Columbus, OH 43215
Phone: 614-224-9101
Fax: 614-222-4040
Robert L. Nichol, Program Coordinator
FIDER Professional Level Program (2000, 2003)
Bachelor of fine arts

Kent State University
Interior Design Program
School of Family and Consumer Studies
College of Fine and Professional Arts
100 Nixson Hall
Kent, OH 44242-0001
Phone: 330-672-2197
Fax: 330-672-2194
Pamela Evans, Program Coordinator
FIDER Professional Level Program (1999, 2005)
Bachelor of arts in Interior Design

The Ohio State University
Interior Design
Department of Industrial, Interior, and Visual Communication Design
380 Hopkins Hall
128 North Oval Mall

Columbus, OH 43210-1318
Phone: 614-292-6746
Fax: 614-292-0217
Susan K. Roth, Chair
FIDER Professional Level Program (1995, 2001)
Bachelor of science in Design

Ohio University
Interior Design Program
School of Human and Consumer Sciences
College of Health and Human Services
108 Tupper Hall
Athens, OH 45701-2979
Phone: 740-593-2870
Fax: 740-593-0289
E-mail: sparkinsol@oak.cats.ohiou.edu
Sharran Parkinson, Area Coordinator
FIDER Professional Level Program (1994, 2000)
Bachelor of science

University of Akron
Interior Design Studies
School of Family and Consumer Sciences
College of Fine and Applied Arts
215 Schrank Hall South
Akron, OH 44325-6103
Phone: 330-972-7864
Fax: 330-972-4934
Robert W. Brown, Director
FIDER Professional Level Program (1997, 2001)
Bachelor of arts in Interior Design

University of Cincinnati
School of Architecture and Interior Design
Department of Interior Design
College of Design, Architecture, Art, and Planning
PO Box 210016
Cincinnati, OH 45221-0016
Phone: 513-556-0222
Fax: 513-556-1230
E-mail: hildebhp@uc.edu
Henry Hildebrandt, Coordinator
FIDER Professional Level Program (1996, 2002)
Bachelor of science in Design, Interior Design

OKLAHOMA

Oklahoma State University
Interior Design Program
Design, Housing, and Merchandising
College of Human Environmental Sciences
431 Human Environmental Sciences
Stillwater, OK 74078-6142
Phone: 405-744-5035
Fax: 405-744-6910
E-mail: cbonnan@okstate.edu
Carol Bonnann, Coordinator
FIDER Professional Level Program (1995, 2001)
Bachelor of science

The University of Oklahoma
Interior Design Division
College of Architecture
830 Van Vleet Oval
Room 162
Norman, OK 73019-0265
Phone: 405-325-6764
Fax: 405-325-7558
Katharine Leigh, Director
FIDER Professional Level Program (1997, 2003)
Bachelor of interior design

OREGON

University of Oregon
Interior Architecture Program
Department of Architecture
1206 University of Oregon
Eugene, OR 97403-1206
Phone: 541-346-3656
Fax: 541-346-3626
Linda Zimmer, Professor and Director
FIDER Professional Level Program (1999, 2005)
Bachelor or master of interior architecture

PENNSYLVANIA

Drexel University
Interior Design Program
Department of Design
Nesbitt College of Design Arts
33rd and Market Streets
Philadelphia, PA 19104
Phone: 215-895-2390
Fax: 215-895-4917
Kathryn J. Dethier, Program Director
FIDER Professional Level Program (1999, 2005)
Bachelor of science

La Roche College
Interior Design Department
Division of Graphics, Design, and Communication
9000 Babcock Boulevard
Pittsburgh, PA 15237-5898
Phone: 412-536-1024
Fax: 412-366-6992
E-mail: iddept@laroche.edu
Carolyn Freeman, Department Chair
FIDER Professional Level Program (1999, 2005)
Bachelor of science in Interior Design

Moore College of Art and Design
Interior Design Department
The Parkway at Twentieth Street
Philadelphia, PA 19103
Phone: 215-568-4515
Fax: 215-568-8017
Margaret Leahy, Chair
FIDER Professional Level Program (1997, 2001)
Bachelor of fine arts

Philadelphia University
Interior Design Program
School of Architecture and Design
School House Lane & Henry Avenue
Philadelphia, PA 19144
Phone: 215-951-2896
Fax: 215-951-2110
E-mail: nathanv@philau.edu
Vini Nathan, Director
FIDER Professional Level Program (1994, 2000)
Bachelor of science in Interior Design

SOUTH CAROLINA

Winthrop University
Interior Design Program
Department of Art and Design
College of Visual and Performing Arts
Rock Hill, SC 29733
Phone: 803-323-2126
Fax: 803-323-2333
John Olvera, Program Coordinator
FIDER Professional Level Program (1997, 2000)
Bachelor of fine arts in Interior Design

TENNESSEE

Middle Tennessee State University
Interior Design Program
Department of Human Sciences
Box 86
Murfreesboro, TN 37132
Phone: 615-898-2884
Fax: 615-898-5130
Sharon Scholtes Coleman, Coordinator
FIDER Professional Level Program (1997, 2003)
Bachelor of science

O'More College of Design
Interior Design Program
P. O. Box 908
Franklin, TN 37065
Phone: 615-794-4254
Fax: 615-790-1662
E-mail: swwarne@aol.com
Sara Beth Warne, Chair
FIDER Professional Level Program (1997, 2003)
Bachelor of interior design

University of Tennessee
Interior Design Program
College of Architecture and Planning
224 Art & Architecture Building
Knoxville, TN 37996-2400
Phone: 865-974-3269
Fax: 865-974-0656
E-mail: jrabunl@utk.edu
Josette H. Rabun, Program Coordinator
FIDER Professional Level Program (1998, 2004)
Bachelor of science in Interior Design

Watkins College of Art & Design
Division of Interior Design
100 Powell Place
Nashville, TN 37204
Phone: 615-383-4848
Fax: 615-383-4849 .
Cheryl Gulley, Department Chair
FIDER Pre-Professional Assistant Level Program (1996, 2003)
Associate of fine art in Interior Design

TEXAS

El Centro College
Interior Design Department
Arts & Sciences Division
Main at Lamar Streets
Dallas, TX 75202
Phone: 214-860-2338
Fax: 214-860-2689
Allen Oliver, Coordinator
FIDER Professional Level Program (1997, 2000)
Certificate in interior design

Houston Community College System/Central College
Interior Design Program
1300 Holman MC 1229
P. O. Box 7849
Houston, TX 77270-7849
Phone: 713-718-6038
Fax: 713-718-6188
Dennis McNabb, Associate Chair
FIDER Pre-Professional Assistant Level Program (1995, 2003)
Associate of applied science

Southwest Texas State University
Interior Design Program
Department of Family & Consumer Sciences
Applied Arts & Technology
601 University Drive
San Marcos, TX 78666-4616
Phone: 512-245-2155
Fax: 512-245-3829
Betty McKee Treanor, Coordinator
FIDER Professional Level Program (1999, 2002)
Bachelor of science

Stephen F. Austin State University
Interior Design Program
Department of Human Sciences
P. O. Box 13014 SFA Station
Nacogdoches, TX 75962
Phone: 409-468-4502
Fax: 409-468-2140

Sally Ann Swearingen, Coordinator
FIDER Professional Level Program (1998, 2001)
Bachelor of science

Texas Christian University
Interior Design Program
Department of Design, Merchandising & Textiles
Addran College of Arts and Sciences
P. O. Box 298630
Fort Worth, TX 76129
Phone: 817-257-7499
Fax: 817-257-6330
Gale Van Ackeren, Program Director
FIDER Professional Level Program (1998, 2004)
Bachelor of science

Texas Tech University
Interior Design Program
College of Human Sciences
Box 41162
Lubbock, TX 79409-1162
Phone: 806-742-3050
Fax: 806-742-1639
E-mail: jshroyer@hs.ttu.edu
JoAnn Shroyer, Chair
FIDER Professional Level Program (1999, 2005)
Bachelor of interior design

University of North Texas
Interior Design Program
School of Visual Arts
P. O. Box 305100
Denton, TX 76203-5100
Phone: 940-565-4010
Fax: 940-565-4717
Bruce Nacke, Associate Professor
FIDER Professional Level Program (1996, 2002)
Bachelor of fine arts

The University of Texas at Arlington
Interior Design Program
School of Architecture
P. O. Box 19108
Arlington, TX 76019-0108
Phone: 817-272-2801
Fax: 817-272-5098
E-mail: marianm@uta.edu
Marian McKeever Millican, Director
FIDER Professional Level Program (1999, 2002)
Bachelor of science in Interior Design

The University of Texas at Austin
Interior Design Program
School of Architecture
115 Gearing Hall
Austin, TX 78712
Phone: 512-471-6249
Fax: 512-471-0716
Nancy Kwallek, Director
FIDER Professional Level Program (1995, 2001)
Bachelor of science in Interior Design

The University of Texas at San Antonio
Interior Design Program
Division of Architecture and Interior Design
6900 North Loop 1604 West
San Antonio, TX 78249-0642
Phone: 210-458-4299
Fax: 210-458-4760
Michael F. Kelly, Interim Director
FIDER Professional Level Program (2000, 2003)
Bachelor of science in Interior Design

UTAH

Utah State University
Interior Design Program
Human Environments Department
Family Life College
Logan, UT 84322-2910
Phone: 435-797-1558
Fax: 435-797-3845

Tom Peterson, Director
FIDER Professional Level Program (1998, 2001)
Bachelor of science and bachelor of arts in Interior Design

VIRGINIA

James Madison University
Interior Design Program
Harrisonburg, VA 22807
Phone: 540-568-6216
Fax: 540-568-6598
Gary Chatelain, Interior Design Coordinator
FIDER Professional Level Program (1995, 2001)
Bachelor of fine arts

Marymount University
Interior Design Department
School of Arts and Sciences
2807 North Glebe Road
Arlington, VA 22207-4299
Phone: 703-284-1565
Fax: 703-284-3859
Jean Parker Freeman, Department Chair
FIDER Professional Level Program (1993, 2000)
Bachelor of arts

Virginia Commonwealth University
Department of Interior Design
School of the Arts
325 North Harrison Street
Richmond, VA 23284-2519
Phone: 804-828-1713
Fax: 804-225-4736
E-mail: bharwood@saturn.vcu.edu
Buie Harwood, Professor and Chair
FIDER Professional Level Program (1998, 2004)
Bachelor of fine arts

Virginia Polytechnic Institute and State University
Department of Near Environments (0410)
College of Human Resources and Education
101 Wallace Hall
Blacksburg, VA 24061-0410
Phone: 540-231-6164
Fax: 540-231-3250
E-mail: mebrock@vt.edu
Mike Ellerbrock, Interim Department Head
FIDER Professional Level Program (1999, 2005)
Bachelor of science

WASHINGTON

Washington State University
Interior Design Program
Apparel, Merchandising, and Interior Design
Agriculture and Home Economics
White Hall 202
P.O. Box 642020
Pullman, WA 99164-2020
Phone: 509-335-1162
Fax: 509-335-7299
E-mail: jturpin@wsu.edu
John C. Turpin, Coordinator
FIDER Professional Level Program (2000, 2003)
Bachelor of arts in Interior Design

WEST VIRGINIA

West Virginia University
Interior Design
Division of Family & Consumer Sciences
College of Agriculture, Forestry & Consumer Sciences
704-L Allen Hall
PO Box 6124
Morgantown, WV 26506-6124
Phone: 304-293-3402
Fax: 304-293-2750
Ronald C. Mowat, Program Coordinator
FIDER Professional Level Program (1999, 2002)
Bachelor of science in Family & Consumer Sciences

WISCONSIN

Mount Mary College
Interior Design Program
Art Department
2900 North Menomonee River Parkway
Milwaukee, WI 53222
Phone: 414-256-1213
Fax: 414-256-1224
E-mail: steffenp@mtmary.edu
Pamela S. Smith-Steffen, Director
FIDER Professional Level Program (1996, 2002)
Bachelor of arts in Interior Design

University of Wisconsin, Madison
Interior Design Major
Environment, Textiles, and Design Department
Room 234
1300 Linden Drive
Madison, and WI 53706
Phone: 608-262-2651
Fax: 608-262-5335
E-mail: jhdohr@facstaff.wisc.edu
Joy H. Dohr
FIDER Professional Level Program (1998, 2004)
Bachelor of science in Environment Textiles & Design-Interior Design

University of Wisconsin, Stevens Point
Interior Architecture Program
Division of Interior Architecture
101 College of Professional Studies
Stevens Point, WI 54481
Phone: 715-346-4600
Fax: 715-346-3751
Kathe Stumpf, Associate Dean
FIDER Professional Level Program (1999, 2005)
Bachelor of science and bachelor of arts

University of Wisconsin, Stout
Interior Design Program
Art Program Direction Office
325 Applied Arts Building
Menomonie, WI 54751
Phone: 715-232-1477
Fax: 715-232-1669
E-mail: delongp@uwstout.edu
Paul DeLong, Art Program Director
FIDER Professional Level Program (2000, 2006)
Bachelor of fine arts in Art/Interior Design

CANADA

Dawson College
Interior Design Department
3040 Sherbrooke Street West
Westmount, PQ H3Z 1A4
Phone: 514-931-8731
Fax: 514-931-3567
Tiiu Poldma, Chairperson
FIDER Professional Level Program (1994, 2000)
Diplome d'études collegiales

Humber College
The Interior Design Program
School of Applied Technology
205 Humber College Boulevard
Etobicoke, ON M9W 5L7
Phone: 416-675-6622 ext. 4355
Fax: 416-675-6357
E-mail: eggins@admin.humberc.on.ca
Connie Eggins, Manager Learning Operations
FIDER Professional Level Program (2000, 2006)
Diploma of interior design

International Academy of Design, Toronto
Interior Design Program
31 Wellesley Street E
Toronto, ON M4Y 1G7
Phone: 416-927-7811
Fax: 416-927-9244

E-mail: jokeefe@iaod.com
Joyce O'Keefe, Chair
FIDER Professional Level Program (1996, 2002)
Diploma in interior design

Lakeland College
Interior Design Department
5707 47 Avenue West
Vermilion, AB T9X 1K5
Phone: 780-853-8522
Fax: 780-853-8710
E-mail: cindi.plant@lakelandc.ab.ca
Cindi Plant, Chair
FIDER Pre-Professional Assistant Level Program (1996, 2003)
Diploma in interior design (Assistant)

Mount Royal College
Department of Interior Design
Faculty of Arts
4825 Richard Road SW
Calgary, AB T3E 6K6
Phone: 403-240-6100
Fax: 403-240-6939
Frank Harks, Chair
FIDER Pre-Professional Assistant Level Program (1995, 2003)
Applied degree in interior design

Kwantlen University College
Professional Level Interior Design Program
Interior Design Department
8771 Lansdowne Road
Richmond, BC V6X 3V8
Phone: 604-599-2542
Fax: 604-599-2716
Sooz Klinkhamer, Chair
FIDER Professional Level Program (2000, 2006)
Bachelor of applied design in Interior Design

Ryerson Polytechnic University
Interior Design Program
School of Interior Design
350 Victoria Street
Toronto, ON M5B 2K3
Phone: 416-979-5188
Fax: 416-979-5240
George Verghese, Chair
FIDER Professional Level Program (1998, 2004)
Bachelor of applied arts in Interior Design

University of Manitoba
Department of Interior Design
216 Architecture II Building
Winnipeg, MB R3T 2N2
Phone: 204-474-6435
Fax: 204-474-7533
E-mail: chalmers@cc.umanitoba.ca
Lynn Chalmers, Head
FIDER Professional Level Program (1994, 2001)
Bachelor of interior design

APPENDIX K
SOURCES

Source: The American Institute of Architects, AIA

AIA

The American Institute of Architects
1735 New York Avenue, N.W.
Washington, DC 20006-5292
(202) 626-7300

AIA Advantage Programs
(202) 626-7438

AIA Press
(202) 626-7427

AIA Publications and Information
(800) 365-ARCH
AIA Pressbooks, professional development
publications, and AIA Documents, as well as
books, gifts, posters, and videos sold through
the AIA Bookstore, can be ordered with a
credit card 24 hours a day, 7 days a week, by
calling (800) 365-ARCH [2724].

Information about architects, architecture, and
professional practice can be obtained from the
AIA Library by calling (202) 626-7492.

AIA Trust [*insurance information*]
(800) 343-2972

American Architectural Foundation
(202) 626-7318

Association Members Retirement Program
(800) 532-1125

Bookstore
(800) 365-ARCH [2724]

College of Fellows
(202) 626-7445

Community Design and Development
(202) 626-7468

Convention
(202) 626-7396

Design Awards and Fellowship Nominations
(202) 626-7586

Electronic Documents (AIA/EDS)
(800) 365-ARCH

Government Affairs
(202) 626-7403

Internship Programs
(202) 626-7345

Library and Archives
(202) 626-7492

MasterSpec and SpecSystems
(800) 424-5080

Membership Recruitment
(202) 626-7390

Membership Services
(800) AIA-DUES

Octagon Museum Prints and
Drawings Collection
(202) 626-7571

AIA OnLine computer network
(800) 864-7753

Professional Interest Areas
(202) 626-7456

Public Affairs
(202) 626-7461

Scholarship Programs
(202) 626-7511

State and Local AIA
Components information
(202) 626-7378

AIA-Related Organizations

AIA/ACSA Council on
   Architectural Research
c/o Association of Collegiate Schools
   of Architecture
1735 New York Avenue, N.W.
Washington, DC 20006
(202) 785-2324

The American Architectural
Foundation (AAF)
1735 New York Avenue, N.W.
Washington, DC 20006
(202) 626-7318

Council of Architecture Component
Executives (CACE)
1735 New York Avenue, N.W.
Washington, DC 20006
(202) 626-7377

Society of Architectural
Administrators (SAA)
1735 New York Avenue, N.W.
Washington, DC 20006
(202) 626-7300

For the names of AIA state and regional
components, call the AIA, (202) 626-7351

Collateral Organizations

The American Institute of Architecture
Students (AIAS)
1735 New York Avenue, N.W.
Washington, DC 20006
(202) 626-7472

The Association of Collegiate Schools
of Architecture (ACSA)
1735 New York Avenue, N.W.
Washington, DC 20006
(202) 785-2324

National Architectural Accrediting
Board (NAAB)
1735 New York Avenue, N.W.
Washington, DC 20006
(202) 783-2007

National Council of Architectural
Registration Boards (NCARB)
1735 New York Avenue, N.W.
Washington, DC 20006
(202) 783-6500

State Registration Boards

Jim H. Seay, Sr., *Secretary*
Alabama Board for Registration of Architects
RSA Plaza
770 Washington Avenue, Suite 150
Montgomery, AL 36130
(205) 242-4179
(205) 242-4531 *fax*

Mark Hymer, *Licensing Examiner*
Alaska Board of Architects,
  Engineers and Land Surveyors
Department of Commerce
P.O. Box 110806
Juneau, AK 99811-0806
(907) 465-2540
(907) 465-2974 *fax*

Ronald Dalrymple, *Executive Director*
Arizona State Board for Technical
  Registration of Architects
1951 West Camelback Road, Suite 250
Phoenix, AZ 85015
(602) 255-4053
(602) 255-4051 *fax*

Bonnie Griffin, *Executive Director*
Arkansas State Board of Architects
1515 Building, Room 512
1515 West Seventh Street
Little Rock, AR 72201
(501) 375-1310
(501) 375-4218 *fax*

Stephen P. Sands, *Executive Officer*
California Board of Architectural Examiners
400 R Street, Suite 4000
Sacramento, CA 95814-6238
(916) 327-3147
(916) 445-8524 *fax*

Mary Lou Burgess, *Program Administrator*
Colorado Board of Examiners of Architects
1560 Broadway, Suite 1370
Denver, CO 80202
(303) 894-7801
(303) 894-7790 *fax*

Cathryn Nuckols, *Executive Secretary*
Connecticut Architectural Licensing Boar
State Office Building, Room G-1
165 Capitol Avenue
Hartford, CT 06106
(203) 566-2093
(203) 566-7630 *fax*

Sheila Wolfe, *Administrative Assistant*
Delaware Board of Architects
Margaret O'Neil Building
Box 1401
Dover, DE 19903
(302) 739-4522
(302) 739-6148 *fax*

Harriet Andrews, *Contact Representative*
DC Department of Consumer and
    Regulatory Affairs
Occupational and Professional
    Licensing Administration
P.O. Box 37200, Room 923
Washington, DC 20013-7200
(202) 727-7468
(202) 727-7009 *fax*

Angel Gonzalez, *Executive Director*
Florida Board of Architecture and
    Interior Design
The Northwood Center
1940 North Monroe, Suite 60
Tallahassee, FL 32399-0751
(904) 488-6685
(904) 922-2918 *fax*

Barbara Wilkerson, *Executive Director*
Georgia State Board of Architects
Examining Boards Division
166 Pryor Street, S.W.
Atlanta, GA 30303
(404) 656-2281
(404) 651-9532 *fax*

Amor A. Pakingan,
    Administrative Services Officer
Territorial Board of Registration
    for Engineering, Architects and
    Land Surveyors
Department of Public Works
Government of Guam
P.O. Box 2950
Agana, GU 96910
(011) + country code
(671) 646-3138
(671) 649-6178 *fax*

Constance Cabral, *Executive Secretary*
Hawaii Board of Registration of
    Professional Engineers,
    Architects, Surveyors and
    Landscape Architects
P.O. Box 3469
Honolulu, HI 96801
(808) 586-2702
(808) 586-2689 *fax*

Carmen Westberg, *Chief*
Bureau of Occupational Licenses
Owyhee Plaza
1109 Main Sreet, Suite 220
Boise, ID 83702
(208) 334-3233
(208) 334-3945 *fax*

Thelma Barrington, *Administrator*
Department of Professional Regulation
320 West Washington Sreet, Third Floor
Springfield, IL 62786
(217) 524-3211
(217) 232-2312 *fax*

Gregory Hill, *Deputy Director*
Indiana Professional Licensing Agency
Indiana Government Center South
302 West Washington Street, Room E034
Indianapolis, IN 46204-2246
(317) 232-3894
(317) 232-2312 *fax*

K. Marie Thayer, *Executive Secretary*
Architectural Examining Board
Division of Professional Licensing
1918 S.E. Hulsizer Avenue
Ankeny, IA 50021
(515) 281-5596
(515) 281-7372 *fax*

Betty Rose, *Executive Director*
Kansas State Board of Technical Professions
900 Jacksons Street, Suite 507
Topeka, KS 66612-1257
(913) 296-3053

L. Wayne Tune, *Executive Director*
State Board of Examiners and
    Registration of Architects
P.O. Box 22097-40522
    (3302 Brookhill Circle
    Lexington, KY 40502)
Lexington, KY 40522
(606) 277-3312

Teeny Simmons, *Executive Director*
Louisiana State Board of
    Architectural Examiners
8017 Jefferson Highway, Suite B-2
Baton Rouge, LA 70809
(504) 925-4802
(504) 925-4804 *fax*

Sandra Leach, *Board Clerk*
Maine State Board for Registration
    of Architects and Landscape Architects
Department of Professional and
    Financial Regulation
State House Station #35
Augusta, ME 04333
(207) 582-8723
(207) 582-5415 *fax*

Sue Mays, *Executive Director*
Maryland Board of Architects
Division of Occupational and
    Professional Licensing
501 St. Paul Place, Room 902
Baltimore, MD 21202
(410) 333-6322
(410) 333-6314 *fax*

Jack Sharpe, *Administrative Secretary*
Bureau of Occupational and
    Professional Regulation
P.O. Box 30018
    (611 West Ottawa
    Lansing, MI 48933)
Lansing, MI 48909
(517) 335-1669
(517) 373-2795 *fax*

Pamela Smith, *Executive Secretary*
Board of Architecture, Engineering,
    Land Surveying, Landscape Architecture
    and Certified Interior Design
133 Seventh Sreet, East
St. Paul, MN 55101-2333
(612) 296-2388
(612) 297-5310 *fax*

Karen Owen, *Board Administrator*
Mississippi State Board of Architecture
239 North Lamar Sreet, Suite 502
Jackson, MS 39201-1311
(601) 359-6020
(601) 359-6159 *fax*

Shirley Cramer-Benson, *Executive Director*
Missouri Board for Architects,
    Professional Engineers and
    Land Surveyors
P.O. Box 184
    (3605 Missouri Boulevard
    Jefferson City, MO 65109)
(314) 751-0047
(314) 751-8046 *fax*

Lisa F. Casman, *Administrator*
Board of Architects
Department of Commerce
Arcade Building, Lower Level
111 North Jackson
Helena, MT 59620-0407
(406) 444-3745

Charles Nelson, *Executive Director*
Nebraska State Board of Examiners
    for Engineers and Architects
P.O. Box 94751
Lincoln, NE 68509
(402) 471-2021
(402) 471-0787 *fax*

Gloria Armendariz, *Executive Director*
State Board of Architecture
2080 East Flamingo Road, Suite 310
Las Vegas, NV 89119
(702) 486-7300
(702) 486-7304 *fax*

Sue Ann Sargent, *Administrator*
Joint Board of Engineers, Architects,
    Land Surveyors, Natural Scientists
    and Foresters
57 Regional Drive
Concord, NH 03301
(603) 271-2219
(603) 271-2856 *fax*

Kevin B. Earle, *Executive Director*
State Board of Architects and
    Certified Landscape Architects
Department of Law and Public Safety
P.O. Box 45001
    (124 Halsey Street
    Newark, NJ 07102)
Newark, NJ 07101
(201) 504-6385
(201) 648-3536 *fax*

John Seaver, *Director*
Board of Examiners for Architects
P.O. Box 509
    (491 Old Santa Fe Trail
    Santa Fe, NM 87501)
Santa Fe, NM 87504
(505) 827-6375
(505) 827-6373 *fax*

William Martin, *Executive Secretary*
State Board of Architecture
State Education Department
Cultural Education Center, Room 3019
Albany, NY 12230
(518) 474-3930
(518) 473-0578 *fax*

Kathleen Hansinger, *Executive Director*
North Carolina Board of Architecture
501 North Blount Sreet
Raleigh, NC 27604
(919) 733-9544
(919) 733-1272 *fax*

Delton Torno, *Secretary/Treasurer*
North Dakota State Board of Architecture
2705 Fourth Avenue, N.W.
Minot, ND 58701
(701) 852-4178
(701) 852-4179 *fax*

Florence Bocago, *Administrator*
Board of Professional Licensing
First Floor, Torres Building
P.O. Box 2078
Saipan, Northern Mariana Islands 96950
(670) 234-5897
(670) 234-6040 *fax*

William N. Wilcox, *Executive Director*
Ohio State Board of Examiners of Architec
77 South High Street, 16th Floor
Columbus, OH 43266-0303
(614) 466-2316
(614) 644-9048 *fax*

Jean Williams, *Executive Director*
Board of Governors of Licensed Architects
    and Landscape Architects of Oklahoma
6801 North Broadway, Suite 201
Oklahoma City, OK 73116-9037
(405) 848-6596
(405) 843-6278 *fax*

Eleanor Gundran, *Administrator*
Oregon Board of Architect Examiners
750 Front Street, N.E., Suite 260
Salem, OR 97310
(503) 378-4270
(503) 364-6891 *fax*

Cheryl B. Lyne, *Board Administrator*
Pennsylvania State Architects
  Licensure Board
Department of State
P.O. Box 2649
  (Room 613
  Transportation Building
  Commonwealth and Forster Sreets
  Harrisburg, PA 17120)
Harrisburg, PA 17105-2649
(717) 783-4866
(717) 787-7769 *fax*

Luís A. Isaac-Sanchez, *Director*
Board of Engineers,
  Architects and Land Surveyors
Old San Juan Station
P.O. Box 3271
San Juan, PR 00902-3271
(809) 722-2122 ext. 325

Lorraine Garvey, *Administrator*
Board of Examination and
  Registration of Architects
50 Holden Street
Providençe, RI 02908
(401) 277-6198
(401) 273-7156 *fax*

Barbara P. Harper, *Executive Director*
State Board of Architectural Examiners
3710 Landmark Drive, Suite 206
Columbia, SC 29204
(803) 734-9750
(803) 734-9371 *fax*

Ann Whipple, *Executive Director*
Engineering, Architectural and
  Land Surveying Examiners
2040 West Main Street, Suite 304
Rapid City, SD 57702-2447
(605) 394-2510
(605) 394-2509 *fax*

Betty A. Smith, *Administrator*
State Board of Architecture and
  Engineering Examiners
Third Floor, Volunteer Plaza
500 James Robertson Parkway
Nashville, TN 37243-1142
(615) 741-3221   (615) 741-6470 *fax*

LaVonne Garland, *Intern Director*
Texas Board of Architectural Examiners
8213 Shoal Creek Boulevard, Suite 107
Austin, TX 78758
(512) 458-1363   (512) 458-1375 *fax*

David B. Fairhurst, *Bureau Manager*
Utah Architects Examining Board
Division of Occupational and
  Professional Licensing
P.O. Box 45805
  (160 East 300 South
  Salt Lake City, UT 84111)
Salt Lake City, UT 84145-0805
(801) 530-6628

Peggy Atkins, *Staff Assistant*
State Board of Architects
Licensing Division
Office of the Secretary of State
109 State Street
  (26 Terrace Street
  Montpelier, VT 05609-1106)
Montpelier, VT 05602
(802) 828-2373

Marylyn A. Stapleton, *Assistant Commissioner*
Department of Licensing and
  Consumer Affairs
Property and Procurement Building, #1
Number 1 Sub Base, Room 205
St. Thomas, VI 00802
(809) 774-3130

Willie Fobbs, III, *Assistant Director*
Virginia Board of Architects,
  Professional Engineers, Land Surveyors,
  and Landscape Architects
Seaboard Building, Fifth Floor
3600 West Broad Street
Richmond, VA 23230-4917
(804) 367-8514

James Hanson, *Program Administrator*
Washington Department of Licensing
Professional Licensing Services
P.O. Box 9045
   (2424 Bristol Court
   Olympia, WA 98502)
Olympia, WA 98507-9045
(206) 753-6967
(206) 586-0998 *fax*

Jane Eschleman, *Administrator*
West Virginia Board of Architects
910 Fourth Avenue, Suite 412
Huntington, WV 25701-1434
(304) 528-5825
(304) 528-5826 *fax*

Patricia Reuter, *Bureau Director*
Wisconsin Bureau of Business
   and Design Professionals
P.O. Box 8935
   (1400 East Washington Avenue
   Madison, WI 53702)
Madison, WI 53708-8935
(608) 266-0609

Veronica Skoranski, *Administrator*
Wyoming State Board of Architects
   and Landscape Architects
The Barrett Building, Third Floor
2301 Central Avenue
Cheyenne, WY 82002
(307) 777-7788
(307) 777-6005 *fax*

Architecture Schools with NAAB-accredited Professional Degree Programs

Andrews University
Department of Architecture
Berrien Springs, MI 49104-0450
(616) 471-3309

University of Arizona
College of Architecture
Tucson, AZ 85721
(602) 621-6751

Arizona State University
School of Architecture
Tempe, AZ 85287-1605
(602) 965-3536

University of Arkansas
School of Architecture
100 Vol Walker Hall
Fayetteville, AR 72701
(501) 575-4945

Auburn University
School of Architecture
202 Dudley Commons
Auburn, AL 36849-5316
(205) 844-4524

Ball State University
College of Architecture and Planning
Muncie, IN 47306
(317) 285-5861

Boston Architectural Center
320 Newbury Street
Boston, MA 02115
(617) 536-3170

University of California, Berkeley
Department of Architecture
232 Wurster Hall
Berkeley, CA 94720
(510) 642-4942

University of California, Los Angeles
Graduate School of Architecture and
   Urban Planning
405 Hilgard Avenue
Los Angeles, CA 90024-1467
(310) 825-4091

California College of Arts and Crafts
School of Architectural Studies
1700 17th Street
San Francisco, CA 94103
(415) 703-9561

California State Polytechnic University,
  San Luis Obispo
Architecture Department
San Luis Obispo, CA 93407
(805) 756-1316

California State Polytechnic University,
  Pomona
Department of Architecture
3801 West Temple Avenue
Pomona, CA 91768-4048
(909) 869-2682

Carnegie Mellon University
Department of Architecture
201 College of Fine Arts
Pittsburgh, PA 15213-3890
(412) 268-2355

Catholic University of America
School of Architecture and Planning
620 Michigan Avenue, N.E.
Washington, DC 20064
(202) 319-5188

University of Cincinnati
School of Architecture and Interior Design
Cincinnati, OH 45221-0016
(513) 556-6426

City College of the City University
  of New York
School of Architecture and
  Environmental Studies
New York, NY 10031
(212) 650-7118

Clemson University
College of Architecture
Clemson, SC 29634-0501
(803) 656-3082

University of Colorado at Denver
College of Architecture and Planning
Campus Box 126
P.O. Box 173364
Denver, CO 80217-3364
(303) 556-3382

Columbia University
Graduate School of Architecture Planning
  and Preservation
New York, NY 10027
(212) 854-3510

Cooper Union
The Irwin S. Chanin School of Architecture
New York, NY 10003-7183
(212) 353-4220

Cornell University
Department of Architecture
143 East Sibley
Ithaca, NY 14853-6701
(607) 255-5236

University of Detroit Mercy
School of Architecture
4001 West McNichols Road
P.O. Box 19900
Detroit, MI 48219-0900
(313) 993-1532

Drexel University
Department of Architecture
Philadelphia, PA 19104
(215) 895-2409

Drury College
Hammons School of Architecture
Springfield, MO 65802
(417) 865-8731

University of Florida
Department of Architecture
Gainesville, FL 32611-2004
(904) 392-0205

Florida A&M University
School of Architecture
Tallahassee, FL 32307
(904) 599-3244

Georgia Institute of Technology
College of Architecture
Atlanta, GA 30332-0155
(404) 894-3881

Hampton University
Department of Architecture
Hampton, VA 23668
(804) 727-5440

Harvard University
Department of Architecture
48 Quincy Street
Cambridge, MA 02138
(617) 495-2591

University of Hawaii at Manoa
School of Architecture
1859 East-West Road
Honolulu, HI 96822
(808) 956-7225

University of Houston
College of Architecture
Houston, TX 77204-4431
(713) 743-2400

Howard University
School of Architecture and Planning
Washington, DC 20059
(202) 806-7420

University of Idaho
Department of Architecture
Moscow, ID 83844-2451
(208) 885-6781

University of Illinois at Chicago
School of Architecture
845 West Harrison Street
Chicago, IL 60607-7024
(312) 996-3335

University of Illinois at Urbana-Champaig
School of Architecture .
608 East Lorado Taft Drive
Champaign, IL 61820
(217) 333-1330

Illinois Institute of Technology
College of Architecture
3360 South State
Chicago, IL 60616
(312) 567-3260

Iowa State University
Department of Architecture
156 College of Design
Ames, IA 50011-3093
(515) 294-4717

University of Kansas
School of Architecture and Urban Design
Lawrence, KS 66045
(913) 864-4281

Kansas State University
College of Architecture and Design
Manhattan, KS 66506
(913) 532-5953

Kent State University
School of Architecture and
    Environmental Design
Kent, OH 44242
(216) 672-2917

University of Kentucky
College of Architecture
Pence Hall
Lexington, KY 40506-0041
(606) 257-7617

Lawrence Technological University
College of Architecture and Design
21000 West Ten Mile Road
Southfield, MI 48075
(313) 356-0200, ext. 2800

Louisiana State University
College of Design
Baton Rouge, LA 70803
(504) 388-5400

Louisiana Tech University
Department of Architecture
P.O. Box 3175 T. S.
Ruston, LA 71272
(318) 257-2816

University of Maryland
School of Architecture
College Park, MD 20742-1411
(301) 405-6284

Massachusetts Institute of Technology
Department of Architecture
77 Massachusetts Avenue
Cambridge, MA 02139
(617) 253-7791

University of Miami
School of Architecture
P.O. Box 249178
Coral Gables, FL 33124
(305) 284-5001

Miami University
Department of Architecture
125 Alumni Hall
Oxford, OH 45056
(513) 529-6426

University of Michigan
College of Architecture and
   Urban Planning
Ann Arbor, MI 48109-2069
(313) 764-1300

University of Minnesota
Department of Architecture
89 Church Street, S.E.
Minneapolis, MN 55455
(612) 624-7866

Mississippi State University
School of Architecture
P.O. Drawer AQ
Mississippi State, MS 39762
(601) 325-2202

Montana State University
School of Architecture
Bozeman, MT 59717
(406) 994-4255

Morgan State University
Institute of Architecture and Planning
Baltimore, MD 21239
(410) 319-3225

University of Nebraska
College of Architecture
Lincoln, NE 68588-0106
(402) 472-3592

New Jersey Institute of Technology
School of Architecture
Newark, NJ 07102
(201) 596-3079

University of New Mexico
School of Architecture and Planning
2414 Central Southeast
Albuquerque, NM 87131
(505) 277-2903

New York Institute of Technology
School of Architecture and Fine Arts
Old Westbury, NY 11568
(516) 686-7593

University of North Carolina at Charlotte
College of Architecture
Charlotte, NC 28223
(704) 547-2358

North Carolina State University
Department of Architecture
P.O. Box 7701
Raleigh, NC 27695-7701
(919) 515-2201

North Dakota State University
Department of Architecture and
   Landscape Architecture
SU Station, P.O. Box 5285
Fargo, ND 58105
(701) 237-8614

University of Notre Dame
School of Architecture
Notre Dame, IN 46556
(219) 631-6137

Ohio State University
Department of Architecture
Columbus, OH 43210
(614) 292-5567

University of Oklahoma
College of Architecture
Norman, OK 73019-0265
(405) 325-2444

Oklahoma State University
School of Architecture
Stillwater, OK 74078-0185
(405) 744-6043

University of Oregon
Department of Architecture
Eugene, OR 97403
(503) 346-3656

University of Pennsylvania
Department of Architecture
207 Meyerson Hall
Philadelphia, PA 19104-6311
(215) 898-5728

Pennsylvania State University
Department of Architecture
206 Architecture Unit C
University Park, PA 16802
(814) 865-9535

Prairie View A&M University
Department of Architecture
P.O. Box 397
Prairie View, TX 77446-0397
(409) 857-2014

Pratt Institute
School of Architecture
200 Willoughby Avenue
Brooklyn, NY 11205
(718) 636-3404

Princeton University
School of Architecture
Princeton, NJ 08544
(609) 258-3741

University of Puerto Rico
School of Architecture
P.O. Box 21909
San Juan, PR 00931-1909
(809) 250-8581

Rensselaer Polytechnic Institute
School of Architecture
110 8th Street
Troy, NY 12180-3590
(518) 276-6466

Rhode Island School of Design
Division of Architecture and Design
2 College Street
Providence, RI 02903
(401) 454-6280

Rice University
School of Architecture
P.O. Box 1892
Houston, TX 77251-1892
(713) 527-4044

Roger Williams University
School of Architecture
1 Ferry Road
Bristol, RI 02809
(401) 254-3605

Savannah College of Art and Design
Department of Architecture
201 West Charlton Street
Savannah, GA 31402-3146
(912) 238-2400

University of South Florida
FAMU/USF Cooperative Master
    of Architecture Program
3702 Spectrum Boulevard, Suite 180
Tampa, FL 33612
(813) 974-4031

University of Southern California
School of Architecture
Los Angeles, CA 90089-0291
(213) 740-2723

Southern California Institute
of Architecture
5454 Beethoven Street
Los Angeles, CA 90066
(310) 574-1123

Southern University and A&M College
School of Architecture
Baton Rouge, LA 70813
(504) 771-3015

University of Southwestern Louisiana
School of Architecture
Lafayette, LA 70504-3850
(318) 231-6225

State University of New York at Buffalo
School of Architecture and Planning
112 Hayes Hall
3435 Main Street
Buffalo, NY 14214-3087
(716) 829-3483, ext. 104

Syracuse University
School of Architecture
103 Slocum Hall
Syracuse, NY 13244 1230
(315) 443-2256

Temple University
Architecture Program
12th and Norris Streets
Philadelphia, PA 19122
(215) 204-8813

University of Tennessee
College of Architecture and Planning
Knoxville, TN 37996-2400
(615) 974-5265

University of Texas at Arlington
School of Architecture
Box 19108
Arlington, TX 76019
(817) 273-2801

University of Texas at Austin
School of Architecture
Goldsmith Hall 2.308
Austin, TX 78712
(512) 471-1922

Texas A&M University
Department of Architecture
College Station, TX 77843-3137
(409) 845-1015

Texas Tech University
College of Architecture
P.O. Box 42091
Lubbock, TX 79409-2091
(806) 742-3136

Tulane University
School of Architecture
Richardson Memorial Hall
New Orleans, LA 70118-5671
(504) 865-5389

Tuskegee University
School of Engineering and Architecture
Tuskegee, AL 36088
(205) 727-8329

University of Utah
Graduate School of Architecture
Salt Lake City, UT 84112
(801) 581-8254

University of Virginia
School of Architecture
Campbell Hall
Charlottesville, VA 22903
(804) 924-3715

Virginia Polytechnic Institute and
State University
College of Architecture and Urban Studies
Blacksburg, VA 24061-0205
(703) 231-6416

University of Washington
Department of Architecture
Seattle, WA 98195
(206) 543-4180

Washington State University
School of Architecture
Pullman, WA 99164-2220
(509) 335-5539

Washington University
School of Architecture
One Brookings Drive
St. Louis, MO 63130
(314) 935-6200

Wentworth Institute of Technology
Department of Architecture
550 Huntington Avenue
Boston, MA 02115-5998
(617) 442-9010

University of Wisconsin-Milwaukee
Department of Architecture
P.O. Box 413
Milwaukee, WI 53201
(414) 229-5564

Yale University
School of Architecture
180 York Street
New Haven, CT 06520
(203) 432-2288

Other Professional Organizations

Accreditation Board for Engineering
   and Technology (ABET)
345 East 47th Street
New York, NY 10017
(212) 705-7685

Acoustical Society of America (ASA)
500 Sunnyside Boulevard
Woodbury, NY 11797
(516) 576-2360

The Alliance to Save Energy
1725 K Street, N.W., Suite 509
Washington, DC 20006
(202) 857-0666
(202) 331-9588 *fax*

American Arbitration Association (AAA)
140 West 51st Street
New York, NY 10020
(212) 484-4000

American Association of
   Engineering Societies (AAES)
345 East 47th Street
New York, NY 10017
(212) 705-7840

American Association of Homes
   for the Aging (AAHA)
901 E Street, N.W., Suite 500
Washington, DC 20004
(202) 783-2242

American Association of
   Housing Educators (AAHE)
c/o Dr. Paul Woods
Department of Construction Science
Texas A&M University
College Station, TX 77843-3137
(409) 845-1017

American Bar Association (ABA)
Construction Industry Forum
750 North Lake Shore Drive
Chicago, IL 60611
(312) 988-5579
(312) 988-5677 *fax*

American Congress on Surveying
   and Mapping
5410 Grosvenor Lane, Suite 100
Bethesda, MD 20814
(301) 493-0200

American Consulting Engineers Council
   (ACEC)
1015 15th Street, N.W.
Washington, DC 20005
(202) 347-7474

American Council for
   Construction Education (ACCE)
901 Hudson Lane
Monroe, LA 71201
(318) 323-2413

American Council for an
  Energy-Efficient Economy (ACEEE)
1001 Connecticut Avenue, N.W., Suite 801
Washington, DC 20036
(202) 429-8873
(202) 429-2248 *fax*

American Hospital Association (AHA)
American Society for Hospital Engineering
840 North Lake Shore Drive
Chicago, IL 60611
(312) 280-6000

American Institute of Certified
  Design Accountants
P.O. Box 328
Edmond, OK 73083-0328
(405) 848-8404

American Institute for Conservation
1717 K Street, N.W., Suite 301
Washington, DC 20036
(202) 452-9545
(202) 452-9328 *fax*

American Institute of Plant Engineers (AIPE)
8180 Corporate Park Drive, Suite 305
Cincinnati, OH 45242
(513) 489-2473

American National Metric Council (ANMC)
4330 East-West Highway, Suite 1117
Bethesda, MD 20814
(301) 718-6508

American National Standards Institute (ANSI)
11 West 42nd Street, 14th Floor
New York, NY 10036
(212) 642-4900

American Planning Association (APA)
1776 Massachusetts Avenue, N.W., #704
Washington, DC 20036
(202) 872-0611

American Society of Architectural
  Perspectivists (ASAP)
320 Newbury Street
Boston, MA 02115
(617) 846-4766

American Society of Civil Engineers (ASCE)
345 East 47th Street
New York, NY 10017
(212) 705-7496
(212) 980-4681 *fax*

American Society of Consulting Planners
  (ASCP)
1773 Massachusetts Avenue, N.W., 4th Floor
Washington, DC 20036
(202) 872-1498

American Society of Engineering Education
  (ASEE)
1818 N Street, N.W., Suite 600
Washington, DC 20036
(202) 331-3500

American Society of Golf Course Architects
  (ASGCA)
221 North LaSalle Street, 35th Floor
Chicago, IL 60601
(312) 372-7090
(312) 372-6160 *fax*

American Society of Heating,
  Refrigerating and Air-Conditioning
  Engineers (ASHRAE)
1791 Tullie Circle, N.E.
Atlanta, GA 30329
(404) 636-8400
(404) 321-5478 *fax*

American Society of Interior Designers
  (ASID)
608 Massachusetts Avenue, N.E.
Washington, DC 20002
(202) 546-3480

American Society of Landscape Architects
  (ASLA)
4401 Connecticut Avenue, N.W.
Washington, DC 20008
(202) 686-2752

American Society of Mechanical Engineers
  (ASME)
1828 L Street, N.W., Suite 906
Washington, DC 20006
(202) 785-3756

American Society for Quality Control
611 East Wisconsin Avenue
Milwaukee, WI 53202
(800) 952-6587

American Society for Testing and Materials
  (ASTM)
1916 Race Street
Philadelphia, PA 19103
(215) 299-5400
(215) 977-9679 *fax*

American Solar Energy Society (ASES)
2400 Central Avenue, Suite G-1
Boulder, CO 80301
(303) 443-3130
(303) 443-3212 *fax*

American Subcontractors Association
1004 Duke Street
Alexandria, VA 22314-3512
(703) 684-3450
(703) 836-3482 *fax*

Architects, Designers,
  and Planners for Social Responsibility
175 Fifth Avenue, Suite 2210
New York, NY 10010
(212) 924-7893

Architectural Research Centers
  Consortium, Inc. (ARCC)
c/o Julia W. Robinson
College of Architecture and
  Landscape Architecture
University of Minnesota
89 Church Street
Minneapolis, MN 55455
(612) 624-7866

ASFE/Association of Engineering Firms
  Practicing in the Geosciences
8811 Colesville Road, Suite G106
Silver Spring, MD 20910
(301) 565-2733

Associated Builders and Contractors (ABC)
1300 North 17th Street
Rosslyn, VA 22209
(703) 812-2000

The Associated General Contractors
  of America (AGC)
1957 E Street, N.W.
Washington, DC 20006
(202) 393-2040

Associated Specialty Contractors
3 Bethesda Metro Center, Suite 1100
Bethesda, MD 20814-3299
(301) 657-3110

Association of Collegiate Schools
  of Planning (ACSP)
c/o Katherine Ross
Georgia Institute of Technology
Graduate City Planning Program
Atlanta, GA 30332-0155
(404) 894-1702

Association for Community Design
c/o AIA Urban Design Programs
1735 New York Avenue, N.W.
Washington, DC 20006
(202) 626-7300

Association of Computer-Aided Design
  in Architecture (ACADIA)
c/o John McIntosh
College of Architecture and
  Environmental Design
Arizona State University
Tempe, AZ 85287
(602) 965-1344

The Association of Energy Engineers
4025 Pleasantdale Road, Suite 420
Atlanta, GA 30340
(404) 447-5083
(404) 446-3969 *fax*

Association of Higher Education
  Facilities Officers (APPA)
1446 Duke Street
Alexandria, VA 22314
(703) 684-1446

Association for Preservation
   Technology (APT)
P.O. Box 8178
Fredericksburg, VA 22404
(703) 373-1621

Association for Quality and Participation
801-B West Eighth Street, Suite 501
Cincinnati, OH 45203
(513) 381-1959

Association of University Architects (AUA)
c/o Austus G. Kellogg, AIA
Yale University College of Medicine
533 Cedar Street
New Haven, CT 06510
(203) 785-4667

Building Officials and Code
   Administrators International, Inc. (BOCA)
4051 West Flossmoor Road
Country Club Hills, IL 60478
(708) 799-2300

Building Owners and Managers
   Association International, Inc. (BOMA)
1201 New York Avenue, N.W., Suite 300
Washington, DC 20005
(202) 408-2662

Building Seismic Safety Council (BSSC)
National Institute of Building Sciences
1201 L Street, N.W., 4th Floor
Washington, DC 20005
(202) 289-7800
(202) 289-1092 fax

Canadian Council of University Schools
   of Architecture (CCUSA)
School of Architecture
University of Toronto
230 College Street
Toronto M5F 1A1, Canada
(416) 978-3089

Canadian Homebuilders Association (CHBA)
150 Laurier Avenue West, #3200
Ottawa, Ontario K I P 5J4, Canada
(613) 230-3060

Canadian Institute of Planners (CIP)
541 Suffix Drive, 2nd Floor
Ottawa, Ontario K I N 6Z6, Canada
(613) 562-4646

Canadian Society of Landscape Architects
   (CSLA)
P.O. Box 870, Station B
Ottawa, Ontario K I P 5P9, Canada
(613) 232-6342

Canadian Standards Association (CSA)
178 Rexdale Boulevard
Rexdale, Ontario M 9 W 1R3, Canada
(416) 747-4000

Construction Industry Institute (CII)
3208 Red River, Suite 300
Austin, TX 78705-2650
(512) 471-4319

Construction Specifications Institute (CSI)
601 Madison Street
Alexandria, VA 22314
(703) 684-0300

Council of American Building Officials
   (CABO) ·
5203 Leesburg Pike, Suite 708
Falls Church, VA 22041
(703) 931-4533

Council of Educational Facility Planners
   (CEFP)
641 Chatham Lane, Suite 217
Columbus, OH 43221
(614) 792-8103

Council of Landscape Architecture
   Registration Boards (CLARB)
12700 Fair Lake Circle, Suite 110
Fairfax, VA 22033
(703) 818-1300
(703) 318-1309 fax

Council of Planning Librarians (CPL)
c/o American Planning Association
1313 East 60th Street
Chicago, IL 60637
(312) 955-9100

Edison Electric Institute (EEI)
701 Pennsylvania Avenue, N.W.
Washington, DC 20004-2696
(202) 508-5000
(202) 508-5030 *fax*

Electric Power Research Institute (EPRI)
Technical Information Center
P.O. Box 10412
Palo Alto, CA 94303
(415) 855-2411

Energy-Efficient Building Association (EEBA)
Northcentral Technical College
1000 Campus Drive
Wassau, WI 54401
(715) 675-6331
(715) 675-9776 *fax*

Environmental Design Research Association
   (EDRA)
P.O. Box 24083
Oklahoma City, OK 73124
(405) 843-4863

Federación de Colegios de Arquitectos
   de La República Mexicana
Avenida Veracruz, 24
Mexico City, Mexico DF 06700
52-5-211-5519
52-5-211-5809 *fax*

Financial Managers' Group
425 West Wilshire
Oklahoma City, OK 73116
(405) 848-1111
(405) 848-4329 *fax*

Forum for Health Care Planning
2111 Wilson Boulevard, Suite 850
Arlington, VA 22201
(703) 516-6192

Foundation for Interior Design
   Education Research (FIDER)
60 Monroe Center, N.W., Suite 300
Grand Rapids, MI 49503-2920
(616) 458-0400

Gas Research Institute
8600 West Bryn Mawr Avenue
Chicago, IL 60631
(312) 399-8100
(312) 399-8170 *fax*

The Governing Board for
   Contract Interior Design Standards
341 Merchandise Mart
Chicago, IL 60654
(312) 527-0517

Heritage Canada Foundation
412 MacLaren Street
Ottawa, Ontario K2P 0M8, Canada
(613) 237-1066

Historic American Buildings Survey/
   Historic American Engineering Record
   (HABS/HAER)
National Park Service
P.O. Box 37127
Washington, DC 20013
(202) 343-9618

Historic Preservation Education Foundation
Box 27080, Central Station
Washington, DC 20038
(301) 587-5164

Illuminating Engineering Society
   of North America (IES)
120 Wall Street
New York, NY 10005
(212) 248-5000
(212) 248-5017 *fax*

Industrial Designers Society of America
   (IDSA)
1142-E Walker Road
Great Falls, VA 22066
(703) 759-0100

Industrial Development Research Council
40 Technology Park/Atlanta, Suite 200
Norcross, GA 30092
(404) 446-6996
(404) 263-8825 *fax*

Institute of Business Designers (IBD)
341 Merchandise Mart
Chicago, IL 60654
(312) 467-1950

Institute of Electrical and
   Electronics Engineers (IEEE)
445 Hoes Lane
P.O. Box 1331
Piscataway, NJ 08854
(800) 678-4333
(908) 562-3800
(908) 562-1571 *fax*

Intelligent Buildings Institute (IBI)
2101 L Street, N.W.
Washington, DC 20037
(202) 457-1988

Interior Design Educators Council (IDEC)
14252 Culver Drive, Suite A-331
Irvine, CA 92714
(714) 551-1622

International Association
   of Lighting Designers (IALD)
18 East 16th Street, Suite 208
New York, NY 10003
(212) 206-1281

International Conference
   of Building Officials (ICBO)
5360 Workmen Mill Road
Whittier, CA 90601-2298
(310) 699-0541
(310) 692-3853 *fax*

International Council for
   Building Research Studies
   and Documentation (CIB)
U.S. Office
c/o J. G. Gross
Building and Fire Research Laboratory
National Institute of Standards
   and Technology
Building 226, Room B250
Gaithersburg, MD 20899
(301) 975-5902

International Facility Management
   Association (IFMA)
1 East Greenway Plaza, Suite 1100
Houston, TX 77046
(713) 623-4362

International Institute for
   Energy Conservation (IIEC)
750 First Street, N.E., Suite 900
Washington, DC 20002
(202) 842-3388
(202) 842-1565 *fax*

International Society of
   Interior Designers (ISID)
1933 South Broadway, Suite 138
Los Angeles, CA 90007
(213) 744-1313

International Union of Architects (UIA)
51, rue Raynouard
75016 Paris
France

Junior Engineering Technical Society (JETS)
1420 King Street, Suite 405
Alexandria, VA 22314-2794
(703) 548-5387

Juran Institute, Inc.
11 River Road
P.O. Box 811
Wilton, CT 06897-0811
(800) 338-7726

Lighting Research Institute (LRI)
120 Wall Street
New York, NY 10005
(212) 248-5014

National Association of Home Builders
   (NAHB)
1201 15th Street, N.W.
Washington, DC 20005
(202) 822-0254

National Association of Housing and
Redevelopment Officials (NAHRO)
1320 18th Street, N.W., Suite 500
Washington, DC 20036
(202) 429-2960

National Association of Industrial and
Office Parks
2201 Cooperative Way, 3rd Floor
Herndon, VA 22071
(703) 904-7100

National Association of
Surety Bond Producers
5301 Wisconsin Avenue, N.W., Suite 450
Washington, DC 20015
(202) 686-3700

National Conference of State Historic
Preservation Officers (NCSHPO)
Suite 342, Hall of the States
444 North Capitol Street, N.W.
Washington, DC 20001-1512
(202) 624-5465

National Conference of States on
Building Codes and Standards (NCSBCS)
505 Huntmar Park Drive, Suite 210
Herndon, VA 22070
(703) 437-0100
(703) 481-3596 *fax*

National Council of Acoustical Consultants
(NCAC)
66 Morris Avenue, Suite 1A
Springfield, NJ 07081
(201) 564-5859
(201) 564-7480 *fax*

National Council for
Interior Design Qualification (NCIDQ)
50 Main Street
White Plains, NY 10606
(914) 948-9100

National Fire Protection Association (NFPA)
1 Batterymarch Park
Quincy, MA 02269
(617) 770-3000
(800) 344-3555
(617) 770-0070 *fax*

National Institute for
Architectural Education (NIAE)
30 West 22nd Street
New York, NY 10010
(212) 924-7000

National Institute of Building Sciences (NIBS)
1201 L Street, N.W., Suite 400
Washington, DC 20005
(202) 289-7800
(202) 289-1092 *fax*

National Organization of
Minority Architects (NOMA)
c/o Robert Easter
101 West Broad Street, Suite 101
Richmond, VA 23220
(804) 788-0338

National Research Council Canada
Institute for Research in Construction
Ottawa, K1A 0R6, Canada
(613) 993-2463

National Society of Professional Engineers
(NSPE)
1420 King Street
Alexandria, VA 22314-2715
(703) 684-2800

National Trust for Historic Preservation
1785 Massachusetts Avenue, N.W.
Washington, DC 20036
(202) 673-4000

Northeast Sustainable Energy Association
(NESEA)
23 Ames Street
Greenfield, MA 01301
(413) 774-6051

Passive Solar Industries Council
1090 Vermont Avenue, Suite 1200
Washington, DC 20005
(202) 393-5043

Professional Photographers of America
57 Forsyth Street, N.W., Suite 1600
Atlanta, GA 30303
(404) 522-8600

Professional Services Management
Association (PSMA)
4726 Park Road, Suite A
Charlotte, NC 28209
(704) 521-8822

Project Management Institute (PMI)
130 South State Road
Upper Darby, PA 19082
(215) 622-1796

Rocky Mountain Institute
1739 Snowmass Creek Road
Snowmass, CO 81654
(303) 927-3851

Society of Architectural Historians (SAH)
1232 Pine Street
Philadelphia, PA 19107
(215) 735-0224

Society for College and University Planning
(SCUP)
2026 M School of Education Building
University of Michigan
610 East University Avenue
Ann Arbor, MI 48109-1259
(313) 763-4776

Society of Environmental Graphic Designers
(SEGD)
1 Story Street
Cambridge, MA 02138
(617) 868-3381

Society of Fire Protection Engineers (SFPE)
One Liberty Square
Boston, MA 02109
(617) 482-0686

Society for Marketing Professional Services
(SMPS)
99 Canal Center Plaza, Suite 250
Alexandria, VA 22314
(703) 549-6117

Southern Building Code Congress
International (SBCC)
900 Montclair Road
Birmingham, AL 35213-1206
(205) 591-1853

Surety Association of America
100 Wood Avenue South
Iselin, NJ 08830-2773
(908) 494-7600
(908) 494-7609 *fax*

Underwriters Laboratories, Inc. (UL)
333 Pfingsten Road
Northbrook, IL 60062
(708) 272-8800, ext. 2612 or 2622
(708) 272-8129 *fax*

United States Committee of
the International Council on
Monuments and Sites (US/ICOMOS)
Decatur House
1600 H Street, N.W.
Washington, DC 20006
(202) 842-1866

U.S. Metric Association
10245 Andasol Avenue
Northbridge, CA 91325-1504
(818) 363-5606

Urban Land Institute (ULI)
625 Indiana Avenue, N.W., Suite 400
Washington, DC 20004
(202) 624-7000
(202) 624-7140 *fax*

Victor O. Schinnerer & Company, Inc.
Two Wisconsin Circle
Chevy Chase, MD 20815-7003
(301) 961-9800

Volunteers in Technical Assistance
1600 Wilson Boulevard, Suite 500
Arlington, VA 22209
(703) 276-1800

Federal Government

Advisory Council on Historic Preservation
1100 Pennsylvania Avenue, N.W., Suite 809
Washington, DC 20004
(202) 606-8503

Americans with Disabilities Act
Information Office
U.S. Department of Justice
Civil Rights Division
P.O. Box 66738
Washington, DC 20035
(202) 514-0301

Architectural and Transportation Barriers
Compliance Board
1331 F Street, N.W., Suite 1000
Washington, DC 20004
(202) 272-5434

Building Research Board (BRB)
2101 Constitution Avenue, N.W.
Washington, DC 20418
(202) 334-3376

Department of Energy (DOE)
Forrestal Building
1000 Independence Avenue, S.W.
Washington, DC 20585
(202) 586-5000

Department of Energy
Conservation and Renewable
Energy Inquiry and Referral Service
P.O. Box 8900
Silver Spring, MD 20907
(800) 523-2929

Department of Energy
Office of Scientific and
Technical Information
Box 62
Oak Ridge, TN 37831
(615) 576-1178

Department of Health and
Human Services (HHS)
Division of Health Facilities Planning
Parklawn Building, Room 17A10
5600 Fishers Lane
Rockville, MD 20857
(301) 443-2265

Department of Housing and
Urban Development (HUD)
451 7th Street, S.W.
Washington, DC 20410
(202) 708-1422

Environmental Protection Agency (EPA)
401 M Street, S.W.
Washington, DC 20460
(202) 260-7751 Public Information Center
(202) 233-9030 Indoor Air Division
(202) 233-9370 Radon Division
(202) 554-1404 Toxic Materials Hotline

Federal Bureau of Prisons
Facilities Development Division
320 First Street, N.W., Room 5008
Washington, DC 20534
(202) 514-6460

Federal Emergency Management Agency
(FEMA)
500 C Street, S.W.
Washington, DC 20472
(202) 646-2500

General Services Administration (GSA)
18th and F Streets, N.W.
Washington, DC 20405
(202) 708-5082

Lawrence Berkeley Laboratory (LBL)
1 Cyclotron Road
Berkeley, CA 94720
(510) 486-5388 Lighting Systems Group
(510) 486-5605 Windows and
Daylighting Group
(510) 486-6940 *fax*

National Appropriate Technology
Assistance Service
U.S. Department of Energy
P.O. Box 2525
Butte, MT 59702

National Endowment for the Arts (NEA)
1100 Pennsylvania Avenue, N.W., Room 624
Washington, DC 20506
(202) 682-5442

National Institute of Corrections
U.S. Department of Justice
1860 Industrial Circle, Suite A
Longmont, CO 80501
(303) 682-0213

National Institute of Standards
    and Technology (NIST)
Building and Fire Research Laboratory
Building 226, Room B216
Gaithersburg, MD 20899
(301) 975-6850

National Institute of Standards
    and Technology (NIST)
Standards and Codes
Building 411, Room A163
Gaithersburg, MD 20899
(301) 975-4040

NIST Publications and Program Inquiries
(301) 975-3058

National Renewable Energy Laboratory
    (NREL)
1617 Cole Boulevard
Golden, CO 80401
(303) 231-7000
(303) 231-1199 *fax*

National Technical Information Service
    (NTIS)
5285 Port Royal Road
Springfield, VA 22161
(703) 487-4650

Occupational Safety and
    Health Administration (OSHA)
820 1st Street, N.E., Suite 440
Washington, DC 20002-1205
(202) 523-1452

Veterans Administration Architectural
    Service (VA)
Construction Management Office
Department of Veterans Affairs
810 Vermont Avenue, N.W.
Washington, DC 20420
(202) 233-83663

Trade Press

Architectural Record
1221 Avenue of the Americas
New York, NY 10020
(212) 512-4686

Architecture
1130 Connecticut Avenue, N.W.
Washington, DC 20006
(202) 828-0993

Building Design and Construction
P.O. Box 5080
Des Plaines, IL 60017
(708) 635-8800

Construction Specifier
Construction Specifications Institute (CSI)
601 Madison Street
Alexandria, VA 22314
(703) 684-0300
(703) 684-0465 *fax*

*CRIT: The Journal of The American
    Institute of Architecture Students*
1735 New York Avenue, N.W.
Washington, DC 20006
(202) 626-7472

ENR: Engineering News-Record
1221 Avenue of the Americas
New York, NY 10020
(212) 512-2000

Journal of Architectural Education
Association of Collegiate Schools
    of Architecture
1735 New York Avenue, N.W.
Washington, DC 20006
(202) 785-2324

Progressive Architecture (P/A)
600 Summer Street
P.O. Box 1361
Stamford, CT 06904
(203) 348-7531

APPENDIX L

HOW TO CALCULATE FIRE RATING FOR CONCRETE BLOCK

Source: Alabama Masonry Institute

How To Calculate Fire Ratings For Concrete Block

STANDARD BUILDING CODE
Southern Building Code Congress International
1991 Edition Chapter 31, Section 3103.1.1

3103.1. The fire resistance ratings of walls and partitions constructed of concrete masonry units shall be determined from Table 3103.1. The rating shall be based on the equivalent thickness of the masonry and type of aggregate used.

TABLE 3103.1 Minimum Equivalent Thickness (Inches) of Loadbearing or Nonloadbearing Concrete Masonry Walls*				
	Fire Resistance Rating (hours)			
Type of Aggregate	**1**	**2**	**3**	**4**
Expanded Shale, Clay** or Slate	2.6	3.6	4.4	5.1

* Values between those shown in the table can be determined by
  direct interpolation.

**Contact producer to verify aggregate and net volume.
  Certifications provided by each producer member as requested.

Thickness shown for concrete masonry is equivalent thickness defined as the average thickness of solid material in the wall and is represented by the formula:

$$T_E = \frac{V_n}{L \times H}$$

Where:
   T_E = Equivalent thickness, in inches
   V_n = Net volume (gross volume less volume of voids), in cubic inches*
   L = Length of block, in inches
   H = Height of block, in inches

Source: SBCCI
     For more information contact AMI
     205-265-0501

Concrete Masonry Unit Terms

A. Scored   F. Rectangular Core
B. Stretcher End (Mortar Groove)   G. Pear Core
C. Breaker   H. Split Face
D. Sash Groove   I. Fluted (8 Rib Shown)
E. Plain End   J. Bullnose (Double Shown)

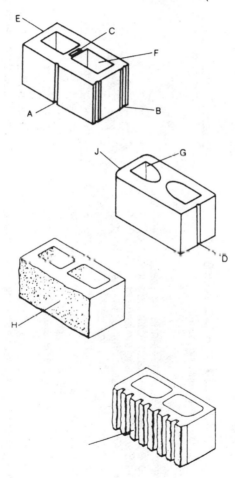

Compressive Strength Of Concrete Masonry, (PSI*)
Gross Area To Net Area Conversion

*based on average of 3 units 4" height and above

Comment: ASTM C-90 is the standard of masonry production specifications in the United States. With the approval of ACI 530.1-88 specifications and the issue of ASTM C-90-91 there is one major specification change to note. In the past block compressive strength (psi) was based on gross area requiring an average 1000 psi. The strength requirements have not changed but the measurement has. All new specifications now are based on net area of 1900 psi.

To assist you in calculating the net area please follow the formula below.

Given the gross area compressive strength you may determine the net area by knowing 1) percent solids of unit, or 2) equivalent thickness of unit.

Example: 8" cmu with a known 1100 psi gross area at 52% solids.

$$\frac{\text{Compressive Strength (Gross Area)}}{\text{(\%) Percent Solids}} \times 100 = \text{Compressive Strength (Net Area)}$$

$$\frac{1100 \text{ psi}}{52\%} \times 100 = 2115 \text{ psi}$$

Example: 8" cmu with (7.625 actual size) with a known 1100 psi gross area with an equivalent thickness of 4.0".

$$\frac{\text{Compressive Strength (Gross Area)}}{\text{Equivalent Thickness}} \times \frac{\text{Actual}}{\text{Thickness}} = \text{Compressive Strength (Net Area)}$$

$$\frac{1100 \text{ psi}}{4.0} \times 7.625 = 2097 \text{ psi}$$

Block manufacturers have gross area psi data as well as solids and equivalent strength numbers. Most will have the net area compressive strength psi with future test results.

APPENDIX M
TABLE 2304.7(2-5)

Source: ICC, International Building Code 2000

TABLE 2304.7(2)

SHEATHING LUMBER, MINIMUM GRADE REQUIREMENTS: BOARD GRADE

SOLID FLOOR OR ROOF SHEATHING	SPACED ROOF SHEATHING	GRADING RULES
Utility	Standard	NLGA, WCLIB, WWPA
4 common or utility	3 common or standard	NLGA, WCLIB, WWPA, NSLB or NELMA
No. 3	No. 2	SPIB
Merchantable	Construction common	RIS

TABLE 2304.7(3)
ALLOWABLE SPANS AND LOADS FOR WOOD STRUCTURAL PANEL SHEATHING AND SINGLE-FLOOR GRADES CONTINUOUS OVER TWO OR MORE SPANS WITH STRENGTH AXIS PERPENDICULAR TO SUPPORTS[a,b]

SHEATHING GRADES		ROOF[c]				FLOOR[d]
		Maximum span (inches)		Load[e] (psf)		
Panel span rating roof/floor span	Panel thickness (inches)	With edge support[f]	Without edge support	Total load	Live load	Maximum span (inches)
12/0	5/16	12	12	40	30	0
16/0	5/16, 3/8	16	16	40	30	0
20/0	5/16, 3/8	20	20	40	30	0
24/0	3/8, 7/16, 1/2	24	20[g]	40	30	0
24/16	7/16, 1/2	24	24	50	40	16
32/16	15/32, 1/2, 5/8	32	28	40	30	16[h]
40/20	19/32, 5/8, 3/4, 7/8	40	32	40	30	20[h,i]
48/24	23/32, 3/4, 7/8	48	36	45	35	24
54/32	7/8, 1	54	40	45	35	32
60/32	7/8, 1 1/8	60	48	45	35	32

M.3

TABLE 2304.7(3)
ALLOWABLE SPANS AND LOADS FOR WOOD STRUCTURAL PANEL SHEATHING AND SINGLE-FLOOR GRADES CONTINUOUS OVER TWO OR MORE SPANS WITH STRENGTH AXIS PERPENDICULAR TO SUPPORTS[a,b]

SINGLE FLOOR GRADES		ROOF[c]				FLOOR[d]
		Maximum Span (inches)		Load[e] (psf)		
Panel span rating	Panel thickness (inches)	With edge support[f]	Without edge support	Total load	Live load	Maximum span (inches)
16 oc	$1/2$, $19/32$, $5/8$	24	24	50	40	16[h]
20 oc	$19/32$, $5/8$, $3/4$	32	32	40	30	20[h,i]
24 oc	$23/32$, $3/4$	48	36	35	25	24
32 oc	$7/8$, 1	48	40	50	40	32
48 oc	$13/32$, $11/8$	60	48	50	40	48

For SI: 1 inch = 25.4 mm, 1 pound per square foot = 0.0479 kN/m².

a. Applies to panels 24 inches or wider.

b. Floor and roof sheathing conforming with this table shall be deemed to meet the design criteria of Section 2304.7.

c. Uniform load deflection limitations 1/180 of span under live load plus dead load, 1/240 under live load only.

d. Panel edges shall have approved tongue-and-groove joints or shall be supported with blocking unless $1/4$-inch minimum thickness underlayment or $11/2$ inches of approved cellular or lightweight concrete is placed over the subfloor, or finish floor is $3/4$-inch wood strip. Allowable uniform load based on deflection of 1/360 of span is 100 pounds per square foot (psf) except the span rating of 48 inches. on center is based on a total load of 65 psf.

e. Allowable load at maximum span.

f. Tongue-and-groove edges, panel edge clips (one midway between each support, except two equally spaced between supports 48 inches on center), lumber blocking, or other. Only lumber blocking shall satisfy blocked diaphragms requirements.

g. For $1/2$-inch panel, maximum span shall be 24 inches.

h. Is permitted to be 24 inches on center where $3/4$-inch wood strip flooring is installed at right angles to joist.

i. Is permitted to be 24 inches on center for floors where $11/2$ inches of cellular or lightweight concrete is applied over the panels.

M.4

TABLE 2304.7(4)
ALLOWABLE SPAN FOR WOOD STRUCTURAL PANEL COMBINATION SUBFLOOR-UNDERLAYMENT (SINGLE FLOOR)[a,b]
(Panels Continuous over Two or More Spans and Strength Axis Perpendicular to Supports)

IDENTIFICATION	MAXIMUM SPACING OF JOISTS (inches)				
	16	20	24	32	48
Species group[c]	Thickness (inches)				
1	$1/2$	$5/8$	$3/4$	—	—
2, 3	$5/8$	$3/4$	$7/8$	—	—
4	$3/4$	$7/8$	1	—	—
Single floor span rating[d]	16 o.c.	20 o.c.	24 o.c.	32 o.c.	48 o.c.

For SI: 1 inch = 25.4 mm, 1 pound per square foot = 0.0479 kN/m².

a. Spans limited to value shown because of possible effects of concentrated loads. Allowable uniform loads based on deflection of 1/360 of span is 100 pounds per square foot (psf) except allowable total uniform load for $1^1/_8$-inch wood structural panels over joists spaced 48 inches on center is 65 psf. Panel edges shall have approved tongue-and-groove joints or shall be supported with blocking, unless $1/_4$-inch minimum thickness underlayment or $1^1/_2$ inches.

b. Floor panels conforming with this table shall be deemed to meet the design criteria of Section 2304.7.

c. Applicable to all grades of sanded exterior-type plywood. See DOC PS 1 for plywood species groups.

d. Applicable to Underlayment grade, C–C (Plugged) plywood, and Single Floor grade wood structural panels.

TABLE 2304.7(5)
ALLOWABLE LOAD (PSF) FOR WOOD STRUCTURAL PANEL ROOF SHEATHING CONTINUOUS OVER TWO OR MORE SPANS AND STRENGTH AXIS PARALLEL TO SUPPORTS
(Plywood structural panels are five-ply, five-layer unless otherwise noted)[a,b]

PANEL GRADE	THICKNESS (inch)	MAXIMUM SPAN (inches)	LOAD AT MAXIMUM SPAN (psf)	
			Live	Total
Structural I Sheathing	7/16	24	20	30
	15/32	24	35[c]	45[c]
	1/2	24	40[c]	50[c]
	19/32, 5/8	24	70	80
	23/32, 3/4	24	90	100
Sheathing, other grades covered in DOC PS 1 or DOC PS 2	7/16	16	40	50
	15/32	24	20	25
	1/2	24	25	30
	19/32	24	40[c]	50[c]
	5/8	24	45[c]	55[c]
	23/32, 3/4	24	60[c]	65[c]

For SI: 1 inch = 25.4 mm, 1 pound per square foot = 0.0479 kN/m².

a. Roof sheathing conforming with this table shall be deemed to meet the design criteria of Section 2304.7.

b. Uniform load deflection limitations: 1/180 of span under live load plus dead load, 1/240 under live load only. Edges shall be blocked with lumber or other approved type of edge supports.

c. For composite and four-ply plywood structural panel, load shall be reduced by 15 pounds per square foot.

M.6

APPENDIX N

IBC TABLE 2304.9(1)

Source: ICC, International Building Code 2000

TABLE 2304.9.1
FASTENING SCHEDULE

CONNECTION	FASTENING[a, m]	LOCATION
1. Joist to sill or girder	3-8d common 3 - 3" × 0.131" nail 3 - 3" 14 gage staple	toenail
2. Bridging to joist	2-8d common 2 - 3" × 0.131" nail 2 - 3" 14 gage staple	toenail each end
3. 1" × 6" subfloor or less to each joist	2-8d common	face nail
4. Wider than 1" × 6" subfloor to each joist	3-8d common	face nail
5. 2" subfloor to joist or girder	2-16d common	blind and face nail
6. Sole plate to joist or blocking	16d at 16" o.c. 3" × 0.131" nail at 8" o.c. 3" 14 gage staple at 12" o.c.	typical face nail
Sole plate to joist or blocking at braced wall panel	3-16d per 16" 3" × 0.131" nail per 16" 3" 14 gage staple per 16"	braced wall panels
7. Top plate to stud	2-16d common 3 - 3" × 0.131" nail 3 - 3" 14 gage staple	end nail
8. Stud to sole plate	4-8d common 4 - 3" × 0.131" nail 3 - 3" 14 gage staple 2-16d common 3 - 3" × 0.131" nail 3 - 3" 14 gage staple	toenail end nail

TABLE 2304.9.1—continued
FASTENING SCHEDULE

CONNECTION	FASTENING[a, m]	LOCATION
9. Double studs	16d at 24" o.c. 3" × 0.131" nail at 8" o.c. 3" 14 gage staple at 8" o.c.	face nail
10. Double top plates	16d at 16" o.c. 3" × 0.131" nail at 12" o.c. 3" 14 gage staple at 12" o.c.	typical face nail
Double top plates	8-16d common 12 - 3" × 0.131" nail 12 - 3" 14 gage staple typical face nail	lap splice
11. Blocking between joists or rafters to top plate	3-8d common 3 - 3" × 0.131" nail 3 - 3" 14 gage staple	toenail
12. Rim joist to top plate	8d at 6" (152 mm) o.c. 3" × 0.131" nail at 6" o.c. 3" 14 gage staple at 6" o.c.	toenail
13. Top plates, laps and intersections	2-16d common 3 - 3" × 0.131" nail 3 - 3" 14 gage staple	face nail
14. Continuous header, two pieces	16d common	16" o.c. along edge
15. Ceiling joists to plate	3-8d common 5 - 3" × 0.131" nail 5 - 3" 14 gage staple	toenail

TABLE 2304.9.1—continued
FASTENING SCHEDULE

16. Continuous header to stud	4-8d common	toenail
17. Ceiling joists, laps over partitions (See Section 2308.10.4.1, Table 2308.10.4.1)	3-16d common minimum, Table 2308.10.4.1 4 - 3" × 0.131" nail 4 - 3" 14 gage staple	face nail
18. Ceiling joists to parallel rafters (See Section 2308.10.4.1, Table 2308.10.4.1)	3-16d common minimum, Table 2308.10.4.1 4 - 3" × 0.131" nail 4 - 3" 14 gage staple	face nail
19. Rafter to plate (See Section 2308.10.1, Table 2308.10.1)	3-8d common 3 - 3" × 0.131" nail 3 - 3" 14 gage staple	toenail
20. 1" diagonal brace to each stud and plate	2-8d common 2 - 3" × 0.131" nail 2 - 3" 14 gage staple face nail	face nail
21. 1" × 8" sheathing to each bearing wall	2-8d common	face nail
22. Wider than 1" × 8" sheathing to each bearing	3-8d common	face nail
23. Build-up corner studs	16d common 3" × 0.131" nail 3" 14 gage staple	24" o.c. 16" o.c. 16" o.c.

TABLE 2304.9.1—continued
FASTENING SCHEDULE

CONNECTION	FASTENING[a, m]	LOCATION
24. Built-up girder and beams	20d common 32" o.c. 3" × 0.131" nail 24" o.c. 3" 14 gage staple 24" o.c.	face nail at top and bottom staggered on opposite sides
	2-20d common 3 - 3" × 0.131" nail 3 - 3" 14 gage staple	face nail at ends and at each splice
25. 2" planks	16d common	at each bearing
26. Collar tie to rafter	3-10d common 4 - 3" × 0.131" nail 4 - 3" 14 gage staple face nail	face nail
27. Jack rafter to hip	3-10d common 4 - 3" × 0.131" nail 4 - 3" 14 gage staple	toenail
	2-16d common 3 - 3" × 0.131" nail 3 - 3" 14 gage staple	face nail
28. Roof rafter to 2-by ridge beam	2-16d common 3 - 3" × 0.131" nail 3 - 3" 14 gage staple	toenail
	2-16d common 3 - 3" × 0.131" nail 3 - 3" 14 gage staple	face nail

N.5

TABLE 2304.9.1—continued
FASTENING SCHEDULE

29. Joist to band joist	3-16d common 5 - 3" × 0.131" nail 5 - 3" 14 gage staple	face nail
30. Ledger strip	3-16d common 4 - 3" × 0.131" nail 4 - 3" 14 gage staple	face nail
31. Wood structural panels and particleboard:[b] Subfloor, roof and wall sheathing (to framing):	$\frac{1}{2}$" and less $^{19}/_{32}$" to $\frac{3}{4}$" $\frac{7}{8}$" to 1"	6d[e,l] $2^{3}/_{8}$" × 0.113" nail[n] $1^{3}/_{4}$" 16 gage[o] 8d[d] or 6d[e] $2^{3}/_{8}$" × 0.113" nail[p] 2" 16 gage[e] 8d[e]	
Single Floor (combination subfloor-underlayment to framing):	$1\frac{1}{8}$" to $1\frac{1}{4}$" $\frac{3}{4}$" and less $\frac{7}{8}$" to 1" $1\frac{1}{8}$" to $1\frac{1}{4}$"	10d[d] or 8d[e] 6d[e] 8d[e] 10d [d] or 8d[e]	
32. Panel siding (to framing)	$\frac{1}{2}$" or less $\frac{5}{8}$"	6d[f] 8d[f]	
33. Fiberboard sheathing:[g]	$\frac{1}{2}$" $^{25}/_{32}$"	No. 11 gage roofing nail[h] 6d common nail No. 16 gage staple[i] No. 11 gage roofing nail[h] 8d common nail No. 16 gage staple[i]	
34. Interior paneling	$\frac{1}{4}$" $\frac{3}{8}$"	4d[j] 6d[k]	

NOTES TO TABLE 2304.9.1

For SI: 1 inch = 25.4 mm.

a. Common or box nails are permitted to be used except where otherwise stated.

b. Nails spaced at 6 inches on center at edges, 12 inches at intermediate supports except 6 inches at supports where spans are 48 inches or more. For nailing of wood structural panel and particleboard diaphragms and shear walls, refer to Section 2305. Nails for wall sheathing are permitted to be common, box or casing.

c. Common or deformed shank.

d. Common.

e. Deformed shank.

f. Corrosion-resistant siding or casing nail.

g. Fasteners spaced 3 inches on center at exterior edges and 6 inches on center at intermediate supports.

h. Corrosion-resistant roofing nails with $^7/_{16}$-inch diameter head and $1^1/_2$ inch length for $^1/_2$-inch sheathing and $1^3/_4$ inch length for $^{25}/_{32}$-inch sheathing.

i. Corrosion-resistant staples with nominal $^7/_{16}$-inch crown and $1^1/_8$ inch length for $^1/_2$-inch sheathing and $1^1/_2$ inch length for $^{25}/_{32}$-inch sheathing. Panel supports at 16 inches (20 inches if strength axis in the long direction of the panel, unless otherwise marked).

j. Casing or finish nails spaced 6 inches on panel edges, 12 inches at intermediate supports.

k. Panel supports at 24 inches. Casing or finish nails spaced 6 inches on panel edges, 12 inches at intermediate supports.

l. For roof sheathing applications, 8d nails are the minimum required for wood structural panels.

m. Staples shall have a minimum crown width of $^7/_{16}$ inch.

n. For roof sheathing applications, fasteners spaced 4 inches on center at edges, 8 inches at intermediate supports.

o. Fasteners spaced 4 inches on center at edges, 8 inches at intermediate supports for subfloor and wall sheathing and 3 inches on center at edges, 6 inches at intermediate supports for roof sheathing.

p. Fasteners spaced 4 inches on center at edges, 8 inches at intermediate.

N.7

APPENDIX O

IBC TABLE 2308.10.2(1-2)

Source: ICC, International Building Code 2000

TABLE 2308.10.2(1)
CEILING JOIST SPANS FOR COMMON LUMBER SPECIES
(Uninhabitable Attics Without Storage, Live Load = 10 pounds per square foot, $L/\Delta = 240$)

CEILING JOIST SPACING (inches)	SPECIES AND GRADE		DEAD LOAD = 5 pounds per square foot			
			Maximum ceiling joist spans			
			2x4	2x6	2x8	2x10
			(ft-in)	(ft-in)	(ft-in)	(ft-in)
12	Douglas Fir-Larch	SS	13-2	20-8	Note a	Note a
	Douglas Fir-Larch	#1	12-8	19-11	Note a	Note a
	Douglas Fir-Larch	#2	12-5	19-6	25-8	Note a
	Douglas Fir-Larch	#3	10-10	15-10	20-1	24-6
	Hem-Fir	SS	12-5	19-6	25-8	Note a
	Hem-Fir	#1	12-2	19-1	25-2	Note a
	Hem-Fir	#2	11-7	18-2	24-0	Note a
	Hem-Fir	#3	10-10	15-10	20-1	24-6
	Southern Pine	SS	12-11	20-3	Note a	Note a
	Southern Pine	#1	12-8	19-11	Note a	Note a
	Southern Pine	#2	12-5	19-6	25-8	Note a
	Southern Pine	#3	11-6	17-0	21-8	25-7
	Spruce-Pine-Fir	SS	12-2	19-1	25-2	Note a
	Spruce-Pine-Fir	#1	11-10	18-8	24-7	Note a
	Spruce-Pine-Fir	#2	11-10	18-8	24-7	Note a
	Spruce-Pine-Fir	#3	10-10	15-10	20-1	24-6
16	Douglas Fir-Larch	SS	11-11	18-9	24-8	Note a
	Douglas Fir-Larch	#1	11-6	18-1	23-10	Note a
	Douglas Fir-Larch	#2	11-3	17-8	23-0	Note a
	Douglas Fir-Larch	#3	9-5	13-9	17-5	21-3
	Hem-Fir	SS	11-3	17-8	23-4	Note a
	Hem-Fir	#1	11-0	17-4	22-10	Note a
	Hem-Fir	#2	10-6	16-6	21-9	Note a
	Hem-Fir	#3	9-5	13-9	17-5	21-3
	Southern Pine	SS	11-9	18-5	24-3	Note a
	Southern Pine	#1	11-6	18-1	23-1	Note a
	Southern Pine	#2	11-3	17-8	23-4	Note a
	Southern Pine	#3	10-0	14-9	18-9	22-2
	Spruce-Pine-Fir	SS	11-0	17-4	22-10	Note a
	Spruce-Pine-Fir	#1	10-9	16-11	22-4	Note a
	Spruce-Pine-Fir	#2	10-9	16-11	22-4	Note a
	Spruce-Pine-Fir	#3	9-5	13-9	17-5	21-3

TABLE 2308.10.2(1)
CEILING JOIST SPANS FOR COMMON LUMBER SPECIES
(Uninhabitable Attics Without Storage, Live Load = 10 pounds per square foot, L/Δ = 240)

Spacing (inches)	Species	Grade				
19.2	Douglas Fir-Larch	SS	11-3	17-8	23-3	Note a
	Douglas Fir-Larch	#1	10-10	17-0	22-5	Note a
	Douglas Fir-Larch	#2	10-7	16-7	21-0	25-8
	Douglas Fir-Larch	#3	8-7	12-6	15-10	19-5
	Hem-Fir	SS	10-7	16-8	21-11	Note a
	Hem-Fir	#1	10-4	16-4	21-6	Note a
	Hem-Fir	#2	9-11	15-7	20-6	25-3
	Hem-Fir	#3	8-7	12-6	15-10	19-5
	Southern Pine	SS	11-0	17-4	22-10	Note a
	Southern Pine	#1	10-10	17-0	22-5	Note a
	Southern Pine	#2	10-7	16-8	21-11	Note a
	Southern Pine	#3	9-1	13-6	17-2	20-3
	Spruce-Pine-Fir	SS	10-4	16-4	21-6	Note a
	Spruce-Pine-Fir	#1	10-2	15-11	21-0	25-8
	Spruce-Pine-Fir	#2	10-2	15-11	21-0	25-8
	Spruce-Pine-Fir	#3	8-7	12-6	15-10	19-5
24	Douglas Fir-Larch	SS	10-5	16-4	21-7	Note a
	Douglas Fir-Larch	#1	10-0	15-9	20-1	24-6
	Douglas Fir-Larch	#2	9-10	14-10	18-9	22-11
	Douglas Fir-Larch	#3	7-8	11-2	14-2	17-4
	Hem-Fir	SS	9-10	15-6	20-5	Note a
	Hem-Fir	#1	9-8	15-2	19-7	23-11
	Hem-Fir	#2	9-2	14-5	18-6	22-7
	Hem-Fir	#3	7-8	11-2	14-2	17-4
	Southern Pine	SS	10-3	16-1	21-2	Note a
	Southern Pine	#1	10-0	15-9	20-10	Note a
	Southern Pine	#2	9-10	15-6	20-1	23-11
	Southern Pine	#3	8-2	12-0	15-4	18-1
	Spruce-Pine-Fir	SS	9-8	15-2	19-11	25-5
	Spruce-Pine-Fir	#1	9-5	14-9	18-9	22-11
	Spruce-Pine-Fir	#2	9-5	14-9	18-9	22-11
	Spruce-Pine-Fir	#3	7-8	11-2	14-2	17-4

For SI: 1 inch = 25.4 mm, 1 foot = 304.8 mm, 1 pound per square foot = 47.9 N/m^2.

a. Span exceeds 26 feet in length. Check sources for availability of lumber in lengths greater than 20 feet.

TABLE 2308.10.2(2)
CEILING JOIST SPANS FOR COMMON LUMBER SPECIES
(Uninhabitable Attics With Limited Storage, Live Load = 20 pounds per square foot, $L/\Delta = 240$)

CEILING JOIST SPACING (inches)	SPECIES AND GRADE		DEAD LOAD = 10 pounds per square foot			
			Maximum ceiling joist spans			
			2x4	2x6	2x8	2x10
			(ft-In)	(ft-In)	(ft-In)	(ft-In)
12	Douglas Fir-Larch	SS	10-5	16-4	21-7	Note a
	Douglas Fir-Larch	#1	10-0	15-9	20-1	24-6
	Douglas Fir-Larch	#2	9-10	14-10	18-9	22-11
	Douglas Fir-Larch	#3	7-8	11-2	14-2	17-4
	Hem-Fir	SS	9-10	15-6	20-5	Note a
	Hem-Fir	#1	9-8	15-2	19-7	23-11
	Hem-Fir	#2	9-2	14-5	18-6	22-7
	Hem-Fir	#3	7-8	11-2	14-2	17-4
	Southern Pine	SS	10-3	16-1	21-2	Note a
	Southern Pine	#1	10-0	15-9	20-10	Note a
	Southern Pine	#2	9-10	15-6	20-1	23-11
	Southern Pine	#3	8-2	12-0	15-4	18-1
	Spruce-Pine-Fir	SS	9-8	15-2	19-11	25-5
	Spruce-Pine-Fir	#1	9-5	14-9	18-9	22-11
	Spruce-Pine-Fir	#2	9-5	14-9	18-9	22-11
	Spruce-Pine-Fir	#3	7-8	11-2	14-2	17-4
16	Douglas Fir-Larch	SS	9-6	14-11	19-7	25-0
	Douglas Fir-Larch	#1	9-1	13-9	17-5	21-3
	Douglas Fir-Larch	#2	8-9	12-10	16-3	19-10
	Douglas Fir-Larch	#3	6-8	9-8	12-4	15-0
	Hem-Fir	SS	8-11	14-1	18-6	23-8
	Hem-Fir	#1	8-9	13-5	16-10	20-8
	Hem-Fir	#2	8-4	12-8	16-0	19-7
	Hem-Fir	#3	6-8	9-8	12-4	15-0
	Southern Pine	SS	9-4	14-7	19-3	24-7
	Southern Pine	#1	9-1	14-4	18-11	23-1
	Southern Pine	#2	8-11	13-6	17-5	20-9
	Southern Pine	#3	7-1	10-5	13-3	15-8
	Spruce-Pine-Fir	SS	8-9	13-9	18-1	23-1
	Spruce-Pine-Fir	#1	8-7	12-10	16-3	19-10
	Spruce-Pine-Fir	#2	8-7	12-10	16-3	19-10
	Spruce-Pine-Fir	#3	6-8	9-8	12-4	15-0

TABLE 2308.10.2(2)
CEILING JOIST SPANS FOR COMMON LUMBER SPECIES
(Uninhabitable Attics With Limited Storage, Live Load = 20 pounds per square foot, L/Δ = 240)

Spacing	Species and grade				
19.2	Douglas Fir-Larch	SS	8-11	14-0	18-5	23-4
	Douglas Fir-Larch	#1	8-7	12-6	15-10	19-5
	Douglas Fir-Larch	#2	8-0	11-9	14-10	18-2
	Douglas Fir-Larch	#3	6-1	8-10	11-3	13-8
	Hem-Fir	SS	8-5	13-3	17-5	22-3
	Hem-Fir	#1	8-3	12-3	15-6	18-11
	Hem-Fir	#2	7-10	11-7	14-8	17-10
	Hem-Fir	#3	6-1	8-10	11-3	13-8
	Southern Pine	SS	8-9	13-9	18-1	23-1
	Southern Pine	#1	8-7	13-6	17-9	21-1
	Southern Pine	#2	8-5	12-3	15-10	18-11
	Southern Pine	#3	6-5	9-6	12-1	14-4
	Spruce-Pine-Fir	SS	8-3	12-11	17-1	21-8
	Spruce-Pine-Fir	#1	8-0	11-9	14-10	18-2
	Spruce-Pine-Fir	#2	8-0	11-9	14-10	18-2
	Spruce-Pine-Fir	#3	6-1	8-10	11-3	13-8
24	Douglas Fir-Larch	SS	8-3	13-0	17-1	20-11
	Douglas Fir-Larch	#1	7-8	11-2	14-2	17-4
	Douglas Fir-Larch	#2	7-2	10-6	13-3	16-3
	Douglas Fir-Larch	#3	5-5	7-11	10-0	12-3
	Hem-Fir	SS	7-10	12-3	16-2	20-6
	Hem-Fir	#1	7-6	10-11	13-10	16-11
	Hem-Fir	#2	7-1	10-4	13-1	16-0
	Hem-Fir	#3	5-5	7-11	10-0	12-3
	Southern Pine	SS	8-1	12-9	16-10	21-6
	Southern Pine	#1	8-0	12-6	15-10	18-10
	Southern Pine	#2	7-8	11-0	14-2	16-11
	Southern Pine	#3	5-9	8-6	10-10	12-10
	Spruce-Pine-Fir	SS	7-8	12-0	15-10	19-5
	Spruce-Pine-Fir	#1	7-2	10-6	13-3	16-3
	Spruce-Pine-Fir	#2	7-2	10-6	13-3	16-3
	Spruce-Pine-Fir	#3	5-5	7-11	10-0	12-3

For SI: 1 inch = 25.4 mm, 1 foot = 304.8 mm, 1 pound per square foot = 47.9 N/m².

a. Span exceeds 26 feet in length. Check sources for availability of lumber in lengths greater than 20 feet.

APPENDIX P

SECTION 3409 COMPLIANCE ALTERNATIVES

Source: ICC, International Building Code 2000

3409.1 Compliance. The provisions of this section are intended to maintain or increase the current degree of public safety, health and general welfare in existing buildings while permitting repair, alteration, addition and change of occupancy without requiring full compliance with Chapters 2 through 33, or Sections 3401.3 through 3406, except where compliance with other provisions of this code is specifically required in this section.

3409.2 Applicability. Structures existing prior to [****DATE TO BE INS-ERTED BY THE JURISDICTION.] [Note: It is recommended that this date coincide with the effective date of building codes within the jurisdiction**] in which there is work involving additions, alterations, or changes of occupancy shall be made to conform to the requirements of this section or the provisions of Sections 3402 through 3406.

The provisions in Sections 3409.2.1 through 3409.2.5 shall apply to existing occupancies that will continue to be, or are proposed to be, in Groups A, B, E, F, M, R, S, and U. These provisions shall not apply to buildings with occupancies in Groups H or I.

3409.2.1 Change in occupancy. Where an existing building is changed to a new occupancy classification and this section is applicable, the provisions of this section for the new occupancy shall be used to determine compliance with this code.

3409.2.2 Part change in occupancy.   Where a portion of the building is changed to a new occupancy classification, and that portion is separated from the remainder of the building with fire barrier walls assemblies having a fire resistance rating as required by Table 302.3.3 for the separate occupancies, or with approved compliance alternatives, the portion changed shall be made to conform to the provisions of this section.

Where a portion of the building is changed to a new occupancy classification, and that portion is not separated from the remainder of the building with fire separation assemblies having a fire resistance rating as required by Table 302.3.3 for the separate occupancies, or with approved compliance alternatives, the provisions of this section which apply to each occupancy shall apply to the entire building. Where there are conflicting provisions, those requirements which secure the greater public safety shall apply to the entire building or structure.

3409.2.3 Additions.   Additions to existing buildings shall comply with the requirements of this code for new construction. The combined height and area of the existing building and the new addition shall not exceed the height and area allowed by Chapter 5. Where a fire wall that complies with Section 705 is provided between the addition and the existing building, the addition shall be considered a separate building.

3409.2.4 Alterations and repairs.   An existing building or portion thereof, which does not comply with the requirements of this code for new construction, shall not be altered or repaired in such a manner that results in the building being less safe or sanitary than such building is currently. If, in the alteration or repair, the current level of safety or sanitation is to be reduced, the portion altered or repaired shall conform to the requirements of Chapters 2 through 12 and Chapters 14 through 33.

3409.2.5 Accessibility requirements.   All portions of the buildings proposed for change of occupancy shall conform to the accessibility provisions of Chapter 11.

3409.3 Acceptance.   For repairs, alterations, additions and changes of occupancy to existing buildings that are evaluated in accordance with this section, compliance with this section shall be accepted by the building official.

34093.3.1 Hazards.   Where the building official determines that an unsafe condition exists, as provided for in Section 115, such unsafe condition shall be abated in accordance with Section 115.

3409.3.2 Compliance with other codes.   Buildings that are evaluated in accordance with this section shall comply with the *International Fire Code* and *International Property Maintenance Code.*

3409.4 Investigation and evaluation. For proposed work covered by this section, the building owner shall cause the existing building to be investigated and evaluated in accordance with the provisions of this section.

3409.4.1 Structural analysis. The owner shall have a structural analysis of the existing building made to determine adequacy of structural systems for the proposed alteration, addition or change of occupancy. The existing building shall be capable of supporting the minimum load requirements of Chapter 16.

3409.4.2 Submittal. The results of the investigation and evaluation as required in Section 3409.4, along with proposed compliance alternatives, shall be submitted to the building official.

3409.4.3 Determination of compliance. The building official shall determine whether the existing building, with the proposed addition, alteration, or change of occupancy, complies with the provisions of this section in accordance with the evaluation process in Sections 3409.5 through 3409.9.

3409.5 Evaluation. The evaluation shall be comprised of three categories: fire safety, means of egress, and general safety, as defined in Sections 3409.5.1 through 3409.5.3.

3409.5.1 Fire safety. Included within the fire safety category are the structural fire resistance, automatic fire detection, fire alarm and fire suppression system features of the facility.

3409.5.2 Means of egress. Included within the means of egress category are the configuration, characteristics, and support features for means of egress in the facility.

3409.5.3 General safety. Included within the general safety category are the fire safety parameters and the means of egress parameters.

3409.6 Evaluation process. The evaluation process specified herein shall be followed in its entirety to evaluate existing buildings. Table 3409.7 shall be utilized for tabulating the results of the evaluation. References to other sections of this code indicate that compliance with those sections is required in order to gain credit in the evaluation herein outlined. In applying this section to a building with mixed occupancies, where the separation between the mixed occupancies does not qualify for any category indicated in Section 3409.6.16, the score for each occupancy shall be determined and the lower score determined for each section of the evaluation process shall apply to the entire building.

Where the separation between the mixed occupancies qualifies for any category indicated in Section 3409.6.16, the score for each occupancy shall apply to each portion of the building based on the occupancy of the space.

3409.6.1 Building height. The value for building height shall be the lesser value determined by the formula in Section 3409.6.1.1. Chapter 5 shall be used to determine the allowable height of the building, including allowable increases due to automatic sprinklers as provided for in Section 504.2. Subtract the actual building height from the allowable and divide by 12½ feet. Enter the height value and its sign (positive or negative) in Table 3409.7 under Safety Parameter 34-1.6.1, Building Height, for fire safety, means of egress, and general safety. The maximum score for a building shall be 10.

> 3409.6.1.1 HEIGHT FORMULA. The following formulas shall be used in computing the building height value.

$$\text{Height value, feet} = \frac{(AH)-(EBH)}{12.5} \times CF$$

Height value, stories = $(AS\text{-}EBS) \times CF$

(Equation 34-1)

where:

AH = Allowable height in feet from Table 503.
EBH = Existing building height in feet.
AS = Allowable height in stories from Table 503.
EBS = Existing building height in stories.
CF = 1 if (AH) - (EBH) is positive.
CF = Construction-type factor shown in Table 3409.6.6(2) if (AH) - (EBH) is negative.

Note. Where mixed occupancies are separated and individually evaluated as indicated in Section 3409.6, the values AH, AS, EBH, and EBS shall be based on the height of the fire area of the occupancy being evaluated.

3409.6.2 Building area. The value for building area shall be determined by the formula in Section 3409.6.2.2. Section 503 and the formula in Section 3409.6.2.1 shall be used to determine the allowable area of the building. This shall include any allowable increases due to open perimeter and automatic sprinklers as provided for in Section 506. Subtract the actual building area from the allowable area and divide by 1200 square feet (112 m^2). Enter the area value and its sign (positive or negative) in Table 3409.7 under Safety Parameter 34-1.6.2, Building Area, for fire safety, means of egress and general safety. In determining the area value, the maximum permitted positive value for area is 50 percent of the fire safety score as listed in Table 3409.8, Mandatory Safety Scores.

3409.6.2.1 ALLOWABLE AREA FORMULA. The following formula shall be used in computing allowable area:

$$AA = \frac{(SP + OP - HR + 100) \times (area, Table\ 503)}{100}$$

(Equation 34-2)

where:

AA = Allowable area.
SP = Percent increase for sprinklers (Section 506.3).
OP = Percent increase for open perimeter (Section 506.2).

Note. Where mixed occupancies are separated and individually evaluated as indicated in Section 3409.6, the value for HR shall be based on the height of the fire area of the occupancy being evaluated.

5409.6.2.2 AREA FORMULA. The following formula shall be used in computing the area value. Determine the Area Value for each occupancy fire area on a floor by floor basis. For each occupancy, choose the minimum Area Value of the set of values obtained for the particular occupancy.

$$Area\ value\ i = \frac{Allowable\ area_i}{1{,}200\ square\ feet} \left[1 - \left(\frac{Actual\ area_i}{Allowable\ area_i} + ... + \frac{Actual\ area_n}{Allowable\ area_n} \right) \right]$$

(Equation 34-3)

where:
i = value for an individual separated occupancy on a floor.
n = number of separated occupancies on a floor.

3409.6.3 *Compartmentation.* Evaluate the compartments created by fire barrier walls which comply with Sections 3409.6.3.1 and 3409.5.3.2 and which are exclusive of the wall elements considered under Sections 3409.6.4 and 3409.6.5. Conforming compartments shall be figured as the net area and do not include shafts, chases, stairways, walls, or columns. Using Table

3409.6.3, determine the appropriate compartmentation value (CV) and enter that value into Table 3409.7 under Safety Parameter 34-1.6.3, Compartmentation, for fire safety, means of egress, and general safety.

3409.6.3.1 WALL CONSTRUCTION. A wall used to create separate compartments shall be a fire barrier conforming to Section 706 with a fire resistance rating of not less than 2 hours. Where the building is not divided into more than one compartment, the compartment size shall be taken as the total floor area on all floors. Where there is more than one compartment within a story, each compartmented area on such story shall be provided with a horizontal exit conforming to Section 1005.3.5. The fire door serving as the horizontal exit between compartments shall be so installed, fitted, and gasketed that such fire door will provide a substantial barrier to the passage of smoke.

3409.6.3.2 FLOOR/CEILING CONSTRUCTION. A floor/ceiling assembly used to create compartments shall conform to Section 710 and shall have a fire resistance rating of not less than 2 hours.

3409.6.4 Tenant and dwelling unit separations. Evaluate the fire resistance rating of floors and walls separating tenants, including dwelling units, and not evaluated under Sections 3409.6.3 and 3409.6.5. Under the categories and occupancies in Table 3409.6.4, determine the appropriate value and enter that value in Table 3409.7 under Safety Parameter 34-1.6.4, Tenant and Dwelling Unit Separation, for fire safety, means of egress, and general safety.

3409.6.4.1 CATEGORIES. The categories for tenant and dwelling unit separations are:

1. Category a—No fire partitions; incomplete fire partitions; no doors; doors not self-closing or automatic closing.

2. Category b—Fire partitions or floor assembly less than 1-hour fire resistance rating or not constructed in accordance with Sections 708 or 710, respectively.

3. Category c—Fire partitions with 1 hour or greater fire resistance rating constructed in accordance with Section 708 and floor assemblies with 1-hour but less than 2-hour fire resistance rating constructed in accordance with Section 710, or with only one tenant within the fire area.

4. Category d—Fire barriers with 1-hour but less than 2-hour fire resistance rating constructed in accordance with Section 706 and floor assemblies with 2-hour or greater fire resistance rating constructed in accordance with Section 710.

5. Category e—Fire barriers and floor assemblies with 2-hour or greater fire resistance rating and constructed in accordance with Sections 706 and 710, respectively.

TABLE 3409.6.4
SEPARATION VALUES

OCCUPANCY	CATEGORIES				
	a	b	c	d	e
A1	0	0	0	0	1
A2	-5	-3	0	1	3
R	-4	-2	0	2	4
A3, A4, B, E, F, M, SI	-4	-3	0	2	4
S2	-5	-2	0	2	4

TABLE 3409.6.3
COMPARTMENTATION VALUES

OCCUPANCY	a Compartment size equal to or greater than 15,000 square feet	b Compartment size of 10,000 square feet	c Compartment size of 7,500 square feet	d Compartment size of 5,000 square feet	e Compartment size of 2,500 square feet or less
	CATEGORIES				
A1, A3	0	6	10	14	18
A2	4	4	10	14	18
A4, B, E, S2	0	5	10	15	20
F, M, R, S1	0	4	10	16	22

For SI: 1 square foot = 0.0929 m².

a. For areas between categories, the compartmentation value shall be obtained by linear interpolation

3409.6.5 Corridor walls. Evaluate the fire resistance rating and degree of completeness of walls which create corridors serving the floor, and constructed in accordance with Section 1004. This evaluation shall not include the wall elements considered under Sections 3409.6.3 and 3409.6.4. Under the categories and Groups in Table 3409.6.5, determine the appropriate value and enter that value into Table 3409.7 under Safety Parameter 34-1.6.5, Corridor Walls, for fire safety, means of egress, and general safety.

3409.6.5.1 CATEGORIES. The categories for corridor walls are:

1. Category a—No fire partitions; incomplete fire partitions; no doors; or doors not self-closing.

2. Category b—Less than 1-hour fire resistance rating or not constructed in accordance with Section 708.4.

3. Category c— 1-hour to less than 2-hour fire resistance rating, with doors conforming to Section 714 or without corridors as permitted by Section 1004.

4. Category d—2-hour or greater fire resistance rating, with doors conforming to Section 714.

TABLE 3409.6.5
CORRIDOR WALL VALUES

OCCUPANCY	CATEGORIES			
	a	b	c[a]	d[a]
A-1	-10	-4	0	2
A-2	-30	-12	0	2
A-3, F, M, R, S-1	-7	-3	0	2
A-4, B, E, S-2	-5	-2	0	5

a. Corridors not providing at least one-half the travel distance for all occupants on a floor shall use Category b.

3409.6.6 Vertical openings. Evaluate the fire resistance rating of vertical exit enclosures, hoistways, escalator openings, and other shaft enclosures within the building, and openings between two or more floors. Table 3409.6.6(1) contains the appropriate protection values. Multiply that value by the construction-type factor found in Table 3409.6.6(2). Enter the vertical opening value and its sign (positive or negative) in Table 3409.7 under Safety Parameter 34-1.6.6, Vertical Openings, for fire safety, means of egress, and general safety. If the structure is a one-story building, enter a value of 2. Unenclosed vertical openings that conform to the requirements of Section 707 shall not be considered in the evaluation of vertical openings.

3409.6.6.1 VERTICAL OPENING FORMULA. The formula on page P.9 shall be used in computing vertical opening value.

3409.6.7 HVAC systems. Evaluate the ability of the HVAC system to resist the movement of smoke and fire beyond the point of origin. Under the categories in Section 3409.6.7.1, determine the appropriate value and enter that value into Table 3409.7 under Safety Parameter 34-1.6.7, HVAC Systems, for fire safety, means of egress, and general safety.

3409.6.7.1 CATEGORIES. The categories for HVAC systems are:

1. Category a—Plenums not in accordance with Section 602 of the International Mechanical Code. –10 points.

$$VO = PV \times CF \qquad \text{(Equation 34-4)}$$

VO = Vertical opening value.
PV = Protection value [Table 3409.6.6(1)]
CF = Construction type factor [Table 3409.6.6(2)]

TABLE 3409.6.6(1)
VERTICAL OPENING PROTECTION VALUE

PROTECTION	VALUE
None (unprotected opening)	-2 times number floors connected
Less than 1 hour	-1 times number floors connected
1 to less than 2 hours	1
2 hours or more	2

TABLE 3409.6.6(2)
CONSTRUCTION-TYPE FACTOR

FACTOR	TYPE OF CONSTRUCTION								
	1A	1B	2A	2B	3A	3B	4	5A	5B
	1.2	1.5	2.2	3.5	2.5	3.5	2.3	3.3	7

2. Category b—Air movement in egress elements not in accordance with Section 1004.3.2.4. –5 points.

3. Category c—Both categories a and b are applicable. –15 points.

4. Category d—Compliance of the HVAC system with Section 1004.3.2.4 and Section 602 of the *International Mechanical Code*. 0 points.

5. Category e—Systems serving one story; or a central boiler/chiller system without ductwork connecting two or more stories. +5 points.

5409.6.8 Automatic fire detection. Evaluate the smoke detection capability based on the location and operation of automatic fire detectors in accordance with Section 907 and the *International Mechanical Code*. Under the categories and occupancies in Table 3409.6.8, determine the appropriate value and enter that value into Table 3409.7 under Safety Parameter 34-1.6.8, Automatic Fire Detection, for fire safety, means of egress, and general safety.

3409.6.8.1 CATEGORIES. The categories for automatic fire detection are:

1. Category a—None.

2. Category b—Existing smoke detectors in HVAC systems and maintained in accordance with the *International Fire Code.*

3. Category c—Smoke detectors in HVAC systems. The detectors are installed in accordance with the requirements for new buildings in the *International Mechanical Code.*

4. Category d—Smoke detectors throughout all floor areas other than individual guest rooms, tenant spaces and dwelling units.

5. Category e—Smoke detectors installed throughout the fire area.

TABLE 3409.6.8
AUTOMATIC FIRE DETECTION VALUES

OCCUPANCY	CATEGORIES				
	a	b	c	d	e
A1, A3, F, M, R, S1	-10	-5	0	2	6
A2	-25	-5	0	5	9
A4, B, E, S2	-4	-2	0	4	8

3409.6.9 Fire alarm systems. Evaluate the capability of the fire alarm system in accordance with Section 907. Under the categories and occupancies in Table 3409.6.9, determine the appropriate value and enter that value into Table 3409.7 under Safety Parameter 34-1.6.9, Fire Alarm, for fire safety, means of egress, and general safety.

3409.6.9.1 CATEGORIES. The categories for fire alarm systems are:

1. Category a—None.

2. Category b—Fire alarm system with manual fire alarm boxes in accordance with Section 907.3 and alarm notification appliances in accordance with Section 907.9.

3. Category c—Fire alarm system in accordance with Section 907.

4. Category d—Category c plus a required emergency voice/alarm communications system and a fire command station that conforms to Section 403.8 and contains the emergency voice/alarm communications system controls, fire department communication system controls and any other controls specified in Section 911 where those systems are provided.

TABLE 3409.6.9
FIRE ALARM SYSTEM VALUES

OCCUPANCY	CATEGORIES			
	a	b[a]	c	d
A-1, A2, A3, A4, B, E, R	-10	-5	0	5
F, M, S	0	5	10	15

a. For buildings equipped throughout with an automatic sprinkler system, add 2 points for activation by a sprinkler water flow device.

3409.6.10 Smoke control. Evaluate the ability of a natural or mechanical venting, exhaust or pressurization system to control the movement of smoke from a fire, Under the categories and occupancies in Table 3409.6.10, determine the appropriate value and enter that value into Table 3409.7 under Safety Parameter 34-1.6.10, Smoke Control, for means of egress and general safety.

TABLE 3409.6.10
SMOKE CONTROL VALUES

OCCUPANCY	CATEGORIES					
	a	b	c	d	e	f
A1, A2, A3	0	1	2	3	6	6
A4, E	0	0	0	1	3	5
B, M, R	0	2[a]	3[a]	3[a]	3[a]	4[a]
F, S	0	2[a]	2[a]	3[a]	3[a]	3[a]

a. This value shall be 0 if compliance with Category d or e in Section 3409.6.8.1 has not been obtained.

3409.6.10.1 CATEGORIES. The categories for smoke control are:

1. Category a—None.

2. Category b—The building is equipped throughout with an automatic sprinkler system. Openings are provided in exterior walls at the rate of 20 square feet (1.86 m^2) per 50 linear feet (15 240 mm) of exterior wall in each story and distributed around the building perimeter at intervals not exceeding 50 feet (15 240 mm). Such openings shall be readily openable from the inside without a key or separate tool and shall be provided with ready access thereto. In lieu of operable openings, clearly and permanently marked tempered glass panels shall be used.

3. Category c—One enclosed exit stairway, with ready access thereto, from each occupied floor of the building. The stairway has operable exterior windows and the building has openings in accordance with Category b.

4. Category d—One smokeproof enclosure and the building has openings in accordance with Category b.

5. Category e—The building is equipped throughout with an automatic sprinkler system. Each fire area is provided with a mechanical air-handling system designed to accomplish smoke containment. Return and exhaust air shall be moved directly to the outside without recirculation to other fire areas of the building under fire conditions. The system shall exhaust not less than six air changes per hour from the fire area. Supply air by mechanical means to the fire area is not required. Containment of smoke shall be considered as confining smoke to the fire area involved without migration to other fire areas. Any other tested and approved design which will adequately accomplish smoke containment is permitted.

6. Category f—Each stairway shall be one of the following: a smokeproof enclosure in accordance with Section 1005.3.2.5; pressurized in accordance with Section 909.20.5; or shall have operable exterior windows.

3409.6.11 Means of egress capacity and number. Evaluate the means of egress capacity and the number of exits available to the building occupants. In applying this section, the means of egress are required to conform to Sections 1004 (with the exception of Section 1004.2.4), 1003 (except that the minimum width required by this section shall be determined solely by the width for the required capacity in accordance with Table 1003.2.3, 1005 and 1006. The number of exits credited is the number that is available to each occupant of the area being evaluated. Existing fire escapes shall be accepted as a component in the means of egress when conforming to Section 3403. Under the categories and occupancies in Table 3409.6.11, determine the appropriate value and enter that value into Table 3409.7 under Safety Parameter 34-1.6.11, Means of Egress Capacity, for means of egress and general safety.

3409.6.11.1 CATEGORIES. The categories for means of egress capacity and number of exits are:

1. Category b—Capacity of the means of egress complies with Section 1003 and the number of exits complies with the minimum number required by Section 1005.

2. Category c—Capacity of the means of egress is equal to or exceeds 125 percent of the required means of egress capacity, the means of egress complies with the minimum required width dimensions specified in the code and the number of exits complies with the minimum number required by Section 1005.

3. Category d—The number of exits provided exceeds the number of exits required by Section 1005. Exits shall be located a distance apart from each other equal to not less than that specified in Section 1004.2.2.

4. Category e—The area being evaluated meets both Categories c and d.

TABLE 3409.6.11
MEANS OF EGRESS VALUES

OCCUPANCY	CATEGORIES				
	a	b	c	d	e
A1, A2, A3, A4, E	-10	0	2	8	10
M	-3	0	1	2	4
B, F, S	-1	0	0	0	0
R	-3	0	0	0	0

a. The values indicated are for buildings six stories or less in height. For buildings over six stories in height, add an additional -10 points.

3409.6.12 Dead ends. In spaces required to be served by more than one means of egress, evaluate the length of the exit access travel path in which the building occupants are confined to a single path of travel. Under the categories and occupancies in Table 3409.6.12, determine the appropriate value and enter that value into Table 3409.7 under Safety Parameter 34-1.6.12, Dead Ends, for means of egress and general safety.

3409.6.12.1 CATEGORIES. The categories for dead ends are:

1. Category a—Dead end of 35 feet (10 670 mm) in unsprinklered buildings or 70 feet (21 340 mm) in sprinklered buildings.

2. Category b—Dead end of 20 feet (6096 mm); or 50 feet 15 240 mm) in Group B in accordance with Section 1004.3.2.3, exception 2.

3. Category c—No dead ends; or ratio of length to width (*l/w*) is less than 2.5:1.

TABLE 3409.6.12
DEAD-END VALUES

OCCUPANCY	CATEGORIES		
	a	b	c
A1, A3, A4, B, E, F, M, R,S	-2	0	2
A2, E	-2	0	2

a. For dead-end distances between categories, the dead-end value shall be obtained by linear interpolation.

3409.6.13 Maximum travel distance to an exit. Evaluate the length of exit access travel to an approved exit. Determine the appropriate points in accordance with the following equation and enter that value into Table 3409.7 under Safety Parameter 34-1.6.13, Maximum Exit Access Travel Distance, for means of egress and general safety. The maximum allowable exit access travel distance shall be determined in accordance with Section 10004.2.4.

$$\text{Points} = 20 \times \frac{\text{Maximum allowable travel distance} - \text{Maximum actual travel distance}}{\text{Max. allowable travel distance}}$$

3409.6.14 Elevator control. Evaluate the passenger elevator equipment and controls that are available to the fire department to reach all occupied floors. Elevator recall controls shall be provided in accordance with the *International Fire Code*. Under the categories and occupancies in Table 3409.6.14, determine the appropriate value and enter that value into Table 3409.7 under Safety Parameter 34-1.6.14, Elevator Control, for fire safety, means of egress, and general safety. The values shall be zero for a single-story building.

3409.6.14.1 CATEGORIES. The categories for elevator controls are:

1. Category a—No elevator.
2. Category b—Any elevator without Phase I and II recall.
3. Category c—All elevators with Phase I and II recall as required by the *International Fire Code*.
4. Category d—All meet Category c; or Category b where permitted to be without recall; and at least one elevator that complies with new construction requirements serves all occupied floors.

TABLE 3409.6.14
ELEVATOR CONTROL VALUES

ELEVATOR TRAVEL	CATEGORIES			
	a	b	c	d
Less than 25 feet of travel above or below the primary level of elevator access for emergency fire-fighting or rescue personnel	-2	0	0	+2
Travel of 25 feet or more above or below the primary level of elevator access for emergency fire-fighting or rescue personnel	-4	NP	0	+4

For SI: 1 foot = 304.8 mm.

3409.6.15 Means of egress emergency lighting. Evaluate the presence of and reliability of means of egress emergency lighting. Under the categories and occupancies in Table 3409.6.15, determine the appropriate value and enter that value into Table 3409.7 under Safety Parameter 34-1.6.15, Means of Egress Emergency lighting, for means of egress and general safety.

3409.6.15.1 CATEGORIES. The categories for means of egress emergency lighting are:

1. Category a—Means of egress lighting and exit signs not provided with emergency power in accordance with Section 2702.
2. Category b—Means of egress lighting and exit signs provided with emergency power in accordance with Section 2702.
3. Category c—Emergency power provided to means of egress lighting and exit signs which provides protection in the event of power failure to the site or building.

TABLE 3409.6.15
MEANS OF EGRESS EMERGENCY LIGHTING VALUES

NUMBER OF EXITS REQUIRED BY SECTION 1010	CATEGORIES		
	a	b	c
Two or more exits	NP	0	4
Minimum of one exit	0	1	1

3409.6.16 Mixed occupancies.   Where a building has two or more occupancies that are not in the same occupancy classification, the separation between the mixed occupancies shall be evaluated in accordance with this section. Where there is no separation between the mixed occupancies or the separation between mixed occupancies does not qualify for any of the categories indicated in Section 3409.6.16.1, the building shall be evaluated as indicated in Section 3409.6 and the value for mixed occupancies shall be zero. Under the categories and occupancies in Table 34-1.6.16, determine the appropriate value and enter that value into Table 3409.7 under Safety Parameter 34.1.6.16, Mixed Occupancies, for fire safety and general safety. For buildings without mixed occupancies, the value shall be zero.

3409.6.16.1 CATEGORIES. The categories for mixed occupancies are:

1. Category a—Minimum 1-hour fire barriers between occupancies.

2. Category b—Fire barriers between occupancies in accordance with Section 302.3.3.

3. Category c—Fire barriers between occupancies having a fire resistance rating of not less than twice that required by Section 302.3.3.

TABLE 3409.6.16
MIXED OCCUPANCY VALUES[a]

OCCUPANCY	CATEGORIES		
	a	b	c
A1, A2, R	-10	0	10
A3, A4, B, E, F, M, S	-5	0	5

a. For fire-resistance ratings between categories, the value shall be obtained by linear interpolation.

3409.6.17 Sprinklers.   Evaluate the ability to suppress a fire based on the installation of an automatic sprinkler system in accordance with Section 903.3.1.1. "Required sprinklers" shall be based on the requirements of this code. Under the categories and occupancies in Table 3409.6.17, determine the appropriate value and enter that value into Table 3409.7 under Safety Parameter 34-1.6.17, Automatic Sprinklers, for fire safety, means of egress divided by 2, and general safety.

3409.6.17.1 CATEGORIES. The categories for automatic sprinkler system protection are:

1. Category a—Sprinklers are required throughout; sprinkler protection is not provided or the sprinkler system design is not adequate for the hazard protected in accordance with Section 903.

2. Category b—Sprinklers are required in a portion of the building; sprinkler protection is not provided or the sprinkler system design is not adequate for the hazard protected in accordance with Section 903.

3. Category c—Sprinklers are not required; none are provided.

4. Category d—Sprinklers are required in a portion of the building; sprinklers are provided in such portion; the system is one which complied with the code at the time of installation and is maintained and supervised in accordance with Section 903.

5. Category e—Sprinklers are required throughout; sprinklers are provided throughout in accordance with Chapter 9.

6. Category f—Sprinklers are not required throughout; sprinklers are provided throughout in accordance with Chapter 9.

TABLE 3409.6.17
SPRINKLER SYSTEM VALUES

OCCUPANCY	CATEGORIES					
	a	b	c	d	e	f
A1, A3, F, M, R, S1	-6	-3	0	2	4	6
A2	-4	-2	0	1	2	4
A4, B, E, S2	-12	-6	0	3	6	12

3409.6.18 Incidental use. Evaluate the protection of incidental use areas in accordance with Section 302.1.1. Do not include those where this code requires suppression throughout the building including covered mall buildings, high-rise buildings, public garages and unlimited area buildings. Assign the lowest score for the building or fire area being evaluated. If there area no specific occupancy areas in the building or fire area being evaluated, the value shall be zero.

3409.7 Building score. After determining the appropriate data from Section 3409.6, enter those data in Table 3409.7 and total the building score.

3409.8 Safety scores. The values in Table 3409.8 are the required mandatory safety scores for the evaluation process listed in Section 3409.6

3409.9 Evaluation of building safety. The mandatory safety score in Table 3409.8 shall be subtracted from the building score in Table 3409.7 for each category. Where the final score for any category equals zero or more, the building is in compliance with the requirements of this section for that category. Where the final score for any category is less than zero, the building is not in compliance with the requirements of this section.

3409.9.1 Mixed occupancies. For mixed occupancies, the following provisions shall apply:

1. Where the separation between mixed occupancies does not qualify for any category indicated in Section 3409.6.16, the mandatory safety scores for the occupancy with the lowest general safety score in Table 3409.8 shall be utilized. (See Section 3409.6.)

2. Where the separation between mixed occupancies qualifies for any category indicated in Section 3409.6.16, the mandatory safety scores for each occupancy shall be placed against the evaluation scores for the appropriate occupancy.

TABLE 3409.6.18
INCIDENTAL USE AREA VALUES[a]

PROTECTION REQUIRED BY TABLE 302.1.1	PROTECTION PROVIDED						
	None	1 Hour	AFSS	AFSS with SP	1 Hour and AFSS	2 Hours	2 Hours and AFSS
2 Hours and AFSS	-4	-3	-2	-2	-1	-2	0
2 Hours, or 1 Hour and AFSS	-3	-2	-1	-1	0	0	0
1 Hour and AFSS	-3	-2	-1	-1	0	-1	0
1 Hour	-1	0	-1	0	0	0	0
1 Hour, or AFSS with SP	-1	0	-1	0	0	0	0
AFSS with SP	-1	-1	-1	0	0	-1	0
1 Hour or AFSS	-1	0	0	0	0	0	0

a. AFSS = Automatic fire suppression system; SP = Smoke partitions (See Section 302.1.1.1).
Note: For Table 3409.7, see page 676.

TABLE 3409.8
MANDATORY SAFETY SCORES[a]

OCCUPANCY	FIRE SAFETY (MFS)	MEANS OF EGRESS (MME)	GENERAL SAFETY (MGS)
A1	16	27	27
A2	19	30	30
A3	18	29	29
A4, E	23	34	34
B	24	34	34
F	20	30	30
M	19	36	36
R	17	34	34
S1	15	25	25
S2	23	33	33

a. MFS = Mandatory Fire Safety;
   MME = Mandatory Means of Egress;
   MGS = Mandatory General Safety.

TABLE 3409.9
EVALUATION FORMULAS[a]

FORMULA		T. 3409.7	T. 3409.8		SCORE	PASS	FAIL
FS-MFS ≥	0	____ (FS) -	____ (MFS) =		____	____	____
ME-MME ≥	0	____ (ME) -	____ (MME)=		____	____	____
GS-MGS ≥	0	____ (GS) -	____ (MGS) =		____	____	____

a.　FS = Fire Safety　　　　　　　MFS = Mandatory Fire Safety
　　ME = Means of Egress　　　　MME = Mandatory Means of Egress
　　GS = General Safety　　　　　MGS = Mandatory General Safety

TABLE 3409.7
SUMMARY SHEET — BUILDING CODE

Existing occupancy _____　　Proposed occupancy _____

Year building was constructed _____　　Number of stories _____　Height in feet _____

Type of construction _____　　Area per floor _____

Percentage of open perimeter _____%　　　　　Percentage of height reduction _____ %

Completely suppressed:　Yes _____　　No _____　　Corridor wall rating _____

Compartmentation:　　Yes _____　　No _____　　Required door closers: Yes _____　　No ____

Fire resistance rating of vertical opening enclosures _____

Type of HVAC system _____,　serving number of floors _____

Automatic fire detection:　Yes _____　　No _____,　　type and location _____

Fire alarm system:　　Yes _____　　No _____,　　type _____

Smoke control:　　　Yes _____　　No _____,　　type _____

Adequate exit routes:　Yes _____　　No _____　　Dead ends: _____ Yes _____ No _____

Maximum exit access travel distance _____　Elevator controls:　Yes _____　· No _____

Means of egress emergency lighting:　Yes ____　No _____　　Mixed occupancies: Yes ____　No ____

SAFETY PARAMETERS	FIRE SAFETY (FS)	MEANS OF EGRESS (ME)	GENERAL SAFETY (GS)
3409.6.1 Building Height 3409.6.2 Building Area 3409.6.3 Compartmentation			
3409.6.4 Tenant and Dwelling Unit Separations 3409.6.5 Corridor Walls 3409.6.6 Vertical Openings			
3409.6.7 HVAC Systems 3409.6.8 Automatic Fire Detection 3409.6.9 Fire Alarm System			
3409.6.10 Smoke control 3409.6.11 Means of Egress 3409.6.12 Dead ends	* * * * * * * * * * * *		
3409.6.13 Maximum Exit Access Travel Distance 3409.6.14 Elevator Control 3409.6.15 Means of Egress Emergency Lighting	* * * * * * * *		
3409.6.16 Mixed Occupancies 3409.6.17 Automatic Sprinklers 3409.6.18 Incidental Use Area Protection		* * * * ÷ 2 =	
Building score — total value			

* * * *No applicable value to be inserted.

APPENDIX Q

REFERENCED STANDARDS

Source: ICC, International Building Code 2000

REFERENCED STANDARDS

This chapter lists the standards that are referenced in various sections of this document. The standards are listed herein by the promulgating agency of the standard, the standard identification, the effective date and title, and the section or sections of this document that reference the standard. The application of the referenced standards shall be as specified in Section 102.8.

AA

Aluminum Association
900 - 19th Street N.W., Suite 300
Washington, DC 20006

Standard reference number	Title	Referenced in code section number
AA–94	Aluminum Design Manual: Part 1-A Aluminum Structures, Allowable Stress Design; and Part 1- B—Aluminum Structures, Load and Resistance Factor Design of Buildings and Similar Type Structures	1604.3.5, 2002.1
AA ASM 35–80	Aluminum Sheet Metal Work in Building Construction.	2002.1

AAMA

American Architectural Manufacturers Association
1827 Waldon Office Square Suite 104
Schaumberg, IL 60173

Standard reference number	Title	Referenced in code section number
AAMA 1001–97	Design Load of Metal Flag Poles (was NAAMM)	1609.1.1
AAMA 1402–86	Aluminum Siding, Soffit and Fascia	1404.5.1
AAMA/NWWDA 10-97	Voluntary Specifications for Aluminum Sliding Vinyl PVC Wood Windows and Glass Doors	1714.5.1

ACI

American Concrete Institute
P.O. Box 9094
Farmington Hills, MI 48333-9094

Standard reference number	Title	Referenced in code section number
ACI 216.1–97	Standard Method for Determining Fire Resistance of Concrete and Masonry Construction Assemblies	Table 719.1(2), 720.1
ACI 318–99	Building Code Requirements for Structural Concrete	1604.3.2, 1604.3.4, 1605.2.1, Table 1617.6, 1617.6.4.3, Table 1704.3, 1704.4.1, Table 1704.4, 1708.3, 1805.4.2.6, 1805.9, 1807.2.23.2, 1808.2.3.2, 1808.2.3.2.2, 1811.8, 1901.2, 1901.3, 1901.4, 1902, 1903.1, 1903.2, 1903.3, 1903.4, 1903.5.1, 1903.6, 1904.4.2, 1905.1.4, 1905.3, 1905.4, 1905.5, 1905.6.5.5, 1905.8.3, 1905.11.3, 1906.1.5, 1906.3, 1906.4.3, 1907.1, 1907.2, 1907.4.1, 1907.6, 1907.7.2, 1907.7.3, 1907.7.4, 1907.8, 1907.9, 1907.10, 1907.11, 1907.12, 1907.13, 1908, 1909.1, 1909.3, 1909.4, 1909.5, 1909.6, 1910.1, 1910.2.1, 1910.2.3, 1910.2.4, 1910.3.1, 1910.4.2, 1910.4.3, 1910.4.4, 1910.4.4.1, 1910.5.2, 1913.1, 1913.2.1, 1913.3.2, 1913.4.4, 1913.4.5, 1913.5.2.7, 1913.8.1

Standard reference number	Title	Referenced in code section number
ACI 530-99	Building Code Requirements for Masonry Structures	1405.5, 1405.5.3, 1405.5.3.1, 1405.9, 1604.3.4, 1704.5, 1704.5.1, 1704.5.2, 1704.5.3, Table 1704.5.1, Table 1704.5.3, 1708.1.1, 1708.1.2, 1708.1.3, 1708.1.4, 1805.5.2, 1811.7, 2101.2.3, 2101.2.4, 2104.1, 2104.1.1, 2106.1.1, 2106.1.1.1, 2106.1.1.2, 2106.1.1.3, 2106.1.1.4, 2106.1.1.5, 2106.1.2, 2106.1.2.1, 2106.1.2.2, 2106.1.2.3, 2106.2, 2106.4.2.1, 2106.4.2.2, 2106.5.1, 2107.1, 2107.2, 2107.2.1, 2107.2.2, 2107.2.3, 2107.2.4, 2107.2.5, 2108.6.5, 2108.7.2, 2109.1, 2109.2.3.1
ACI 530.1-99	Masonry Structures	1405.5.2, 1405.9.1, Table 1704.5.1, Table 1704.5.3, 1805.5.2, 2104.1, 2104.1.1 2108.7.2, 2109.1, 2109.2.3.1

AF&PA

American Forest & Paper Association
1111 19th St, NW Suite 800
Washington, DC 20036

Standard reference number	Title	Referenced in code section number
AF&PA/ASCE 16-95	Standard for Load and Resistance Factor Design (LRFD) for Engineered Wood Construction	2307.1
No. 4-89	Plank and Beam Framing for Residential Buildings	2306.1.2
WFCM	Wood Frame Construction Manual for One-and Two-family Dwellings, 1995 SBC High-wind Edition, Copyright 1996	1609.1.1, 2308.2
Technical Report 7-87	Basic Requirements for Permanent Wood Foundation System	1805.4.6, 1806.2, 2304.9.5
AF&PA NDS-97	Wood Construction and Supplement	720.6.3.2, 1715.1.1, 1715.1.4, 1805.4.5, 1808.1, 2306.1, 2306.2.1, 2306.3.2, Table 2306.3.1, Table 2306.4.1, 2306.3.4, 2306.3.5, 2306.4.1, 2308.2.1, Table 2308.9.3(4)
AF&PA	Span Tables for Joists and Rafters	2306.1.1, 2308.8, 2308.10.2, 2308.10.3

AHA

American Hardwood Association
1210 West N.W. Highway
Palatine, IL 60067

Standard reference number	Title	Referenced in code section number
AHA A135.4–95	Basic Hardware	1404.3.1, 2303.1.6
AHA A135.5–95	Prefinished Hardboard Paneling	2303.1.6, 2304.6.2
AHA A135.6–98	Hardboard Siding	1404.3.2, 2303.1.6
AHA 194.1–85	Cellulosic Fiber Board	2303.1.5

AISC

American Institute of Steel Construction
One East Wacker Drive, Suite 3100
Chicago, IL 60601-2001

Standard reference number	Title	Referenced in code section number
AISC ASD (1989)	Structural Steel Buildings—Allowable Stress Design, Plastic Design	1604.3.3, 1621.3.13.2, Table 1617.6, Table 1704.3, 2203.2, 2204
AISC LRFD (1993)	Load and Resistance Factor Design for Structural Steel Buildings, including Supplement No. 1 Dated January 1998	1604.3.3, Table 1617.6, Table 1704.3, 2203.2, 2204, 2213.1
AISC HSS (1997)	Specification for the Design of Steel Hollow Structural Sections	1604.3.3, Table 1617.6, 2203.2, 2204
AISC Seismic (1997)	Seismic Provisions for Structural Steel Buildings, including Supplement No. 1 dated 1999	Table 1617.6, 1622.3.4.1, 1707.2, 1708.4, 2212.1.1, 2212.1.2, 2213.1, 2213.2

AISI

American Iron and Steel Institute
1101 - 17th Street, N.W., Suite 1300
Washington, DC 20036-4700

Standard reference number	Title	Referenced in code section number
AISI (1996)	Specification for Design of Cold-formed Steel Structural Members	1604.3.3, 2205.1, 2211.1

AITC

American Institute of Timber Construction
Suite 140
7012 S. Revere Parkway
Englewood, CO 80112

Standard reference number	Title	Referenced in code section number
ANSI/AITC A 190.1–92	Structural Glued Laminated Timber	2303.1.3, 2306.1
AITC Technical Note 7–1996	Calculation of Fire Resistance of Glued Laminated Timbers	720.6.3.3
AITC 104–84	Typical Construction Details	2306.1
AITC 110–97	Standard Appearance Grades for Structural Glued Laminated Timber	2306.1
AITC 112–93	Standard for Tongue-and-groove Heavy Timber Roof Decking	2306.1
AITC 113–93	Standard for Dimensions of Structural Glued Laminated Timber	2306.1
AITC 117–93	Standard Specifications for Structural Glued Laminated Timber of Softwood Species — Design, with February 27, 1993 Addendum Standard Specifications for Structural Glued Laminated Timber of Softwood Species — Manufacturing	2306.1
AITC 119–96	Standard Specifications for Structural Glued Laminated Timber of Hardwood Species	2306.1
AITC 200–92	Inspection Manual	2306.1
AITC 500–91	Determination of Design Values for Structural Glued Laminated Timber	2306.1

ALI

Automotive Lift Institute
P.O. Box 33116
Indialantic, FL 32903-3116

Standard reference number	Title	Referenced in code section number
ALI ALCTV-98	Standard for Automobile Lifts–Safety Requirements for the Construction, Testing and Validation	3001.2

ANSI

American National Standards Institute
11 West 42nd Street
New York, NY 10036

Standard reference number	Title	Referenced in code section number
ANSI A 13.1–96	Scheme for Identification of Piping Systems	415.9.6.4
ANSI A 42.2–71	Portland Cement and Portland Cement Lime Plastering, Exterior (Stucco) and Interior	2109.8.4.6
ANSI A 42.3–71	Lathing and Furring for Portland Cement and Portland Cement Lime Plastering, Exterior Stucco and Interior	2109.8.4.6
ANSI A 108.1A&B–92	Glazed Wall Tile, Ceramic Mosaic Tile, Quarry Tile and Paver Tile Installed with Portland Cement Mortar	2103.9
ANSI A 108.4–92	Ceramic Tile Installed with Organic Adhesives or Water-cleanable Tile Setting Epoxy Adhesives	2103.9.7
ANSI A 108.5–92	Ceramic Tile Installed with Dry-set Portland Cement Mortar or Latex Portland Cement Mortar	2103.9.1, 2103.9.2, 2103.9.3

ASAE

American Society of Agricultural Engineers
2950 Niles Road
St. Joseph, MI 49085-9659

Standard reference number	Title	Referenced in code section number
ASAE EP 484.2	Diaphragm Design of Metal-Clad, Post-Frame Rectangular Buildings	2306.1
ASAE 559	Design Requirements and Bending Properties for Mechanically Laminated Columns	2306.1

ASCE

American Society of Civil Engineers
1801 Alexander Bell Drive
Reston, VA 20191-4400

Standard reference number	Title	Referenced in code section number
ASCE 3–84	Standard for the Structural Design of Composite Slabs	1604.3.3, 2205.2
ASCE 5–99	Building Code Requirements for Masonry Structures	1405.5, 1405.5.3, 1405.5.3.1, 1405.9 1604.3.4, 1704.5, 1704.5.1, 1704.5.2, 1704.5.3, Table 1704.5.1, Table 1704.5.3, 1708.1.1, 1708.1.2, 1708.1.3, 1708.1.4, 1811.7, 2101.2.3, 2101.2.4, 2106.1.1, 2106.1.1.1, 2106.1.1.2, 2106.1.1.3, 2106.1.1.4, 2106.1.1.5, 2106.1.2, 2106.1.2.1, 2106.1.2.2, 2106.1.2.3, 2106.2, 2106.4.2.1, 2106.4.2.2, 2106.5.1, 2107.1, 2107.2, 2107.2.1, 2107.2.2, 2107.2.3, 2107.2.4, 2107.2.5, 2108.6.5, 2109.1, 2109.2.3.1
ASCE 6–99	Masonry Structures	1405.5.2, 1405.9.1, Table 1704.5.1, Table 1704.5.3, 1805.5.2, 2104.1, 2104.1.1, 2108.7.2

ASCE 7-98	Minimum Design Loads for Buildings and Other Structures	1605.2.1, 1605.2.2, 1605.3.1.2, 1605.3.2, 1605.3.3, 1608.1, 1608.3, 1608.3.4, 1608.3.5, 1608.4, 1608.5, 1608.6, 1608.7, 1608.8, 1608.9, 1609.1.1, 1609.2, 1609.3, 1609.7.3, 1612.2, 1619
ASCE 8-90	Design of Cold-formed Stainless Steel Structural Members	1604.3.3, 2205.1, 2211.1
ASCE 16-95	Standard for Load Resistance Factor Design (LRFD) for Engineered Wood Construction	2307.1
ASCE 19-95	Structural Applications of Steel Cables for Buildings	2207.1, 2207.2
ASCE 24-98	Flood Resistance Design and Construction Standard	1202.3.2, 1612, 1612.4, 1612.5, 3001.2

ASME

American Society of Mechanical Engineers
Three Park Avenue
New York, NY 10016-5990

Standard reference number	Title	Referenced in code section number
ASME A17.1-96	Safety Code for Elevators and Escalators — with A17.1a-97 and A17.1b-98 Addenda	1607.8.1, 1621.3.14, 1621.3.14.1, 1621.3.14.3, 1003.2.13.3, 1003.2.13.4, 3001.2, 3001.4, 3002.5, 3003.2, 3408.7.1, 3408.7.2
ASME A90.1-97	Safety Standard for Belt Manlifts — with A90.1a-95 Addendum	3001.2
ASME B 16.18-84 (R94)	Cast Copper Alloy Solder Joint Pressure Fittings	909.13.1
ASME B 16.22-95	Wrought Copper and Copper Alloy Solder Joint Pressure Fittings with B16.22-98 Addendum	909.13.1
ASME B 20.1-97	Safety Standard for Conveyors and Related Equipment — with B20.1a-94 Addendum	3001.2, 3005.3
ASME B31.1-98	Power Piping	1621.3.10.2

Q.14

Q.15

Q.19

AWPA

American Wood-Preservers' Association
P.O. Box 5690
Grandbury, TX 76049

Standard reference number	Title	Referenced in code section number
AWPA C1–98	All Timber Products-Preservative Treatment by Pressure Processes	1403.6, 1505.6.1, 2303.1.8
AWPA C2–98	Lumber, Timber, Bridge Ties and Mine Ties-Preservative Treatment by Pressure Processes	1403.6, Table .1507.9.5, 1805.4.5, 1805.7.1, 2303.1.8, 2304.11.2, 2304.11.4, 2304.11.7
AWPA C3–97	Piles-Preservative Treatment by Pressure Processes	1403.6, 1805.4.5, 1808.1.2, 2303.1.8
AWPA C4–95	Poles-Preservative Treatment by Pressure Processes	1403.6, 1805.7.1, 1808.1.2, 2303.1.8
AWPA C9–97	Plywood-Preservative Treatment by Pressure Processes	1403.6, 2303.1.8, 2304.11.2, 2304.11.4, 2304.11.7
AWPA C14–90	Wood for Highway Construction, Preservative Treatment	2303.1.8
AWPA C15–98	Wood for Commercial-Residential Construction Preservative Treatment by Pressure Process	1403.6, 2303.1.8
AWPA C16–90	Wood Used on Farms, Pressure Treatment	2303.1.8
AWPA C18–95	Standard for Pressure Treated Material in Marine Construction	1403.6
AWPA C20–98	Structural Lumber-Fire Retardant Treatment by Pressure Processes	1805.4.6, 2303.2, 2303.1.8
AWPA C22–96	Lumber and Plywood for Permanent Wood Foundations-Preservative Treatment by Pressure Processes	1403.6, 1805.4.6, 2303.1.8
AWPA C23–94	Round Poles and Posts Used in Building Construction-Preservative Treatment by Pressure Processes	2303.1.8
AWPA C24–96	Sawn Timber Piles Used for Residential Commercial Building	1403.6, 1808.1.2, 2303.1.8
AWPA C27–88	Plywood-Fire-Retardant Treatment by Pressure Process	2303.2
AWPA C28–99	Standard for Preservative Treatment of Structural Glued Laminated Members and Laminations before Glueing of Southern Pine, Coastal Douglas-Fir, Hemfir and Western Hemlock by Pressure Processes	1403.6, 2303.1.8
AWPA M4–95	Standard for the Care of Preservative-Treated Wood Products	1808.1.2, 2303.1.8
AWPA P1/13–95	Standard for Coal Tar Creosote for Land and Fresh Water and Marine (Coastal Water) Use	1403.6, 2303.1.8

AWPA P2–98	Standard for Creosote Solutions	1403.6, 2303.1.8
AWPA P5–95	Standard for Waterborne Preservatives	2303.1.8
AWPA P8–95	Standard for Oil-borne Preservatives	2303.1.8
AWPA P9–92	Standard for Solvents and Formulations for Organic Preservative Systems	2303.1.8

AWS

American Welding Society
550 N.W. LeJeune Road
Miami, FL 33126

Standard reference number	Title	Referenced in code section number
D1.1-98	Structural Welding Code—Steel	Table 1704.3, 1704.3.1, 1708.4
D1.3-98	Structural Welding Code—Sheet Steel	Table 1704.3
D1.4-98	Structural Welding Code—Reinforcing Steel	Table 1704.3, 1903.5.2, 2108.9.2.11, Item 2

BHMA

Builders Hardware Manufacturers' Association
355 Lexington Avenue, 17th Floor
New York, NY 10017-6603

Standard reference number	Title	Referenced in code section number
A 156.10-85	Power Operated Pedestrian Doors	1003.3.1.3.2
A 156.19-97	Power Assist and Low Energy Operated Doors	1003.3.1.3.2

CGSB

Canadian General Standards Board
222 Queens Street
14th Floor, Suite 1402
Ottawa, Ontario, Canada KIA 1G6

Standard reference number	Title	Referenced in code section number
37-52M-84	Roofing and Waterproofing Membrane, Sheet Applied, Elastomeric	1504.6, 1507.12.2
37-54M-79	Roofing and Waterproofing Membrane, Sheet Applied, Flexible, Polyvinyl Chloride	1507.13.2
37-56M-80	Membrane, Modified, Bituminous, Prefabricated, and Reinforced for Roofing —with December 1985 Amendment	1507.11.2

CISCA

Ceiling and Interior Systems Construction Association
1500 Lincoln Highway, Suite 202
St Charles, IL 60174

Standard reference number	Title	Referenced in code section number
02–91	Recommendations for Direct-hung Acoustical Tile and Lay-in panel ceilings	1621.2.5.2.1
3-4–91	Guidelines for Seismic Restraint Direct Hung Suspended Ceiling Assemblies	1621.2.5.2.2

CPSC

Consumer Product Safety Commission
4330 East West Highway
Bethesda, MD 20814–4408

Standard reference number	Title	Referenced in code section number
16 CFR 107–97	Room Fire Test Standard for Garage Doors Using Foam Plastic Insulation	2603.4.1.9
16 CFR 1201–77	Safety Standard for Architectural Glazing	2406.1, 2406.1.2, 2407.1, 2408.2
16 CFR 1209–79	Interim Safety Standard for Cellulose Insulation	718.6
16 CFR 1404–79	Cellulose Insulation	718.6
16 CFR 1500–91	Hazardous Substance and Articles; Administration and Enforcement Regulations	307.2
16 CFR 1500 44–91	Method for Determining Extremely Flammable and Flammable Solids	307.2
16 CFR 1507–91	Fireworks Devices	307.2
16 CFR 1630–70 (DOC FF-1-70)–98	Standard for the Surface Flammability of Carpets and Rugs	804.5.1

CSSB

Cedar Shake and Shingle Bureau
P.O. Box 1178
Sumas, WA 98295-1178

Standard reference number	Title	Referenced in code section number
CSSB-97	Grading Rules	Table 1507.8.4, Table 1507.9.5

DASMA

Door and Access Systems Manufacturer's
Association International
1300 Summer Avenue
Cleveland, OH 44115-2851

Standard reference number	Title	Referenced in code section number
107-97	Room Fire Test Standard for Garage Doors Using Foam Plastic Insulation	2603.4.1.9

DOC

U.S. Department of Commerce
National Institute of Standards and Technology
100 Bureau Drive Stop 3460
Gaithersburg, MD 20899

Standard reference number	Title	Referenced in code section number
PS-1–95	Construction and Industrial Plywood	2211.3.1, 2303.1.4, 2304.6.2, Table 2304.7(4), 2306.3.2
PS-2–92	Performance Standard for Wood-based Structural-use Panels	1808.1.1, 2211.3.1, 2303.1.4, 2304.6.2, Table 2304.7(4), Table 2304.7(5), Table 2306.3.1, 2306.3.2
PS 20–99	American Softwood Lumber Standard	1808.1.1, 2302, 2303.1.1

DOL

U.S. Department of Labor
c/o Superintendent of Documents
U.S. Government Printing Office
Washington, DC 20402-9325

Standard reference number	Title	Referenced in code section number
29 CFR 1910.1000–74	Air Contaminants	902.1

DOTn

U.S. Department of Transportation
c/o Superintendent of Documents
U.S. Government Printing Office
Washington, DC 20402-9325

Standard reference number	Title	Referenced in code section number
49 CFR (173-178)–88 UN 0335, UN 0336	Specification of Transportation of Explosive and Other Dangerous Articles, Shipping Containers	307.2
49 CFR(172)–88	Hazardous Materials Tables, Special Provisions, Hazardous Materials Communications, Emergency Response Information and Training Requirements	307.2

EIA

Electronics Industries Association
2500 Wilson Boulevard
Arlington, VA 22201-3834

Standard reference number	Title	Referenced in code section number
EIA/TIA 222-E–91	Structural Standards for Steel Antenna Towers and Antenna Supporting Structures	3108.4

EWA

APA - Engineered Wood Association
P.O. Box 11700
Tacoma, WA 98411-0700

Standard reference number	Title	Referenced in code section number
APA PDS-97	Plywood Design Specification.	2306.1, Table 2306.3.1, 2306.3.2, 2306.3.4, 2306.3.5, 2306.4.1
	Supplement 1-Design and Fabrication of Plywood Curved Panels	2306.1
	Supplement 2-Design and Fabrication of Plywood-lumber beams	2306.1
	Supplement 3-Design and Fabrication of Plywood Stressed-skin Panels	2306.1
	Supplement 4-Design and Fabrication of Plywood Sandwich Panels	2306.1
	Supplement 5-Design and Fabrication of All-plywood Beams	2306.1
EWS X440–98	Product and Application Guide	2306.1
EWS R540–96	Builders Tips: Proper Storage and Handling of Glulam Beams	2306.1
EWS T300–99	Glulam Connection Details	2306.1
EWS S475–99	Data File: Glued Laminated Beam Design Tables	2306.1
EWS X445–97	Glulams in Residential Construction — Southern Edition	2306.1
EWS S560–99	Field Notching and Drilling of Glued Laminated Timber Beams	2306.1
EWS X450–97	Glulams in Residential Construction — Western Edition	2306.1

FEMA

Federal Emergency Management Agency
Federal Center Plaza
500 C Street S.W.
Washington, DC 20472

Standard reference number	Title	Referenced in code section number
FEMA 302	NEHRP Recommended Provisions for Seismic Regulations for New Buildings and Other Structures........................Figure 1615(7), Figure 1615(8), Figure 1615(9), Figure 1615(10)	

FM

Factory Mutual
Standards Laboratories Department
1151 Boston-Providence Turnpike
Norwood, MA 02062

Standard reference number	Title	Referenced in code section number
4450–90	Approval Standard for Class 1 Insulated Steel Deck Roofs—with Supplements thru 7/92............	1504.3.1, 1508.1, 2603.3, 2603.4.1.5
4470–86	Approval Standard for Class 1 Roof Coverings—with Supplements thru August 1992............	1504.3.1, 1504.6
4880–94	Approval Standard for Class 1:a) Insulated Wall or Wall and Roof/Ceiling Panels, b) Plastic Interior Finish Materials, c) Plastic Exterior Building Panels, d) Wall/Ceiling Coating Systems and e) Interior or Exterior Finish Systems	2603.4, 2603.7

GA

Gypsum Association
810 First Street N.E. #510
Washington, DC 20002-4268

Standard reference number	Title	Referenced in code section number
GA 216-96	Application and Finishing of Gypsum Board	Table 2508.1, 2509.1.2
GA 600-97	Fire-resistance Design Manual, 15th Edition, April, 1997	Table 719.1(1), Table 719.1(2), Table 719.1(3)

HPVA

Hardwood Plywood Veneer Association
1825 Michael Faraday Drive
Reston, VA 20190-5350

Standard reference number	Title	Referenced in code section number
ANSI/HPVA HP-1–1994	The American National Standard for Hardwood and Decorative Plywood	2303.3, 2304.6.2

ICC

International Code Council
5203 Leesburg Pike, Suite 708
Falls Church, VA 22041

Standard reference number	Title	Referenced in code section number
ICC A 117.1–98	Accessible and Usable Buildings and Facilities	406.2.2, 907.9.1.3, 1003.2.13.5.5, 1003.3.4, 1003.3.4.5.5, 1003.3.4.8, 1101.2, 1102.1, 1104.2.1, 1104.3.1, 1105.1, 1105.2, 1105.3, 1105.4, 1106.2, Table 1106.2, 1106.3, 1106.4, 1106.4.8, 1106.5, 1106.6, 1107.2, 1107.3, 1107.5.4, 1108.1, 1108.2, 1108.2.1.1, 1108.2.2, 1108.3, 1108.4, 1108.8, 1109.2.1, 1109.2.2.1, 1109.2.2.2, 1109.2.2.3, 1109.2.3, 1109.2.5, 1109.2.8, 1110.2, 1110.4, 1405.10.4, 1607.7, 3001.3, 3408.7.1, 3408.7.2
ICC EC–2000	ICC Electrical Code™	101.4.1, 904.3.1, 907.5, 909.11, 909.12.1, 909.16.3, 1204.4.1, 1003.2.10.5, 1003.2.11.2, 1405.10.4, 2701.1, 2702.1, 3401.3
IECC–2000	International Energy Conservation Code™	101.4.7, 1202.3.2, 1301.1.1, 1403.2
IFC–2000	International Fire Code®	101.4.6, 102.6, 307.2, 307.9, Table 307.7(1), Table 307.7(2), 403.8, 404.2, 406.5.1, 410.3.7, 411.1, 412.4.1, 413.1, 414.1.1, 414.1.2, 414.2.4, Table 414.2.4, 414.3, 414.5, Table 414.5.1, 414.5.2, 414.5.4, 414.5.5, 414.6, 415.1, 415.3, Table 415.3.1, 415.7, 415.7.1, 415.7.1.4, 415.7.2, 415.7.2.3, 415.7.2.5, 415.7.2.7, 415.7.2.8, 415.7.2.9, 415.7.3, 415.7.3.3, 415.7.3.5, 415.7.4, 415.8, 415.9.1, 415.9.2.7, 415.9.5.1, 415.9.7.2, 704.8.2, 901.2, 901.3, 901.5, 903.2.6.1, 903.2.13, Table 903.2.15, 903.5, 905.1, 904.2.1, 906.1, 907.2.5, 907.2.12.2, 907.2.14, 907.2.16, 907.19, 909.20, 910.2.3, Table 910.3, 1001.3, 1202.4.2, 1202.5, 2702.2.8, 2702.2.10, 2702.2.11, 2702.12, 2702.3, 3102.1, 3103.1, 3309.2, 3401.3, 3409.3.2, 3409.6.8.1, 3409.6.14, 3409.6.14.1
IFGC–2000	International Fuel Gas Code®	101.4.2, 201.3, 307.9, 415.7.3, 2113.11.2, 2801.1, 3401.3
IMC–2000	International Mechanical Code®	101.4.3, 201.3, 307.9, 406.4.2, 406.6.3, 409.3, 412.4.6, 414.1.2, 414.3, 415.7.1.4, 415.7.2.8, 415.7.3, 415.7.4, 415.9.11.1, 416.3, 603.1, 707.2, 715.2.2, 715.5.4, 715.6.1, 715.6.2, 715.6.3, 716.5, 718.1, 903.2.14.1, 904.2.1, 908.6, 909.1, 909.10.2, 1004.3.2.4, 1007.3, 1202.1, 1202.2.1, 1202.4.2, 1202.4.2.1, 1202.5, 1208.3, 2304.5, 2801.1, 3004.3.1, 3401.3, 3409.6.7.1, 3409.6.8, 3409.6.8.1
IPC–2000	International Plumbing Code®	101.4.4, 102.6, 103.3, 201.3, 415.7.4, 716.5, 903.3.5, 1205.3.3, 1503.4, 1611.1, 1806.4.3, 2901.1, 3305.1, 3401.3, 3409.3.2

IPMC–2000	International Property Maintenance Code® 101.4.5, 102.6, 3401.3, 3409.3.2
IPSDC–2000	International Private Sewage Disposal Code® 101.4.4, 2901.1, 3401.3
IRC–2000	International Residential Code™ 101.2, 2113.15, 3401.3
SBCCI SSTD 7–99	Standard for Soil Expansion Index Test 1802.3.2
SBCCI SSTD 10–99	Standard for Hurricane Resistant Residential Construction 1609.1.1, 2308.2.1
SBCCI SSTD 11–97	Test Standard for Determining Wind Resistance of Concrete or Clay Roof Tiles 1715.2.1, 1715.2.2
SBCCI SSTD 12–97	Standard for Determining Impact Resistance from Windborne Debris. 1609.1.1
UBC Standard 18–2	Expansion Index Test 1802.3.2
UBC 26-4–97	Method of Test for the Evaluation of Flammability Characteristics of Exterior, Nonload-Bearing Wall Panel Assemblies Using Foam Plastic Insulation 2603.5.5
UWIC–2000	Urban Wildland Interface Code™ . . . . Table 1505.1

NBS

National Bureau of Standards
U.S. Department of Commerce
Superintendent of Documents
Government Printing Office
Washington, DC 20401

Standard reference number	Title	Referenced in code section number
BMS 71–41	Fire Tests of Wood and Metal-framed Partitions	720.7
TRBM-44-46	Fire-resistance and Sound-insulation Ratings for Walls, Partitions and Floors	720.7

NCMA

National Concrete Masonry Association
2302 Horse Pen Road
Herndon, VA 22071-3499

Standard reference number	Title	Referenced in code section number
NCMA-TEK 5-8 (1978)	Design Details for Concrete Masonry Fire Walls	Table 719.1(2)

NEMA

National Electrical Manufacturers Association
2101 L Street, N.W., Suite 300
Washington, DC 20037

Standard reference number	Title	Referenced in code section number
NEMA-250-97	Enclosures for Electrical Equipment (1000 volts, Max)	1621.3.13.1
NEMA ICS 6-93	Industrial Control and System Enclosures	1621.3.13.1

NFPA

National Fire Protection Association
1 Batterymarch Park
Quincy, MA 02269-9101

Standard reference number	Title	Referenced in code section number
NFPA 11–98	Low Expansion Foam	904.7
NFPA 11A–99	Medium- and High-expansion Foam Systems	904.7
NFPA 12–98	Carbon Dioxide Extinguishing Systems	904.8, 904.11
NFPA 12A–98	Halon 1301 Fire Extinguishing Systems	904.9
NFPA 13–96	Installation of Sprinkler Systems	704.12, 707.2, 903.3.1.1, 903.3.2, 903.3.5.1.1, 904.11, 907.8, 1621.3.10.1, 3104.5, 3104.9
NFPA 13D–96	Installation of Sprinkler Systems in One- and Two-family Dwellings and Manufactured Homes	903.1.2, 903.3.1.3, 903.3.5.1.1
NFPA 13R–96	Installation of Sprinkler Systems in Residential Occupancies Up to and Including Four Stories in Height	903.1.2, 903.3.1.2, 903.3.5.1.1, 903.3.5.1.2, 903.4
NFPA 14–96	Standpipe and Hose System	905.2, 905.3.2, 905.3.5, 905.4.2, 905.8
NFPA 16–99	Installation of Deluge Foam-water Sprinkler and Foam-water Spray Systems	904.7, 904.11
NFPA 17–98	Dry Chemical Extinguishing Systems	904.6, 904.11
NFPA 17A–98	Wet Chemical Extinguishing Systems	904.5, 904.11
NFPA 30–96	Flammable and Combustible Liquids Code	307.9, 415.3
NFPA 30B–98	Manufacture and Storage of Aerosol Products	307.9
NFPA 32–96	Dry Cleaning Plants	415.7.4
NFPA 33–95	Spray Application Using Flammable and Combustible	307.9, 416.1
NFPA 34–95	Dipping and Coating Processes Using Flammable or Combustible Liquid.	307.9, 416.1

PCI

Precast Prestressed Concrete Institute
175 W. Jackson Boulevard, Suite 1859
Chicago, IL 60604-9773

Standard reference number	Title	Referenced in code section number
MNL 124–1977	Design for Fire Resistance of Precast Prestressed Concrete	720.2.3.1

PTI

Post-Tensioning Institute
1717 W. Northern Avenue, Suite 114
Phoenix, AZ 85021

Standard reference number	Title	Referenced in code section number
PTI-1996	Design and Construction of Post-tensioned Slabs-on-ground, 2nd Edition	1805.8.2

RMA

Rubber Manufacturers Association
1400 K. Street, N.W. #900
Washington, DC 20005

Standard reference number	Title	Referenced in code section number
RP-1-90	Minimum Requirements for Non-reinforced Black EPDM Rubber Sheets	1507.12.2
RP-2-90	Minimum Requirements for Fabric-reinforced Black EPDM Rubber Sheets	1507.12.2
RP-3-85	Minimum Requirements for Fabric-reinforced Black Polychloroprene Rubber Sheets	1507.12.2
RMA/SPRI RP-4-1988	Wind Design Guide for Ballasted Single-ply Roofing Systems	1504.4

RMI

Rack Manufacturers Institute
8720 Red Oak Boulevard, Suite 201
Charlotte, NC 28217

Standard reference number	Title	Referenced in code section number
RMI (1997)	Design, Testing and Utilization of Industrial Steel Storage Racks	2210, 1622.3.4

SAE

Society of Automotive Engineers
400 Common Wealth Drive
Warrendale, PA 15096

Standard reference number	Title	Referenced in code section number
SAE J78–79	Steel Self Drilling Tapping Screws	2211.2, 2211.3.3

SJI

Steel Joist Institute
3127 10th Avenue, North
Myrtle Beach, SC 29577-5760

Standard reference number	Title	Referenced in code section number
SJI–1994	Standard Specification, Load Tables and Weight Tables for Steel Joists and Joist Girders	1604.3.3, 2206
SJI–1994	Open Web Steel Joists, K Series	2206
SJI–1994	Longspan Steel Joists, LH Series and Deep Longspan Steel Joists, DLH Series	2206

SMACNA

Sheet Metal & Air Conditioning Contractor's National Assn., Inc.
4201 Lafayette Center Drive
Chantilly, VA 20151

Standard reference number	Title	Referenced in code section number
SMACNA-HVAC–1995	HVAC Duct Construction Standards, Metal and Flexible	1621.3.9
SMACNA-Seismic–1998	Seismic Restraint Manual Guidelines for Mechanical Systems, 1991, including Appendix B, 1998	1621.3.9

TIA

Telecommunications Industry Association
2500 Wilson Boulevard
Arlington, VA 22201-3834

Standard reference number	Title	Referenced in code section number
EIA-TIA 222-E-91	Structural Standards for Steel Antenna Towers and Antenna Supporting Structures	3108.4

TMS

The Masonry Society
3970 Broadway, Unit 201-D
Boulder, CO 80304-1135

Standard reference number	Title	Referenced in code section number
0216–97	Standard Method for Determining Fire Resistance of Concrete and Masonry Construction Assemblies	Table 719.1(2), 720.1
402–99	Building Code Requirements for Masonry Structures	1405.5, 1405.5.3, 1405.5.3.1, 1405.9; 1604.3.4, 1704.5, 1704.5.1, 1704.5.2, 1704.5.3, Table 1704.5.1, Table 1704.5.3, 1708.1.1, 1708.1.2, 1708.1.3, 1708.1.4, 1805.5.2, 1811.7, 2101.2.3, 2101.2.4, 2106.1.1, 2106.1.1.1, 2106.1.1.2, 2106.1.1.3, 2106.1.1.4, 2106.1.1.5, 2106.1.2, 2106.1.2.1, 2106.1.2.2, 2106.1.2.3, 2106.2, 2106.4.2.1, 2106.4.2.2, 2106.5.1, 2107.1, 2107.2, 2107.2.1, 2107.2.2, 2107.2.3, 2107.2.4, 2107.2.5, 2108.6.5, 2109.1, 2109.2.3.1
602–99	Specification for Masonry Structures	1405.5.2, 1405.9.1, Table 1704.5.1, Table 1704.5.3, 2104.1, 2104.1.1, 2108.7.2

TPI

Truss Plate Institute
583 D'Onofrio Drive, Suite 200
Madison, WI 53719

Standard reference number	Title	Referenced in code section number
TPI 1–1995	National Design Standards for Metal-Plate-Connected Wood Truss Construction	2303.4, 2306.1

UL

Underwriters Laboratories
333 Pfingsten Road
Northbrook, IL 60062-2096

Standard reference number	Title	Referenced in code section number
UL 10A–9ᵖ	Tin Clad Fire Doors	714.2
UL 10B–97	Fire Tests of Door Assemblies	714.2.2
UL 10C–98	Posture Pressure Fire Tests of Door Assemblies	714.2.1, 714.2.3
UL 14B–96	Sliding Hardware for Standard Horizontally Mounted Tin Clad Fire Doors	714.2
UL 14C–96	Swinging Hardware for Standard Tin Clad Fire Doors Mounted Single and in Pairs	714.2
UL 103–98	Chimneys, Factory-Built, 1 Residential Type and Building Heating Appliance —with Revisions through March 1999	716.2.5
UL 127–99	Factory-built Fireplaces	716.2.5
UL 268–96	Smoke Detectors for Fire Protective SignalingSystems-with Revisions Through January 1999	407.6, 907.2.6.1
UL 300–96	Fire Testing of Fire Extinguishing Systems for Protection of Restaurant Cooking Areas —with Revisions through December 1998	904.11
UL 555–95	Fire Dampers	715.3
UL 555C–96	Ceiling Dampers	715.3, 715.6.2
UL 555S–96	Leakage Rated Dampers for Use in Smoke Control Systems	715.3, 715.3.1.1
UL 580–94	Test for Uplift Resistance of Roof Assemblies—with Revisions through April 1995	1504.3.1, 1504.3.2

ULC

Underwriters Laboratories of Canada
7 Crouse Road
Scarborough, Ontario, Canada M1R3A9

USC

United States Code
c/o Superintendent of Documents
U.S. Government Printing Office
Washington, DC 20402-9325

Standard reference number	Title	Referenced in code section number
USC Title 18: Chapter 40–70	Importation, Manufacture, Distribution and Storage of Explosive Materials	307.2

WRI

Wire Reinforcement Institute, Inc.
203 Loudon Street, S.W.
2nd Floor, Suite 203C
Leesburg, VA 22075

Standard reference number	Title	Referenced in code section number
WRI/CRSI–81	Design of Slab-on-ground Foundations	1805.8.2

APPENDIX R
METRIC CONVERSIONS

Source: SBCCI, Standard Building Code Commentary, 1997

METRIC CONVERSIONS

	MULTIPLY	BY	TO GET
Length	inches	25.4	mm
	ft	0.3048	m
Area	sq in	645.16	mm²
	sq ft	0.0929	m²
Volume	cu in	0.01639	L
	cu ft	28.3169	L
	cu ft	0.02832	m³
	gal	3.785	L
	gal	0.003785	m³
Mass	lb	0.4536	kg
Mass/unit length	plf (lb/ft)	1.4882	kg/m
Mass/unit area	psf (lb/sq ft)	4.882	kg/m²
Mass density	pcf (lb/cu ft)	16.02	kg/m³
Force	lb	4.4482	N
Force/unit length	plf (lb/ft)	14.5939	N/m
Pressure, stress, modulus of elasticity	psi	6.895	kPa
	psf (lb/sq ft)	47.88	Pa
Second moment of area	in⁴	416,231	mm⁴
Section modulus	in³	16,387.064	mm³
Temperature	°F−32	5/9	°C
	(°F-32) + 273.15	5/9	K
Energy, work, quantity of heat	kWh	3.6	MJ
	Btu	1055	J
	ft • lb (force)	1.3558	J
Power	ton (refrig)	3.517	kW
	Btu/s	1.0543	kW
	hp (electric)	745.7	W
	Btu/h	0.2931	W

METRIC CONVERSIONS *(Continued)*

	MULTIPLY	BY	TO GET
Thermal conductance (U value)	Btu/f^2 • h • °F	5.6783	W/m^2 •K
Thermal resistance (R value)	ft^2 • h • °F/Btu	0.1761	m^2 • K/W
Flow	gpm cfm	0.0631 0.4719	L/s L/s
Illuminance	footcandle (lm/sq ft)	10.76	lx (lux)
Velocity (speed)	mph	0.447	m/s
Plane angle	°(angle)	0.01745	rad

INDEX